Language Learning Strategies in Independent Settings

SECOND LANGUAGE ACQUISITION
Series Editor: Professor David Singleton, *Trinity College, Dublin, Ireland*

This series brings together titles dealing with a variety of aspects of language acquisition and processing in situations where a language or languages other than the native language is involved. Second language is thus interpreted in its broadest possible sense. The volumes included in the series all offer in their different ways, on the one hand, exposition and discussion of empirical findings and, on the other, some degree of theoretical reflection. In this latter connection, no particular theoretical stance is privileged in the series; nor is any relevant perspective – sociolinguistic, psycholinguistic, neurolinguistic, etc. – deemed out of place. The intended readership of the series includes final-year undergraduates working on second language acquisition projects, postgraduate students involved in second language acquisition research, and researchers and teachers in general whose interests include a second language acquisition component.

Other Books in the Series
Language Learners in Study Abroad Contexts
  Margaret A. DuFon and Eton Churchill (eds)
Age and the Rate of Foreign Language Learning
  Carmen Muñoz (ed.)
Investigating Tasks in Formal Language Learning
  María del Pilar García Mayo (ed.)
Input for Instructed L2 Learners: The Relevance of Relevance
  Anna Nizegorodcew
Cross-linguistic Similarity in Foreign Language Learning
  Håkan Ringbom
Second Language Lexical Processes
  Zsolt Lengyel and Judit Navracsics (eds)
Third or Additional Language Acquisition
  Gessica De Angelis
Understanding Second Language Process
  ZhaoHong Han (ed.)
Japan's Built-in Lexicon of English-based Loanwords
  Frank E. Daulton
Vocabulary Learning Strategies and Foreign Language Acquisition
  Višnja Pavičić Takač
Foreign Language Input: Initial Processing
  Rebekah Rast
Morphosyntactic Issues in Second Language Acquisition
  Danuta Gabryś-Barker (ed)
Investigating Pragmatics in Foreign Language Learning, Teaching and Testing
  Eva Alcón Soler and Alicia Martínez-Flor (eds)
Language Learners with Special Needs: An International Perspective
  Judit Kormos and Edit H. Kontra (eds)
Socializing Identities through Speech Style: Learners of Japanese as a Foreign Language
  Haruko Minegishi Cook

For more details of these or any other of our publications, please contact:
Multilingual Matters, St Nicholas House, 31-34 High Street,
Bristol, BS1 2AW, England
http://www.multilingual-matters.com

SECOND LANGUAGE ACQUISITION 33
Series Editor: David Singleton, *Trinity College, Dublin, Ireland*

Language Learning Strategies in Independent Settings

Edited by
Stella Hurd and Tim Lewis

MULTILINGUAL MATTERS
Bristol • Buffalo • Toronto

Library of Congress Cataloging in Publication Data
Language Learning Strategies in Independent Settings / Edited by Stella Hurd and Tim Lewis. 1st ed.
Second Language Acquisition: 33
Includes bibliographical references and index.
1. Language and languages–Study and teaching. 2. Independent study.
3. Second language acquisition. I. Hurd, Stella. II. Lewis, Tim
P53.445.L36 2008
418.0071–dc22   2008012751

British Library Cataloguing in Publication Data
A catalogue entry for this book is available from the British Library.

ISBN-13: 978-1-84769-098-2 (hbk)
ISBN-13: 978-1-84769-097-5 (pbk)

Multilingual Matters
UK: St Nicholas House, 31-34 High Street, Bristol, BS1 2AW.
USA: UTP, 2250 Military Road, Tonawanda, NY 14150, USA.
Canada: UTP, 5201 Dufferin Street, North York, Ontario M3H 5T8, Canada.

Copyright © 2008 Stella Hurd, Tim Lewis and the authors of individual chapters.

All rights reserved. No part of this work may be reproduced in any form or by any means without permission in writing from the publisher.

Typeset by Techset Composition Ltd.
Printed and bound in Great Britain by the Cromwell Press Ltd.

Contents

The Contributors vii
Introduction xii

Part 1: Language Learning Strategies: Theory, Research and Practice

1 Language Learning Strategies in Independent Language Learning: An Overview
  Cynthia White 3

2 Individual Variation and Language Learning Strategies
  Phil Benson and Xuesong Gao 25

3 Hero With a Thousand Faces: Learner Autonomy, Learning Strategies and Learning Tactics in Independent Language Learning
  Rebecca L. Oxford 41

Part 2: Strategies for Skills Development in Independent Language Learning

4 Independent Second Language Reading as an Interdependent Process
  Carolyn Gascoigne 67

5 Learning Strategies for Listening Comprehension
  Larry Vandergrift 84

6 Second Language Composition in Independent Settings: Supporting the Writing Process with Cognitive Strategies
  Melanie Bloom 103

7 Speaking Strategies for Independent Learning: A Focus on Pragmatic Performance
  Andrew D. Cohen 119

8 Bringing the Learner Back Into the Process: Identifying Learner Strategies for Grammatical Development in Independent Language Learning
  Elspeth Broady and Nick Dwyer 141

9 Deliberate and Incidental: Vocabulary Learning Strategies
   in Independent Second Language Learning
   John Klapper 159

10 Strategies for Acquiring Intercultural Competence
   Inma Álvarez, Tita Beaven and Cecilia Garrido. 179

Part 3: Strategies for Learner Self-Management
11 Learning Logs and Strategy Development for Distance
   and Other Independent Language Learners
   Linda Murphy 199

12 Affect and Strategy Use in Independent Language Learning
   Stella Hurd. 218

13 Collaborative Language Learning Strategies in an
   Email Tandem Exchange
   Ursula Stickler and Tim Lewis. 237

14 Self-correction Strategies in Distance Language Learning
   Mike Truman 262

15 Strategies for Online Learning Environments
   Mirjam Hauck and Regine Hampel 283

16 Integrating Strategy Instruction into Learning Materials
   Linda Murphy 303

Index 321

The Contributors

Inma Álvarez is a Lecturer in Spanish in the Department of Languages at The Open University, UK. She has researched and published on the incorporation of the intercultural dimension in the modern languages curriculum. In particular she has investigated the role of translation skills, web-based activities, reading literature and the new training needs for teachers and learners that come with the development of intercultural skills.

Tita Beaven is a Lecturer in Spanish at the Open University. She has extensive experience of writing distance educational materials. Her research interests include the development of intercultural competence, and the teaching of Spanish as a world language.

Phil Benson is a Professor in the English Department at the Hong Kong Institute of Education. He has published widely on the subject of autonomy, including the book *Teaching and researching autonomy in language learning* (Pearson, 2001). His current research interests include language learning histories, and he is co-editor of the recent collection *Learners' Stories: Difference and Diversity in Language Learning* (Cambridge University Press, 2005).

Melanie Bloom is an Assistant Professor of Spanish at the University of Nebraska at Omaha. In addition, she serves as the Graduate Programme Chair for the Master of Arts in Language Teaching programme. Her research interests include teacher-research, second language writing, curriculum development, language teaching methodology and service-learning in language education.

Elspeth Broady studied French and Linguistics and then worked at universities in the UK and in Belgium, teaching English, French and Second Language Acquisition. She became Head of the School of Language, Literature and Communication at the University of Brighton in 2003. Elspeth has published textbooks for independent learners and has worked with several Open University French course teams. She has also published work on learner autonomy. Her current interests lie in the development of learners' grammatical concepts.

Andrew D. Cohen (Professor, Second Language Studies, University of Minnesota) has published on language learner strategies, pragmatics, language testing, bilingual and immersion education, and research methods. Recent efforts include *Language Learner Strategies: 30 Years of Research and Practice* (co-edited with Ernesto Macaro, Oxford University Press, 2007) and an online course on assessing language ability in adults in the ELT Advantage series (a joint venture between Heinle/Cengage Learning and TESOL).

Nick Dwyer is a Senior Lecturer in English Language Learning and Teaching at the University of Brighton. His current teaching includes training ELT professionals on Diploma and MA programmes, particularly in the area of SLA. He has conducted research into the use of chatrooms in language teaching, and is currently developing an area of research interest involving cognitive linguistic perspectives on language acquisition.

Cecilia Garrido is Associate Dean and Senior Lecturer in Spanish in the Faculty of Education and Language Studies at the Open University. She has extensive experience in the teaching of Spanish as a foreign language. Her research and publications are mostly in the area of intercultural competence and the implications it has for curriculum design, materials development and teacher education.

Carolyn Gascoigne is a Kiewit Professor and Chair of the Department of Foreign Languages at the University of Nebraska at Omaha. Her research centres on second language reading and writing at the post-secondary level, and programme articulation. Her research has appeared in publications such as the *French Review, Foreign Language Annals* and *Hispania*.

Xuesong (Andy) Gao did his doctoral research on mainland Chinese students' language learning strategy use in Hong Kong at English Centre/Faculty of Education, the University of Hong Kong. He has papers published or accepted in journals including *ELT Journal, System* and *Teaching and Teacher Education*. He joined the English Department, Hong Kong Institute of Education in January 2008.

Regine Hampel is a Senior Lecturer in Modern Languages at the Open University, UK. Her research explores theoretical and practical issues around the use of new technologies in language learning and teaching, focusing in particular on affordances of the new media, task design, tutor training, and learner interaction. She has written a number of articles and book chapters as well as a book, *Online Communication for Language Learning and Teaching* with Marie-Noëlle Lamy (Palgrave).

Mirjam Hauck is a Senior Lecturer and an Associate Head in the Department of Languages at the Open University, UK where she has been investigating virtual environments such as audio-graphic conferencing for the learning of languages and cultures for almost a decade. She is currently carrying out research into two interrelated areas: the role of metacognitive strategies – learner self-management in particular – in online and face-to-face language learning contexts, and the interdependence of multimodal and intercultural competence in telecollaboration.

Stella Hurd is a Senior Lecturer in the Department of Languages at the Open University, UK, where she has worked since 1994, after many years of teaching languages in adult education. Her research interests include learner autonomy, learner difference, learning strategies, metacognition and affect in self-access and distance language learning. Publications include journal articles, edited books and book chapters on all these topics. She has also co-edited three books on adult language learning (1992, 2001 and 2005).

John Klapper is Professor of Foreign Language Pedagogy, Director of the Centre for Modern Languages and a member of the Department of German Studies, University of Birmingham, UK. He is a HEFCE National Teaching Fellow. His research interests include the development of foreign language proficiency, language teacher education, language teaching methodology, the teaching of grammar, immersion learning and 20th century German literature.

Tim Lewis is a Lecturer in French at the Open University, UK. He founded and was the first Director of the Modern Languages Teaching Centre of the University of Sheffield (1993–2001). His research interests are in learner and teacher autonomy, collaborative learning and online language learning. Tim has previously co-edited volumes on *Autonomous Language Learning in Tandem* (Academy, 2003) and *Technology and the Advanced Language Learner* (AFLS/CiLT[1], 2000).

Linda Murphy is a Senior Lecturer in the Department of Languages at the Open University, UK, where she is a member of the regional academic staff based in Oxford. She has previously worked in teaching, teacher training and educational management in Adult and Further Education in the areas of adult learning, language learning and English as an Additional Language. Her current research focuses on the development of language learning and teaching strategies to support self-direction and learner autonomy in distance language learning.

Rebecca L. Oxford is Professor and Distinguished Scholar-Teacher at the University of Maryland. She is the author of books and articles on language learning strategies, motivation, cultural identity, and learning technologies. She served as series editor of an ESL/EFL program, *Tapestry*, published by Heinle/Thomson Learning and received a Lifetime Achievement Award, which states: 'Rebecca Oxford's research on learning strategies has changed the way the world teaches languages'.

Ursula Stickler is a Lecturer in German at the Open University, UK. Her research interests are in the areas of independent language learning, including technology enhanced language learning and Tandem learning. She is currently involved in projects researching interaction in online and face-to-face language tutorials and the use of VLE tools for language learning. She has published book chapters and articles in all the above areas.

Mike Truman has been a Lecturer in Spanish in the Department of Languages at the Open University in the UK since 1998. He has contributed to a number of publications on assessment and feedback in open and distance learning language learning, and has co-authored several course books for students of Spanish in higher education. His other research interests include translation and political discourse.

Larry Vandergrift is Professor at the University of Ottawa, Canada. His research on L2 listening has been published widely in applied linguistics journals. He is a co-editor of the *Canadian Modern Language Review* and Director of the Centre canadien des études et de recherche en bilinguisme et aménagement linguistique (CCERBAL), the research centre at the University's Institute of Official Languages and Bilingualism.

Cynthia White is Professor in the School of Language Studies, Massey University, New Zealand. She has research interests in language learning strategies, distance and online language learning, metacognition and teacher cognition. In 2004 Cynthia received the International TESOL Virginia French Allen Award for Scholarship and Service. In 2003 her book *Language Learning in Distance Education* was published by Cambridge University, and a co-edited book entitled *Languages and Distance Education: Evolution and Change* appeared with Multilingual Matters in 2005.

Email addresses

adcohen@umn.edu
b.c.garrido@open.ac.uk
C.J.White@massey.ac.nz
cgascoigne@mail.unomaha.edu
elspeth_broady@msn.com
i.alvarez@open.ac.uk
j.m.klapper@bham.ac.uk
l.m.murphy@open.ac.uk
lvdgrift@uottawa.ca
m.c.beaven@open.ac.uk
m.hauck@open.ac.uk
m.s.hurd@open.ac.uk
m.truman@open.ac.uk

melaniebloom@mail.unomaha.edu
n.dwyer@brighton.ac.uk
pbenson@ied.edu.hk
r.hampel@open.ac.uk
rebecca_oxford@yahoo.com
t.w.lewis@open.ac.uk
u.stickler@open.ac.uk
xsgao@ied.edu.hk

Note

1. The Centre for Language Teaching and Research (CILT) changed its name to The National Centre for Languages (CiLT) in 2003. For ease of reference, the current name is used throughout.

Introduction

Language learning strategies have long been the subject of research. However, the majority of studies and overviews have been based on classroom contexts, and less attention has been paid to strategies appropriate for independent language learning settings, where for all, most or some of the time the teacher is physically absent. These settings include all those that require students to take a degree of responsibility for their learning, and cover self-access, self-directed, resource-based and distance learning environments. The acknowledged link between strategic competence in language learning, learner autonomy and successful outcomes is a powerful argument for bringing together state-of-the-art research into the theory and practice of language learning strategies in learning environments that do not rely on the physical presence of a teacher.

This volume of collected papers covers language learning strategies from a variety of standpoints in an international context. Its contributors are researchers and practitioners from the UK, the United States, Hong Kong, New Zealand and Canada, all of whom have written extensively in the field. Two of them (Andrew Cohen and Cynthia White) were keynote speakers at the 'Independent Language Learning: New Research Directions' conference hosted by the Open University, UK in December 2003. Others have been invited to contribute on the basis of their previously published work. A number of chapters are written by members of the Department of Languages at the Open University, who have considerable experience of the theory and practice of distance language learning. Their inputs are equally applicable to other independent settings.

The book is divided into three sections: Part 1 sets out the theoretical context in terms of the setting, the impact of individual difference on strategy choice and use, and the links between strategies and autonomy. Part 2 concentrates on strategies involving cognitive and metacognitive development in relation to the four language skills, grammar, vocabulary and intercultural learning. Metacognitive and affective strategies for self-management in independent learning contexts are the focus of Part 3, and these include learning logs, self-correction, collaborative and online strategies. The final chapter of the book examines ways of integrating strategies into independent learning.

Language Learning Strategies: Theory, Research and Practice

In Chapter 1, Cynthia White gives a comprehensive overview of the field of language learning strategies in independent learning. She starts with three dimensions of independent language learning (ILL) – context, philosophy and attributes – and explores the ways in which all of these contribute to a wider understanding of the concept and, in the case of learner attributes, relate to learning strategies, learner autonomy and learner support. Her learner-context interface theory provides a framework for understanding ILL from a learner perspective in which learners draw on their metacognitive knowledge of self, task and strategy use in order to develop 'a meaningful interface with the learning environment' as autonomous agents in their own learning. White's discussion of selected landmark studies within the field of ILL focuses on two broad areas: first, the strategies learners use to respond to their particular learning contexts, and second, strategy training to enhance learner independence. She concludes that, as the field of ILL continues to evolve and diversify, sustained research is needed into the ways in which learners engage with ILL contexts, both real and virtual.

Phil Benson and Xuesong Gao investigate the interaction between individual variation and language learning strategies in Chapter 2. In the absence of research into strategy use in structured as opposed to naturalistic independent settings, their stated aim is to 'clear the theoretical ground for further studies in this area'. From an individual differences perspective, they explore internal, external, task and contextual factors moving on to learner experience and agency. They postulate that patterns of strategy preference and use are acquired, socially constructed and context-sensitive, but highlight the difficulty of establishing a consensual view. Issues of personal and social identity are raised in their examination of studies using qualitative research methods to investigate strategy use from a sociocultural perspective, leading to a discussion of the role of agency, and the ways in which individual strategy use can change over time in response to different language learning settings. Referring to White's (1999) learner-context interface theory, they suggest that independent language learners need to act strategically to 'create' environments that suit their own individual needs and the specificities of the learning setting.

Rebecca Oxford explores in Chapter 3 the relationship between independent language learning, autonomy and learning strategies. Her 'hero with a thousand faces' is a visual metaphor for the learner in a 'massive globally scattered, independent L2 learning enterprise'. Oxford guides us first through the concept of multiple autonomies, including stage theories, autonomy as an element in a spiral, autonomy by degree, decision-making, and individual autonomy versus social autonomy. She then goes on to discuss learning strategies and tactics (the use of specific strategies for particular tasks, problems and situations), focusing on strategies with particular relevance to independent language learning. Following an examination of learner development for autonomy through strategy instruction and learner reflection, Oxford moves on to a discussion of learning strategies to promote autonomous practice in six 'sample' independent learning settings, including self-access, online and distance. In conclusion, she calls for more mixed methods studies of variables likely to influence autonomy, with a stronger socio-cultural focus, and greater coordination to encourage comparability and ensure a more coherent approach.

Strategies for Skills Development in Independent Language Learning

In Chapter 4, Carolyn Gascoigne discusses reading as an interdependent process. She explores first two well-known models of reading. The first of these is 'bottom-up' and text-driven. The second is 'top-down', focuses on the reader and can be understood in terms of 'schemata', the mental frameworks that organise our world and can explain underlying connections or relationships. She then focuses on interactive models which involve the reader engaging with the text, and therefore involve both bottom-up and top-down processes working interdependently, as readers autonomously negotiate and co-construct meanings. Gascoigne goes on to identify global, interactive and metacognitive reading strategies, tools and techniques that emphasise the reflective and creative aspects of the reading process and can thus enable learners to become successful readers in independent, including technologically-mediated, learning environments. She concludes that independent learners need to be guided in reading strategy development to help them manage this aspect of their learning.

Strategies for listening comprehension are the subject of Chapter 5. Here, Larry Vandergrift presents an overview of listening strategies and how independent learners can acquire them. He highlights the multidimensional nature of listening comprehension and the subsequent need to take control of listening through acquiring word recognition and segmentation skills, as well as metacognitive strategies specific to L2 listening which enable learners to interpret what they hear. He focuses in particular on the development of metacognitive awareness about listening processes and its link with reflection, motivation and learner autonomy. The learning cycle he presents guides learners through the planning, predicting, monitoring, verification and reflection stages needed to acquire good listening skills and knowledge of the metacognitive processes related to them, as skilled autonomous learners.

In Chapter 6 Melanie Bloom discusses cognitive strategies to support the writing process. She makes a strong case for writing strategies to have a more central place in ILL than they are currently afforded in conventional contexts. Bloom looks first at the theory of second language writing, before exploring ways in which cognitive strategies used in conventional learning settings could be adapted for independent contexts. She categorises these under pre-writing (e.g. resourcing, analysing, elaborating and grouping), writing (e.g. rereading, substitution and strategic use of the L1), and revising between drafts (e.g. guided proofreading, resourcing and recombining). Bloom concludes that the interrelated characteristics of L2 writing – communicative, cultural, social and linguistic – call for a range of cognitive strategies, and that independent language learners need, in addition, to develop metacognitive knowledge and strategies such as self-evaluation and planning to give them more control over their learning.

Andrew Cohen presents an original approach in Chapter 7 to the development of speaking strategies through the use of pragmatics in virtual environments. He demonstrates how speech acts are dependent on the socio-cultural situation in which they are being performed. Cohen emphasises the need to support learners in developing the strategies needed for learning and performing speech acts in different cultural settings and the ability to monitor and evaluate pragmatic performance (metapragmatic strategies). His innovative project *Dancing with words* takes us into Second Life where students can communicate in an online virtual world via avatars, and through taking part in role-plays, develop strategies to improve their speaking skills in given socio-cultural contexts. Cohen concludes with a focus on the key role of language learning strategies in enhancing pragmatic performance and the benefits of different technologies for pragmatic and cultural instruction in independent language learning contexts.

Elspeth Broady and Nick Dwyer 'bring the learner back into the process' in Chapter 8 in their discussion of strategies for grammatical development in independent learning. Their overview of the research relevant to grammatical development takes us from the 'good language learner' equipped with cognitive grammar-focused strategies, to the metacognitively aware learner who is, in addition, able to plan, orchestrate and monitor his or her strategy use. Broady and Dwyer suggest that there is an important role for metacognitive awareness in the area of grammar, particularly for independent learners who need to adopt meaning-focused strategies which 'overcome the limitations of decontextualised grammatical practice', while at the same time making choices about when and how to focus on grammatical form. They conclude with an outline of the context for future research which will mark a renewed focus on learners' own interventions in this highly complex area.

Strategies for vocabulary acquisition are the topic of Chapter 9. In this chapter, John Klapper reviews current research into vocabulary learning strategies (VLS) and evaluates its relevance for independent language learners. He discusses the complementarity of explicit and implicit approaches to vocabulary learning, the concept of 'deep' and 'shallow' processing in relation to VLS, and the various attempts made to categorise strategies, in particular Schmitt's (2000) strategy taxonomy which, in concentrating on explicit, deliberate approaches, is particularly appropriate for learners in independent settings. Strategies for implicit learning such as guessing from context and reading for pleasure make up the final sections of Klapper's chapter. He argues in conclusion that independent language learners need to employ a range of both deliberate and incidental VLS in order to acquire the vocabulary they need for effective language use.

In Chapter 10, Inma Alvarez, Tita Beaven and Cecilia Garrido discuss strategies for acquiring intercultural competence, an area that is under-researched in the literature. They refer to Byram's (1997) definition of intercultural communicative competence based on cultural knowledge, attitudes and skills, and the concept of the 'intercultural speaker' who is aware of the constantly changing nature of culture, the contribution of individual cultural input to language interactions, and the power of different cultures to shape language identities. Alvarez *et al.* focus on strategies that enable language learners to become independent in developing a 'cross-cultural mind', engaging critically with 'otherness', and negotiating meaning in intercultural communication. They emphasise throughout the link between language learning and culture learning strategies, and highlight the need for a cultural dimension in any strategies-based approach to independent language learning.

Strategies for Learner Self-management

Linda Murphy explores the use of learning logs in Chapter 11, as a means of supporting language learning strategies and as a strategy in its own right. Her chapter starts with an elaboration of the concept of a learning log and other terms such as 'journal', 'diary' and 'portfolio', which are all used to record students' feelings and reactions to their learning, and can thus be instrumental in helping students to engage in critical reflection, which is closely linked to autonomy. Murphy explores the context, framework and language for reflection, and then examines the practice of reflective learning logs to develop metacognitive strategies, including planning, monitoring and self-assessment. Her later sections focus on the use of learning logs to develop specific language skills such as listening, reading, speaking and writing. She concludes that there is a clear link between the strategic use of learning logs, conscious critical reflection and effective language learning.

In Chapter 12, Stella Hurd examines the concept of affect and its interrelationship with cognition, explores classifications of strategies in relation to affect, and discusses self-regulation in terms of affective control. Hurd focuses in particular on strategies to cope with language anxiety and maintain motivation at a distance. She highlights the potential of virtual learning environments to provide opportunities for peer support, as well as the critical role of the tutor in building confidence, providing feedback and promoting a sense of community. The second half of her chapter reports on a study using think-aloud verbal protocols to investigate affect and strategy use among a small group of distance language learners. In conclusion, Hurd calls for a more holistic approach which gives greater recognition to the importance of affect in independent learning settings and recognises the integral relationship between affective and cognitive aspects of language learning.

Collaborative language learning strategies are discussed in Chapter 13. Ursula Stickler and Tim Lewis provide a history of Tandem learning and set out the two key principles of Tandem learning – autonomy and reciprocity. They then report the findings of a study in which the exchanges between six Tandem learners taking part in a German/English project were analysed to reveal the type of language learning strategies employed and the frequency of their use. Using an adapted version of Oxford's (1990) strategy inventory, they were able to provide a detailed and comprehensive picture of these. Social strategies were found to be the most widely used, indicating the highly social nature of Tandem learning. In conclusion, they emphasise that success in email Tandem learning is reliant on the use of a distinctive set of strategies: 41% of strategy use was found to be specific to the online or Tandem learning environment.

Mike Truman in Chapter 14 develops the theme of self-management in his discussion of an area of particular significance in independent settings, that of self-correction. He explores self-correction as a key process in independent language learning, and the relationships between this process, self-regulation and the development of learner autonomy. Truman focuses on learner-centred approaches to dealing with linguistic faults, such as co-operative learning, collaboration and, in particular, learner–teacher interaction in relation to focus on form, noticing and attention, and feedback to encourage self-correction. He examines both tutor interventions (repetition, incorporation, self-repair and peer-repair) and computerised 'intelligent' automated feedback, which can increase learners' control over learning. Finally, using examples from learning materials in different environments, Truman highlights both the pedagogical and communication dimensions of self-correction and, in conclusion, returns to the theme of self-correction as interaction, which he sees as encompassing both dimensions of this highly complex concept.

Strategies for online language learning environments are the subject of Chapter 15. Based on the findings from a telecollaboration project involving participants from France, the UK and the United States, Mirjam Hauck and Regine Hampel discuss the specific challenges of computer-mediated communication (CMC) and the ways in which these may influence strategy use. Taking Oxford's (1990) strategy inventory, they focus in their study on participants' affective and social strategies, and the additional strategies students use to manage their learning online. A new cluster of strategies which they grouped together as 'facilitating interaction' emerged from analysis, as well as other online-specific strategies which they termed 'socio-environmental' and which contributed to establishing a sense of community. Hauck and Hampel conclude that strategies cannot simply be transferred from face-to-face to virtual contexts and argue for strategy training geared to the specific context of online language learning.

The final chapter of the volume addresses issues around the integration of language learning strategies into learning materials. In this chapter, Linda Murphy looks first at research into strategy instruction, and the divergent opinions on whether instruction should be an explicit, informed and integral part of learning materials or allowed to develop implicitly in an informal and 'uninformed' way. She discusses the widely held view that learners need to be given opportunities to try out strategies, in addition to developing a better awareness of the potential of strategies to improve their own learning. Her final sections examine integration in practice for independent language learners, using examples from Open University and other materials. In her conclusion, she draws together key considerations for strategy instruction, such as balance (between strategy instruction and language instruction), task design, and assessment, while warning of the dangers of attempting to adopt a 'one-size fits all' policy.

Language Learning Strategies in Independent Settings offers a rich and varied landscape presented by a number of experienced and committed authors. Our hope is that it will contribute to a fuller understanding of the role of language learning strategies in independent settings, provoke thought and stimulate new developments in what is an exciting and evolving field.

Stella Hurd and Tim Lewis

Part 1
Language Learning Strategies: Theory, Research and Practice

Chapter 1
Language Learning Strategies in Independent Language Learning: An Overview

CYNTHIA WHITE

Introduction

The notions of independence, autonomy and control in learning experiences have come to play an increasingly important role in language education. A number of principles underpin independent language learning – optimising or extending learner choice, focusing on the needs of individual learners, not the interests of a teacher or an institution, and the diffusion of decision-making to learners. Independent language learning (ILL) reflects a move towards more learner-centred approaches viewing learners as individuals with needs and rights, who can develop and exercise responsibility for their learning. An important outgrowth of this perspective has been the range of means developed to raise learners' awareness and knowledge of themselves, their learning needs and preferences, their beliefs and motivation and the strategies they use to develop target language (TL) competence. In this chapter I begin with an overview of the concept of independent language learning, and of the particular contribution of language learning strategies to this domain. I argue that a fundamental challenge of independent language learning is for learners to develop the ability to engage with, interact with, and derive benefit from learning environments which are not directly mediated by a teacher. Drawing on learner conceptualisations of distance language learning I argue that learners develop this ability largely by constructing a personally meaningful interface with the learning context, and that strategies play a key role in this regard. In the latter half of the chapter I focus on a series of landmark studies, identifying how they illuminate important aspects of independent language learning, extend our understanding of strategies and strategy development and provide insights into how students use strategies within independent learning contexts. The following three sections provide historical and theoretical background, while the two main sections in the remainder of the chapter provide a state of the art overview of language learning strategies in ILL.

The Emergence of Independent Language Learning

Concern for the individual learner and for learner choice, control and responsibility has been a pervasive influence on language learning and teaching for more than three decades (Brindley, 1989; Holec, 1981, 1987; Holec *et al.*, 1996; Nunan, 1988; Rubin, 1975; Tudor, 1996), and is central to the idea and practice of independent language learning. The expectation that language learners can be independent, and that this is an important attribute and goal, underlies much of the writing on learner autonomy (Benson, 2001; Broady & Kenning, 1996; Little, 1991; Wenden, 1991), self-access learning (Sheerin, 1997), distance learning (Hurd, 2005; Murphy, 2005a, 2005b; Vanijdee, 2003; White, 2003, 2006), resource-based learning (Guillot, 1996), self-directed learning (Carver, 1984) and different forms of online learning such as tandem partnerships (Lewis & Walker, 2003). But independent in what sense? Here I explore three broad interpretations of independent language learning, the first concerning the learning context, the second outlining a philosophy of learning and the third based on learner attributes (see Figure 1.1).

Independent language learning can refer to a context or setting for language learning (Benson & Voller, 1997; Wright, 2005) in which learners develop skills in the TL often, though not always, individually. The emphasis here is on independence from the mediating presence of a teacher during the course of learning. In addition, the degree of freedom

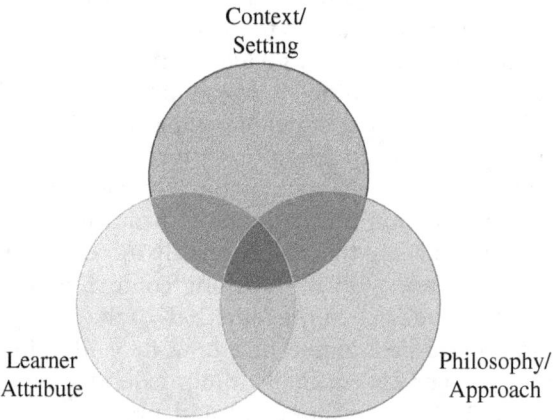

Figure 1.1   Interrelated dimensions of independent language learning

learners have to make choices (Anderson & Garrison, 1998), to select learning opportunities and to use resources according to need is highlighted. Self-access learning (Gardner, 2007), distance learning (White, 2007) and language advising (Gremmo & Castillo, 2006) represent ways of organising learning aligned to this interpretation, each of which has its own strong tradition in cultures as diverse as those of Scandinavia, the People's Republic of China, New Zealand and France.

A second dimension of independent language learning refers to a philosophy or approach to learning which aims to develop and foster independence in learners, who may or may not be in independent learning settings. Dickinson (1994), for example, argues that the most effective way of developing favourable attitudes towards independence is for teachers to prepare language learners to think about their needs and objectives and then to learn how to structure their learning. From another perspective, Candy (1991) argues that independent learning can be both a goal and a process and that the two are intertwined. Paul (1990: 37) captures both goal and process aspects, suggesting that the most important criterion for success in distance education should relate to learner independence and that 'the ultimate challenge ... is to develop each individual's capacity to look after his or her own learning needs'. This approach, promoting learner independence, has been highly influential within the learner autonomy movement (Benson, 2001). I shall shortly return to examining the relationship between learner autonomy and learner independence.

The third dimension of ILL refers to learner attributes and skills which can be acquired and used in self-directed learning, and it is here that the link with strategies and strategy instruction is most commonly drawn; independence involves developing the attitudes, beliefs, knowledge and strategies needed by learners to take actions dealing with their own learning. Independent learning in this sense is based on students' understanding of their own needs and interests and is fostered by creating the opportunities and experiences which encourage student choice and self-reliance and which promote the development of learning strategies and metacognitive knowledge. Many learner support initiatives (see e.g. Dreyer *et al.*, 2005) are focused on developing this dimension of learner independence. A further distinction is important here, namely the difference between disposition and ability highlighted by Sheerin (1997: 57): 'Learner independence is a complex construct, a cluster of dispositions and abilities to undertake certain activities. It is important to distinguish between disposition and ability because a learner may be disposed to be independent in an activity such as setting objectives, but lack the technical ability – may be an independent learner in intention but not in practice ...' While ILL as a philosophy and as an attribute may both be significant aspects of particular language learning arrangements, it is useful to maintain the distinction between the two: the former emphasises the ways in which learning is configured to promote independence in learners, while the latter focuses on the contribution learners themselves make to ILL.

Within the research literature, the relationship between independence and autonomy is both diverse and contested: Little (1991) writing on learner autonomy emphasises 'interdependence' over 'independence' in learning; Dickinson (1994), associates independence with active responsibility for one's learning and autonomy with the idea of learning alone; and Littlewood (1997: 81) sees autonomy in the context of language acquisition as involving 'an ability to operate independently with the language and use it to communicate personal meanings in real, unpredictable situations'. More recently Lamb and Reinders (2006: viii) in the introduction to their edited volume on supporting independent language learning use autonomy suggest there are 'two strands of independence/autonomy', one concerned with language learning as essentially an independent process, the other concerned with ways of organising learning to take place independently of teacher control. They highlight the 'contextual nature of autonomy, and indeed independence' (Lamb & Reinders, 2006: vii) and argue that given the complexity of the field, it is impossible to arrive at a definitive definition of either independent language learning or autonomy, echoing Aoki's (2003) argument that there are only multiple views of autonomy rather than a single authoritative characterisation. It is not unusual for learner autonomy and learner independence to be used interchangeably, as synonyms, or near synonyms (see e.g. Fisher *et al.*, 2007; Mozzon-McPherson, 2007). Further perspectives on individual difference and learner autonomy are to be found in Chapters 2 and 3.

There have also been a number of critiques of the notion of independence and the way it has been conceptualised and applied within learning contexts. Arguing that independence implies 'an unavoidable dependence on one level on authorities for information and guidance' Boud (1988: 29) sees interdependence as a stage of development that transcends independence and as an essential component of autonomy. In a similar vein, Anderson and Garrison (1998) critique the emphasis placed on learner independence in distance contexts, noting that a concern with independence has not been sufficiently matched with a concern for the demands placed on learners in independent learning contexts. They posit that the goal should not be learner independence, but developing control of learning experiences by the learners themselves; this requires a combination of independence (the opportunity to explore and make choices), proficiency (the ability and competence to engage in learning experiences) and support (resources that facilitate personally meaningful learning). An important question arising from this perspective is the extent to which, in any form of independent language learning, learners can participate in and control their learning experiences, whether in terms of opportunity, disposition or ability. This question will be examined and revisited at different points in the chapter, alongside the related contribution of learning strategies.

Conceptualising Independent Language Learning: Learner Perspectives

As we have just seen, researchers and theorists have conceptualised independent learning as a particular context for learning, and as a philosophy or approach to learning including as a goal of education. It has also been interpreted as referring to qualities or attributes of learners: as skills and abilities which can be learned, developed and used in working independently and as individuals taking responsibility for their learning. These ways of thinking about independent learning tell us little, however, about how learners conceptualise independent learning and the meanings and significance it holds for them. While a substantial body of research into learner beliefs about language learning exists (Abraham & Vann, 1987; Barcelos, 2003; Benson & Lor, 1999; Kalaja, 1995; Wenden, 1986), including beliefs about strategy use (Riley, 1997; Victori, 1995; Yang, 1999), learner beliefs and representations of independent language learning remain relatively unexplored. Such a gap in our understanding is rather curious given that the purpose of independent language learning, however defined, is to enhance the learning experiences and opportunities of the key participants, the learners.

One framework for understanding the essentials of independent language learning and the critical contribution of language learning strategies comes from the learner-context interface theory (White, 2003, 2005) based on a phenomenographic study into how students perceive, experience and conceptualise their learning in an independent setting (for details see White, 1999). Within the reports of learners, independent language learning was not defined as a specific setting, or philosophy, or set of learner attributes. Rather, the essence of independent language learning involved constructing and assuming control of a personally meaningful and effective interface between themselves, their attributes and needs, and the features of the learning context. Independent language learning according to this view is based around learners as active agents who evaluate the potential affordances within their environments and then create, select and make use of tasks, experiences, and interlocutors in keeping with their needs, preferences, and goals as learners. The ways in which learners do this, and the composition of each interface is likely to differ between learners and over time. The constructed interface then guides and informs learning and develops with new learning experiences. Establishing an interface requires knowledge of self and of the environments and the skills to establish congruence between those two dimensions. The construction of the interface is also closely related to the use of learning strategies and the development of metacognitive knowledge and this is discussed in the next section.

The Contribution of Language Learning Strategies

Until the mid-1970s, a major focus of applied linguistics research was classroom-based language teaching methodology with the possible significance of alternative learning contexts or learner contributions such as motivation, learning styles and language learning strategies largely overlooked. From the mid-1970s the emphasis moved from a concern with the methods and products of language teaching to a focus on the learner, with growing inquiry into how language learners process, store, retrieve and use TL material. One dimension of this research involved attempts to find out how language learners manage their learning and the strategies they use as a means of improving TL competence. Various lists and taxonomies of strategy use have been developed as a result of these enquiries the two most influential being O'Malley and Chamot's (1990) distinction between metacognitive, cognitive and socio-affective strategies, and Oxford's (1990) *Strategy Inventory for Language Learning* (SILL) comprising direct strategies (memory, cognitive and compensation strategies) and indirect strategies (metacognitive, affective and social). More recently, specific taxonomies have been produced for particular areas of language use, such as listening (Vandergrift *et al.*, 2005) – the topic of Chapter 5 in this volume – and reading (Sheory & Mokhtari, 2001), which Chapter 4 addresses. As research in this field developed, researchers quickly established the link between strategy use and learner independence: Holec (1981), for example, argued that learners need methodological preparation for self-directed learning and this includes facility in the use of learning strategies. 'Learning how to learn' then came to be seen as a critical and necessary component of the language learning process, from which the idea of learner training and strategy instruction emerged (Ellis & Sinclair, 1989; Weaver & Cohen, 1997). Learning strategy research and strategy instruction are central to developing understanding of how to tackle learning a language in a range of contexts, including independent settings. In addition, the distinctive contribution of metacognitive strategies and metacognitive knowledge to independent language learning has been a recurrent theme in the literature (Hurd, 2001; Victori & Lockart, 1995; Wenden, 1999; White, 1995, 1997, 1999).

The lack of consensus in defining the term strategy first noted by Wenden (1991) has been echoed by other researchers (Dörnyei, 2005; Ellis, 1994; McDonough, 1995). Strategy researchers have addressed this criticism (Grenfell & Macaro, 2007), and have also explored the ways in which second language acquisition researchers conceptualise, define, operationalise and use the term strategy (Cohen, 2007). Language learning strategies are commonly defined as the operations or processes which are consciously selected and employed by the learner to learn the TL or facilitate a language task. Strategies offer a set of options from which learners consciously select in real time, taking into account changes occurring in the environment, in order to optimise their chances of success in achieving their goals in learning and using the TL. As such the term strategy characterises the relationship between intention and action, and is based on a view of learners as responsible agents who are aware of their needs, preferences, goals and problems.

Students must draw on knowledge of themselves as learners, of the learning task and of appropriate strategies to use in a given context, in order to develop a meaningful interface with the learning environment. An example of the key contribution of strategy use to the development of a productive learner-context interface in independent language learning comes from the work of Harris (1995). In a study of successful learning among adult distance learners of English as a Second Language (ESL) in the Adult Migrant English Programme in Australia Harris noted that while students were highly motivated they found it hard to accept the role of being a distance student and struggled to develop for themselves the conditions and characteristics associated with being a distance learner.

Interviews with the students revealed that for many this was a painful process of adjustment as they held on to the view that the ideal learning environment is provided by face-to-face teacher-mediated language classes with immediate support from the teacher, opportunities for regular commitment to study, language practice in a non-threatening situation and the opportunity to make social contacts. Those adult distance learners of English who may have resisted this form of learning but succeeded 'had found ways to re-create for themselves the "study-nurturing" environment needed for success' (Harris, 1995: 52). Strategies were central to this process and distance learning only became a viable option for those students who were able to 'match the level of the course and teacher support with their own self-supporting strategies' (Harris, 1995: 88). For example, successful students actively created for themselves a study-nurturing environment, in ways which approximated their idea of the kind of learning environment a teacher develops in face-to-face language classes.

The sustained popularity of language learner strategy research lies in the potential it holds for affecting learning, both in and outside of the classroom, offering information that clearly is useful to both teachers and learners, and that can enhance the processes of language learning (Grenfell & Macaro, 2007). Exploring learning strategies is an important way of gaining insights into independent learning given that researchers and teachers are generally remote from the sites of learning in those contexts. Independent language learning is also particularly challenging for learners (Bown, 2006; Jones, 1994; White, 1995, 1997), and an ongoing concern has been to provide learners with insights into those challenges and the ways they can respond to them through strategy use. Within the field of ILL it is possible to identify a number of landmark studies which have extended our understanding of learning strategies in a range of forms and settings for independent learning; they are also significant in marking out the field of strategy research in independent learning. The studies have focused on two broad domains: the strategies learners use, and ways of enhancing independent language learning through strategy training and strategy development. The remainder of the chapter is devoted to an overview of learning strategies in ILL, seen in terms of these two domains.

Strategy Use in Independent Language Learning

For studies within the first domain (see Table 1.1) the focus has been not only on strategy use, but on how those strategies contribute to learners' progress, how strategy use changes over time and how it relates to the learning environment and individual differences. A hallmark of these studies has been the largely contextual approach they take to view strategy use as the result of not only learners' cognitive choices but also of the mediation of their particular communities (White *et al.*, 2007). The value of a contextual approach is to reveal the extent to which language learning

Table 1.1 Language learning strategies in independent language learning: research context and focus

Researcher(s)	*Context*	*Focus*
Bown (2006)	Self-instructed university language learning	Locus of learning and affective strategy use
Carson & Longhini (2002)	Immersion language learning	Strategy use in a naturalistic, immersion setting
Jones (1994)	Self-study of Hungarian	Diary study focusing on learning strategies
Rowsell & Libben (1994)	Independent language learning over six months in a university course	Strategy use of high- and low-achievers
White (1995)	Dual-mode university foreign language learning	Comparative study of strategy use of classroom and distance language learners

strategies are part of students' experiences, interrelated with their environment, and also to reveal how strategies function in different aspects of language learning. Methodologies used include diaries, case studies, and interviews, all of which aim to access students' strategies through their own interpretative meanings and perspectives.

The studies reviewed here reveal how learners develop creative language use strategies to build a rich interface with the learning context (Rowsell & Libben, 1994), how strategy use functions as a means of matching learning needs with affordances of the context (Carson & Longhini, 2002; Jones, 1994), and changes in strategy use over time (Carson & Longhini, 2002; Jones, 1994). The studies also reveal how metacognitive strategy use, in particular self-management strategies, enables learners to respond to the demands of an independent learning context (White, 1995, 1997). Affective strategies are also seen to assist learners in managing the isolated aspects of independent learning and to contribute to the development of an effective interface with the features of those contexts (Bown, 2006; White, 1995, 1997).

A landmark study, focusing explicitly on independent language learning comes from Rowsell and Libben (1994) with the intriguing title of 'The sound of one hand clapping: How to succeed in independent language learning'. It deals with the behaviours of high-achieving independent learners. While in the body of the article the researchers largely eschew the use of the term strategy since they claim it is strongly associated with classroom procedures, the abstract begins with: 'This paper describes the self-reported strategies of thirty adults who were independent language learners for a period of six months' (Rowsell & Libben, 1994: 668). The term they prefer to use is autonomously controlled task (ACT) to represent independent learning behaviour which takes place outside the classroom environment. The undergraduate students in the study were assigned the task of choosing a foreign language to study on their own for six months without the aid of a teacher; they kept diaries of how they carried out their learning and how they approached the issue of being communicative in isolation. The significant differences between high and low achievers were not in how they treated the learning materials they chose, but rather in their meaningful use of language. High achievers showed more instances of what they termed 'communication-making' and 'context-making' activities (Rowsell & Libben, 1994: 668); they often created imaginary partners in imaginary settings to converse with and they treated language as functional, as a medium of communication rather than content to be memorised. The learners used ACTs which required creative language use in context, and this ability was not developed by the low achievers who used more restricted strategies such as memorising phrases. Functional ACTs were a powerful acquisition technique in Rowsell and Libben's study enabling learners to develop a rich interface with the learning context; by bringing into play imagined contextualised communication successful learners participated in a form of practice which developed a positive affective relationship to the task, and which treated language as a medium to be used creatively.

Another early study comes from Jones (1994) who explores his own self-study of Hungarian as a 'lone language learner' over a period of eleven months. Analysing his diary entries, he notes his reliance on intensive vocabulary learning strategies for the first few months; once his goal of about 2000 word-families had been reached, there was a 'radical paradigm shift' (Jones, 1994: 441) in his strategies. This was made possible by the crossing of two linguistic thresholds: sufficient knowledge of word roots to support the guessing of meaning of many compound lexical items, and the ability to read authentic texts. Jones argues that both types of strategies – studial strategies (textbook-centred strategies) and strategies related to comprehensible input – were equally valuable but at different stages of his independent language learning trajectory. Jones' study is illuminating not only in terms of strategy use and the nature of independent learning, but in terms of how strategy use functions as a key means of matching individual needs with the opportunities and constraints of the learning environment. Strategies for developing writing skills and for grammatical and vocabulary development are explored in Chapters 6, 8 and 9 of this volume.

Relatively few studies have focused on naturalistic independent learning in an immersion context where learners have no access to formal instruction. An important piece of research in this area comes from Carson and Longhini (2002) who provide a longitudinal account of the learning styles and strategies of an adult learner of Spanish, Joan, immersed in the TL in Argentina over a period of eight weeks. A distinctive feature of the diary study is the attention given to the learning context – described as 'a rich target language environment with continuous communicative demands' (Carson & Longhini, 2002: 432). Carson and Longhini also focus on the contribution of the interlocutors and what they afford in terms of learning opportunities and explanations of language phenomena, especially pragmatics and nuances in the semantic lexicon. Key factors in the development of the learner-context interface in this study are Joan's preferences as a learner and the continuous need to communicate in an immersion context. An important finding was that while learning style remained relatively constant throughout the study, strategy use was variable. In the initial stages the primary strategy reported was 'compensating for missing knowledge' attributed to the communicative demands of an immersion context and Joan's lack of effective memory strategies. In later stages, Joan's cognitive strategies had increased and her command of the TL had improved meaning she was less reliant on compensation strategies. The study provides clear evidence that strategy choice was influenced by learning in a naturalistic environment, with much less use of studial strategies associated with classroom learning contexts. Within the diary entries by far the most recurrent strategies were in the metacognitive group (examples include organising and evaluating strategies), comprising 40% of total reported strategy use. The high frequency of metacognitive strategies is attributed to individual learner characteristics, namely Joan's interests as a learner and her understanding of the contribution of metacognitive strategies to her experience as a language learner. The study provides a fascinating look into the world of the independent language learner in a TL immersion context. It reveals the learner's awareness of the affordances of the learning context, and of the ways particular speakers can contribute to her growing expertise in the language. It also reveals the learner's awareness of her strategy preferences, the gaps in the repertoire of strategies she was prepared to use, and the overriding influence of learning style on strategy choice and use.

The influence of an independent learning context on strategy use was the focus of a large-scale study carried out by White (1995, 1997) in a dual-mode university, offering language courses to both distance and face-to-face students. Using both quantitative and qualitative measures White compared the strategy use of distance ($n = 274$) and face-to-face ($n = 143$) language learners enrolled in the same foreign language courses. Results revealed a highly significant difference between the two groups in terms of metacognitive strategy use on a number of measures. Distance learners reported four times the use of metacognitive strategies compared to classroom learners. This is aligned with Hurd's (2001) observation that metacognitive strategies have special significance for students in open and distance contexts. There were also differences in the kinds of metacognitive strategies used by the two groups: self-management was the metacognitive strategy most frequently used by distance learners, but accounted for a low proportion of the metacognitive strategy use of classroom learners. In order to deploy self-management strategies, learners need to know how they learn best, and need to have the necessary procedural skills to set up optimal learning conditions. Distance learners made significantly greater use of self-management strategies which involved working out how they learned best, then incorporating these conditions into their interactions with the TL. This was also very evident in the verbal reports produced by distance learners. The wider and increased use of metacognitive control by distance learners found in this study can be seen as a response to the demands placed on those learners by the independent learning context and as an important means for them to set up and manage an effective interface with the learning context. White (1999) extended this study to gain further insights into the kinds of metacognitive knowledge novice distance learners use, or attempt to gain, to ensure their learning processes are effective in the relatively unfamiliar self-instruction context.

The final study in this section highlights the importance of self-regulation of affect through the use of affective strategies in independent language learning. Writing from the context of a university individualised instruction programme in Russian, Bown (2006) explores the affective strategies students use and the contribution of those strategies to their learning experiences. She uses Richards and Renandya's (2002: 121) definition of affective strategies as those that 'serve to regulate emotions, attitude and motivation' including, for example, positive self-talk. Within the Russian programme, students receive course materials and a specially prepared handbook to guide them through the course, they work on their own at their own pace and have a set number of meetings with instructors for conversational practice and assessment. Noting Knowles' (1975) observation that students often feel angry, confused or disoriented when beginning to work in a self-directed environment, Bown focuses on how students use affective strategies to cope with emotional states they may experience in the programme. Bown's study provides rich insights into how students regulate affect in self-instruction, and the aspects of self-instruction which give rise to negative emotions. Isolation from a learning group meant many students struggled to maintain motivation and the absence of self-referencing opportunities to assess progress. In that isolation some students developed negative beliefs about their own abilities, comparing themselves unfavorably to imagined 'idealised' learners who proceed with few difficulties. Interestingly Bown notes that all students experienced ambiguity and demotivation as a result of isolation from their peers, but it was the more successful students who reported use of strategies to help them cope with negative emotions, including the uncertainty that arose from the lack of benchmarks. So control and management of affect were critical to students developing an effective interface with the self-instruction learning context. Specifically they did this through such strategies as self-encouragement and self-talk strategies that evaluated and adjusted their expectations of themselves. Bown provides insights into the way affective strategies contributed to the development of an effective interface between learners and the self-instruction context: they provided encouragement and reduced anxiety; they gave students a sense that they could do the work, and enhanced their motivation and enjoyment of learning. Her findings are congruent with those of Harris (1995), namely that independent language learning presents significant challenges to learners and that the ability to manage affective responses to these challenges is crucial for persistence, satisfaction and success. For Ushioda (1996: 54), the experience of success, the ability to minimise the impact of negative experiences, to reflect and to take personal control of 'affective conditions and experiences' are all keys to the development of motivational autonomy in L2 learners. Chapter 12 on affective strategies develops and extends many of these points.

The findings from these studies reveal much about strategy use in independent learning contexts, and the ways in which learners use strategies to respond to the particular features and demands of those settings. Another important research avenue has also been pursued which focuses on providing learners with opportunities to raise their awareness of and involvement in their learning and to develop their strategic repertoires. Identifying optimal ways of learner development in and for independent learning runs through these studies to which I now turn.

Strategy Development and Independent Language Learning

The second domain of studies (see Table 1.2) concerns ways of enhancing ILL through strategy training and strategy development. In these

Table 1.2 Strategy development in independent language learning: Research context and focus

Researcher(s)	*Context*	*Focus*
Cohen and White (2008)	Self-selected language learning contexts	Fostering learner awareness and choice, including strategic awareness
Harris (2003)	Independent language learning at a distance	Strategy instruction to support adults at diverse levels of competence learning a range of languages
Hurd *et al.* (2001)	Distance foreign language learning	Learner support, course development and strategy training
Hyland (2001)	Distance learning of English	Feedback to distance learners linked to learning strategies
Paige *et al.* (2004)	Study abroad	A strategy-based curriculum on language and culture learning
Rowsell and Libben (1994)	Independent language learning over six months in a university course	Strategy use of high- and low-achievers
Pujolà (2002)	Independent language learning in ImPRESSions, a web-based multimedia CALL programme	Strategy use and use of online help facilities with learner training components

studies researchers have explored ways of best providing strategy instruction for particular independent language learning environments, the role of the teacher in that process and the relationship between feedback and strategy development. The issue of implicit learner training in strategies was touched on in the work of Hyland (2001) as part of a study of feedback provided to distance learners of English in Hong Kong. She sees feedback as relating to two broad categories: the product and the learning process. In an independent learning context the need for learners to establish effective ways of working to develop TL skills means that feedback relating to process (i.e. the strategies and actions students should take to improve their language) is particularly important. In spite of the fact that tutors in the study had been encouraged to focus on feedback relating to the learning process less than 17% of teacher comments addressed this area. When teachers did focus on this area Hyland notes they provided encouragement and suggested specific learning strategies and, as a best practice, related this feedback to specific parts of the learning materials. Hyland (2001: 246) concludes that 'learning a language through the distance-learning mode is a challenging task and the feedback we offer students ... may be crucial to them ... in terms of helping them to improve their learning strategies'.

To date, few further studies have focused on the relationship between learner feedback and strategy development, despite this being a promising avenue for research and practice. For an extended discussion of the role of self-correction strategies in ILL see Chapter 14.

Hurd *et al.* (2001) address the issue of providing strategy development opportunities to distance language learners, in the context of the Open University, UK's language courses. They argue that in recognition of the level of strategic competence required for distance study, strategy development and a reflective approach to learning need to be incorporated into the course materials. The overall aim is to scaffold opportunities for learners to manage their independence in optimal ways, by acquiring 'a series of strategies and skills that will enable them to work individually' (Hurd *et al.*, 2001: 341). Hurd *et al.* provide a range of approaches to strategy development and learner training: a learning strategies guide,[1] a contextualised approach to strategy instruction distributed throughout the course, and opportunities for students to think about how they learn – in the form of a learning diary. In addition there is an emphasis on self-evaluation and self-assessment, together with language awareness activities requiring students to relate what they are learning to what they already know. The approach aims to initiate students into a more independent form of learning focusing on learners' ability to organise and reflect on learning, monitor progress, identify gaps and solve problems. To do this students are encouraged to learn about themselves as language learners and to use this individualised self-knowledge to enhance the interface they develop with the learning context. This approach relates closely to the findings of White (1995) that distance language learners need to be able to manage the process of language learning based on their understandings of how they learn best; they then draw on this understanding to set up learning experiences which are favourable, though not necessarily ideal.

A different approach to learner training comes from Harris (2003) who explores the interesting question of how best to provide strategy instruction for adult distance learners in Europe. The situation is still more complex than in the work of Hurd *et al.* (2001) in that the audience are learners in diverse distance contexts, learning different languages at different levels of proficiency and with different needs, expectations and prior experiences. Under the aegis of the European Commission's Grundtvig Programme, Harris and her INSTAL project partners decided to develop a stand-alone handbook and CD-Rom to develop the ability of adult learners to work more effectively with the distance learning resources available to them.[2] As Harris reflects critically on the process of adapting classroom-based models of strategy instruction she explores central dilemmas that arise: strategy instruction could not be contextualised and it was to take place without the mediating presence of a teacher or of a learning group; the instruction was 'stand-alone' in that it did not relate to a particular language or level of proficiency; it was not embedded in a specific language course; it was to be accessed by learners working independently of a teacher or peers. In terms of approach, the first two parts of the handbook aim to raise learners' awareness of themselves as learners, including their motivation, beliefs, learning style, prior experiences and the affective dimension of learning. The third section focusing directly on strategy instruction allows students to navigate their own paths through the handbook, according to their needs. Still, a number of important questions remained which had to be resolved in developing the content: What level of language learner to focus on, elementary, intermediate or advanced? How encompassing should the strategy training be? Is it possible to include enough not to be overwhelming but also enough to allow most students to extend their strategic repertoire? What sort of language should the handbook be couched in – so that it is transparent, clear and also translatable to other languages? These issues are highlighted as crucial because of the absence of teacher mediation to make the bridge between students' needs, abilities and preferences and strategy instruction, and to scaffold ongoing strategy development. Viewing Harris' approach in terms of the learner-context interface model, it is the students who have to create a meaningful interface between themselves and the strategy instruction modalities, and then use this to enhance their own interactions with the TL, improving that interface. Harris concludes that while initially she identified ways of contextualising strategy instruction as the key issue, as experience within the project developed this was less problematic than the absence of teacher mediation to scaffold learner self-management. This conclusion lends support to an interface-based model of independent language learning, of the roles and requirements placed on learners, and of how strategy instruction can be directed at enhancing the learner-context interface. The final chapter of this volume, Chapter 16, deals with the integration of strategy instruction into learning materials for independent users.

The relationship between computer-based language learning and strategy development has been the subject of a number of studies (Meskill, 1991; Pujolà, 2002; Ulitsky, 2000). Pujolà (2002) explores the use of strategy help facilities within a Web-based programme for English language learners intended for self-study. ImPRESSions is a multimedia programme consisting of video, audio and written text using multimedia – TV, radio and newspapers – as a source of language input. Pujolà notes that the design of ImPRESSions makes it a powerful tool for independent language learning in terms of the combination of media which support learners in working on TL tasks. Of particular interest for independent learning are the help facilities including a learner training facility called Ask-the-Experts the main purpose of which is to develop learners' metacognitive knowledge regarding comprehension strategies. The form that the advice takes is an interesting feature of the study. Pujolà observes that, based on experience, learners pay more attention to tutors' advice in class rather than advice in handbooks or texts, so in ImPRESSions a video format was chosen. Two experienced teachers gave unscripted responses to such questions for reading as: 'What can I do when unfamiliar information is given?' and for listening: 'How can I improve listening to news on the radio?' Students were free to Ask-the Experts at any point within a module. Students' computer movements were digital-video screen recorded, and this together with direct observation and retrospective questions provided detailed insights into students' learning strategies. Pujolà notes the challenge of providing appropriate strategy training for all users: while most students found the facility interesting, providing strategic information they were not aware of, more strategically knowledgeable students reported it was of little use. The study also demonstrates the tensions students experience in distributing attention optimally to language practice and learner training: those students who never accessed the Ask-the-Experts facility cited time constraints and were concerned to devote enough time to the comprehension tasks. For a fuller discussion of strategies for online environments, see Chapter 15.

A further development in independent language learning has been the growth in study abroad learning opportunities. Paige et al. (2004) assess the impact of a strategy-based curriculum on language and culture learning when students are on study abroad. Students were required twice a week to reflect on assigned sections of a self-study guide which included a strategies-based approach to language and culture learning. In addition, they were asked to reflect online on their own experiences, and their experiences in relation to the assigned reading using e-journals. The e-journals were complemented by another qualitative method, interviews, and quantitative measures such as questionnaires and profiles. Preliminary analysis of the e-journals suggests that students valued the way in which the journalling enabled them to make links between the world of learning in the guide, and their lived experiences during study abroad; e-journalling was useful not only as a means of accessing students' reflections in the field, but also of structuring their reflections and use of the guide. Based on the students' qualitative reports Paige *et al.* (2004) provide examples of how language and culture learning strategies helped students better understand differences in communication styles, gave students a perspective on their experiences, and on ways of improving their language skills, and encouraged them to seek out native speakers to support them. A discussion of strategies for intercultural learning is given in Chapter 10.

An innovative approach to learner development comes from Cohen and White (2008) who focus on learners as they exercise choice in independent language learning. As background to the study twenty-first century language learners are positioned as 'informed consumers' facing multiple options, both real and virtual, for learning languages. Central to the idea of the informed consumer is that making choices places demands on language learners, and needs to be underpinned by knowledge and abilities which cannot be assumed. Cohen and White explore the idea that learners can become skilled in choosing appropriate learning environments, and then within those elected environments can also become more skilled in learning how to make best use of them. A pilot undergraduate course was developed by Cohen to develop student expertise and know-how about language learning in both in-class and out-of-class contexts. As part of the course students conducted explorations of different language learning opportunities in their immediate environment – many of which involved independent language learning. One component of the course concerns strategies and how they contribute to different aspects of language learning processes in different environments. Cohen and White's study provides a broadened sense of what is required of learners in independent language learning, in selecting particular learning environments, in combining them with other learning opportunities, in critically reflecting on what those environments afford them, and in finding ways to add value to their experiences. Through the reports of students we have insights into the means by which they actively construct, fashion and enhance a way of learning for themselves based on the alternatives available. This view of language learners as individuals who actively seek out and evaluate the possibilities for language learning in their context, characterises many of the key processes required of students in independent language learning.

Conclusion

The theory and practice of independent language learning has focused on particular contexts or settings for learning, particular philosophies or approaches, and particular attributes of learners, whether these be dispositions, skills or goals. The nature of independent learning requires learners to develop the ability to engage with and derive benefit from TL sources and contexts which are not directly mediated by a teacher. Within applied linguistics there has been a sustained commitment to find out how learners succeed in ILL and to find ways of enabling learners to manage the challenges of language learning in those contexts through the decisions they make and the actions they take as learners. In this chapter I have provided an overview of landmark studies in learning strategies in ILL, focusing on both the strategies learners use and on ways of enhancing ILL through strategy development. Investigating how learners develop their abilities to direct and derive benefit from independent learning experiences is a particularly illuminating approach to understanding such diverse opportunities for language learning as immersion contexts, self-access settings and virtual learning environments. The studies reviewed here provide insights into the operations or processes used by learners, and into the nature of independent language learning itself, providing a solid basis for future enquiry. As contexts for language learning, both real and virtual, continue to expand and diversify, continued research and reflection on how learners develop the ability to engage with independent learning contexts deserves to remain high on emerging research agendas.

Notes

1. This has now been replaced with *Success with Languages* (Hurd & Murphy, 2005), a set book for language students at beginner level and recommended to language students at all other levels.
2. Grundtvig project no. 87400-CP-1-2000-1-AT-GRUNDTVIG-ADU ran from 2000 to 2002. Its acronym, INSTAL, stood for Individualising Strategies for Adult Learners in Language and ICT Learning. For a statement of aims and details of the project partners see http://www.isoc.siu.no/isocii.nsf/projectlist/87400.

References

Abraham, R. and Vann, R. (1987) Strategies of two language learners: A case study. In A. Wenden and J. Rubin (eds) *Learner Strategies in Language Learning* (pp. 85–102). London: Prentice Hall.

Anderson, T. and Garrison, D. (1998) Learning in a networked world: New roles and responsibilities. In C. Gibson (ed.) *Distance Learners in Higher Education: Institutional Responses for Quality Outcomes*. Madison Wisconsin: Atwood Publishing.

Aoki, N. (2003) Expanding space for reflection and collaboration. In A. Barfield and M. Nix (eds) *Learner and Teacher Autonomy in Japan 1: Autonomy You Ask!* (pp. 189–196). Tokyo: JALT.

Barcelos, A. (2003) Researching beliefs about SLA: A critical review. In P. Kalaja and A. Barcelos (eds) *Beliefs About SLA: New Research Approaches* (pp. 7–33). Netherlands: Kluwer.

Benson, P. (2001) *Teaching and Researching Autonomy in Language Learning*. Harlow: Longman.

Benson, P. and Lor, W. (1999) Conceptions of language and language learning. *System* 27, 459–472.

Benson, P. and Voller, P. (1997) Introduction: Autonomy and independence in language learning. In P. Benson and P. Voller (eds) *Autonomy and Independence in Language Learning* (pp. 1–17). Harlow, Essex: Addison Wesley Longman.

Boud, D. (1988) Moving towards autonomy. In D. Boud (ed.) *Developing Student Autonomy in Learning* (pp. 17–39). London: Kogan Page.

Bown, J. (2006) Locus of learning and affective strategy use: Two factors affecting success in self-instructed language learning. *Foreign Language Annals* 39 (4), 640–659.

Brindley, G. (1989) *Assessing Achievement in the Learner-Centered Curriculum, Sydney NSW*. Sydney: Macquarie University, National Centre for English Language Teaching and Research.

Broady, E. and Kenning, M. (1996) Learner autonomy: An introduction to the issues. In E. Broady and M. Kenning (eds) *Promoting Learner Autonomy in University Language Teaching* (pp. 9–22). London: Association for French Language Studies (AFLS) in association with The National Centre for Languages (CiLT).

Candy, P. (1991) *Self-Direction for Lifelong Learning*. San Francisco: Jossey-Bass.

Carson, J. and Longhini, A. (2002) Focusing on learning styles and strategies: A diary study in an immersion setting. *Language Learning* 52 (2), 401–438.

Carver, D. (1984) Plans, learner strategies and self-direction in language learning. *System* 12 (2), 123–131.

Cohen, A. (2007) Coming to terms with language learner strategies: Surveying the experts. In A. Cohen and E. Macaro (eds) *Language Learner Strategies: 30 Years of Research and Practice* (pp. 29–46). Oxford: Oxford University Press.

Cohen, A. and White, C. (2008) Language learners as informed consumers of language instruction. In I. Kupferberg and A. Stavans (eds) *Festschrift for Elite Olshtain* (pp. 185–206). Jerusalem, Israel: Magness, Hebrew University Press.

Dickinson, L. (1994) Preparing learners: Toolkit requirements for preparing/orienting learners. In E. Esch (ed.) *Self-Access and the Adult Language Learner* (pp. 39–49). London: The National Centre for Languages (CiLT).

Dörnyei, Z. (2005) *The Psychology of the Language Learner: Individual Differences in Second Language Acquisition*. Mahwah, NJ: Lawrence Erlbaum.

Dreyer, C., Bangeni, N. and Nel, C. (2005) A framework for supporting students studying English via a mixed-mode delivery system. In B. Holmberg, M. Shelley and C. White (eds) *Distance Education and Languages: Evolution and Change* (pp. 92–118). Clevedon: Multilingual Matters.

Ellis, G. and Sinclair, B. (1989) *Learning to Learn English: A Course in Learner Training*. Cambridge: Cambridge University Press.

Ellis, R. (1994) *The Study of Second Language Acquisition*. Oxford: Oxford University Press.

Fisher, D., Hafner, C. and Young, J. (2007) Integrating independent learning: Lessons learned and implications for the classroom. In D. Gardner (ed.) *Learner Autonomy 10: Integration and Support* (pp. 33–55). Dublin: Authentik.

Gardner, D. (2007) Integrating self-access learning into an ESP course. In D. Gardner (ed.) *Learner Autonomy 10: Integration and Support* (pp. 8–32). Dublin: Authentik.

Gremmo, M-J. and Castillo, D. (2006) Advising in a multilingual setting: New perspectives for the role of the advisor. In T. Lamb and H. Reinders (eds) *Supporting Independent Learning: Issues and Interventions* (pp. 21–36). Frankfurt: Peter Lang.

Grenfell, M. and Macaro, E. (2007) Claims and critiques. In A. Cohen and E. Macaro (eds) *Language Learner Strategies: 30 Years of Research and Practice* (pp. 9–28). Oxford: Oxford University Press.

Guillot, M. (1996) Resource-based language learning: Pedagogic strategies for Le Monde sur CD-Rom. In E. Broady and M. Kenning (eds) *Promoting Learner Autonomy in University Language Teaching* (pp. 139–158). London: Association for French Language Studies (AFLS) in association with The National Centre for Languages (CiLT).

Harris, C. (1995) 'What do the learners think?': A study of how It's Over To You learners define successful learning at a distance. In S. Gollin (ed.) *Language in Distance Education. How Far Can We Go? Proceedings of the NCELTR Conference* (pp. 44–54). Sydney: NCELTR.

Harris, V. (2003) Adapting classroom-based strategy instruction to a distance learning context. *Tesl-EJ* 7 (2). On WWW at http://cwp60.berkeley.edu:16080/TESL-EJ/ej26/a1.html. Accessed 15.04.08.

Holec, H. (1981) *Autonomy and Foreign Language Learning*. Oxford: Pergamon.

Holec, H. (1987) The learner as manager: Managing learning or managing to learn? In A. Wenden and J. Rubin (eds) *Learner Strategies in Language Learning* (pp. 145–156). London: Prentice Hall.

Holec, H., Little, D. and Richterich, R. (eds) (1996) *Strategies in Language Learning and Use*. Strasbourg: Council of Europe Publishing.

Hurd, S. (2001) Managing and supporting language learners in open and distance learning environments. In M. Mozzon-McPherson and R. Vismans (eds) *Beyond Language Teaching Towards Language Advising* (pp. 135–148). London: The National Centre for Languages (CiLT) in association with the University of Hull.

Hurd, S. (2005) Autonomy and the distance language learner. In B. Holmberg, M. Shelley and C. White (eds) *Distance Education and Languages: Evolution and Change* (pp. 1–19). Clevedon: Multilingual Matters.

Hurd, S., Beaven, T. and Ortega, A. (2001) Developing autonomy in a distance language learning context: Issues and dilemmas for course writers. *System* 29 (3), 341–355.

Hyland, F. (2001) Providing effective support: Investigating feedback to distance language learners. *Open Learning* 16 (3), 233–247.

Jones, F. (1994) The lone language learner: A diary study. *System* 22 (4), 441–454.

Kalaja, P. (1995) Student beliefs (or metacognitive knowledge) about SLA reconsidered. *International Journal of Applied Linguistics* 5 (2), 191–204.

Knowles, M. (1975) *Self-Directed Learning: A Guide for Learners and Teachers*. New York: The Adult Education Company.

Lamb, T. and Reinders, H. (2006) Introduction. In T. Lamb and H. Reinders (eds) *Supporting Independent Learning: Issues and Interventions* (pp. vii–xi). Frankfurt: Peter Lang.

Lewis, T. and Walker, L. (eds) (2003) *Autonomous Language Learning in Tandem*. Sheffield: Academy Electronic Publications.

Little, D. (1991) *Learner Autonomy: Definitions, Issues and Problems*. Dublin: Authentik.

Littlewood, W. (1997) Self-access: Why do we want it and what can it do? In P. Benson and P. Voller (eds) *Autonomy and Independence in Language Learning* (pp. 79–92). London: Longman.

McDonough, S. (1995) *Strategy and Skill in Learning a Foreign Language*. London: Arnold.

Meskill, C. (1991) Language learning strategies advice: A study of the effects of on-line messaging. *System* 19, 277–287.
Mozzon-McPherson, M. (2007) Supporting independent learning environments: An analysis of structures and roles of language learning advisers. *System* 35, 66–92.
Murphy, L. (2005a) Attending to form and meaning: The experience of adult distance learners of French, German and Spanish. *Language Teaching Research* 9 (3), 295–327.
Murphy, L. (2005b) Critical reflection and autonomy: A study of distance learners of French, German and Spanish. In B. Holmberg, M. Shelley and C. White (eds) *Distance Education and Languages: Evolution and Change* (pp. 20–39). Clevedon: Multilingual Matters.
Nunan, D. (1988) *The Learner-centred Curriculum: A Study in Second Language Teaching*. Cambridge: Cambridge University Press.
O'Malley, J. and Chamot, A. (1990) *Learning Strategies in Second Language Acquisition*. Cambridge: Cambridge University Press.
Oxford, R. (1990) *Language Learning Strategies: What Every Teacher Should Know*. New York: Newbury House.
Paige, R., Cohen, A. and Shively, R. (2004) Assessing the impact of a strategies-based curriculum on language and culture learning abroad. *Frontiers: The Interdisciplinary Journal of Study Abroad* 10, 253–276.
Paul, R. (1990) Towards a new measure of success: Developing independent learners. *Open Learning* 5 (1), 31–38.
Pujolà, J-T. (2002) CALLing for help: Researching language learning strategies using help facilities in a web-based multimedia program. *ReCALL* 14 (2), 235–262.
Richards, J. and Renandya, W. (2002) *Methodology in Language Teaching: An Anthology of Current Practice*. Cambridge: Cambridge University Press.
Riley, P. (1997) 'BATs' and 'BALLs': Beliefs about talk and beliefs about language learning. Conference Proceedings. Bangkok: Thonburi. In L. Dickinson (ed.) *Autonomy 2000: The Development of Learning Independence in Language Learning*. Bangkok: King Mongkut's Institute of Technology.
Rowsell, L. and Libben, G. (1994) The sound of one hand clapping: How to succeed in independent language learning. *Canadian Modern Language Review* 50 (4), 668–687.
Rubin, J. (1975) What the "good language learner" can teach us. *TESOL Quarterly* 9, 41–51.
Sheerin, S. (1997) An exploration of the relationship between self-access and independent learning. In P. Benson and P. Voller (eds) *Autonomy and Independence in Language Learning* (pp. 54–65). Harlow, Essex: Addison Wesley Longman.
Sheory, R. and Mokhtari, K. (2001) Differences in the metacognitive awareness of reading strategies among native and non-native readers. *System* 29 (4), 431–449.
Tudor, I. (1996) *Learner-Centredness as Language Education*. Cambridge: Cambridge University Press.
Ulitsky, H. (2000) Language learner strategies with technology. *Journal of Educational Computing Research* 22 (3), 285–322.
Ushioda, E. (1996) *Learner Autonomy 5: The Role of Motivation*. Dublin: Authentik.
Vandergrift, L., Goh, C., Mareschal, C. and Hassantafaghodtari, M. (2005) *The Metacognitive Awareness Listening Questionnaire (malq). Development and Validation*. Paper presented at International Association of Applied Linguistics, Madison WI, 26 July 2005.
Vanijdee, A. (2003) Thai distance English learners and learner autonomy. *Open Learning* 18 (1), 75–84.

Victori, M. (1995) *EFL Writing Knowledge and Strategies: An Integrative Study Doctoral Dissertation*. Universitat Autonoma de Barcelona (available at Dissertation Abstracts International. UMI number: 9804043).

Victori, M. and Lockart, W. (1995) Enhancing metacognition in self-directed learning. *System* 23 (2), 223–234.

Weaver, S. and Cohen, A. (1997) *Strategies-Based Instruction: A Teacher-Training Manual*. Minneapolis, MN: Center for Advanced Research on Language Acquisition, University of Minnesota.

Wenden, A. (1986) What do second language learners know about their learning?: A second look at retrospective accounts. *Applied Linguistics* 7, 186–205.

Wenden, A. (1991) *Learner Strategies for Learner Autonomy*. Englewood Cliffs, NJ: Prentice Hall.

Wenden, A. (1999) An introduction to metacognitive knowledge and beliefs in language learning: Beyond the basics. *System* 27 (4), 435–441.

White, C. (1995) Autonomy and strategy use in distance foreign language learning: Research findings. *System* 23, 207–221.

White, C. (1997) Effects of mode of study on foreign language learning. *Distance Education* 18 (1), 178–196.

White, C. (1999) The metacognitive knowledge of distance learners. *Open Learning* 14 (3), 37–47.

White, C. (2003) *Language Learning in Distance Education*. Cambridge: Cambridge University Press.

White, C. (2005) Towards a learner-based theory of distance language learning: The concept of the learner-context interface. In B. Holmberg, M. Shelley and C. White (eds) *Distance Education and Languages: Evolution and Change* (pp. 55–71). Clevedon: Multilingual Matters.

White, C. (2006) Robinson Crusoe and the challenges of supported distance language learning. In T. Lamb and H. Reinders (eds) *Supporting Independent Learning: Issues and Interventions* (pp. 55–72). Frankfurt: Peter Lang.

White, C. (2007) Autonomy, independence and control: Mapping the future of distance language learning. In D. Gardner (ed.) *Learner Autonomy 10: Integration and Support* (pp. 56–71). Dublin: Authentik.

White, C., Schramm, K. and Chamot, A. (2007) Research methods in strategy research: Re-examining the toolbox. In A. Cohen and E. Macaro (eds) *Language Learner Strategies: 30 Years of Research and Practice* (pp. 93–116). Oxford: Oxford University Press.

Wright, V. (2005) Independent learning. In J. Coleman and J. Klapper (eds) *Effective Learning and Teaching in Modern Languages* (pp. 133–141). London: Routledge.

Yang, N-D. (1999) The relationship between EFL learners' beliefs and learning strategy use. *System* 27 (4), 515–535.

Chapter 2
Individual Variation and Language Learning Strategies

PHIL BENSON and XUESONG GAO

Introduction

This chapter is concerned with the interaction between two important areas of second language learning research: learning strategies, the theme of this book, and individual variation in language learning. Interest in individual variation as an essential element in second language learning has gained ground in recent years in the light of critiques of the idea that the most important SLA processes have a 'universal' character (e.g. Block, 2003; Breen, 2001; Ellis, 1999; Firth & Wagner, 1997; Norton & Toohey, 2001; Zuengler & Miller, 2006). Although this interest takes a number of forms, learning strategy research provides us with some of the most powerful evidence that we have for individual variation at the level of the learning process. Instruments such as the Strategy Inventory for Language Learning (SILL) (Oxford, 1990), for example, tend to reveal considerable variations within and among the populations they are administered to. But how are these variations to be explained? In this chapter, we will explore three major approaches to this question: the first focusing on internal and external factors influencing strategy use, the second on the ways in which strategy use is situated within specific contexts and tasks, and the third on learner experience and agency. We will also attempt to identify the different views of 'language learners as individuals' underlying each of these approaches.

Internal and External Influences on Strategy Use

At the heart of the approach discussed in this section is the idea of 'individual differences', a term that has been used to tie together a number of independent fields of research (Dörnyei, 2005; Dörnyei & Skehan, 2003; Ehrman et al., 2003; Ellis, 1994, 2004; Gardner, 1997; Larsen-Freeman, 2001; Skehan, 1989). Reviews of the literature tend to reserve the term 'individual differences' for internal, biological or psychological attributes that are assumed to influence language learning outcomes. Research on variation in strategy use, however, has extended this assumption in two major directions: first, by treating strategy use as a variable outcome of individual differences and, second, by considering external, social or situational, factors as influences on strategies alongside factors of individual difference.

Ellis explains the basic idea behind individual difference research as follows:

> In the case of L1 acquisition, children vary in their rate of acquisition but all, except in cases of severe environmental deprivation, achieve full competence in their mother tongue; in the case of L2 acquisition (SLA), learners vary not only in the speed of acquisition but also in their ultimate level of achievement, with a few achieving native-like competence and others stopping far short. How can we explain these differences in achievement? (Ellis, 2004: 525)

Individual difference research is, therefore, ultimately concerned with relationships between learner attributes and what Larsen-Freeman (2001: 12) calls 'differential success' in second language learning. Although researchers have begun to use qualitative approaches to explore these relationships more deeply, quantitative methods have hitherto dominated the field. As Ellis puts it:

> The favoured method is a survey questionnaire consisting of Likert scale items that require learners to self-report on some aspect of their language learning.... The data obtained from questionnaires and tests are submitted to correlational analysis (e.g. Pearson Product Moment correlation, exploratory and confirmatory factor analysis, or multiple regression), the purpose of which is to identify relationships among individual difference variables and/or the relationship between a specific factor (such as motivation) and a measure of L2 achievement or proficiency. (Ellis, 2004: 526–527)

Reviews of research differ both in the variables they place under the heading of individual differences and in the ways in which they group these variables together. Here we divide the most frequently discussed individual difference variables into two major groups:

- attributes that are typically supposed to be innate, such as gender, age, language learning aptitude, personality and learning styles;
- attributes that are typically supposed to be acquired, such as attitudes, motivation, beliefs, and strategy use.

Although strategy use, itself, is treated as an individual difference variable in many reviews, Dörnyei (2005: 162) questions whether it should be, because strategies are 'an aspect of the learning process rather than being learner attributes proper'. The counter-argument is, perhaps, that questionnaire instruments such as the SILL identify strategy preferences more than strategy use and that strategy preferences are, in fact, a psychological attribute akin to learner beliefs.

The innate-acquired distinction can also be expressed in other ways: as, for example, a distinction between biologically-determined and socially-constructed, or context-free and context-sensitive, attributes. Viewed as binary distinctions these are somewhat problematic. Gender, age, language learning aptitude, personality and learning styles can be viewed as biologically fixed and context free, but their effects are socially-constructed and context-sensitive. In the case of gender, for example, biological sex, *per se*, may be of less significance as an individual difference variable than the social construction of gender differences and the different expectations of, and opportunities for, males and females with respect to second language learning in particular contexts (e.g. Rao, 2005). What seems clear, however, is that patterns of strategy preference and use are acquired, socially-constructed and context-sensitive. As Wenden (2002: 45) argues, while many of the attributes on the list of individual difference factors appear to 'operate below consciousness and are not easily changed', with the identification of learning strategies as an individual difference variable, 'a learner difference that is accessible and changeable has been added to this list of factors'.

Although individual difference research is ultimately concerned with variable success in language learning, primarily measured through variables of proficiency, there has also been a good deal of research into the interaction between individual difference factors. And because learning strategies appear to be especially malleable, much of this research has focused on the ways in which strategy use is influenced by other individual differences. Although Ellis (2004: 545) is critical of the dominance of survey questionnaires in strategy research, he also notes that they have facilitated systematic investigation of factors influencing strategy use, including 'learner age, stage of learning, gender, the target language, learner cognition, learning style, cultural background, personality, previous experience of language learning, and the setting in which learning takes place'. Dörnyei (2005: 171) also describes this as 'the most fruitful research direction in the area of learning strategies' and reviews a number of studies on the influence of gender, cultural background and motivation. In most of these studies, strategy use is assessed using the SILL or similar instruments and strategies are treated as the independent variable, with many also treating proficiency levels as a potential influence.

Contextual factors such as stage of learning, target language, cultural background, previous experience, and setting tend to fall outside the scope of individual difference research proper, because they are viewed as being external to language learning as a cognitive process. Nevertheless, Larsen-Freeman (2001: 23) describes the extent to which individual difference factors are altered by contextual factors as 'an enormously important, yet vexing, question'. Studies of variation in learning strategies have also begun to break down the distinction between internal and external influences by incorporating both individual differences and social and situational factors. Below, we summarise two studies investigating some of these potential influences on learning strategies, Yang (1999) and Shmais (2003), in order to illustrate how this kind of research works.

Focusing on relationships between learner beliefs, motivation and strategy use, Yang (1999) used a questionnaire incorporating Horwitz's (1988) Beliefs About Language Learning Inventory (BALLI), the SILL, and a number of self-designed questions on learner background and motivation. The subjects were 405 students of English (194 male and 211 female) attending six different Taiwanese universities. Yang used statistical procedures to identify four factors in the BALLI data: (1) self-efficacy and expectation about learning English, (2) perceived value and nature of learning spoken English, (3) beliefs about foreign language aptitude, and (4) beliefs about formal structural studies. Factors identified in the SILL data were: functional practice, cognitive-memory, metacognitive, formal oral-practice, social, and compensation strategies. Correlation analysis revealed significant statistical correlations between self-efficacy beliefs and all six strategy factors and between beliefs about the value and nature of learning spoken English and formal oral-practice strategies. The study also revealed one conflict between beliefs and strategy use; whereas most of the students believed that memorisation was important in language learning, they used a limited number of memory strategies. Interpreting the main findings from the data, Yang noted that the first and second belief factors, which correlated most strongly with strategy use, consisted mainly of 'motivational beliefs', while the third and fourth consisted mainly of 'metacognitive beliefs'. From this, Yang hypothesised a cyclical process, in which beliefs and high levels of motivation lead to strategy use, while strategy use modifies beliefs and in turn enhances motivation.

Our second example, Shmais (2003), focuses on relationships between strategy use and gender and proficiency among 99 English major students (80 female and 19 male) at university in Palestine. Strategy use was assessed using a modified version of the SILL, to which 10 strategies specific to the local setting were added. Three measures of proficiency were used: cumulative university assessment scores, year of study and self-efficacy ratings on a three-point scale ('very good', 'good' and 'poor'). Statistical correlations showed no significant relationship between gender and any of the six groupings on the SILL. The results relating to proficiency variables showed no significant overall correlation with strategy use, although significant correlations were established between low university scores and affective strategies, and high self-efficacy ratings and cognitive strategies.

Reviews of studies based on statistical correlations between internal or external variables and scores on strategy instruments such as the SILL suggest that variation in strategy use correlates with a wide range of variables (Dörnyei, 2005; Ellis, 2004). But to date, no clear overall pattern of influences has emerged from this research and, looking closely at examples of studies of this kind, we can see a number of difficulties in establishing a consensual view along these lines. Yang's (1999) and Shmais's (2003) studies, for example, are non-comparable, because they examine different variables. Studies of the same variables can also be difficult to compare, because they use different instruments or interpret results in particular ways (e.g. Yang's use of factor analysis to draw conclusions about motivation from a learner beliefs questionnaire). Interpreting correlational data in terms of causality is a persistent problem and we may note, for example, that Yang's hypothesis about the cyclical relationship involving strategies, motivation and beliefs is not derived from data reported in the study, which at best shows no more than correlations among these variables. And, as in Yang's and Shmais's studies, the significant correlations that are found are often between particular aspects of the individual difference or contextual variables and results on particular sections of the strategy questionnaire. Lastly, there are persistent methodological problems concerned with sample size and the validity and reliability of the instruments. Although Shmais's (2003) findings on gender, for example, run counter to those of the majority of studies, which have tended to show that females use more strategies than males, this may be no more than an artefact of the research design, in particular the small sample size and the imbalance between the number of male and female subjects.

In conclusion to this section, we want to look more at the view of learners as individuals that emerges from this kind of research. Each of the factors identified as potential influences on strategy use divides up the general population of second and foreign language learners in a particular way. Gender, for example, divides this population roughly into two groups on the basis of an observable biological characteristic. Cultural background divides up the same population according to observations based on geographical setting, ethnicity and first language. Factors such as language learning aptitude, learning style, motivation and beliefs divide the population into psychological types, usually on the basis of categories derived from responses to questionnaires. Lastly, situational variables divide the population according to the types of teaching and learning environments in which learners find themselves at any particular moment in time. Considered independently of each other, each of these factors potentially accounts for strategy use variations among groups or types of learners of various kinds. But at the level of the individual, we must assume that all of these factors will be operating at any moment in time. It is perhaps, then, simply the sheer number of factors at issue and the complexity of interaction among them that accounts for individual variation in learning strategy use. This presupposes, however, that learners' individual identities are constituted within, or even determined by, unique configurations of biological, psychological, social and situational variability. In the following sections, we will explore how some learning strategy researchers have begun to see this as a problematic view of learner individuality, especially in respect to its treatment of context and agency.

Context and Tasks

Language learning strategy questionnaires typically invite students to describe their strategy use in a general way. And although questionnaire items often presuppose specific situation or task types, students are again invited to describe their strategic responses to them in a general way. Strategy questionnaires, therefore, tend to be context-insensitive to the extent that students do not have the opportunity to say that they use particular strategies on some occasions but not on others. Most strategy questionnaires, for example, ask students how frequently they guess the meanings of unknown words when reading, to which they might reply 'sometimes'. But they do not inquire into the meaning of this response: whether the students use the strategy only with certain kinds of texts, when reading for particular purposes, or in particular environmental conditions, and so on. In the approach discussed in the previous section, context feeds into variation in strategy use through the learner's identity. But here again, it tends to have a very general character. Cultural background and teaching and learning settings are among the most important contextual factors identified in the literature. Levine *et al.* (1996), for example, found that recent immigrants to Israel from the former Soviet Union tended to prefer 'traditional' strategies, such as memorisation of grammar rules and doing grammar exercises, whereas learners who had spent five years or more in Israel showed a preference for more 'communicative' strategies. Explaining the preferences of the Soviet sample in terms of 'cultural-educational' factors, they suggested that 'learners studying in a highly structured and uniform educational system would develop learning strategies reflecting that system' (Levine *et al.*, 1996: 45). The assumption here appears to be that prolonged experience of types of educational environments will eventually become a factor of cultural identity, albeit one that is susceptible to change in new contexts of culture (Bedell & Oxford, 1996).

It is in this sense that strategy questionnaires appear to address strategy preferences, or predispositions to adopt certain strategies independently of the situation or task at hand, rather than strategy use. In so far as it is concerned with context, correlational research also pays more attention to broad or macro-contextual factors contributing to learner identity than it does to more immediate or micro-contextual factors. More recently, however, there has been growing interest in the ways in which individuals vary their strategy use in response to particular situations or tasks (Donato & McCormick, 1994; Gao, 2003, 2006; Gillette, 1994; Gu, 2003; Oxford et al., 2004; Parks, 2000; Parks & Raymond, 2004). Oxford et al. (2004), for example, compared students' strategy use when dealing with reading tasks of three difficulty levels and found that the differences among learners of different proficiency levels was less marked when they were working on an easy task than when they were working on a more difficult one. Although this is essentially a finding from empirical data, interest in the micro-contextual aspects of variation in strategy use has also been fuelled at the theoretical level by insights from sociocultural theory.

In a seminal paper published in the mid-1990s, Donato and McCormick (1994) outlined what they understood to be the implications of three of the major planks of sociocultural theory for language learning strategy research: the principle of 'genetic explanation' and the notions of 'activity' and 'mediation'. Genetic explanation, they argued, 'maintains that psychological phenomena (e.g. language learning strategies) can be understood only by examining their genesis in a culturally-specific situated activity', which implies a research approach involving 'documenting strategic development in situ' (Donato & McCormick, 1994: 454). The notion of 'activity' (derived from Leontiev's Activity Theory) implied principally that strategies are 'actions motivated by specific objectives and instrumental to fulfilling specific goals' (Donato & McCormick, 1994: 455). A strategy such as guessing words in context could, for example, be used in order to save time during a reading assignment rather than to enhance second language reading proficiency (Gillette, 1994). In this sense, Activity Theory 'provides a framework for *situating* strategy use within the total context of an individual's language learning activity' (Donato & McCormick, 1994: 455). Lastly, mediation involves the idea that higher mental processes, which include learning strategies, develop through interactions with material tools, symbolic systems such as language and discourse, and the behaviour of other human beings. All forms of mediation, they argue, are 'embedded in some context that makes them inherently sociocultural processes' and learning strategies are, therefore, the outcome of processes 'analogous to other forms of socioculturally mediated development, such as initiation into a professional community, the construction of cultural beliefs and values, or ways of relating to others' (Donato & McCormick, 1994: 456). In sum, Donato and McCormick argue for an approach to research in which the emergence of strategies is viewed as a 'by-product of goal-directed situated activity in which mediation through artefacts, discourse, or others plays a central role in apprenticing novices into a community of practice' (Donato & McCormick, 1994: 456), or put more simply, as 'a process directly connected to the practices of cultural groups' (Donato & McCormick, 1994: 453). Below we look at two studies that have applied this view of strategy development 'in context' to investigation of variations in strategy use.

Adopting a sociocultural perspective, Parks and Raymond (2004) investigated how the strategies used by Chinese students enrolled on an MBA course at a Canadian University developed as they moved from sheltered classes into electives in which they studied alongside native-speakers of English. The study involved multiple data collection procedures including interviews with students, EAP teachers and MBA professors, class observations and collection of documents such as course outlines and samples of student work. Parks and Raymond observed changes in strategy use in three main areas. One of the main changes related to reading; in order to cope with the quantity of reading in the MBA electives, and with the goal of passing the course in mind, the students became highly selective in what they read. They also developed a variety of strategies for speaking out in participatory lectures that were influenced by re-evaluations of their ability to interact in English; the students' lack of participation in sheltered lectures had been noted by their professors and their researchers and, as Parks and Raymond put it, with the presence of native speakers in lectures 'the students themselves henceforth perceived their lack of involvement as an issue' (Parks & Raymond, 2004: 384). Lastly, the students developed strategies for coping with the demands of teamwork including avoidance of groups containing Canadians and more positive strategies through which they repositioned themselves as competent team members. One of the major conclusions of Parks and Raymond's study was that strategy use is 'a more complex, socially-situated phenomenon' (Parks & Raymond, 2004: 387) than it often appears to be in the learning strategies literature. Emphasising the mediating role of the presence of native-speakers of English in this particular situation, Parks and Raymond suggested that the students' use or non-use of strategies was also mediated by issues of personal and social identity implicated, for example, in their views of appropriate classroom behaviour, their assessments of Canadian students' behaviour and the attitudes of the Canadian students and professors towards them.

Whereas Parks and Raymond (2004) investigated changes in Chinese students' strategy use within an overseas setting, Gao (2006) investigated changes in strategy use among Chinese undergraduate and postgraduate students when they moved from China to a university in the United Kingdom. The data were collected through interviews in which the students were asked to describe their approaches to learning English in these settings. The changes Gao observed were first interpreted in terms of factors of psychological and social difference (Gao, 2003), but in

Gao (2006) the data were revisited from a sociocultural perspective. The focus of this second study was on how strategy use was mediated through discourses, goals and agents in the learning process in China and the United Kingdom. Gao found that in China a tendency to favour memorisation and practice strategies was mediated through discourses that emphasised the value of English as a 'tool' for educational and social advancement, an orientation towards the goal of passing English examinations, and the direction and advice of teachers, language learning experts and family members. Once the students moved to the United Kingdom, however, the force of these mediating factors diminished, because the students had largely achieved the opportunities for advancement that English offered them in China and because assessment practices shifted from tests of English to assessment of coursework through the medium of English. In the United Kingdom, the students also appeared to divide into two groups: a group whose use of strategies was considerably reduced and who often felt 'lost' in their learning of English, and a group who shifted towards greater use of social strategies and sought out opportunities for interacting with English speakers. Gao also described how this shift was facilitated by interactions with supportive English speakers. One of the important differences between the two groups, he argues, was that the first tended to be more oriented towards the goal of gaining academic qualifications through the medium of English, while the second were more strongly oriented towards learning English as a goal in its own right.

One of the more important features distinguishing the approaches discussed in this section and the next from those discussed earlier is the use of qualitative research methods. Whereas quantitative strategy research methods tend to describe broad strategy preferences, qualitative studies tend to describe the strategic behaviours of individuals in some detail. The view of language learners as individuals that emerges from this kind of research, therefore, foregrounds the idea that language learners should be viewed as 'people' with particular goals, motives and rationales (Lantolf & Pavlenko, 2001). Yet at the same time, the focus on micro-contextual explanation in sociocultural theory means that researchers have tended to foreground variations *within* individual strategy use over variation *among* individuals. Although the presentation of detailed qualitative data in Parks and Raymond (2004) and Gao (2006) conveys a picture of strategy use being forged within micro-contextual experiences in uniquely individual ways, at the level of interpretation the individuality of the students tends to be obscured by an emphasis on the ways in which these experiences influenced the group as a whole. We have not yet, in other words, arrived at the point where individual learners are viewed as being fundamentally different from each other prior to and within contextual experiences of these kinds.

Experience and Agency

Although our third approach to the explanation of variation in strategy use emphasises micro-contextual experience, it also involves a methodological focus on individual learners. The studies we are concerned with here are generally case studies of single learners, as opposed to studies of teaching and learning situations that draw on qualitative data from a number of individuals. For this reason, they convey a stronger sense of variations in strategy use developing over time as a consequence of experience. They also convey a stronger sense of the ways in which individual agency informs strategy use.

Lantolf and Pavlenko (2001) point to narratives of long-term experiences of learning as a potential source of insight into relationships between context, experience and agency in language learning, but there are as yet no individual case studies of learning strategy use in the sociocultural tradition. There are, however, a number of studies of this kind outside this tradition, using introspective or autobiographical methods (Carson & Longhini, 2002; He, 2002), biographical methods (Malcolm, 2005; Murray & Kojima, 2006) or review of published biographies (Takeuchi, 2003) to explore the long-term development of strategy use in individual learners. And even when they are not explicitly focused on this topic, introspective diary studies and (auto)biographical studies, especially, can have a great deal to say about the development of strategic behaviour (see, e.g. Campbell, 1996; Jones, 1994, 1995; Schmidt & Frota, 1986, and contributions to Benson & Nunan, 2002, 2005). Again, we will summarise two of these studies, Carson and Longhini (2002) and He (2002), in order to illustrate how this kind of research works.

Carson and Longhini (2002) is a study of Joan Carson's eight-week stay in Argentina as a Fulbright professor, during which she kept a detailed diary of her efforts to learn and use Spanish. Carson completed the SILL on three occasions, at the beginning, middle and end of her stay, and the Style Analysis Survey at the beginning. Her diary entries were also coded for references to strategies and style by Longhini and a colleague. The main findings of the study were based on statistical analysis of this data: Carson's learning style remained relatively constant, but her strategy use varied over the eight-week period, while remaining consistent with her learning style. Of more interest here, however, is the discussion of Carson's diary extracts in the published paper, which paints a detailed picture of developments in her strategy use. In particular, they show how her confidence in using social strategies developed through a series of small but significant successes, and frustrations, in interactions with strangers and friends. Her growing friendship with Longhini and her family, and Susanna, a former primary school teacher and principal in whose home she stayed, appears to have been an especially important factor here.

In one diary extract, for example, Carson describes Susanna and herself 'settled down in the living room – her with her knitting and me with my needlepoint'. Susanna looks up and says that they look like *'dos abuelitas'*.

> Another word I remembered – grandmother. We looked like two little grandmothers! I laughed and agreed. We talked off and on and I'm surprised by how much information we exchanged. (Carson & Longhini, 2002: 426)

Carson also used Susanna as a 'teacher/informant' and was occasionally frustrated because Susanna 'was unaccustomed to language learners' questions and tended to respond with explanations that would have been more appropriate for a native speaker' (Carson & Longhini, 2002: 406). On the other hand, Susanna is described as 'invaluable both as a source of input and for clarification of semantic nuances in the lexicon' and as 'a life-long teacher and an avid conversationalist' (Carson & Longhini, 2002: 406), who was 'relentless in her corrections' (Carson & Longhini, 2002: 426). What emerges from Carson's diary extracts, then, is not simply a picture of Carson's strategy use changing from one state to another in response to the naturalistic learning setting, but a far more detailed portrait of her strategy use evolving over time through a succession of experiences within this setting, and especially as a consequence of her capacity as an *individual agent* to build friendships and create environments in which she felt a sense of comfort.

He's (2002) autobiographical study of the development of her language learning strategies over the course of her life is divided into six stages: her life as a teenage EFL student in pre-Cultural Revolution China, as an independent learner working on an assembly line in a tractor factory during the Cultural Revolution, as a university student after the Cultural Revolution ended, as a lecturer and postgraduate student in Australia, and as a teacher educator in Hong Kong. Relating changes in her strategy use to the demands of each of these contexts, He explains how she mainly used cognitive and metacognitive strategies in school, but made much greater use of metacognitive strategies as an independent learner. Metacognitive strategies, she explains, continued to play a role when she moved to Australia, but they also became more or less habitual. Urgent communication needs such as writing essays and participating in seminars also shifted her attention to strategies targeting specific skills and tasks, compensation strategies and affective strategies to reduce task anxiety. A second finding of He's study was that in the early stages of her learning in China she did not consciously select the language learning strategies that she used. Instead, they were acquired in the context of instruction and gradually became automatised. In the later stages of her learning, however, with more exposure to alternative options, she became more conscious of her choice of strategies. Although He emphasises the ways in which her strategy use changed in response to different contexts of language learning and use, her article conveys a strong sense of her strategy use developing over time and as a consequence of accumulated experience. Her agency is also very much in evidence in her story: for example, in her decision to continue studying English independently in her spare time while working in a factory in the countryside and in her decisions to move first to Australia and later to Hong Kong.

The approach discussed in this section is by no means contradictory to the sociocultural perspective on variations in strategy use discussed above. Studies focused on individual learners, however, tend to foreground the ways in which strategy use develops through experiences that run through and across contexts, situations and tasks. Covering a relatively short period of time, Carson and Longhini's (2002) study shows how contextually-conditioned changes in an individual's strategy use actually take place over time as a consequence of specific experiences within the context. Covering a much longer period, He's (2002) study shows how her strategy use developed across a succession of contexts. The underlying view of language learners as individuals in studies of this kind is, therefore, one that places emphasis on the lives that they lead and the place of language learning in their lives. From this point of view, it is the accumulation of experiences of various settings, situations and tasks making up a language learning career that contributes most to learner individuality. But agency also appears to play an important part, because what the learner makes of each new context is evidently conditioned by the individuality that has already been acquired through prior experience.

Discussion and Conclusion

In this chapter, we have discussed three approaches to the explanation and investigation of individual variation in strategy use. The second and third approaches, favouring qualitative methods, clearly have more in common with each other than with the first quantitative approach. And arguably we are really dealing with a number of approaches, rather than a single approach, in each case. We acknowledge, therefore, that our tripartite division will doubtless be challenged, particularly with regard to what we have said about the view of 'the learner as individual' underlying each approach. Nevertheless, it is based on at least one fairly robust criterion concerning the ways in which learners appear in strategy research. Paradoxically, research from the 'individual differences' perspective usually involves intact groups or population samples. Although the raw data may provide evidence of individual variation, statistical treatments aim at the identification of group or typological variation. It is also something of a paradox that, although research from the sociocultural perspective treats language learning as a social process, it also pays a good deal of attention to individuals. This research, however, tends to deal with small groups of individuals in particular contexts, with the analytical focus usually falling on the context rather than the individuals. Lastly, the research on personal experience and agency deals with and focuses more directly on individual learners and their lives.

Now, it will be evident from our own contributions to the literature that we favour the second and third approaches over the first. The point that we want to draw out from this review, however, is that although these three approaches are all oriented towards understanding variation in strategy use, they actually investigate three different things: how shared biological and psychological attributes and macro-contextual circumstances correlate with strategies, how strategies are mediated by engagements with particular learning situations and tasks, and how strategies develop over the course of individual learning careers. In this sense, they are complementary approaches, each providing us with potentially useful information. Nevertheless, there is a historical trend towards the adoption of our second and third approaches, even though studies adopting quantitative correlational approaches remain numerically dominant in the literature. The individual difference research tradition on which this approach is based also appears to have reached something of an impasse, with reviews of research repeatedly concluding with calls for more qualitative, naturalistic and holistic studies. As Bailey (1991: 88) argues, 'an appreciation for individual differences ... leads directly to the importance of studying single learners in depth'. There are, however, relatively few studies of variation in strategy use of this kind, and for this reason alone, perhaps, our second and third approaches deserve further attention.

In the context of this volume, we should also point out that there have been very few studies of variations in strategy use among independent learners and, to the best of our knowledge, no studies at all directly addressing this issue in structured, as opposed to naturalistic, independent learning contexts. The aim of this chapter, therefore, has not so much been to explain variations in strategy use among independent learners, as to attempt to clear the theoretical ground for further studies in this area. Although it is difficult to forecast the directions in which such studies will take us, we want to conclude by suggesting the particular importance of understanding how the question of individual variations in strategy use may be different for independent and classroom learners.

Qualitative studies of independent learners' strategy use seem to show, above all, that strategies are woven into contexts of learning in highly specific and essentially unpredictable ways. In Joan Carson's case, for example, one strategy involved sitting with her host at her home and conversing over needlepoint and knitting. The needlepoint and knitting were not incidental to the strategy, we think. They were both a crucial contextual element in a situation that facilitated second language interaction and a symbol of the comfort of Susanna's home as an informal teaching-learning environment. Our point here is that in classroom learning, the situation and environment are usually given and known. But in both structured and unstructured independent learning contexts, learners have to create these environments and situations for themselves and the ways in which they go about this will be part and parcel of the strategic behaviour that we will need to understand. Summarising a theoretical framework for understanding the essentials of distance language learning, White (2006: 250) suggests that in distance learning the learner must 'develop an interface with the learning context that can both guide and be informed by meaningful learning experiences'. Again this seems to be a matter of strategic behaviour. The language learning strategies required of independent learners, therefore, seem to be somewhat different from those required of classroom learners and presumably they also vary according to the mode of independent learning they are engaged in. Part of our problem, in other words, is to determine the important dimensions of strategy use for independent learners, and in order to learn more about this we will undoubtedly have to pay more attention to qualitative investigation of the varied ways in which they go about language learning in their homes, workplaces and lives.

References

Bailey, K.M. (1991) Diary studies of classroom language learning: The doubting game and the believing game. In E. Sadtono (ed.) *Language Acquisition and the Second/Foreign Language Classroom* (pp. 6–102). RELC Anthology Series 28. Singapore: RELC.

Bedell, D.A. and Oxford, R. (1996) Cross-cultural comparisons of language learning strategies in the People's Republic of China and other countries. In R. Oxford (ed.) *Language Learning Strategies Around the World: Cross-Cultural Perspectives* (pp. 47–60). Honolulu: University of Hawaii Press.

Benson, P. and Nunan, D. (eds) (2002) The experience of language learning. Special issue of *Hong Kong Journal of Applied Linguistics*, 7 (2).

Benson, P. and Nunan, D. (eds) (2005) *Learners' Stories: Difference and Diversity in Language Learning*. Cambridge: Cambridge University Press.

Block, D. (2003) *The Social Turn in Second Language acquisition*. Edinburgh: Edinburgh University Press.

Breen, M. (ed.) (2001) *Learner Contributions to Language Learning*. Harlow: Pearson Education.

Campbell, C. (1996) Socializing with the teachers and prior language learning experience: A diary study. In K.M. Bailey and D. Nunan (eds) *Voices from the Language Classroom* (pp. 201–223). Cambridge: Cambridge University Press.

Carson, J.G. and Longhini, A. (2002) Focusing on learning styles and strategies: A diary study in an immersion setting. *Language Learning* 52 (2), 401–438.

Donato, R. and McCormick, D. (1994) A sociocultural perspective on language learning strategies: The role of mediation. *The Modern Language Journal* 78, 453–464.

Dornyei, Z. (2005) *The Psychology of the Language Learner: Individual Differences in Second Language Acquisition*. Mahwah, NJ: L. Erlbaum Associates.

Dörnyei, Z. and Skehan, P. (2003) Individual differences in second language learning. In C.J. Doughty and M.H. Long (eds) *The Handbook of Second Language Acquisition* (pp. 589–630). Oxford: Blackwell.

Ehrman, M.E. Leaver, B.L. and Oxford, R.L. (2003) A brief overview of individual differences in second language learning. *System* 31 (3), 313–330.

Ellis, R. (1994) *The Study of Second Language Acquisition*. Oxford: Oxford University Press.

Ellis, R. (1999) Theoretical perspectives on interaction and language learning. In R. Ellis (ed.) *Learning a Second Language Through Interaction*. Amsterdam: John Benjamins.

Ellis, R. (2004) Individual differences in second language learning. In A. Davies and C. Elder (eds) *The Handbook of Applied Linguistics* (pp. 525–550). Oxford: Blackwell Publishing.

Firth, A. and Wagner, J. (1997) On discourse, communication and (some) fundamental concepts in SLA research. *The Modern Language Journal* 81 (3), 285–300.

Gao, X. (2003) Changes in Chinese learners' learner strategy use after arrival in the UK: A qualitative enquiry. In D. Palfreyman and R.C. Smith (eds) *Learner Autonomy Across Cultures: Language Education Perspectives* (pp. 41–57). Basingstoke: Palgrave MacMillan.

Gao, X. (2006) Understanding changes in Chinese students' uses of learning strategies in China and Britain: A socio-cultural re-interpretation. *System* 34 (1), 55–67.

Gardner, R.C. (1997) Individual differences and second language learning. In R.G. Tucker and D. Corson (eds) *Encyclopedia of Language and Education. Volume 4. Second Language Education* (pp. 33–42). Amsterdam: Kluwer Academic.

Gillette, B. (1994) The role of learner goals in L2 success. In J.P. Lantolf and G. Appel (eds) *Vygotskian Approaches to Second Language Research* (pp. 195–214). Norwood: Ablex.

Gu, Y. (2003) Fine brush and freehand: The vocabulary-learning art of two successful Chinese EFL learners. *TESOL Quarterly* 37 (1), 73–104.

He, A. (2002) Learning English in different linguistic and socio-cultural contexts. *Hong Kong Journal of Applied Linguistics* 7 (2), 107–121.

Horwitz, E.K. (1988) Beliefs about language learning of beginning university foreign language students. *The Modern Language Journal* 72 (3), 283–294.

Jones, F. (1994) The lone language learner: A diary study. *System* 22 (4), 441–454.

Jones, F. (1995) Learning an alien lexicon: A single-subject case study. *Second Language Research* 11 (2), 95–111.

Lantolf, J.P. and Pavlenko, A. (2001) (S)econd (L)anguage (A)ctivity theory: Understanding second language learners as people. In M. Breen (ed.) *Learner Contributions to Language Learning: New Directions in Research* (pp. 141–158). London: Pearson Education.

Larsen-Freeman, D. (2001) Individual cognitive/affective learner contributions and differential success in second language acquisition. In M.P. Breen (ed.) *Learner Contributions to Language Learning: New Directions in Research* (pp. 12–24). London: Longman.

Levine, A., Reves, T. and Leaver, B.L. (1996) Relationship between language learning strategies and Israeli versus Russian cultural-educational factors. In R. Oxford (ed.) *Language Learning Strategies around the World: Cross-Cultural Perspectives* (pp. 35–45). Honolulu: University of Hawaii Press.

Malcolm, D. (2005) An Arabic-speaking learner's path to autonomy through reading. In P. Benson and D. Nunan (eds) *Learners' Stories: Difference and Diversity in Language Learning* (pp. 69–82). Cambridge: Cambridge University Press.

Murray, G. and Kojima, M. (2006) Out-of-class language learning: One learner's story. In P. Benson (ed.) *Insider Perspectives on Learner and Teacher Autonomy* (pp. 26–40). Dublin: Authentik.

Norton, B. and Toohey, K. (2001) Changing perspectives on good language learners. *TESOL Quarterly* 35, 307–321.

Oxford, R. (1990) *Language Learning Strategies: What Every Teacher Should Know.* New York: Newbury House/Harper and Row.

Oxford, R., Cho, Y., Leung, S. and Kim, H. (2004) Effects of the presence and difficulty of task on strategy use: An exploratory study. *International Review of Applied Linguistics in Language Teaching* 42 (1), 1–47.

Parks, S. (2000) Same task, different activities: Issues of investment, identity and use of strategy. *TESL Canada Journal* 17 (2), 64–88.

Parks, S. and Raymond, P.M. (2004) Strategy use by non-native English speaking students in an MBA program: Not business as usual. *The Modern Language Journal* 88 (3), 374–389.

Rao, Z. (2005) Gender, academic major, and Chinese students' use of language learning strategies: Social and educational perspectives. *The Journal of Asia TEFL* 2 (3), 115–138.

Schmidt, R. and Frota, S. (1986) Developing basic conversational ability in a second language: A case study of an adult learner of Portuguese. In R. Day (ed.) *Talking to Learn* (pp. 237–326). Rowley, MA: Newbury House.

Skehan, P. (1989) *Individual Differences in Second-Language Learning.* London: Edward Arnold.

Shmais, W.A. (2003) Language learning strategy use in Palestine. *TESL-EJ* 7 (2), A–3. On WWW at http://www-writing.berkeley.edu/TESL-EJ/ej26/a3.html. Accessed 08.09.07.

Takeuchi, O. (2003) What can we learn from good foreign language learners?: A qualitative study in the Japanese foreign language context. *System* 31 (3), 385–392.

Wenden, A. (2002) Learner development in language learning. *Applied Linguistics* 23 (1), 32–55.

White, C. (2006) State-of-the-art review article: The distance learning of foreign languages. *Language Teaching* 39 (4), 247–264.

Yang, N-D. (1999) The relationship between EFL learners' beliefs and learning strategy use. *System* 27 (4), 515–535.

Zuengler, J. and Miller, E.R. (2006) Cognitive and sociocultural perspectives: Two parallel SLA worlds. *TESOL Quarterly* 40 (1), 35–58.

Chapter 3
Hero With a Thousand Faces: Learner Autonomy, Learning Strategies and Learning Tactics in Independent Language Learning

REBECCA L. OXFORD

Introduction

As I complete this chapter and return to where I began, a kaleidoscopic image whirls to mind of Joseph Campbell's (1972) 'hero with a thousand faces', the mythic, journeying hero with different faces, male and female, in all cultures, times and places. As the kaleidoscope turns, I see the faces of busy, independent second or foreign language (L2) learners of many colours and ages in different sociocultural settings around the world. On their own or with help from a distance, they heroically crack the code of their new language or push themselves to greater fluency and accuracy. I see laughing faces in a study group at a café. I see a woman's intent face as she consults a tutor by telephone. I glimpse a teenage boy, emailing his tandem-learning partner three countries away. I see individual college students, retirees and refugees, dispersed, in unconventional spaces and moments, reading and studying alone or with peers.

These independent L2 learners are developing *learner autonomy* (taking responsibility for their learning), which involves, at least in part, deciding upon and using *learning strategies and tactics* that are relevant to their tasks and goals. L2 learning strategies are the goal-oriented actions or steps (e.g. plan, evaluate, analyse) that learners take, with some degree of consciousness, to enhance their L2 learning. Tactics are the highly specific versions of those actions applied to particular L2 tasks, problems, or situations (e.g. analysing a section of the newspaper *Izvestia*, to practise distinguishing between facts and opinions while reading Russian).

The people described above are embedded in their varied cultural and social settings and are influenced – though not necessarily bound – by the attitudes, values and beliefs prevalent in those settings. They are creating unique tales of linguistic-cultural being and becoming part of the massive, globally scattered, independent L2 learning enterprise. Their incipient linguistic-cultural identities grow, shift, and sometimes clash with their other identities and roles (see e.g. Norton, 2000, 2001; Norton & Toohey, 2002).[1]

For the purpose of this chapter, independent L2 learning is the learning of an additional language, usually without the involvement of a teacher. Such learning can occur alone or with other learners. It can be formal or informal. It can use technologies such as print, internet, compact disc, television, radio, video (e.g. VHS, DVD), phone or a combination. Examples of additional supports that might be offered to independent L2 learners include a self-access centre, a tutor via email or (periodically) in person, a learner support group, a chat room, a printed or Web-based guidebook on how to learn and other media support. However, the amount and nature of additional support varies greatly for L2 learners, from none to very extensive.

The overall purpose of this chapter is to show connections among three phenomena: (1) independent L2 learning, (2) learner autonomy, and (3) L2 learning strategies. The first section explains theories associated with autonomy/autonomies in independent L2 learning. The second section is primarily practical and focuses on L2 learning strategies and tactics for autonomy in independent L2 learning. The final section serves as a synthesis by describing a handful of specific examples of independent L2 learning arrangements, along with the autonomies and learning strategies likely to be associated with those arrangements.

Figure 3.1 presents relationships among the constructs in this chapter. Independent learning and classroom learning, the latter of which is not discussed in detail here, are in two separate circles. The autonomy circle bridges the two types of learning, although (as shown) autonomy is more widely associated with independent learning than with classroom learning. Autonomy can and should be employed in independent and classroom learning, although the number and types of decisions made by the learner might differ in the two situations. The use of learning strategies can both reflect and further promote learner autonomy. There is a caveat, however: There are different levels of 'depth' in strategies, as explained in the second section of this chapter.

Theories: Learner Autonomies in Independent L2 Learning

Many researchers stress the importance of learner autonomy for effective L2 learning in general (e.g. Cotterall & Crabbe, 1999; Dam, 1995; Esch, 1996; Holec, 1981; Little 1991, 1996, 1999a, 1999b, 2000a, 2000b; Wenden, 1991). However, learner autonomy has a myriad of different meanings, as shown here. This theoretical section presents and critiques (1) images of learner autonomy, (2) types of decisions, and (3) individual versus social autonomy.

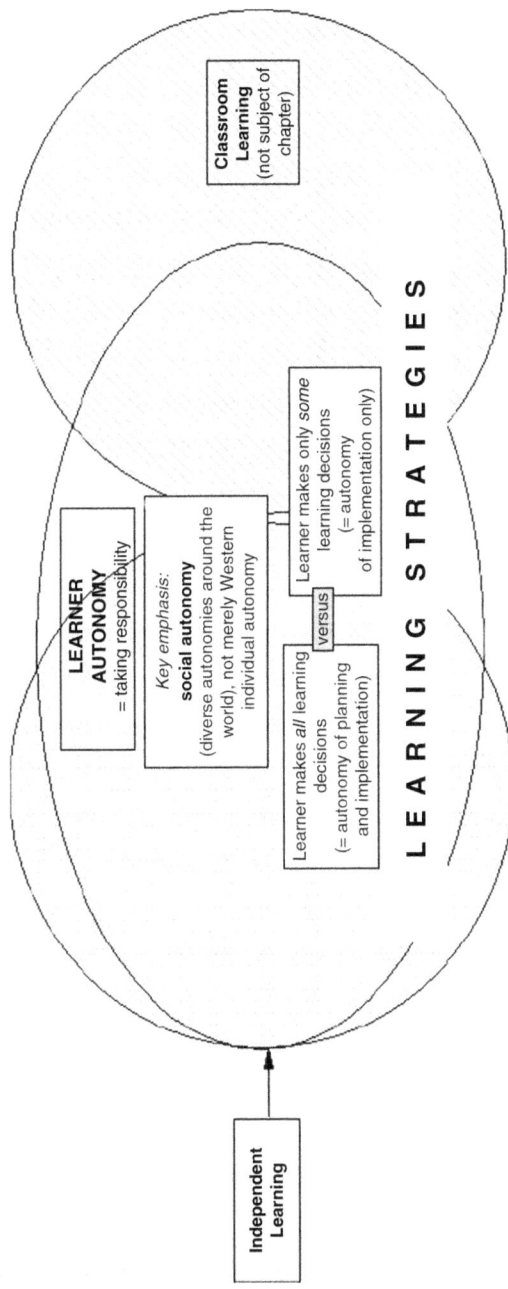

Figure 3.1 Relationships among main ideas: independent learning, learner autonomy and learning strategies
Note: As shown, learner autonomy is widely employed in independent learning. While learner autonomy is also very important for classroom learning, it is not as widely used there as it should be. The use of learning strategies can strongly both reflect and further promote learner autonomy.

Metaphors for autonomy; multiple autonomies

In this section, I present some pictures of autonomy in the literature: as stages, as part of a spiral and as degrees. These are visual metaphors, just as the hero with a thousand faces is a visual metaphor of independent L2 learning.

Stage theories[2]

Vygotsky (1978, 1981) presents a social-constructivist theory of stages of development of internal self-regulation, which is akin but not identical to autonomy. In Vygotsky's view, learning occurs within a sociocultural environment through the learner's dialogues with a more competent person, who 'mediates' the learning. Self-regulation is achieved by moving through three stages: (1) *social speech*, that is, interaction with the more capable person, who models higher-order thinking skills; (2) *egocentric speech*, that is, overtly giving oneself instructions for applying such skills; and (3) *inner speech*, that is, mental self-guidance, a sign that the learner has fully internalised such skills. Vygotsky's theory implies a rather close relationship between the more competent person and the learner. However, in the independent L2 learning situation such a relationship is difficult or rare because the tutor, if one exists, often tends to be at a distance and does not work constantly with the learner, although s/he might still have an important role as the more competent person. Learning in independent L2 situations might be mediated primarily by computer programmes, textbooks, handbooks, videos, websites, and so on, and some independent learners do not have access to a tutor. However, constructivist logic would argue that these mediating tools bear the ongoing imprint of the highly competent people who created them and that the learner, when using these tools, is interacting with and 'co-constructing' with those creators. In this way, independent L2 learning might actually follow the Vygotskyian sequence of stages.

Another stage theory is presented by Nunan (1997). This theory concentrates on classroom-based L2 learners, whose autonomy grows and changes through five stages. For present purposes, Nunan's work has been substantially modified to fit the situations of independent L2 learning, while retaining the five-stage structure (see Table 3.1) and adding another option: 'No Stage'. In my version, Stages 1–4 describe independent learners who are enrolled in or receiving support from established independent L2 learning systems.[3] Arguably, the independent learner can enter the autonomy sequence at any stage from 1 to 4, depending on the type and number of decisions he or she makes about learning (or is allowed to make by the system). For instance, when Mario starts learning Mandarin independently, he can choose his own goals from a list and select tasks from a given set; therefore he enters independent learning at Stage 2. In contrast, Xiaomei begins to study English independently with a different system, which

Table 3.1 Oxford's adaptation of Nunan's stages of autonomy to fit independent L2 learning

Level	Learner action	Learner role	Goals, which lead to → → → → →	Tasks	Comments regarding scope of decisions and responsibility
1	Become aware Nunan: Awareness	Recipient of information	The independent learning system explains the official goals.	The independent learning system provides the task(s) and explains the reason for doing the task(s).	Learners can decide how to do the task and possibly when. They can make few other decisions about learning. Most decisions are made by the independent learning system.
2	Select Nunan: Involvement	Reviewer and selector among system-given options	Learners choose their own goals from a range of official goals.	Learners choose which tasks (or part of tasks) from given alternatives as ways to achieve the goals. They choose the order in which to do the tasks or parts of tasks.	The scope of decision-making and responsibility expands as learners select from a set of given options provided by the system.
3	Adapt Nunan: Intervention	Adaptor	Learners adapt (but do not eliminate) official goals.	Learners adapt given tasks, a little or a lot, as means of achieving the goals.	Learners remain in the established system but adapt it, making more decisions on their own and taking more responsibility.
4	Create Nunan: Creation	Inventor, originator, Creator	Learners create their own goals.	Learners create or decide on their own tasks to fulfill the goals.	This is the apex of decision-making within an independent L2 learning system. The system might provide support, but learners make all decisions and take maximum responsibility.

(Continued)

Table 3.1 (Continued)

Level	Learner action	Learner role	Goals, which lead to → → → → →	Tasks	Comments regarding scope of decisions and responsibility
5	Transcend Nunan: Transcendence	World-seeker, Researcher, Teacher	Learners identify their own interests and create goals relevant to those.	Learners seek and perform tasks in the outside world that involve creating new knowledge and helping others to learn the L2.	These learners leave the established independent L2 learning system. They are autonomous in a larger sphere. They seek resources, challenges, and ways to help in the world.
NO STAGE	Decide	Master decision-maker, free learner	Learners identify their own interests and create goals relevant to those.	Learners seek and do learning tasks in the outside world	**These learners do not enter the established independent L2 learning system in the first place.** They make all decisions for themselves. They seek resources anywhere they can find them and decide on their own independent learning path from the start. Motivation might help compensate for the lack of formal support in learning.

IMPORTANT: (a) Stages 1–4 are within an established independent L2 learning system. Stage 5 transcends the system. **(b)** Learners do not have to go through all stages. They can start their independent learning at *any stage* and can move to higher stages, depending on the type and number of decisions they make about their learning. Sometimes the independent L2 learning system limits the decision-making to only certain types of decisions. **(c)** It is conceivable that a person might be in different stages in relation to decision-making about goals and tasks. **(d)** 'No Stage' means that the learner *never* enters an established independent L2 learning system, does not go through stages, and is responsible for all learning decisions from the start.

encourages learners to create their own goals and tasks; thus, she is at Stage 4 without having gone through earlier stages. Stage 5 is for the person who has been in an established independent learning system but is now leaving it for larger horizons, while in Nunan's theory, Stage 5 is for the person who has achieved autonomy in the classroom and seeks greater challenges outside. The new 'No Stage' descriptor is for learners who have not received help from an established independent L2 learning system while learning the current L2, so they are not linked with system-related stages.

Stage theories remind us that autonomy and independent L2 learning are not 'all-or-nothing' phenomena. However, they need to be tempered with the knowledge that it is very difficult for any stage theory to fully describe the complexities of a given learning situation. For some theories, the stages blend or change depending on the proficiency the learner has attained, the person's learning style and time pressures, and the sometimes shifting reasons for learning the language.

Autonomy as an element in a spiral

Extending Vygotskian social-constructivist theory and the notion of interdependence, Little (2000b) uses the image of autonomy as part of a learning spiral. In the spiral, the learner progresses to new levels of independence only by first moving through additional phases of interdependence (with a teacher or others). This suggests that autonomy is not a linear matter of stages or degrees (see below) but instead part of the constant, curving movement of the spiral.

Autonomy by degree

A number of authors have stated that L2 learner autonomy is a matter of degree (see e.g. Farmer, 1994; Farmer & Sweeney, 1994; Pierson, 1996). Learner autonomy is not all-or-nothing, but it cannot be a simple matter of degree, either. Autonomy is not a uniform commodity that can be expressed in degrees, although the 'degree' metaphor might, for some experts, serve as a rough substitute for the much more complicated reality.

Visual images like the ones above are a way of trying to grasp and express as simply as possible the complexity of difficult phenomena. They are pictorial metaphors that point to a certain reality; but, by nature, such images or metaphors cannot be the reality itself.

Decision-making in autonomy

Holec's (1981: 3) commentary about the scope of the autonomous learner's control reflects intellectual autonomy. He states that the autonomous learner has 'the ability to take charge of ... [his or her] learning' in terms of making the following decisions: determining objectives, defining the contents and progressions, selecting methods and techniques, monitoring procedures of acquisition and evaluating what has been acquired. 'The autonomous learner is himself [or herself] capable of making *all* these decisions ... ' (Holec, 1981: 3 – emphasis added). The website of the Centre for Independent Language Learning (CILL) at Hong Kong Polytechnic University (HKPU) describes independent L2 learning similarly:

> Independent Language Learning aims to give learners more control over what, how and when they learn languages. Learners decide on their aims, make plans of what to learn, develop their own methods of learning (learning strategies), assess their own learning, and plan what to learn next. (http://elc.polyu.edu.hk/CILL/whatsILL.htm)

Dickinson (1987: 11), arguing for self-instruction, also stresses that the autonomous learner can make 'all decisions concerned with his/her learning and the implementation of these decisions'.

The list of possible decisions in independent L2 learning grows even longer when details are considered: (1) the language to be learned; (2) the purpose, general content, topics, and specific tasks of the L2 learning; (3) the amount and type of directions the learner needs; (4) the kinds of learning strategies to be used; (5) the nature, frequency, and reporting format of assessment; (6) formality or informality of the learning; (7) timing; and (8) location (e.g. at a self-access centre, on the phone or computer at home, or elsewhere). A reason for becoming an independent learner might include wanting an opportunity to make decisions about and to take greater responsibility for some or all of these factors.

Nonetheless, the ability to decide everything about learning appears to be something of an ideal rather than a reality for most learners. As Holec (1981: 25 – 26) explains, the most common situation 'will be that of learners who are *not yet autonomous* but are involved in the *process of acquiring the ability* to assume responsibility for their learning' (emphasis added). This suggests that most learners at any given time will be only on their way to autonomy and will be able to make some but not all the decisions about L2 learning – yet the goal, implies Holec, is autonomy. However, not all learners have autonomy as their actual goal. Independent L2 learning can open the doors to control or responsibility by learners, but learners must actually want that control or responsibility and actively take it. Some learners are not as ready for autonomy as others (Cotterall, 1995), and some will be prepared to make only some decisions and not others.

I now turn to a discussion of individual autonomy versus social autonomy. This is a fundamental distinction in ways of looking at learner autonomy.

Individual autonomy versus social autonomy

One of the most significant theoretical clashes of recent years in the L2 field has occurred between proponents of (Western-style individual) learner autonomy and advocates of social autonomy. Individual learner autonomy is reflected in a cluster of related concepts: agency, locus of control, attribution of outcomes and self-efficacy. *Agency* is the situation in which the person is the origin of behaviour and has an effect on outcomes, that is, is an agent (Oxford, 2003). The person who has agency is not just a 'pawn' with no power to influence the results, but instead is an 'origin' in the 'autonomy continuum' (de Charms, 1976). In the Western view, the autonomous L2 learner has a sense of agency (Oxford, 2003). *Locus of control* refers to whether a person considers that outcomes are contingent upon what he or she does (internal control orientation) or on events or situations outside the person's control (external control orientation). For example, a student with an internal control orientation might attribute success in a task to working hard, while a student with an external control orientation might believe that success is due to the ease of the task. Internal locus of control is one of the characteristics of autonomy (Fazey & Fazey, 2001). A directly related concept is *attribution* of outcomes (Weiner, 1984, 1992). Attribution can be internal (ability/competence and effort) or external (luck and/or difficulty of the task). Autonomous learners tend to attribute learning success to internal factors rather than external ones. *Self-efficacy* (Bandura, 1997, 2001) is the individual's belief that he or she is sufficiently competent to fulfil a specific task or goal, which again emphasises the importance of individual prowess and control. These individual-autonomy concepts, which are prevalent among many people in Western society, characterise an isolated achiever who concentrates on personal attainment, without focusing on the support or involvement of a group or necessarily contributing to a group.

Pennycook (1997) condemns attempts to push the individual, competitive, Western version of autonomy onto non-Western societies and strongly encourages awareness of cultural alternatives. Esch (2004) critiques the concept of individual autonomy and promotes the idea of social autonomy. Holliday (2003) also promotes the social autonomy approach and describes this approach as assuming the following: (1) different forms of autonomy exist in different sociocultural contexts, (2) autonomy is already present in learners' social worlds, and (3) we should look for and learn from students' own autonomous strategies while sharing other strategies that they might want to know.[4] Smith (2003) discusses 'strong pedagogies', which assume that learners are already autonomous to an extent.

Holliday (2003: 118) states that we should *'presume'* that 'autonomy is a *universal* until there is evidence otherwise ..., thus treating people equally as people' (emphasis in original). Learner autonomy is indeed diverse in nature, difficult to pin down as a single entity (Benson & Voller, 1997), tightly embedded in varied sociocultural contexts, and located around the world, not just in Western societies. Hence the concept of *multiple autonomies*.

Awareness of different cultural values is extremely important in understanding autonomy. Learners' beliefs, which are strongly affected by the sociocultural context, are major influences on autonomy (Cotterall, 1995). Putting it even more broadly, '[T]he social context in which learning takes place is of vital importance to the success of the educational endeavour' (Harmer, 2003: 288), and the social context should therefore be the matrix in which we understand different forms of autonomy. Considering social autonomy rather than constantly focusing on individual autonomy would allow a much clearer understanding of what autonomy means, or could mean, in traditional Asian cultures. Such cultures focus on social factors, including group cohesion and social support within the in-group (see Matsumoto, 2001; Nisbet, 2004). To be applicable to traditional Asian cultures, any concept of autonomy must involve the person in relationship to the group. Politeness rituals, speech acts, interactions with parents and in-laws, dealings with those who are not part of one's in-group, business operations, schooling, religious rites: every aspect of life is influenced by the primacy of the group. What the person does has tremendous ramifications for the group and vice versa. Some theorists argue that group-oriented approaches are valid ways by which Asians manifest autonomy (see Benson, 2007; Palfreyman, 2003; Smith, 2001). Sung Dynasty scholar Chu Hsi (quoted by Pierson, 1996: 56) supported sharp, independent thinking (e.g. 'If you are in doubt, think it out for yourself. Do not depend on others for explanations' [http://elc.polyu.edu.hk/CILL/theory.htm]), but this autonomy does not imply that the individual can operate without consideration of his or her own rank in society and in the family. For varying points of view about autonomy among Asian students, see Gieve and Clark (2005), Ho and Crookall (1995), Holden and Usuki (1999), Littlewood (2000) and Pierson (1996).

By all means, researchers should avoid the biased Western assumption (see Biggs, 1994) that instructional approaches in Asia generally fail to encourage students to take responsibility. It is more accurate to say that the Western concept of individual autonomy does not fit well into many traditional Asian cultures. Following from this, Western attempts to teach students in traditional cultures to accept all the trappings of individual autonomy might be considered as cultural imperialism, or at best culturally inappropriate (see e.g. Holliday, 2003). Researchers should discover the kinds of learning-related decisions students make in traditional cultures and the types of responsibility they take, rather than looking through a biased cultural lens. Researchers should also be aware that in any geographic area, there are many cultures and subcultures, not just one. Moreover, generalisations do not and can never apply to every member of any single culture or subculture. For example, it is highly unlikely that Asian learners can be appropriately viewed *en bloc* or that there is only one Asian form of autonomy, despite the power of tradition.

Western culture is not monolithic, either. Many men and women in Western societies do not feel comfortable with an individual, competitive perspective on autonomy. Feminist versions of autonomy have been mentioned for some years in the West and other parts of the world (see Benson, 2007; Palfreyman & Smith, 2003). There are probably many more autonomies than we can imagine, because responsibility for learning can be taken in widely different ways.

More studies are needed of autonomy in different Asian, African, South American and other contexts around the world. Research involving a sociocultural perspective on autonomy could have particular implications for the social aspects of independent L2 learning, such as the roles of tutors, electronic communication and study groups.[5]

The next section moves away from theoretical issues and discusses L2 learning strategies and tactics for autonomy, as well as learner development. These are highly practical topics which can aid any independent L2 learning programme.

Learning Strategies, Learning Tactics and Learner Development for Autonomy in the Independent L2 Learning Context

For decades researchers have said that effective learners are typically aware of their strategies for learning, can judge the effectiveness of these strategies, and can choose strategies well (Chamot & O'Malley, 1996; Cohen, 1998; O'Malley & Chamot, 1990; Oxford, 1990). Tactics are the specific implementations of strategies as used in particular L2 situations and tasks and learners must quickly identify the relevant tactics in order to be optimally successful. This section addresses the value of learning strategies, shows the relative importance of various kinds of strategies for independent and classroom learning and discusses some principles of learner development.

Value of strategies

Research indicates that more proficient L2 learners tend to have a wider range of strategies and employ them more often than less proficient learners (O'Malley & Chamot, 1990; Oxford, 1990, 1996, 2008 forthcoming). More proficient learners also orchestrate strategy use more effectively, combining strategies into strategy clusters for complex tasks and making sure that any chosen strategy is appropriate at the time. Less proficient L2 learners often use strategies in a desperate way, not knowing how to identify the needed strategies.

A possible reason for the frequently documented effectiveness of learning strategies is that such strategies require the learner to be more active than a learner who is less strategically engaged. The language learner is seen as 'an active participant in the learning process, using various mental strategies in order to sort out the system of the language to be learned' (Williams & Burden, 1997: 13). Rather than mere passive receptacles for knowledge, learners become thinking participants who can influence both the processes and the desired outcome of their own learning: the development of language proficiency. The use of strategies embodies taking active, timely, coordinated responsibility for learning. This is both learnable and teachable.

As noted earlier, learning strategies are generally signs of learner autonomy. However, if a learner uses a strategy merely as a tool to pass a test or get through an assignment, without intending to learn and retain the information, the learner does not take responsibility for learning, and the strategy is not a 'learning strategy' in any deep sense. Schmeck (1988) distinguishes among deep strategies, which lead to long-term learning; surface strategies, which are for superficial uses and do not lead to long-term learning; and achievement strategies, which are merely focused on securing good grades and might or might not lead to long-term learning.

Strategies and their relative importance to independent learning and classroom learning

L2 learning strategies can be placed in four general categories based on their functions:

- metacognitive strategies for guiding the learning process itself, such as *plan* and *evaluate*;
- affective strategies for managing, volition and emotions, such as *develop positive motivation* and *deal with negative emotions*;
- cognitive strategies for mental processing of the L2 and creating cognitive schema (frameworks), such as *analyse* and *synthesise*;
- social-interactive strategies for aiding the learner within the specific sociocultural setting, such as *collaborate* and *notice sociocultural factors.*

Metacognitive strategies and tactics are extremely important for independent L2 learning, even more so than in classroom L2 learning environments. White (1995) compares the strategies used by distance learners (who are often independent learners) to those of classroom language learners. She reports greater use of metacognitive strategies by distance learners and concludes that these strategies are sparked by the need to compensate for lack of a teacher. Here are a few examples of metacognitive strategies and tactics useful for independent L2 learners:

STRATEGY: Plan   TACTIC: I set realistic objectives for this week's two major writing tasks.
STRATEGY: Organise   TACTIC: I organise the computer files on my laptop before doing anything else.

STRATEGY: Monitor	TACTIC: During the reading task, I monitor my energy level and clarity of thought every 20 minutes or so.
STRATEGY: Evaluate	TACTIC: I compare my current listening performance to my listening performance a month ago to evaluate progress.

White (1995) suggests that because of the lack of ready peer social support and interaction, distance learners often have to use *affective strategies*, such as positive self-talk and relaxation strategies, to manage their emotions and motivation, and this is likely to be the case for most independent L2 learners. In the following examples, motivation refers to the pre-task spark, and volition to the drive to continue involvement during the task. For a fuller discussion of the role of affective strategies in independent L2 learning, see Chapter 12.

STRATEGY: Build positive motivation	TACTIC: I search for something about the task that excites my interest
STRATEGY: Maintain positive volition	TACTIC: I use positive self-talk to keep going ('I have done well so far,' 'I can finish the rest,' 'This is easy')
STRATEGY: Deal with negative emotions	TACTIC: I lower any unhelpful anxiety by deep breathing, music, humour, relaxation, meditation, or a short break.

Cognitive strategies and tactics for processing L2 information are equally important in the two settings, independent learning and classroom learning. They are essential for processing language information and for integrating it into long-term memory by means of schemata. Here are a few examples:

STRATEGY: Combine	TACTIC: I combine this week's new phrases to write five different sentences.
STRATEGY: Group	TACTIC: I group the new material I find about the topic and put it into various files so I can find it.
STRATEGY: Analyse	TACTIC: I break today's multisyllabic words into component parts so I can understand and remember them.
STRATEGY: Synthesise	TACTIC: I use topic sentences in paragraphs to help me write a summary of the essay I just read.

Social-interactional strategies might be less important in the independent L2 learning setting than in the classroom setting, although this depends on several factors, such as the amount of social interaction learners enjoy with peers, via email or other means, the role of the tutor (if any), and the degree to which culture learning accompanies L2 learning.

STRATEGY: Ask questions	TACTIC: I ask the tutor the questions and listen well to the answers.
STRATEGY: Collaborate	TACTIC: I respond to other students' postings in the discussion forum.
STRATEGY: Notice sociocultural factors	TACTIC: I ask myself the meaning of certain social behaviours and sayings that I encounter by video.

L2 learners, no matter how autonomous they wish to be, are not born knowing all the strategies and tactics they need. They must learn about these strategies and tactics, a learning process that can be assisted by learner development, as discussed next.

Learner development for autonomy

L2 learning strategy instruction (by this is meant instruction in both strategies and tactics) is often valuable for enhancing learner autonomy in independent L2 settings. It should be part of broad-scale, culturally relevant *learner development*, which involves learners in thinking about themselves as learners, about language, about why they are learning languages, and about how to make the greatest progress in their L2 learning. Although in classrooms some teachers occasionally offer a form of learner development (and this should happen much more often), in the independent L2 learning setting learner development must occur without a teacher. Various ways of integrating strategy instruction into L2 learning are explored in Chapter 16.

First, independent L2 learning programmes can set up learner development tutorial(s) online, or using print or visual media, which deal with how to learn the L2 and offer repeated, light-hearted but targeted reminders about learning strategies and tactics, attitudes, resources and other information by email at periodic intervals. Such learner development can help students identify their current learning strategies and tactics vis-à-vis specific tasks, teach how to discern whether a particular tactic is working well or poorly, indicate how to identify strategies and tactics that might be useful for specific kinds of tasks, and show how to cluster strategies (and their tactics) into 'strategy chains' for complex tasks. Such learning-to-learn offerings, though featuring strategies and tactics as the key element, can also help learners recognise signs of demotivation and flagging volition, identify symptoms of anxiety and decide about help they need from others and help they can give themselves.

Second, independent L2 learning programmes can create print materials to help students learn how to learn. Harris (2003) describes working with others to create a print-based handbook for strategy instruction for use in a distance learning environment. The handbook developed by Harris and her colleagues is free-standing, to be suitable for adults learning different languages, employs user-friendly wording, includes a targeted set of important strategies, and encompasses a set of four simple stages to promote learner self-management. Stage 1 is Explore, which invites learners to reflect on prior L2 learning activities and then do a task with their own current L2 materials, after which they use a strategy checklist to indicate the just-employed strategies. Stage 2 is Read and Think, which provides general, brief advice about the strategies in the handbook. Stage 3 is Practice, which involves practising the handbook's strategies with L2 tasks while communicating with someone, if at all possible. Stage 4 is Reflect, in which diary writing is the means of evaluating the use of strategies. All of the issues Harris raises for the development of the distance-learning strategy instruction handbook are relevant to the independent L2 learning setting, which often requires some form of 'learning how to learn' information.

Third, independent learning tutors, if any, can provide learning tips on an *ad hoc* basis if learners make mistakes, need help, or ask questions. Fourth, learners can participate in online chats or discussion forums about why they are learning the language, what they hope to do with it, and the strategies and tactics they use; and they can receive feedback and more ideas from peers. Fifth, if learners are using a sequence of materials from the independent learning program, learning strategy suggestions (expressed in non-jargon terms such as the ones in Tables 3.3 to 3.6) can be directly included in independent lesson material to help students gain greater autonomy. Sixth, independent L2 programme websites can include whole sections on learning strategies and tactics, possibly categorised by skill (e.g. reading or speaking).

Learner development, no matter how it is delivered, can aid learners in being ready to fulfil existing goals and tasks, identify additional goals, take greater responsibility and control, gain greater competence (Cotterall & Crabbe, 1999), and strengthen motivation. Specific guidelines for strategy instruction, sometimes as part of larger learner development, are readily available from Chamot *et al.* (1996, 1999), Chamot and O'Malley (1996), Cohen (1998), Oxford and Leaver (1996) and others. An important point is that learner development can and must pay attention to cultural beliefs and values (Holliday, 2003). There is no place for cultural imperialism in learner development, strategies, or any other aspect of independent L2 learning. Benson (2007) and Palfreyman and Smith (2003) provide a variety of ideas and sources relevant to learner development for autonomy in different cultures.

The next section offers a series of examples of autonomy in action in independent L2 learning. It reflects Benson and Voller's (1997) call to explore a range of possibilities for autonomy and independence.

A Range of Possibilities for Independent L2 Learning, Autonomies and Strategies

This section presents six sample settings for independent L2 learning, as well as autonomies and strategies potentially associated with them.[6] They include a virtual language advisor, a self-access centre, an online course without a tutor, a distance course with a tutor, online resource websites without a tutor and tandem learning via technology.

One interesting system that helps develop learner autonomy is presented by Hong Kong University of Science and Technology, working with more than a dozen other universities in both Asia and the West. The system is known as the Virtual English Language Advisor (VELA), which enables learners to make some of their own decisions about L2 learning. This is meant to be an independent L2 learning system. VELA is an interactive online system that makes available individual advice to English learners. It is structured to provide three types of practice (focused, transfer and general). It also teaches a problem-solving procedure that highlights a number of metacognitive learning strategies, although other strategy types are also relevant. Learners discover solutions for their own problems with 'appropriately matched strategies and materials' (http://celt.ust.hk/instr/instr_td04.htm). In some instances VELA can involve optional meetings with self-access language advisors. An important point is that VELA does not assume that learners must make all decisions for L2 learning. Becoming autonomous (taking responsibility and making decisions) can occur gradually and in different ways

> Learners [can] take on *some* of the responsibility for making decisions. ... Learners *begin* to actively take control and responsibility for their learning outcomes, and become more skilled in thinking critically about options available to them, planning, monitoring and evaluating the logic of their choices and the effectiveness of their outcomes. (http://celt.ust.hk/instr/instr_td04.htm), emphasis added)

Self-access centres and resource centres also promote learner autonomy. For example, the Languages Resource Centre of Goldsmiths College, University of London, offers self-access materials, videos, full multimedia courses, immediate satellite TV from several countries, and extensive computer-assisted language learning (CALL) packages in many European languages, plus Latin American versions of Spanish. Students can use these self-access resources in a variety of ways (http://www.goldsmiths.ac.uk/language-studies-centre/independent-study.html).

Different autonomies are necessary for benefiting from the varied resources. For instance, if the learner uses the Languages Resource Centre to find excellent materials and videos and makes his or her own judgments about what to learn, which tasks to accomplish, how to do it, when and how to monitor and evaluate the effort, this autonomy has a different flavour from that employed by a learner who comes to the same centre to use a full multimedia course in which many or most of the decisions are already made. Learning strategies would depend on which resources are chosen and for which types of goals.

Though most decisions are pre-established in full multimedia courses, some types of autonomy remain because decisions about when and where to use the course, as well as which learning strategies to use, are often open to the learner. An example of a completely online, self-paced, independent L2 learning course is the BBC's *German Steps* (http://www.bbc.co.uk/languages/german/lj/). In this course, learners encounter a rich, interesting combination of text, audio, video, and graphics in a highly structured, very well organised format. Specific forms of learner self-assessment are included, but there is no tutor to guide the learner or provide feedback. However, the amount of course structure reduces the need for decision-making in setting objectives, finding resources, and identifying assessment tools. Though much is planned for the learner, metacognitive learning strategies are still necessary for such a course. Cognitive and affective strategies also play a role. To the extent that the learner wants to learn the culture, a few of the social-interactional strategies – particularly those focusing on sociocultural issues – might be useful.

The Open University (UK) offers L2 courses, but they are not completely delivered through technology like the BBC course just described. 'Supported open learning' at the Open University offers possibilities for various kinds of independent learning at a distance (http://www.open.ac.uk/about/ou/p5.shtml). The Open University describes its courses as involving 'learning in your own time by reading course material, working on course activities, writing assignments and perhaps working with other students.' Its mission statement – 'open to people, places, methods and ideas' – implies an ethos of inclusion, regardless of social or educational background. The available foreign language courses (http://www3.open.ac.uk/courses/) are highly structured; use prescribed print, audio-visual and online materials; require the submission of written assignments for a tutor to mark; and offer tutor support of various kinds. Learners do not design their own objectives, activities and so on, though they make decisions about where they will learn and the strategies they will use to approach the learning. Many strategies for these courses might be similar to those listed for the BBC course.

Another form of independent L2 learning involves completely open-ended, flexible use of online L2 resource websites without any course or requirements. Among the many examples are *Karen's ESL Partyland*, www.eslpartyland.com; *Grammar Bytes*, www.chompchomp.com; and BBC's *Learning English* (http://www.bbc.co.uk/worldservice/learningenglish/index.shtml). Significant autonomy is necessary to use these sites, because learners must make many decisions as to the learning objectives, which materials on a given website are relevant to these objectives, how to use the materials, which learning strategies are relevant (primarily metacognitive, affective and cognitive), and how to assess whether objectives are met. Of course, some of the materials include assessments, but those might not be related to the learner's own objectives. Such sites can be used in various ways: (1) freely by the learner without connection to a course or (2) as a relatively independent supplement to a regular L2 course.

Yet another intriguing form of independent L2 learning is eTandem learning, which is a distance education format in which two partners want to learn each others' languages. The partners interact via electronic media, which might be e-mail, audio- or video-conferencing. The partners are matched by a central organisation, eTandem Europa (http://www.slf.ruhr-uni-bochum.de/etandem/etdef-en.html). Individuals can register, or teachers can register their whole class to participate and be matched with others. The autonomy or autonomies manifested in eTandem learning depend on how much guidance teachers or tutors give (i.e. who makes which kinds of decisions about learning), if indeed a teacher or tutor is involved at all. eTandem Europa has guidebooks and plenty of information for different ways in which eTandem learning can be accomplished. Social-interactional and perhaps affective strategies are exceptionally important to eTandem learning, as are metacognitive strategies. Chapter 13 explores in detail the collaborative strategies adopted by eTandem learners.

All of these examples are associated with learner autonomy and learning strategies. They represent an illustrative selection of possible models of independent L2 learning.

Conclusion

There is significant interest in learner autonomy in the independent L2 learning area. Learning strategies (and their associated tactics), such as those in the metacognitive, affective, cognitive and social-interactional categories discussed in this chapter, are crucial because they concretely help independent learners become autonomous. This chapter has explored the meaning and importance of learner autonomy and of learning strategies and tactics in independent L2 learning. It has also discussed learner development, which can aid learners in their use of strategies and tactics, and deals with other aspects of L2 learning.

Many more studies are needed of the topics presented here. Mixed-methods studies, which combine qualitative and quantitative methods, are strongly encouraged. Studies should consider a number of variables that are likely to affect learner autonomy and the use of learning strategies and tactics. These variables include not only the geographic area of the world but also socioeconomic background, main discipline of study, gender, age, learning style, goals, interests, travel experience and schooling. Moreover, studies need to address not only trends or commonalities but also variations or differences, both within and across cultural settings, as we saw in Chapter 2, where some of the key theoretical ground for this was explored. The social autonomy approach deserves to be explored in depth. A sociocultural focus would lead beyond the Western stereotype of autonomy and underscore the fact that diverse autonomies exist in many locations around the world.

Teams of researchers representing varied, complementary methodological expertise should try to coordinate their efforts within and across studies. In the current situation, individuals or small numbers of researchers tend to conduct studies that are uncoordinated with the studies of other investigators. This limits the resources available for each study, and leads to lack of comparability across studies and fragmentation in our understanding of complex issues in independent L2 learning, learner autonomy, and learning strategies and tactics.

This chapter has attempted to help readers understand more deeply the complexities of learner autonomy in independent L2 learning and the contributions of learning strategies and tactics to such learning. It promotes and supports the hero with a thousand faces across the globe. Our hero embodies the diverse autonomies and is equipped with a range of learning strategies that empower the multi-faceted independent L2 learner in today's complex communicative world.

Notes

1. Not every metaphorical entailment of the mythic hero's story fits the current chapter, although it might be worthwhile someday to study identity change of L2 learners in that mythic light, as well as in sociocultural ways.
2. Two stage theories are discussed here. An additional stage theory (Sheerin, 1997), focused on learner independence, is less convincing because 'working without supervision' occurs very late in Sheerin's independent learning process.
3. This system might be, for instance, for example, centred at a university, delivered by a commercial company or government agency, or managed by an international programme like eTandem Europa (see later for tandem learning).
4. He also mentions that many international English language educators desire culture-free professionalism, but instead such educators must be constantly and critically aware of the social/cultural implications of what they do.
5. *Proactive autonomy versus reactive autonomy* (Littlewood, 1999) and *intellectual autonomy versus autonomy of means* (Nolen, 1995) are also terms found in the literature. Proactive autonomy and intellectual autonomy are similar in that they involve making decisions about what, where, when, and why to learn, whereas reactive autonomy and autonomy of means involve making decisions about *how* to learn only after other decisions have been made for the learner by someone else. I do not promote the two contrasts, proactive versus reactive and intellectual versus means. The reason is the potentially pejorative connotations of 'reactive autonomy' (in the West, 'proactive' is often the ideal, with

'reactive' as less valued) and 'autonomy of means' (the latter of which is semantically 'non-intellectual' when compared with 'intellectual autonomy'). Terms 'reactive autonomy' and 'autonomy of means' have been attributed to certain populations, but I view these terms as value-laden and capable of cultural harm, regardless of any good intentions lying behind them.
6. Responsibility for these interpretations is my own. I welcome any additions or clarifications.

References

BBC *German Steps*. On WWW at http://www.bbc.co.uk/languages/german/lj/. Accessed 07.09.07.

BBC *Learning English*. On WWW at http://www.bbc.co.uk/worldservice/learningenglish/index.shtml. Accessed 07.09.07.

Bandura, A. (1997) *Self-Efficacy: The Exercise of Control*. New York: Freeman.

Bandura, A. (2001) Social cognitive theory: An agentic perspective. *Annual Review of Psychology* 52, 1–26.

Benson, P. (2007) State-of-the-art article: Autonomy in language teaching and learning. *Language Teaching* 40, 21–40.

Benson, P. and Voller, P. (eds) (1997) *Autonomy and Independence in Language Learning*. London: Longman.

Biggs, J. (1994) What are effective schools?: Lessons from East and West. *Australian Educational Researcher* 21 (1), 19–59.

Campbell, J. (1972) *The Hero with a Thousand Faces*. Princeton, NJ: Princeton University Press.

Centre for Independent Language Learning (n.d.) What is independent language learning? On WWW at http://elc.polyu.edu.hk/CILL/whatsILL.htm. Accessed 07.09.07.

Chamot, A.U., Barnhardt, S., El-Dinary, P. and Robbins, J. (1996) Methods for teaching learning strategies in the foreign language classroom. In R. Oxford (ed.) *Language Learning Strategies around the World: Cross-Cultural Perspectives* (pp. 175–188). Manoa: University of Hawaii Press.

Chamot, A.U., Barnhardt, S., El-Dinary, P. and Robbins, J. (1999) *Learning Strategies Handbook*. White Plains, NY: Addison Wesley Longman.

Chamot, A.U. and O'Malley, J.M. (1996) Implementing the Cognitive Academic Language Learning Approach (CALLA). In R. Oxford (ed.) *Language Learning Strategies Around the World: Cross-Cultural Perspectives* (pp. 167–174). Manoa: University of Hawaii Press.

Cohen, A.D. (1998) *Strategies for Learning and Using a Second Language*. Essex: Longman.

Cotterall, S. (1995) Readiness for autonomy: Investigating learner beliefs. *System* 23 (2), 195–205.

Cotterall, S. and Crabbe, D. (eds) (1999) *Learner Autonomy in Language Learning: Defining the Field and Effecting Change*. Frankfurt am Main: Lang.

Dam, L. (1995) *Learner Autonomy 3: From Theory to Classroom Practice*. Dublin: Authentik.

de Charms, R. (1976) *Enhancing Motivation*. New York: Irvington/Wiley.

Dickinson, L. (1987) *Self-Instruction in Language Learning*. Cambridge: Cambridge University Press.

Esch, E. (1996) Promoting learner autonomy: Criteria for the selection of appropriate methods. In R. Pemberton, E.L. Li, W.W.F. Or and H.D. Pierson (eds) *Taking Control: Autonomy in Language Learning* (pp. 35–48). Hong Kong: Hong Kong University Press.

Esch, E. (2004) Crash or clash? Autonomy ten years on. Paper presented at the Conference on Autonomy in Language Learning – Maintaining Control, Hong Kong University of Science and Technology. On WWW at http://lc.ust.hk/~centre/conf2004/esch.html. Accessed 07.09.07.

eTandem Europa. On WWW at http://www.slf.ruhr-uni-bochum.de/etandem/etdef-en.html. Accessed 07.09.07.

Farmer, R. (1994) The limits of learner independence in Hong Kong. In D. Gardner and L. Miller (eds) *Directions in Self-Access Language Learning* (pp. 13–28). Hong Kong University Press.

Farmer, R. and Sweeney, E. (1994) Self-access in Hong Kong: A square peg in a round hole? *Occasional Papers in Language Teaching* 4 (pp. 24–30). ELT Unit: Chinese University of Hong Kong.

Fazey, D. and Fazey J. (2001) The potential for autonomy in learning. *Studies in Higher Education* 26 (3), 345–361.

Gieve, S. and Clark, R. (2005) The Chinese approach to learning: Cultural trait or situated response? The case of a self-directed learning programme. *System* 33 (2), 261–276.

Harmer, J. (2003) Popular culture, methods, and context. *ELT Journal* 57 (3), 288–294.

Harris, V. (2003) Adapting classroom-based strategy instruction to a distance learning context. *TESL-EJ*, 7 (2). On WWW at http://www-writing.berkeley.edu/TESL-EJ/ej26/a1.html. Accessed 07.09.07.

Goldsmiths College, University of London: Languages Resource Centre. On WWW at http://www.goldsmiths.ac.uk/language-studies-centre/independent-study.html. Accessed 07.09.07.

Grammar Bytes. On WWW at www.chompchomp.com. Accessed 07.09.07.

Ho, J. and Crookall, D. (1995) Breaking with Chinese cultural traditions: Learner autonomy in English language teaching. *System* 23 (2), 235–243.

Holden, B. and Usuki, M. (1999) Learner autonomy in language learning: A preliminary investigation. *Bulletin of Hokuriku University* 23, 191–203.

Holec, H. (1981) *Autonomy in Foreign Language Learning*. Strasbourg: Council of Europe.

Holliday, A. (1996) Developing a sociological imagination: Expanding ethnography in international English language education. *Applied Linguistics* 17 (2), 234–255.

Holliday, A. (2003) Social autonomy: Addressing the dangers of culturism in TESOL. In D. Palfreyman and R.C. Smith (eds) *Learner Autonomy Across Cultures: Language Education Perspectives* (pp. 110–128). London: Palgrave Macmillan.

Hong Kong University of Science and Technology: Virtual English Language Advisor (VELA). On WWW at http://celt.ust.hk/instr/instr_td04.htm. Accessed 07.09.07.

Karen's ESL Partyland. On WWW at www.eslpartyland.com. Accessed 07.09.07.

Little, D. (1991) *Learner Autonomy 1: Definitions, Issues, and Problems*. Dublin: Authentik.

Little, D. (1996) Learner autonomy: Some steps in the evolution of theory and practice. *TEANGA: The Irish Yearbook of Applied Linguistics* 16, 1–13.

Little, D. (1999a) Developing learner autonomy in the foreign language classroom: A social-interactive view of learning and three fundamental pedagogical principles. *Revista Canaria de Estudios Ingleses* 38, 77–88.

Little, D. (1999b) Learner autonomy is more than a Western cultural construct. In S. Cotterall and D. Crabbe (eds) *Learner Autonomy in Language Learning: Defining the Field and Effecting Change* (pp. 11–18). Frankfurt am Main: Lang.

Little, D. (2000a) Learner autonomy and human interdependence: Some theoretical and practical consequences of a social-interactive view of cognition, learning and language. In B. Sinclair, I. McGrath and T. Lamb (eds) *Learner Autonomy, Teacher Autonomy: Future Directions* (pp. 15–23). Harlow: Longman.

Little, D. (2000b) Learner autonomy: Why foreign languages should occupy a central role in the curriculum. In S. Green (ed.) *New Perspectives on Teaching and Learning Modern Languages*. Modern Languages in Practice 13. Clevedon: Multilingual Matters.

Littlewood, W. (1999) Defining and developing autonomy in East Asian contexts. *Applied Linguistics* 20 (1), 71–94.

Littlewood, W. (2000) Do Asian students really want to listen and obey? *ELT Journal* 54 (1), 31–36.

Matsumoto, D. (ed.) (2001) *Handbook of Culture and Psychology*. Oxford: Oxford University Press.

Nisbet, R. (2004) *The Geography of Thought: How Asians and Westerners Think Differently ... and Why*. New York: Free Press.

Nolen, S.B. (1995) Teaching for autonomous learning. In C. Desforges (ed.) *An Introduction to Teaching*. Oxford: Blackwell.

Norton, B. (2000) *Identity and Language Learning: Gender, Ethnicity and Educational Change*. London: Longman.

Norton, B. (2001) Non-participation, imagined communities and the language classroom. In M. Breen (ed.) *Learner Contributions to Language Learning: New Directions in Research* (pp. 159–171). London: Longman.

Norton, B. and Toohey, K. (2002) Identity and language learning. In R. Kaplan (ed.) *The Oxford Handbook of Applied Linguistics*. Oxford: Oxford University Press.

Nunan, D. (1997) Designing and adapting materials to encourage learner autonomy. In P. Benson and P. Voller (eds) *Autonomy and Independence in Language Learning* (pp. 192–203). London: Longman.

O'Malley, J.M. and Chamot, A.U. (1990) *Learning Strategies in Second Language Acquisition*. Cambridge: Cambridge University Press.

Oxford, R.L. (1990) *Language Learning Strategies: What Every Teacher Should Know*. Boston: Heinle & Heinle.

Oxford, R.L. (ed.) (1996) *Language Learning Strategies around the World: Cross-cultural Perspectives*. Manoa: University of Hawaii Press.

Oxford, R.L. (2003) Toward a more systematic model of L2 learner autonomy. In D. Palfreyman and R.C. Smith (eds) *Learner Autonomy Across Cultures: Language Education Perspectives* (pp. 75–91). London: Palgrave Macmillan.

Oxford, R.L. (forthcoming 2008) *Teaching and Researching Language Learning Strategies*. London: Longman.

Oxford, R.L. and Leaver, B.L. (1996) A synthesis of strategy instruction for language learners. In R. Oxford (ed.) *Language Learning Strategies around the World: Cross-Cultural Perspectives* (pp. 227–246). Manoa: University of Hawaii Press.

Palfreyman, D. (2003) Introduction: Culture and learner autonomy. In D. Palfreyman and R.C. Smith (eds) *Learner Autonomy Across Cultures: Language Education Perspectives* (pp. 1–22). London: Palgrave Macmillan.

Palfreyman, D. and Smith, R.C. (eds) (2003) *Learner Autonomy Across Cultures: Language Education Perspectives*. London: Palgrave Macmillan.

Pennycook, A. (1997) Cultural alternatives and autonomy. In P. Benson and P. Voller (eds) *Autonomy and Independence in Language Learning* (pp. 35–53). London: Longman.

Pierson, H.D. (1996) Learner culture and learner autonomy in the Hong Kong Chinese context. In R. Pemberton, E.L. Li, W.W.F. Or and H.D. Pierson (eds) *Taking Control: Autonomy in Language Learning* (pp. 49–58). Hong Kong: Hong Kong University Press.

Schmeck, R. (1988) *Learning Strategies and Learning Styles*. New York: Plenum Press.

Sheerin, S. (1997) An exploration of the relationship between self-access and independent learning. In P. Benson and P. Voller (eds) *Autonomy and Independence in Language Learning* (pp. 54–65). London: Longman.

Smith, R.C. (2001) Group work for autonomy in Asia. *AILA Review* 15, 70–81.

Smith, R.C. (2003) Pedagogy as (becoming-) appropriate methodology. In D. Palfreyman and R.C. Smith (eds) *Learner Autonomy Across Cultures: Language Education Perspectives* (pp. 129–146). London: Palgrave Macmillan.

The Open University (2007) Description of language programmes. On WWW at www.ou.ac.uk. Accessed 07.09.07.

The Open University (2007) Supported open learning. On WWW at http://www.open.ac.uk/about/ou/p5.shtml. Accessed 07.09.07.

Vygotsky, L. (1978) *Mind in Society*. Cambridge, MA: Harvard University Press.

Vygotsky, L. (1981) The genesis of the higher mental functions. In J.V. Wertsch (ed.) *The Concept of Activity in Soviet Psychology*. Armonk, NY: Sharpe.

Weiner, B. (1984) Principles for a theory of student motivation and their application within an attributional framework. In R. Ames and C. Ames (eds) *Research on Motivation in Education: Student Motivation* (Vol. 1). San Diego, CA: Academic Press.

Weiner, B. (1992) *Human Motivation: Metaphors, Theories, and Research*. Newbury Park, CA: Sage.

Wenden, A. (1991) *Learner Strategies for Learner Autonomy*. Englewood Cliffs, NJ: Prentice Hall.

White, C. (1995). Autonomy and strategy use in distance foreign language learning: Research findings. *System* 23, 207–221.

Williams, M. and Burden, R.L. (1997) *Psychology for Language Teachers*. Cambridge: Cambridge University Press.

Part 2
Strategies for Skills Development in Independent Language Learning

Chapter 4
Independent Second Language Reading as an Interdependent Process

CAROLYN GASCOIGNE

Introduction

Language learning is intuitively and rationally considered by most to be interactive in nature. Certainly, we all learned our first language through interaction with parents and caregivers. And, if we are fortunate enough to have mastered a second or third language, they too were most likely acquired either in a natural immersion-like setting, replete with interaction with parents or peers, or in an academic setting traditionally characterised by teacher–student and student–student interaction. Indeed, the role of the 'other' in language learning has rarely been questioned, be it an interlocutor or the author of a printed text (Brown, 2001; Wu, 1992). In truth, what is the point of developing skills in reading, speaking, listening and writing, if there is nobody to speak, to listen, or to write to, or whose works are to be read. However, of all the skills, reading has traditionally been the one most readily assumed to be 'an individual responsibility – a task conducted outside of class' (Swaffar et al., 1991: 117). In fact, Walz (2001: 1202), among others, believes that second language students should be 'encouraged to read critically on their own'. As a consequence, the reading skill has historically received relatively little attention, with many researchers and practitioners assuming that first language (L1) reading skills were easily and automatically applied to new second language situations (Lally, 1998).

Although subject to much debate, Krashen's Input Hypothesis and subsequent research sparked a renewed interest in extensive, as opposed to intensive, or detail-oriented, reading. Indeed, second language students 'need large amounts of comprehensible input [...] and reading materials provide the most readily available source' (Chastain, 1988: 218).

In extensive reading, students are encouraged to read independently by using resources within their reach and that appeal to their personal interests. According to Bell and LeBlanc (2000), increased attention to reading, in general, and self-directed reading, in particular, can also be attributed to developments in technology and the resources it affords the individual learner. Undoubtedly, students 'now have access to authentic texts written by native speakers from around the world' (Bell & LeBlanc, 2000: 274) in endless supply, and at any time. For example, students can obtain 'newspapers, magazines, and books from many sources, and they can read them in the privacy of their own home at their own convenience' (Chastain, 1988: 219). In fact, reading in general and independent reading, in particular, will become ever more important in our high-speed, high-tech and increasingly interdependent world.

For White (1995: 209), success in self-instructional contexts is dependent upon learner autonomy, which relates to 'an attitude on the part of the learner towards taking control of the language learning process and assuming responsibility for the process' (Vanijdee, 2003: 75). In this respect, learner autonomy is intimately related to learning strategies (Huttunen, 1996; Vanijdee, 2003; Wenden, 1991; White, 1995). Therefore, following a brief history of reading models and theories, this chapter will examine the findings of research in second language (L2) reading in order to provide a review of the recommended strategies and skills that can be applied to independent reading contexts, including distance education courses, self-access centres, on-line learning, or the use of independent learning material.

Models of Interdependence: The Reader and the Text

The language teaching profession's understanding and explanation of the nature of the reading process, whether conducted in a traditional classroom or an independent setting, has undergone a noticeable evolution since the 1960s (Brantmeier, 2003a). Fuelled by research in the cognitive sciences, first-language acquisition, and in second language learning, models used to explain the reading process (in both first and second languages) have evolved from being text-driven, to reader-driven, to interactive in nature, and are commonly referred to as bottom-up, top-down, and interactive models, respectively.

Bottom-up models

In a bottom-up model, reading is viewed as a text-driven decoding process. It is considered to be heavily data-driven and dominated by the use of local strategies such as identifying word meanings, sentence structure and the correspondence of letters and pronunciation (Konishi, 2003).

The text is regarded as a 'chain of isolated words, each of which is to be deciphered individually' (Martinez-Lang, 1995: 70), and the reader as someone 'who approaches the text by concentrating exclusively on the combination of letters and words in a purely linear manner' (Martinez-Lang, 1995: 70). Throughout this decoding process, the reader attempts to reconstruct the author's meaning from the smallest textual elements relying on word-order, suprasegmental patterns (stress, rhythm and intonation), structures, and translation of individual words (Shrum & Glisan, 1994). In bottom-up models, the text is considered to be the sole and solemn source of meaning. Moreover, since meaning is believed to be fixed within the letters, words and structures on the printed page or computer screen, it is considered invariable. That is, each and every reader, assuming he or she has the appropriate competencies, should generally reach the same conclusion from any given text regardless of his or her individual experiences or interests. For a true bottom-up model, the way in which a text is written and structured, the vocabulary used and the communicative context are seen as determining its meaning, to the exclusion of any factors deriving from the receptive context. (Gascoigne, 2005: 2).

However, according to Chia (2001), even when students report having no difficulty understanding both the words and sentence structures of a given passage, they often still have trouble reaching a satisfactory interpretation of the text. Clearly, a purely text-driven view of reading does not tell the whole story. Yet, some researchers maintain that the direct teaching of decoding skills should be a part of initial reading instruction, at least until readers have had a chance to build a cache of L2 vocabulary and gain control over basic syntactic structures (Gough, 1972; Orasanu, 1986). For many researchers there is a 'direct causal link between vocabulary and comprehension' (Ahmad & Asraf, 2004: 32), causing reading proficiency to mirror overall language proficiency and requiring that a certain basic level of vocabulary knowledge exist before learners can start to apply reading strategies. Proponents of the next set of models, however, argue that while extremely important, language proficiency is not the only ingredient needed to ensure successful reading comprehension.

Top-down models

Top-down models take the opposite position and have become popular because of the rise of the importance of the learner in second language acquisition research and theory. This group of models came about as the 'language teaching profession became disenchanted with a limited system of normed language and began to value creativity and expression [as well as] cognition and communication' (Lally, 1998: 270). From a top-down perspective, the reader is considered to be the source or the creator of meaning, rather than a mechanical translator of a fixed text (Barnett, 1989;

Brantmeier, 2002, 2003a, 2003b; Goodman, 1968). Top-down models focus on what the reader brings to the reading task in terms of world knowledge, experience, interests and expectations. In a top-down view of the reading process, meaning and comprehension depend so much upon the reader that interpretation of a given text can vary from reader to reader (Brantmeier, 2003a). For extremists, 'the text has little or no meaning in and of itself. Instead, it gives direction to readers concerning how readers should retrieve and construct meaning from their own previously acquired knowledge' (Gascoigne, 2005: 2). Goodman (1968: 126), for example, describes the reading process as 'a psycholinguistic guessing game' in which the reader makes predictions and then samples just enough of the text to inform these predictions. In other words, he or she relies upon general knowledge of the world 'to make intelligent guesses about what might come next in the text [and then] samples only enough of the text to confirm or reject these guesses' (Barnett, 1989: 3).

The importance of the reader and of his or her background knowledge in a top-down model can be explained by *schema theory* (Anderson & Pearson, 1988; Carrell & Eisterhold, 1983; Rumelhart, 1980; Schank & Abelson, 1977). Although schema theory was first made popular in the late 1960s, the concept can already be detected in the 18th century writings of Immanuel Kant in which he proposes the existence of 'innate structures' that organise the world. The notion resurfaces again much later in Bartlett's (1932) work, *Remembering*, where he posits that the 'understanding and remembering of events is shaped by expectations or prior knowledge and that these expectations are presented mentally in some sort of schematic fashion' (Ajideh, 2003: 4).

Schemata are the underlying connections that allow new experiences and information to be aligned with previously acquired knowledge. They are knowledge structures that function as 'ideational scaffolding' (Landry, 2002: 1). Schemata represent commonly accepted connections or relationships among people, things and events. In other words, they are the mental frameworks that organise our world. A script, on the other hand, is a particular type of schema constructed from a standard sequence of familiar events such as dining in a restaurant, driving a car or taking a final exam. Textual schemata are yet another type that represents the expectations that readers have as they encounter different text genres such as 'stories, personal letters, research reports or telegrams' (Amer, 2003: 64). For example, when reading a research paper, readers are likely to expect to see certain elements such as an introduction, a research question, a literature review, a description of the study, findings, implications and a conclusion. More specifically, a story schema is a type of textual schemata that accounts for the mental representation that readers have of a narrative, its parts and their relationships, such as the setting, characters, problem, action and resolution of the problem. Both schemata- and script-based comprehension maintain that in order to understand what is going on, a person must have been in that situation before or, in the case of textual or story schemata, be familiar with the component parts of the text and of their organisation (Schank & Abelson, 1977: 67). Clearly, the importance of the individual reader in terms of his or her experience and expectations in top-down models (and later in interactive models as well) cannot be ignored.

Interactive models

The third type of model is the interactive group. In interactive models, top-down and bottom-up processes complement one another and function interdependently (Bernhardt, 1991; Grabe, 1991; Swaffar *et al.*, 1991: 24). Here, the text gives direction to the reader concerning how he or she should retrieve and construct meaning from his or her previously acquired knowledge and experiences. In other words, text messages interact with reader perceptions to produce meaning. For Swaffar *et al.* (1991), these interactions are comprised of the following eight top-down and bottom-up components attributed to either the reader or the text.

Top-down Factors: Reader

(1) reader background (semantic knowledge)
(2) reader perspective (reading strategies)
(3) cultural knowledge

Top-down Factors: Text

(4) text schema (topic)
(5) text structure (organisational pattern of information)
(6) episodic sequence (scripts or story grammar)

Bottom-up Factors: Text and Reader

(7) illustrative detail (micropropositions)
(8) surface language features of the text in letters, words, and individual sentences
(9) reader language proficiency

The interaction of these text-based and reader-based variables results in comprehension that represents the successful union of the text and the reader's background knowledge and target language proficiency. Specifically, readers co-construct meaning along with the author as they analyse and match letters, words and sentences against the backdrop of their personal knowledge of the world (Brantmeier, 2003a, 2005). Perhaps the relationship between the text and the reader as represented by interactive models, in general, and in Swaffar *et al.*'s procedural model, in particular, is best explained in their car and driver analogy:

> The reader drives, the text transports. The reader decides where to go, but needs a vehicle, some gas in the tank and air in the tires to get anywhere. How fast and how effectively they travel together depends on features of both the reader and the text, and how the two interact. During the journey, text factors will dominate, indeed dictate successful reader behaviour ... At the end of the trip, the reader is again dominant. Like the driver of a car, the initiator and concluder of interaction with the text is always the reader. (Swaffar *et al.*, 1991: 74)

In addition to providing a script for understanding the interdependence inherent in interactive models, the above analogy also points to the priority – although less significant than in pure top-down models – that is still placed on the role of the reader in comprehending text.

As our professional understanding of the second language reading process has evolved from being text- and language-focused, to reader-focused, to interactive, so must our view of the reader evolve from the isolated, autonomous, and unaffected agent to a negotiator of meaning, a co-author, if you will. The reader is not a free agent who methodically and impersonally extracts meaning from the text. Instead, he or she communicates with the text in a give-and-take of information and experience. Even when reading in independent settings – alone in a library, online or in a distance learning course – the reader is engaging with the text and its author and therefore needs to employ interactive strategies and skills in order for successful comprehension to occur. The following sections, therefore, describe strategies, tools and techniques that promote interactive reading in independent settings.

Interdependent Strategies for Independent Reading

Cognitive strategies are direct strategies used to orchestrate the mental processing of a target language. They are the 'specific "attacks" that learners employ' when faced with a learning or comprehension problem (Brantmeier, 2002: 1). Metacognitive strategies, on the other hand, are indirect strategies used to monitor the self while engaged in an activity such as reading. For Swaffar *et al.* (1991: 117) metacognitive awareness of reading is, in essence, 'a dialogue between text and reader'.

Just like models of the reading process, cognitive strategies can be either local (data-driven), global (reader-driven) or interactive in nature. Commonly-cited reading strategies include skimming, scanning, identifying cognates or word families, guessing, reading for meaning, predicting, questioning, rereading words, sentences or entire passages, activating general or background knowledge, making inferences, following references, separating main ideas from detail, and summarising (Barnett, 1989; Brantmeier, 2002).

However, studies in strategy use have produced remarkably consistent descriptions of the tools L2 readers use to manage their interaction with target language texts (Bacon, 1992; Barnett, 1989; Block, 1986; Brantmeier, 2002; Konishi, 2003; Saricoban, 2002; Swaffar *et al.*, 1991). For example, using a strategy use questionnaire, Saricoban (2002) found that successful readers engaged in predicting and guessing, accessed background knowledge related to the text's topic, guessed the meaning of unknown words, reread the entire passage, identified main ideas and monitored comprehension. In short, successful readers employed global top-down strategies that were cognitive, metacognitive and compensatory in nature. Poor readers, on the other hand, tended to process text in a word-for-word fashion, focusing on grammatical structure, sound-letter correspondences, word meaning, and text detail. Barnett (1989) found that less effective readers focused on meaning of individual words, paid attention to text structure, reread isolated sentences or passages, rather than the entire text, never or rarely hypothesised and resisted skipping any unknown words. In other words, less skilled readers tend to employ local, bottom-up strategies, whereas more successful readers use global, interactive and metacognitive reading strategies.

Block (1986) also found that general comprehension strategies (anticipating content, recognising text structure, integrating information, questioning information, distinguishing main ideas from detail, monitoring comprehension, correcting behaviour, focusing on textual meaning as a whole and reacting to the text) were superior to local linguistic strategies (rereading words or sentences, questioning the meaning of words or sentences and solving vocabulary problems). Similarly, Ahmad and Asraf (2004) found that good readers verbalised their comprehension strategies and believed that effective comprehension monitoring instruction was necessary. Ahmad and Asraf (2004: 35) go on to offer five reading comprehension strategies that should be taught to L2 readers and that can be applied to any reading environment: 'determining importance, summarising information, drawing inferences, generating questions, and monitoring comprehension'. Indeed, without the benefit of a teacher or tutor as an external monitor, comprehension monitoring (or metacognitive) strategies, are particularly important for the independent reader.

Transferring Tools and Techniques to Promote Interactive Reading in Independent Settings

Reading skills and strategies commonly attributed to more-skilled readers in traditional reading instruction (that is, top-down and metacognitive strategies) can also be applied to independent and/or technologically-mediated reading contexts. Swaffar *et al.* (1991: 117), for example, stress the 'importance of encouraging problem solving attitudes such as persistence (Keep on reading!), linking global concepts to textual detail, and identifying the structures of messages implied by linguistic patterns'. Indeed, the macrosyntax or rhetorical organisation of a text represents the patterns of dominant relationships between people, institutions, events or ideas as a development (cause/effect, problem/solution), or a description (features/characters/comparisons) that are contained within a text (Swaffar *et al.*, 1991: 121).

A set of techniques that can be used to develop readers' awareness of textual organisation in any environment are those based upon the notion of story grammar (Amer, 2003; Swaffar *et al.*, 1991). The goal of story grammar is to explicitly provide students with the skills necessary to focus upon and understand text structure and organisation. Students are encouraged to attend to textual schemata for various texts such as letters, reports or stories. In story grammar reading comprehension is considered a transaction between the reader and the text and it requires that the reader understand how the author organised his or her ideas within and through the text's structure (Amer, 2003). Text structure, such as narrative or expository organisations, represent the patterns of how concepts are organised and connected. According to Amer (2003: 65), a story schema 'is the mental representation that readers have of a story's parts and their relationships'. Reading strategies that can be applied to narrative texts, whether employed in independent or traditional environments, include the use of guiding questions that encourage consideration of the setting, characters, problems, actions, resolution and theme of a text. In addition to using standard questions to evoke such considerations, visual or graphic representations, such as character or story maps that can be arranged in a vertical flow chart or in a diagram, can also be used to help learners identify which parts of a text are salient and how these salient concepts are related. Commercially-prepared computer programs such as *Inspiration* by Inspiration Software, Inc. (2007) can be used to generate various map structures as well.

Awareness of a text's organisation can help readers focus on main concepts without the distraction of unnecessary details (Gascoigne, 2002b). Story maps and frames, character maps and reading logs can help readers independently develop a level of organisational awareness. A story map, for instance, asks students to identify major story elements such as the title, setting, characters, problems, major events, ending or resolution and overall theme in descending order on a screen or page (see Figure 4.1). A story frame, on the other hand, uses a gap-filling procedure to identify some of the same components and relationships (see Figure 4.2).

A character map asks readers to identify main characters and generate several character traits to be listed under each (see Figure 4.3). An additional

Title: _____

Setting:

_____

Character 1: _____

Character 2: _____

Character 3: _____

Problem/ Major Event:

_____

Secondary Event:

_____

Ending/ Resolution:

_____

Theme:

_____

Figure 4.1   Story map

In this story, the problem starts when……………………………….After that,………………………………………………..Next,…………………………….

…………… Then,……………………………………………..the problem ends with …………………………………………….(Amer, 2003: 67).

Figure 4.2   Story frame

technique, and one that emphasises the reflective and creative aspects of the reading process, is the reading log (see Figure 4.4).

Swaffar *et al.* (1991) recommend that when engaged in pre-, during- or post-reading activities, particularly those that encourage the activation of

Character 1: Emma Bovary

Trait 1: Selfish

Trait 2: Insecure

Trait 3: Vain

Trait 4: Petty

Character 2: Charles Bovary

Trait 1: Simple

Trait 2: Insecure

Trait 3: Naïve

Figure 4.3   Character map

reader background knowledge and metacognition, the reader be allowed to use the L1, especially at early stages of reading instruction.

Although the research is in overwhelming agreement concerning the successful use of top-down and metacognitive strategies by more-skilled readers (Bacon, 1992; Barnett, 1989; Block, 1986; Brantmeier, 2002, 2003b; Chastain, 1988; Chia, 2001; Gascoigne, 2002a, 2005; Konishi, 2003; Lally, 1998; Landry, 2002; Saricoban, 2002; Shrum & Glisan, 1994; Swaffar *et al.*, 1991), as well as the utility of promoting these types of activities among L2 readers, certain bottom-up strategies can nevertheless be extremely useful, especially for the beginning L2 reader. For the novice L2 reader, simple vocabulary recognition is often a major obstacle, 'L1 and L2 studies agree that about 5000 words [. . .] constitute 90% of the words needed to read a text for comprehension [and] the evidence argues for teaching high-frequency vocabulary to a point of automaticity' (Swaffar *et al.*, 1991: 44). Simply put, 'knowing more words is statistically related to better comprehension of text' (Ahmad & Asraf, 2004: 32). Initial L2 reading instruction, therefore, should include a least a minimal amount of decoding strategy assistance (Alyousef, 2005; Ahmed & Asraf, 2004; Eskey, 1988; Gough, 1972; Orasanu, 1986), while resisting the temptation to return to a discrete, text-focused approach. Although reliance upon glosses and bilingual dictionaries has been discouraged by recent research

Independent Second Language Reading 77

While reading, write down everything that goes on in your head in a 'stream of consciousness' style. As you read you should record images, associations, feelings, thoughts, or judgments. This record should contain:

Questions that you ask yourself about characters and events as you read. (Answer these as you can.)

Memories from your own experiences provoked by the reading.

Guesses about how you think the story will develop and why.

Reflections on notable moments or ideas in the reading.

Comparisons between how you behave and how the characters are behaving.

Thoughts and feelings about characters and events.

Comments on how the story is being told, including words, phrases, or passages that made an impression on you, or motifs that the author keeps using.

Connections to other texts, courses, ideas, or experiences.

An Outline of each chapter or major section, no longer than one paragraph each.

Please date each entry and note down the time and the place, as well as the mood you were in while reading (Amer, 2003: 69–70).

Figure 4.4 Reading log

(Ajideh, 2003; Hayati, 2005), electronic environments offer possibilities for vocabulary assistance without the labour, the disconnect, or the text-boundedness often associated with traditional vocabulary lists, glosses or dictionary use. For example, pre-teaching vocabulary in semantically and topically related sets can be facilitated by prepared software or through pre-reading activities mediated by authentic websites. Moreover, because the selection of authentic language texts available through new media has increased exponentially, the use of authentic, rather than prepared or even abridged texts, can help readers contextually guess or predict the meaning of unknown words.

Authentic texts, which tend to be lengthier than standard teacher-prepared selections, often have a natural redundancy of vocabulary, discourse structure, and theme that is useful to the L2 reader. L1 research demonstrates that word recognition is directly and positively correlated to frequency of occurrence (Rubenstein *et al.*, 1970). However, prepared, edited and shortened texts tend to encourage the use of word-level strategies by sanitising the natural repetition of vocabulary, patterns of structure, conceptual redundancy and rhetorical organisation, thus rendering the shortened or edited passage less readable than the original. Indeed, it is the authentic and independent reading done 'outside of class – the daily reading of newspapers and magazines, comics, sensational literature, or trivial texts – that fosters automaticity' in vocabulary recognition (Swaffar *et al.*, 1991: 50–51). In addition to the use of authentic texts to encourage vocabulary and rhetorical structure recognition, other considerations inspired by the reader-centred movement, and easily applicable to independent and/or technological contexts, include the selection of texts for which students have the appropriate background knowledge, and for which steps can be taken to encourage the activation of this knowledge through 'visuals, advance organisers or more actively through discussion and problem solving' (Gascoigne, 2002a: 344). To this end, Swaffar *et al.* (1991: 137–139) offer 10 desirable features of target language texts:

(1) The topic should be familiar to the students.
(2) The topic should be of interest to the students.
(3) The plot or message system should be substantive or readily discernable.
(4) There should be a clear and sequential development (a logical series of events such as those in a fairy-tale or history text).
(5) There should be well-marked episodes (language that signals changes of people, place, topic or action).
(6) There should be a recognisable agent or concrete subject.
(7) There should be a minimal amount of description.
(8) There should be an unambiguous intent (avoiding humour or parody, at least for beginners).
(9) The text should have an appropriate length (rethinking the notion that short readings are preferable to long ones).
(10) Texts should be authentic and unedited.

Certain language features function as more than mere vocabulary; they can also serve as a structural bridge between episodes of a text. In particular, sequence words such as *first, next, later* and *consequently*, or contrast markers such as *despite, but, nonetheless* or *on the other hand*, are important for the identification of rhetorical structure and help readers understand and identify coherent relationships in structure and in meaning (Swaffar *et al.*, 1991: 68). In fact,

> logical connectors are among the vocabulary items the hardest to guess in context yet essential for accurate text construction [...] they must be taught, particularly in pre-reading exercises. And, since intersentence connectors identify relationships between macro- and micropropositions, they are most logically discussed as links between high-, mid- and low-level text structure [...] In building mental representations of text structure, L2 readers need syntactic cohesion factors to connect semantics. (Swaffar *et al.*, 1991: 68)

Activities designed to teach or draw attention to sentence connectors promote awareness of textual organisation, patterns and relationships that extend well beyond the word level and can facilitate comprehension. For the independent learner, who is often unable to ask comprehension questions or receive immediate feedback, awareness of logical connectors is even more urgent.

Interactive Reading in Technologically-Mediated Independent Environments

While the above strategies and techniques can also be applied to independent reading that just happens to take place in an online or electronic context, these media do require additional considerations. For instance, in many technology-mediated independent settings, readers may also need to employ various navigational strategies, such as 'scrolling up and down along a page, moving among pages by clicking on buttons, utilising multiple windows and changing an active window' (Konishi, 2003: 105). In addition, incidental kinesthetic activities such as manipulating a mouse and the occasional use of a keyboard or special key combinations may also need to be employed and monitored.

Konishi (2003) suggests that certain independent on-line environments will require additional levels of flexibility and focus, in that they will allow readers to pursue interests that may or may not be relevant to the original task by accessing hyperlinks. This new option can lead to unexpectedly attractive and useful information, or it can lead independent readers down irrelevant and convoluted paths. Therefore, an additional level of metacognitive awareness and monitoring of the use of hyperlinks (maintaining an awareness of their facilitative and debilitative effects) must be encouraged.

While examining the strategy use of readers as they encounter L2 hypertext, Konishi (2003) found that successful readers rely upon global strategies just as they tend to do in traditional contexts. In fact, despite the unique nature of the text,

> electronic nodes and links, hypertext systems inherently have connectivity and intertextuality. Hypertext is also characterised by multi-linearity and open-endedness [because] there are multiple pathways [with] no mandatory starting point or absolute finishing point, (Konishi, 2003: 109)

successful independent online readers used the same global strategies that they used with print text, such as making inferences connecting new information in the text to their background knowledge, and using meta-cognitive strategies including goal-setting, monitoring understanding, and revising strategy use. Indeed, we are in the midst of a new relationship with text now 'because of the Internet, such that images dominate over the text and the screen dominates over books [...] the screen is a visual entity such that the text that appears is treated as an image [...] with the result that the text plays a secondary role to image in terms of meaning' (Horning, 2003: 75). Still, Konishi believes that because of the characteristics of online reading, 'reading hypertext requires the constant integration of new information and monitoring of understanding to guide comprehension' (Horning, 2003: 113), the process and the skills required are similar to those needed for the reading of printed text.

Like Konishi (2003), Horning (2003) found that reading strategies in electronic environments are consistent with well-established, cognitively-based strategies for reading print. Indeed, interaction 'appears to be important in both book reading and screen reading, making them more alike than they might first appear' (Horning, 2003: 76–77). Just as readers rely upon background knowledge (and text schemata) to recognise the structure of a poem, a fairy tale or a report, so too do they rely upon genre of the internet such as the format of a news site, a shopping site, or a pop-up advertisement. In both 'book reading and screen reading, patterns of many kinds help readers create appropriate expectations of the text, enhancing comprehension' (Horning, 2003: 77). In online environments, Walz (2001) also encourages the consideration of ancillary aspects such as the URL (the address of the site) or the domain name, which can help orient the reader, much like a heading or an image in print.

Conclusion

Skills and strategies needed for the successful comprehension of both text and images, whether on the printed page or the interactive screen, and whether treated in the classroom or in an independent setting, rely upon similar and well-established processes (Horning, 2003) that tend to be interactive and global in nature. The development of global reading strategies, such as the activation of background knowledge, paying attention to meaning, hypothesising, making predictions based on titles or images, skipping or engaging in contextual guessing when faced with unknown vocabulary, selecting texts in which one is interested, with which one is generally familiar, or about which one is motivated to read can and should be encouraged in independent reading as well as traditional contexts (Brantmeier, 2002; Horning, 2003; Konishi, 2003; Walz, 2001). Even in emerging reading environments, with the use of technology, prior knowledge can be activated through visuals, graphics and streamed videos. And, 'hyperlinks can be created to connect the readers to online information about authors, historical periods, and geography' (Brantmeier, 2002: 55). In addition, concept mapping software, such as *Inspiration*, can be used to guide pre-reading brainstorming efforts.

In sum, the commonalities underlying the behaviours and mental processes essential to literacy suggest that while 'the place we are looking at in the "new media age" may be different, i.e., screen rather than page, or image rather than text, the basic processing is the same' (Horning, 2003: 85) and the skills, strategies and behaviours that encourage successful comprehension in traditional reading contexts should be shared with the independent reader as well. The learner autonomy needed for successful reading comprehension in the independent context can be supported and facilitated by the strategies, techniques and tools employed by successful readers in traditional environments. However, the profession cannot afford to assume that all independent readers already and automatically employ these skills. Therefore, proven reading strategies, metacognitive and monitoring strategies in particular, should be provided in order to help guide the independent student in managing his or her own learning experience.

References

Ahmad, I.S. and Asraf, R.M. (2004) Making sense of text: Strategies used by good and average readers. *The Reading Matrix* 4 (1), 26–37.

Ajideh, P. (2003) Schema theory-based pre-reading tasks: A neglected essential in the ESL reading class. *The Reading Matrix* 3 (1), 1–14.

Alyousef, H. (2005) Teaching reading comprehension to ESL/EFL learners. *The Reading Matrix* 5 (2), 143–154.

Amer, A.A. (2003) Teaching EFL/ESL literature. *The Reading Matrix* 3 (2), 63–73.

Anderson, T. and Pearson, P.D. (1988) A schematic-theoretic view of basic processes in reading comprehension. In P. Carrell, J. Devine and D. Eskey (eds) *Interactive Approaches to Second Language Reading* (pp. 37–55). Cambridge: Cambridge University Press.

Bacon, S.M. (1992) Phases of listening to authentic input in Spanish: A descriptive study. *Foreign Language Annals* 25, 317–334.

Barnett, M. (1989) *More than Meets the Eye*. Englewood Cliffs, NJ: Prentice Hall.

Bartlett, F.C. (1932) *Remembering*. Cambridge: Cambridge University Press.

Bell, F. and LeBlanc, L. (2000) The language glosses in L2 reading on computer: Learners' preferences. *Hispania* 83, 274–285.

Bernhardt, E. (1991) *Reading Development in a Second Language: Theoretical, Empirical, and Classroom Perspectives*. New Jersey: Ablex.

Block, E. (1986) The comprehension strategies of second language readers. *TESOL Quarterly* 20, 436–494.

Brantmeier, C. (2002) Second language reading strategy research at the secondary and university levels: Variations, disparities, and generalisability. *The Reading Matrix* 2 (3), 1–13.

Brantmeier, C. (2003a) Beyond linguistic knowledge: Individual differences in second language reading. *Foreign Language Annals* 36 (1), 33–43.

Brantmeier, C. (2003b) Technology and second language reading at the university level: Informed instructors' perceptions. *The Reading Matrix* 3 (3), 50–73.

Brantmeier, C. (2005) Anxiety about L2 reading or L2 reading tasks: A study with advanced language learners. *The Reading Matrix* 5 (2), 67–79.

Brown, H.D. (2001) *Teaching by Principles: An Interactive Approach to Language Pedagogy*. New York: Addison Wesley Longman.

Carrell, P. and Eisterhold, J. (1983) Schema theory and ESL pedagogy. In P. Carrell, J. Devine and D. Eskey (eds) *Interactive Approaches to Second Language Reading* (pp. 73–92). Cambridge: Cambridge University Press.

Chastain, K. (1988) *Developing Second Language Skills: Theory and Practice*. Orlando: Harcourt, Brace and Jovanovich.

Chia, H.L. (2001) Reading activities for effective top-down processing. *FORUM* 39 (1), 1–22.

Eskey, D.E. (1988) Holding in the bottom: An interactive approach to the language problems of second language readers. In P. Carrell, J. Devine and D. Eskey (eds) *Interactive Approaches to Second Language Reading* (pp. 90–100). Cambridge: Cambridge University Press.

Gascoigne, C. (2002a) Reviewing reading: Recommendations versus reality. *Foreign Language Annals* 35 (3), 343–348.

Gascoigne, C. (2002b) Documenting the initial second language reading experience: The readers speak. *Foreign Language Annals* 35 (5), 554–560.

Gascoigne, C. (2005) Toward an understanding of the relationship between L2 reading comprehension and grammatical competence. *The Reading Matrix* 5 (2), 1–14.

Goodman, K.S. (1968) *The Psycholinguistic Nature of the Reading Process*. Detroit: Wayne State University Press.

Gough, P.B. (1972) One second of reading. In J.F. Kavanagh and I.G. Mattingly (eds) *Language by Ear and Eye* (pp. 332–358). Cambridge: Cambridge University Press.

Grabe, W. (1991) Current developments in second language reading research. *TESOL Quarterly* 25, 375–406.

Hayati, A.M. (2005) A comparative study of using bilingual and monolingual dictionaries in reading comprehension of intermediate EFL students. *The Reading Matrix* 5 (2), 61–66.

Horning, A. (2003) Electronic reading: Emergence in online text. *The Reading Matrix* 3 (3), 75–86.

Huttunen, I. (1996) Learning to learn: An overview. *Language Teaching* April, 86–89.

Inspiration (2007) Portland, OR: Inspiration Software, Inc.

Konishi, M. (2003) Strategies for reading hypertext by Japanese ESL learners. *The Reading Matrix* 3 (3), 97–119.

Lally, C. (1998) The application of first language reading models to second language study: A recent historical perspective. *Reading Horizons* 38 (4), 267–277.

Landry, K.L. (2002) Schemata in second language reading. *The Reading Matrix* 2 (3), 1–7.

Martinez-Lang, A. (1995) Benefits of keeping a reading journal in the development of second language reading ability. *Dimension* 95, 65–79.

Orasanu, J. (1986) *Reading Comprehension: From Research to Practice*. Hillsdale, NJ: Lawrence Erlbaum.

Rubenstein, H., Garfield, L. and Millikan, J. (1970) Homographic entries in the internal lexicon. *Journal of Verbal Learning and Verbal Behavior* 9, 487–494.

Rumelhart, D.E. (1980) Schemata: The building blocks of cognition. In R.J. Spiro, B.C. Bruce and W.F. Brewer (eds) *Theoretical Issues in Reading Comprehension: Perspectives from Cognitive Psychology, Linguistics, Artificial Intelligence, and Education* (pp. 35–58). Hillsdale, NJ: Lawrence Erlbaum.

Saricoban, A. (2002) Reading strategies of successful readers through the three phase approach. *The Reading Matrix* 2 (3), 1–13.

Schank, R. and Abelson, R. (1977) *Scripts, Plans, Goals, and Understanding*. Hillsdale, NJ: Lawrence Erlbaum.

Shrum, J.L. and Glisan, E.W. (1994) *Teacher's Handbook: Contextualised Language Instruction*. Boston: Heinle and Heinle.

Swaffar, J.K., Arens, K.M. and Byrnes, H. (1991) *Reading for Meaning: An Integrated Approach to Language Learning*. Englewood Cliffs, NJ: Prentice Hall.

Vanijdee, A. (2003) Thai distance English learners and learner autonomy. *Open Learning* 18 (1), 75–84.

Walz, J. (2001) Critical reading and the Internet. *French Review* 74 (6), 1193–1205.

Wenden, A.L. (1991) *Learner Strategies for Learner Autonomy*. New York: Prentice Hall.

White, C.J. (1995) Autonomy and strategy use in distance foreign language learning: Research findings. *System* 23 (2), 207–221.

Wu, M.H.H. (1992) QUILT *and* QUILL: *Achieving and Maintaining Quality in Language Teaching and Learning*. Hong Kong: Institute of Language.

Chapter 5
Learning Strategies for Listening Comprehension

LARRY VANDERGRIFT

Introduction

Listening is perhaps the most essential skill for second/foreign (L2) language learning, particularly at the beginning stages. It internalises the rules of language and facilitates the emergence of other language skills (e.g. Rost, 2002). Listening is also perceived as the most difficult skill to learn because of its implicit and ephemeral nature (e.g. Graham, 2003). Given the salience of listening in language learning and its perceived difficulty, strategies for effective listening can help L2 learners capitalise on the language input they receive.

This chapter presents an overview of the strategies used in L2 listening and how L2 learners can acquire these strategies. The first section provides an introduction to listening strategies, in particular the metacognitive strategies which are specific to L2 listening, and highlights their importance for independent language learning. The second section discusses the insights provided by research into acquiring word segmentation skills and developing metacognitive awareness about listening processes. The concluding section outlines an approach to teaching listening strategies that can help L2 learners become aware of the processes underlying L2 listening comprehension and acquire the skills needed to control and direct their ability to listen and comprehend.

Listening Strategies

Listening strategies are deliberate procedures used by learners to enhance comprehension, learning and retention of the target language (Rigney, 1978). O'Malley and Chamot (1990) validated a body of learning strategies and an accompanying classification scheme grounded in cognitive theory (Brown & Palincsar, 1982). Based on earlier work in cognitive psychology, O'Malley and Chamot differentiated L2 learning strategies by type of cognitive function: an executive or metacognitive function (metacognitive strategies) and an operative, cognitive processing function (cognitive strategies). Metacognitive strategies involve thinking about and directing the listening process: they include actions such as planning, monitoring, evaluating and problem-solving. These strategies are important because they oversee, regulate or direct the listening comprehension process by orchestrating the deployment of specific cognitive strategies. In addition, the listener uses cognitive strategies to manipulate elements from the listening text (e.g. summarising) or apply a specific technique to the listening task (e.g. inferencing). While metacognitive strategies may direct listening activity, their directive power cannot be realised without the application of appropriate cognitive strategies. Therefore, successful L2 listening involves the careful orchestration of both metacognitive and cognitive strategies.

There is another category of listening strategies, socio-affective strategies, used by L2 listeners primarily in interaction with another speaker (see, e.g. Farrell & Mallard, 2006; Vandergrift, 1997b). These strategies will not be discussed here because this chapter highlights one-way listening, the type of listening that can best be developed in independent language learning settings.

Building on the work of O'Malley and Chamot (1990), Vandergrift (1997a) identified a range of metacognitive and cognitive listening strategies reported by L2 learners thinking aloud while listening to texts in French. Think-aloud sessions, adapted from O'Malley et al. (1989), were conducted on an individual basis with students listening to texts in French. For each text, the tape was stopped at the breaks indicated on the tape script (natural discourse boundaries), and students attempted to verbalise what they were thinking. The investigator used only non-cueing probes, such as 'What are you thinking now?' Great care was taken not to inadvertently plant strategies in the student's mind. A second tape recorder recorded the text, the think-aloud data and any investigator prompts. These data were transcribed and examined for evidence of the strategies outlined by O'Malley and Chamot (1990: 137–138). Definitions of identified strategies were then revised with particular reference to listening, and the inferencing category was further subdivided. Table 5.1 presents the resulting taxonomy of L2 listening strategies, their definitions and representative examples.

Metacognitive Strategies and Skilled L2 Listening

Studies of the differences between more-skilled and less-skilled listeners highlight the importance of metacognitive strategies (see section 1 in Table 5.1) to L2 listening success (Bacon, 1992; Goh, 2000; O'Malley &

Table 5.1 Listening comprehension strategies, definitions and examples

(1) Metacognitive strategies

1.1	**Planning:** Developing an awareness of what needs to be done to accomplish a listening task, developing an appropriate action plan and/or appropriate contingency plans to overcome difficulties that may interfere with successful completion of the task.		
	1.1.1 Advance organisation:	Clarifying the objectives of an anticipated listening task and/or proposing strategies for handling it.	I read over what we have to do. I try to think of questions the teacher is going to ask.
	1.1.2 Directed attention:	Deciding in advance to **attend in general** to the listening task and to ignore irrelevant distracters; maintaining attention while listening.	I listen really hard. I put everything aside and concentrate on what she is saying.
	1.1.3 Selective attention:	Deciding to **attend to specific aspects of** language input or situational details that assist in understanding and/or task completion.	I listen for the key words. I establish the speakers in the conversation, their relationship by tone of voice, how they will address each other. This will limit the topics of discussion (in combination with **planning**, **voice inferencing** and **elaboration**).
1.2	**Monitoring:** Checking, verifying, or correcting one's comprehension or performance in the course of a listening task.		
	1.2.1 Comprehension monitoring:	Checking, verifying, or correcting one's understanding at the local level.	I translate and see if it sounds right. (in combination with **translation**) I just try to put everything together, understanding one thing leads to understanding another.
	1.2.2 Double-check monitoring:	Checking, verifying or correcting one's understanding across the task or during the second time through the oral text.	I might catch it at the end and then I'd go back. Sunny in the morning, that's not making sense ... (earlier) it sounded like a cold front; something doesn't make sense to me any more.

Learning Strategies for Listening Comprehension 87

1.3	Evaluation: Checking the outcomes of one's listening comprehension against an internal measure of completeness and accuracy.	
1.3.1 Performance evaluation:	Judging one's overall execution of the task.	How close was I? (at end of a think-aloud report)
1.3.2 Strategy evaluation:	Judging one's strategy use.	I don't concentrate too much to the point of translation of individual words because then you just have a whole lot of words and not how they're strung together into some kind of meaning.
1.4 Problem solving:	Identifying what needs resolution in a task or identifying an aspect of the task that hinders its successful completion and applying a cognitive strategy; e.g. inferencing.	I missed something in between but I could tell that he didn't know what to tell his teacher so he obviously didn't do his homework because of the apartment.
(2) *Cognitive strategies*		
2.1	Inferencing: Using information within the text or conversational context to guess the meanings of unfamiliar language items associated with a listening task, to predict outcomes, or to fill in missing information.	
2.1.1 Linguistic inferencing:	Using known words in an utterance to guess the meaning of unknown words.	I use other words in the sentence. I try to think of it in context and guess.
2.1.2 Voice and paralinguistic inferencing:	Using tone of voice and/or paralinguistics to guess the meaning of unknown words in an utterance.	I listen to the way the words are said. I guess, using tone of voice as a clue.
2.1.3 Kinesic inferencing:	Using facial expressions, body language and hand movements to guess the meaning of unknown words used by a speaker.	I try to read her body language. I read her face. I use the teacher's hand gestures.

(*Continued*)

Table 5.1 (Continued)

2.1.4 Extralinguistic inferencing:	Using background sounds and relationships between speakers in an oral text, material in the response sheet or concrete situational referents to guess the meaning of unknown words.	I guess on the basis of the kind of information the question asks for. I comprehend what the teacher chooses to write on the board to clarify what she is saying.
2.1.5 Between parts inferencing:	Using information beyond the local sentential level, i.e. co-text, to guess at meaning.	Because in the beginning she said 'course,' so maybe it was, maybe it was a race … may be a horse race … You pick out things you do know and in the whole situation piece it together so that you do know what it does mean.
2.2	**Elaboration:** Using prior knowledge from outside the text or conversational context and relating it to knowledge gained from the text or conversation in order to predict outcomes or fill in missing information.	
2.2.1 Personal elaboration:	Referring to prior experience personally.	I think there is some big picnic or a family gathering, sounds like fun, I don't know … You know … maybe they missed, because that happens to me lots just miss accidentally and then you call up and say. 'Well, what happened?'
2.2.2 World elaboration:	Using knowledge gained from experience in the world.	Recognising the names in sports helps you to know what sport they are talking about. I use the topic to determine the words that I will listen for. (in combination with **selective attention**)
2.2.3 Academic elaboration:	Using knowledge gained in academic situations.	[I know that] from doing telephone conversations in class. I relate the word to a topic we've studied. I try to think of all my background in French.
2.2.4 Questioning elaboration:	Using a combination of questions and world knowledge to brainstorm logical possibilities.	Oh, I think now, she's, it looks like she won something. Like maybe a talk show or something … It's a surprise. I think I heard maybe something about 'gagner' or something, I'm not sure.

Learning Strategies for Listening Comprehension 89

2.2.5 Creative elaboration:	Making up a story line, or adopting a clever, yet plausible, perspective that could explain what the listener heard.	Sounded like introducing something, like it says here is something but I can't figure out what it is, it could be like … one of the athletes, like introducing some person or something.
2.3 Imagery:	Using mental or actual pictures or visuals to represent information; coded as a separate category but viewed as a form of elaboration.	I can picture the words in my mind. I make pictures in my mind for words I know, then I fill in the picture that's missing in the sequence of pictures in my mind.
2.4 Summarisation:	Making a mental or written summary of language and information presented in a listening task.	I remember the key points and run them through my head, 'what happened here and what happened here' and get everything organised in order to answer the questions.
2.5 Translation:	Rendering ideas from one language to another in a relatively verbatim manner.	I translate. I'll say what she says in my head, but in English. A little voice inside me is translating.
2.6 Transfer:	Using knowledge of one language (e.g. cognates) to facilitate listening in another.	I try to relate the words to English. I use my knowledge of other languages: English to understand German and Portuguese (primarily sound) to understand French.
2.7 Repetition:	Repeating a chunk of language (a word or phrase) in the course of performing a listening task.	I sound out the words. I say the word to myself.
2.8 Note taking:	Writing down key words and concepts in abbreviated verbal, graphic, or numerical form to assist performance of a listening task.	I write down the word. When I write it down, it comes to my mind what it means.

Source: Based on Vandergrift (1997a) and O'Malley and Chamot (1990).

Chamot, 1990; Vandergrift, 1997a, 1998). In a more recent study of adolescent learners of French, Vandergrift (2003a) found significant quantitative differences in strategy use: skilled listeners used about twice as many metacognitive strategies as their less-skilled counterparts. Furthermore, there were also differences in the use of specific strategies such as comprehension monitoring, questioning elaboration (flexibility in using a combination of questions and world knowledge in evaluating logical possibilities) and on-line translation (by the less-skilled listener). A qualitative analysis of the think-aloud aloud protocols reinforced these differences and also found that more-skilled listeners used an effective combination of metacognitive and cognitive strategies, 'coupling strategies together like links in a fence' (Murphy, 1985: 38). Goh (2002b) also reported similar findings. Skilled L2 listening, therefore, is more than a question of numbers of strategies used; it involves a skilful orchestration of selected metacognitive and cognitive strategies to regulate learning processes and achieve comprehension.

The use of metacognitive strategies to control learning is closely linked to motivation, self-regulated learning (Pintrich, 1999) and learner autonomy (Dickinson, 1995). In a study correlating listening test scores with student reported levels of motivation (grounded in self-determination theory) and student reported use of cognitive and metacognitive listening strategies, Vandergrift (2005) uncovered an interesting pattern of increasingly higher correlations between each of the three levels of motivation (a continuum of increasing self-determination from amotivation to extrinsic and to intrinsic motivation) and reported use of metacognitive strategies. These patterns of correlation provide some evidence for the hypothesised links between self-determination theory, self-regulated learning, learner autonomy and metacognition. As suggested by Dickinson (1995) and Dörnyei (2001), intrinsically motivated or self-regulated learners are more effective learners because the locus of control is internalised. This would suggest that learning to regulate the metacognitive processes underlying L2 listening is important for taking control of listening development, particularly in independent learning settings. This relates closely to one of the listening goals highlighted by Flowerdew and Miller (2005) for developing learner independence.

Listening is not a uni-dimensional or linear process, however. Buck (2001), among others, emphasises that listening comprehension is multi-dimensional in nature with a number of different information sources informing the comprehension process in no fixed order. Listeners use all the information, inside or outside a text that will help them arrive at what seems to them to be a reasonable interpretation of a text. Therefore, learning to take control of listening also involves the development of perception skills. Only when L2 listeners can begin to identify words in the sound stream (the aural text), can they begin to use their metacognitive and background knowledge (see the strategy of elaboration in Table 5.1) to interpret what they hear. The next section focuses on helping L2 listeners pay attention to the acoustic signal and develop word segmentation skills.

Developing Word Segmentation Skills

Development of word segmentation skills is a major challenge faced by L2 listeners. Unlike readers, listeners do not have the luxury of spaces to help them determine word boundaries. They must parse the sound stream into meaningful units and, owing to stress patterns, elisions and reduced forms, word boundaries are often hard to determine. Even if they can recognise individual words, listeners may not always recognise the same word in connected speech. Word segmentation skills are language-specific, acquired early in life. These procedures are so solidly engrained in the listener's processing system that they are involuntarily applied when listening to a non-native language. Listening to a language that is rhythmically different from one's L1 can be particularly difficult; however, Cutler (2001) found that L2 listeners can learn to inhibit the natural compulsion to apply native language segmentation procedures when listening to another language that is rhythmically different. This promising finding suggests that students can develop word segmentation skills.

Word segmentation skills can be acquired by giving L2 listeners opportunities to 'accumulate and categorise acoustic, phonemic, syllabic, morphological and lexical information' (Hulstijn, 2003: 422). He describes an unsophisticated six-step procedure, particularly suitable for independent language learning: (1) listen to the recording; (2) ask yourself if you have understood; (3) replay the recording as often as necessary; (4) consult the written text to read what you have just heard; (5) recognise what you should have understood; and (6) replay the recording as often as necessary to understand the oral text without written support. This approach also calls attention to the phenomena that make comprehension of connected speech in L2 such a challenge: reduced forms, assimilation, and elision. L2 listeners need to become aware of these phenomena, pay attention to them and, replay them in listening practice exercises so they can puzzle them out for themselves (Field, 2003).

Digital video texts and multimedia can also contribute to listening practice that enhances word recognition skills. Learners can choose to listen to any chunk of text and replay it as often as necessary. Research on the use of videotexts demonstrates, however, that the visual component does not always help L2 listeners in ways that one might expect (Gruba, 2004). Use of video in ESL lecture comprehension demonstrated that listeners needed more than a 'talking head' to comprehend the lecture. Listeners demonstrated better comprehension when questions could be answered using visual aids, such as transparencies, used by the lecturer

(Smidt & Hegelheimer, 2004). In order to verify hypotheses and decipher incomprehensible chunks of text, listeners need to have eventual access to the written text if listening growth is to occur.

Hulstijn (2003) and colleagues have developed a multimedia software program (123LISTEN) that allows learners to segment digitised video or audio texts into short chunks, each segment accompanied by a written transcript of the text. Listeners can choose three modes of listening: (1) nonstop listening without text; (2) listening by segment with delayed text display; and, (3) listening by segment with simultaneous text display. Hulstijn argues that the real value of 123LISTEN is the second mode where students listen first and then try to interpret what they are hearing. However, in order to develop real-life listening skills, listeners should first try to understand what they have heard by using prediction and monitoring strategies and then verify comprehension, using text display to read the words in the segment. In a similar vein, an initiative reported by Hoeflaak (2004) will provide training in perception skills for French, with a detailed feedback function based on a corpus of learner errors. Furthermore, online tutorials (focusing on decoding skills), available through EuroCom (Klein & Robert, 2004) are available for the development of listening and reading competence in Italian, Romanian and Spanish. These initiatives can potentially facilitate the development of L2 listening perception skills in independent learning environments.

Finally, Wilson (2003) has proposed the use of the dictogloss technique as a tool for developing word recognition skills. After listening to the aural text a number of times, L2 listeners, in pairs, reconstruct the text. They are then guided towards noticing the differences between their reconstructed text and a written transcription of the original. This technique can improve perceptual processing skills because learners can attend to the source of their comprehension problems, consider the reasons for their errors and evaluate the importance of these errors.

The next section deals with the development of metacognitive knowledge that familiarises learners with the processes underlying L2 listening.

Developing Metacognitive Knowledge About L2 Listening

Reflection on the process of listening can raise awareness and help L2 learners develop strategic knowledge for successful L2 listening. Students can be encouraged to take responsibility for planning, monitoring and evaluating their own learning, leading to greater success in L2 listening and, concomitantly, greater motivation and increased self-efficacy.

Given the importance of metacognitive awareness in successful listening, Vandergrift (2002, 2003a) investigated the effect of process-based listening instruction on the development of metacognitive knowledge about listening. While students completed listening tasks, they actively engaged in the major processes underlying listening: prediction, monitoring, problem-solving and evaluation. On a very simple level, for example, beginning-level learners of French in primary school listened to a text explaining what they must feed animals in a pet shop (Vandergrift, 2002). Before listening to the text, students studied and completed a matrix of animals (in rows) and foods (in columns), using their world knowledge to predict answers about what each animal would eat or drink, and discussing their predictions with a classmate (planning). They also completed a checklist reminding them of how to concentrate and what to attend to (planning). Students then listened to the text to answer and verify their predictions (monitoring). This was followed by a 'Retour réflexif', in which students again turned their attention to the checklist, noted what they actually did as they listened (evaluating), and then participated in a class discussion on what was easy and what was difficult. The same approach, using more age-appropriate tasks and texts, was used with beginner-level university students of French (Vandergrift, 2003b).

Both groups of students found it motivating to learn to understand rapid, authentic texts, and responded overwhelmingly in favour of this approach to L2 listening. Students noted, in particular, the power of predictions for selective attention to the text (instead of trying to understand every word), the importance of collaboration with a partner for monitoring, and the confidence-building role of this approach. Goh and Taib (2006) noted similar results with primary school students in Singapore. After eight process-based listening lessons, students reported greater awareness of the nature and demands of L2 listening, increased confidence, and better problem-solving abilities. The researchers also noted that the weaker listeners appeared to benefit more from this listening instruction.

Metacognitive knowledge about listening can be developed in other ways. Listening diaries, followed by class discussions, can help listeners to reflect on what they actually do while they listen and distinguish between successful and unsuccessful approaches to a task (Goh, 1997). (See also Chapter 11 on learning logs.) Listeners can also learn about new strategies through teacher-led discussions, as reported by both Vandergrift (2002), and Goh and Taib (2006). For independent learners, these can be held online. Questionnaires, such as the Metacognitive Awareness Listening Questionnaire (MALQ), can stimulate reflection on the listening process (see Appendix A). The MALQ is grounded in research and theory about L2 listening and significantly related to L2 listening success (Vandergrift *et al.*, 2006). Students can use questionnaires for self-assessment purposes, to determine their current level of metacognitive awareness and to chart the development of their strategy use/listening awareness over time. In the latter case, the MALQ can be particularly useful to positively influence students' attitudes and their perceptions of the listening process. Ultimately they can become skilled listeners who automatically regulate metacognitive comprehension processes. Techniques such as diaries, discussions and questionnaires help learners to step back from real-time listening, examine their listening processes, and develop their own metacognitive knowledge about effective L2 listening (Vandergrift & Goh, in press).

The next section discusses a metacognitive cycle for learning to listen in L2 that integrates the development of metacognitive knowledge about L2 listening with the development of word perception skills.

Learning How to Listen

Guidance in the use of listening strategies typically addresses the product of listening: the correct answer. While an emphasis on the product allows comprehension to be verified, the answer (correct or incorrect) reveals nothing about the process used; that is, how students arrived at comprehension. For the listener, an exclusive interest in the right answer often creates a high level of anxiety, especially when rate of speech is challenging. On the other hand, placing an emphasis on the process of listening comprehension through regular practice, unencumbered by the threat of evaluation, can strengthen students' ability to control comprehension processes on their own. Optimum L2 listening practice takes place when students regularly listen to realistic texts for communicative purposes and are sensitised to important issues in listening (Buck, 1995).

The following learning sequence can develop an awareness of the process of (one-way) listening and help listeners acquire the metacognitive knowledge critical to success in listening comprehension. Gruba (2004) has identified many of the same steps taken by listeners in front-to-back (uninterrupted) viewing of digital video media.

Planning for the successful completion of a listening task

Pre-listening activities help listeners make decisions about what to listen for and, subsequently, to attend to meaning while listening (see the strategies associated with this phase in section 1.1 of Table 5.1). During this critical phase of the listening process, listeners prepare themselves for what they will hear and what they are expected to do. To plan for listening, students are encouraged to:

- bring to consciousness their knowledge of the topic and any relevant cultural information;
- familiarise themselves with pertinent cultural content;
- analyse the type of text to which they will listen and recall how information is organised in such a text;
- anticipate possible words that they can identify;

- determine where to pay attention and how much detail to find (based on an authentic purpose for listening) in order to direct listening efforts;
- use all the available information to predict and anticipate what they will hear.

Monitoring comprehension during a listening task

During the listening task itself, listeners monitor their comprehension and make decisions about strategy use (see the strategies associated with this phase in section 1.2 of Table 5.1). Intervention during this phase is virtually impossible because of the ephemeral nature of listening. Listeners need to:

- evaluate continually what they are comprehending through self-questioning activities (questioning elaboration; see 2.2.5 in Table 5.1);
- check for consistency with their predictions, and for internal consistency; that is, the ongoing interpretation of the oral text (co-text);
- verify predictions and accept the fact that they are not going to understand every word;
- check for comprehension of desired information and necessary details.

Evaluating the approach and outcomes of a listening task

Comprehension is demonstrated by using the product, comprehended information, for a functional purpose. In addition, learners need to evaluate the effectiveness of steps taken and decisions made during the listening process (see the strategies associated with this phase in section 1.3 of Table 5.1). In order to do this, listeners can:

- reflect on what was easy and difficult (and why);
- reflect on what went wrong and why;
- confirm comprehension with a transcription of parts or all of the aural text;
- share individual routes leading to success (with other learners on-line); for example, how they guessed (inference) the meaning of a certain word or how they modified a particular strategy;
- set goals for future listening activities; or
- use the MALQ (or other listening questionnaire) for reflection purposes and compare responses to earlier uses of this questionnaire.

During both the monitoring and evaluating phases, listeners are also engaged in problem-solving (see section 1.4 in Table 5.1) as they verify comprehension and reflect on the outcomes of their listening efforts.

This sequence of activities and the metacognitive processes underlying them is encapsulated in the learning cycle set out in Table 5.2. In addition

Table 5.2 Stages for guided listening and related metacognitive processes

Planning/predicting stage (1) Once students know the topic and text type, they predict types of information and possible words they may hear.	(1) Planning and directed attention
First listen/verification stage (2) Students listen to verify initial hypotheses, correct as required and note additional information understood.	(2) Monitoring
(3) Students compare what they have written with peers, modify as required, establish what needs resolution and decide on the important details that still need special attention.	(3) Monitoring, planning and selective attention
Second listen/verification stage (4) Students selectively attend to points of disagreement, make corrections and write down additional details understood.	(4) Monitoring and problem-solving
(5) Discussion in which class members contribute to the reconstruction of the text's main points and most pertinent details, interspersed with reflections on how students arrived at the meaning of certain words or parts of the text.	(5) Monitoring and evaluation
Final listen/verification stage (6) Students listen for the information revealed in the class discussion which they were not able to decipher earlier and/or compare all or selected sections of the aural form of the text with a transcription of the text.	(6) Selective attention and monitoring
Reflection stage (7) Based on the earlier discussion on strategies used to compensate for what was not understood, students write goals for the next listening activity. A discussion on discrepancies between the aural and written forms of the text could also take place at this stage.	(7) Evaluation

Source: Based on Vandergrift (2004).

to developing metacognitive awareness about L2 listening, this cycle develops L2 perception skills and word recognition skills, as recommended by Graham (2006). Through an orchestration of hypothesis formation and verification, accompanied by the judicious application of prior knowledge to compensate for gaps in understanding, listeners are guided in the acquisition of implicit knowledge about listening processes.

Matching all or parts of aural and written forms of the text helps L2 listeners develop awareness of form-meaning relationships and enhances word recognition skills. It is important, however, that the latter step takes place only after listeners have engaged in the cognitive processes underlying comprehension, using only cues that underlie real-life listening. If listeners are allowed access to the written form too early in the cycle, they risk developing an inefficient online translation approach to listening (Eastman, 1991). Given the constraints of working memory, L2 listeners cannot construct meaning when they process connected speech on a word by word basis only (Osada, 2001).

Guiding learners through the comprehension process as part of regular listening activities can improve their listening performance (Field, 2001; Goh, 2002a; Mendelsohn, 1994, 1998; Vandergrift, 2002, 2003a; Wilson, 2003). Students need repeated and systematic practice with a variety of listening tasks that activate the metacognitive processes used by skilled listeners; all tasks, however, should be grounded in the same metacognitive cycle (see Vandergrift, 2003b; Goh, 2002a; and White, 1998 for examples of other tasks). In order to compensate for the peer interaction that may not be present in independent language learning contexts, the element of monitoring could be programmed into the listening tasks through techniques such as 'pop-up windows' of predictions that represent varying degrees of accuracy (based on actual L2 listener predictions). L2 listeners can compare these 'programmed' predictions with their own predictions, resulting in more active monitoring and more directed attention to the text in subsequent listening efforts.

This learning cycle has strong theoretical support in that it closely parallels the research demonstrating implicit learning through task performance (Johnston, 2006). It also has empirical support. In a carefully controlled study conducted over the period of one semester, beginning- and intermediate-level learners of French who were guided through this process approach to listening significantly outperformed learners in the control classes (Vandergrift, 2007). To control for the potentially confounding effects of the teacher variable, both groups were taught by the same teacher using the same texts. The hypothesis that the weaker listeners in the experimental group would make greater gains than the stronger listeners in the experimental group was also confirmed. It appears that weaker L2 listeners may benefit most from this kind of listening practice.

This approach to developing listening skills is not limited to beginning-level language learners; advanced-level L2 listeners can also benefit from this kind of listening practice. Mareschal (2007) found that both a low-proficiency group and a high-proficiency group of learners of French exposed to this learning cycle during an eight-week course were better able to regulate their listening processes. Analysing data from listening questionnaire (MALQ) responses completed over time, stimulated recalls, diaries and a final summative report, she was able to document what impact this approach had on the listeners' self-regulatory ability, strategy use, metacognitive knowledge and listening success, particularly for the low-proficiency group. The aural-written verification stage proved to be particularly valuable to the low-proficiency group for developing auditory discrimination skills and to the high-proficiency group for more refined word recognition skills.

Conclusion

This chapter has presented an overview of the strategies used by L2 listeners to enhance their comprehension of aural texts, with an emphasis on the metacognitive strategies that they can use to successfully direct and control their listening efforts. The learning sequence introduced to help L2 listeners practise the metacognitive strategies necessary for becoming skilled, autonomous second language listeners is of particular relevance for teachers and designers of independent language learning programmes/materials, given the evidence from research studies suggesting that L2 listeners benefit from this approach to listening.

Emerging technologies open up a number of new possibilities for L2 learners in independent learning environments to explore aural and video texts: repeated audio delivery, slowed audio text delivery, transcribed texts to accompany webcasts, captioned video, translation bots and voice chats (Robin, 2007). L2 learners who are metacognitively aware can use the learning sequence to exploit these technological innovations with varying degrees of support, depending on their level of L2 learning and the degree of comprehension detail required. As new research findings are applied more extensively through curriculum, learning and teaching practices in face-to-face and independent language learning contexts, and emerging technologies, further research is likely to refine both conceptual models and teaching methodologies for L2 listening.

References

Bacon, S.M. (1992) The relationship between gender, comprehension, processing strategies, and cognitive and affective response in foreign language listening. *The Modern Language Journal* 76 (2), 160–178.

Brown, A.L. and Palinscar, A.S. (1982) Inducing strategic learning from texts by means of informed, self-control training. *Topics in Learning and Learning Disabilities* 2, 1–17.

Buck, G. (2001) *Assessing Listening*. Cambridge: Cambridge University Press.

Buck, G. (1995) How to become a good listening teacher. In D. Mendelsohn and J. Rubin (eds) *A Guide for the Teaching of Second Language Listening* (pp. 113–128). San Diego, CA: Dominie Press.

Cutler, A. (2001) Listening to a second language through the ears of a first. *Interpreting* 5, 1–23.

Dickinson, L. (1995) Autonomy and motivation: A literature review. *System* 23, 165–174.

Dörnyei, Z. (2001) *Teaching and Researching Motivation*. Essex: Longman.
Eastman, J.K. (1991) Learning to listen and comprehend: The beginning stages. *System* 19, 179–188.
Farrell, T. and Mallard, C. (2006) The use of reception strategies by learners of French as a foreign language. *Modern Language Journal* 90, 338–352.
Field, J. (2001) Finding one's way in the fog: Listening strategies and second-language learners. *Modern English Teacher* 9 (1), 29–34.
Field, J. (2003) Promoting perception: Lexical segmentation in second language listening. *ELT Journal* 57, 325–334.
Flowerdew, J. and Miller, L. (2005) *Second Language Listening: Theory and Practice*. New York: Cambridge University Press.
Goh, C. (1997) Metacognitive awareness and second language listeners. *ELT Journal* 51, 361–369.
Goh, C. (2000) A cognitive perspective on language learners: Listening comprehension problems. *System* 28, 55–75.
Goh, C. (2002a) *Teaching Listening in the Language Classroom*. Singapore: SEAMEO Regional Language Centre.
Goh, C. (2002b) Exploring listening comprehension tactics and their interaction patterns. *System* 30, 185–206.
Goh, C. and Taib, Y. (2006) Metacognitive instruction in listening for young learners. *ELT Journal* 60, 222–232.
Graham, S. (2003) Learner strategies and advanced level listening comprehension. *Language Learning Journal* 28, 64–69.
Graham, S. (2006) Listening comprehension: The learners' perspective. *System* 34, 165–182.
Gruba, P. (2004) Understanding digitised second language videotext. *Computer Assisted Language Learning* 17, 15–82.
Hoeflaak, A. (2004) Computer-assisted training in the comprehension of authentic French speech: A closer view. *Computer Assisted Language Learning* 17, 315–337.
Hulstijn, J.H. (2003) Connectionist models of language processing and the training of listening skills with the aid of multimedia software. *Computer Assisted Language Learning* 16, 413–425.
Johnston, J.D. (2006) Technology-mediated language training: Listening sub-skills technical report. University of Maryland Centre for Advanced Study of Language (CASL) (mimeo).
Klein, H. and Robert, J.M. (2004) L'eurocompréhension (EUROCOM), une méthode de compréhension des langues voisines. *Études de linguistique appliquée* 136, 403–418.
Mareschal, C. (2007) Student perceptions of a self-regulatory approach to second language listening comprehension development. Unpublished doctoral thesis, University of Ottawa.
Mendelsohn, D. (1994) *Learning to Listen: A Strategy-Based Approach for the Second-Language Learner*. San Diego, CA: Dominie.
Mendelsohn, D. (1998) Teaching listening. *Annual Review of Applied Linguistics* 18, 81–101.
Murphy, J.M. (1985) *An Investigation into the Listening Strategies of ESL College Students* (ERIC Document Reproduction Service No. ED 278 275).
O'Malley, J.M. and Chamot, A.U. (1990) *Learning Strategies in Second Language Acquisition*. Cambridge: Cambridge University Press.
O'Malley, J.M., Chamot, A.U. and Küpper, L. (1989) Listening comprehension strategies in second language acquisition. *Applied Linguistics* 10, 418–437.

Osada, N. (2001) What strategy do less proficient learners employ in listening comprehension?: A reappraisal of bottom-up and top-down processing. *Journal of the Pan-Pacific Association of Applied Linguistics* 5, 73–90.

Pintrich, P.R. (1999) The role of motivation in promoting and sustaining self-regulated listening learning. *International Journal of Educational Research* 31, 459–470.

Rigney, J.W. (1978). Learning strategies: A theoretical perspective. In H.F. O'Neill (ed.) *Learning Strategies* (pp. 165–205). New York: Academic Press.

Robin, R. (2007) Learner-based listening and technological authenticity. *Language Learning & Technology* 11 (1), 109–115.

Rost, M. (2002) *Teaching and Researching Listening*. London: Longman.

Smidt, E. and Hegelheimer, V. (2004) Effects of online academic lectures on ESL listening comprehension, incidental vocabulary acquisition and strategy use. *Computer Assisted Language Learning* 17 (5), 517–556.

Vandergrift, L. (1997a) The strategies of second language (French) listeners: A descriptive study. *Foreign Language Annals* 30, 387–409.

Vandergrift, L. (1997b) The Cinderella of communication strategies: Receptive strategies in interactive listening. *Modern Language Journal* 90, 338–352.

Vandergrift, L. (1998) Successful and less successful listeners in French: What are the strategy differences? *The French Review* 71, 370–395.

Vandergrift, L. (2002) It was nice to see that our predictions were right: Developing metacognition in L2 listening comprehension. *Canadian Modern Language Review* 58, 555–575.

Vandergrift, L. (2003a) From prediction through reflection: Guiding students through the process of L2 listening. *Canadian Modern Language Review* 59 (3), 425–440.

Vandergrift, L. (2003b) Orchestrating strategy use: Toward a model of the skilled second language listener. *Language Learning* 53, 463–496.

Vandergrift, L. (2004) Learning to listen or listening to learn? *Annual Review of Applied Linguistics* 24, 3–25.

Vandergrift, L. (2005) Relationships among motivation orientations, metacognitive awareness and proficiency in L2 listening. *Applied Linguistics* 26, 70–89.

Vandergrift, L. (2007) *Teaching Students How to Listen: Effects on Listening Achievement*. Paper presented at the annual meeting of the American Association of Applied Linguistics, Costa Mesa, CA.

Vandergrift, L. and Goh, C. (forthcoming) Teaching and testing listening comprehension. In M. Long and C. Doughty (eds) *Handbook of Second and Foreign Language Teaching*. Cambridge, MA: Blackwell.

Vandergrift, L., Goh, C., Mareschal, C. and Tafaghodatari, M.H. (2006) The Metacognitive Awareness Listening Questionnaire (MALQ): Development and validation. *Language Learning* 56, 431–462.

White, G. (1998) *Listening*. Oxford: Oxford University Press.

Wilson, M. (2003) Discovery listening – improving perceptual processing. *ELT Journal* 57, 335–343.

Appendix A: Metacognitive Awareness Listening Questionnaire (MALQ)*

Please indicate your opinion after each statement by circling the number which best corresponds to your level of agreement with the statement, as follows: 1 = strongly disagree; 2 = disagree; 3 = partly disagree; 4 = partly agree; 5 = agree; 6 = strongly agree.

1. Before I start to listen, I have a plan in my head for how I am going to listen.   1   2   3   4   5   6
2. I focus harder on the text when I have trouble understanding.   1   2   3   4   5   6
3. I find that listening in French is more difficult than reading, speaking, or writing in French.   1   2   3   4   5   6
4. I translate in my head as I listen.   1   2   3   4   5   6
5. I use the words I understand to guess the meaning of the words I don't understand.   1   2   3   4   5   6
6. When my mind wanders, I recover my concentration right away.   1   2   3   4   5   6
7. As I listen, I compare what I understand with what I know about the topic.   1   2   3   4   5   6
8. I feel that listening comprehension in French is a challenge for me.   1   2   3   4   5   6
9. I use my experience and knowledge to help me understand.   1   2   3   4   5   6
10. Before listening, I think of similar texts that I may have listened to.   1   2   3   4   5   6
11. I translate key words as I listen.   1   2   3   4   5   6
12. I try to get back on track when I lose concentration.   1   2   3   4   5   6
13. As I listen, I quickly adjust my interpretation if I realise that it is not correct.   1   2   3   4   5   6
14. After listening, I think back to how I listened, and about what I might do differently next time.   1   2   3   4   5   6
15. I don't feel nervous when I listen to French.   1   2   3   4   5   6
16. When I have difficulty understanding what I hear, I give up and stop listening.   1   2   3   4   5   6
17. I use the general idea of the text to help me guess the meaning of the words that I don't understand.   1   2   3   4   5   6

18. I translate word by word, as I listen.   1   2   3   4   5   6
19. When I guess the meaning of a word,   1   2   3   4   5   6
    I think back to everything else that I have
    heard, to see if my guess makes sense.
20. As I listen, I periodically ask myself if I am 1   2   3   4   5   6
    satisfied with my level of comprehension.
21. I have a goal in mind as I listen.   1   2   3   4   5   6

*To obtain an interpretation guide for the MALQ, please contact the author (lvdgrift@uottawa.ca).

Chapter 6
Second Language Composition in Independent Settings: Supporting the Writing Process with Cognitive Strategies

MELANIE BLOOM

Introduction

Although many aspects of language can be addressed in independent language learning (ILL) settings, it is writing that lends itself most naturally to individual practice. Whereas speaking and listening, for example, normally occur 'in the company of one or more individuals, writing is usually a solitary activity. Students can complete written tasks by themselves' (Chastain, 1988: 248). This would seem to suggest that the discussion of writing in ILL contexts is relatively straightforward. However, this is not necessarily the case. The difficulty in discussing second language (L2) writing in general may be that it is historically the skill that receives the least attention in the second language classroom context (Lally, 2000a; Valdés *et al.*, 1992) and is often treated as a support skill rather than an essential component of second language competence (Scott, 1996). Even within the field of language learning strategies, writing may receive a secondary role. For example, many of the cognitive strategies applied specifically to writing, such as note taking, summarising and highlighting (Oxford, 1990), are writing strategies that support listening and reading comprehension rather than the development of L2 writing competence. Therefore, the question of how we define L2 writing in general and how we discuss strategy use in L2 writing contexts is complicated by the place historically occupied by writing in L2 instruction.

This chapter aims to present a clear description of the theoretical background of the L2 writing process and strategy use in L2 writing in order to discuss both effectively in ILL contexts. It treats L2 writing as a skill to be learned rather than simply support for language learning in general.

Finally, it suggests specific cognitive strategies that independent L2 writers can use to support their writing processes and maximise their self-sufficiency, because if 'active engagement in higher learning implies and requires self-awareness and self-direction' (Angelo & Cross, 1993: 225), as well as effective strategies use, then nowhere is instruction in the use of these skills and strategies more important than in the ILL setting.

Second Language Writing: A Theoretical Background

Few, if any, language educators would disagree with the observation that second language writing instruction has evolved from a pedagogy possessing a static product orientation, to one that emphasises writing as a dynamic, non-linear, recursive process. Indeed the process model has remained dominant in second language writing for the past 30 years (Hyland, 2003). This model encompasses a view of writing in terms of the mental processes it involves, and defines it as a series of steps (pre-writing, writing, reviewing and rewriting) involving multiple drafts. It emphasises the act of writing, rather than just the outcome. According to Flower and Hayes (1981), writing is a complex cognitive process involving the writer's long-term memory where knowledge of the topic, audience and writing plans are stored; the task environment, including the rhetorical problem and the text produced so far; and writing subprocesses such as idea-generation, goal-setting, organising, reviewing, evaluating and revising. The writing process is therefore 'quite cognitively complex as writers move their thoughts back and forth between [stages and] components, always returning to and redefining their higher goals' (Barnett, 1989: 35).

The process model has also met with criticism on the grounds that it focuses on cognitive processes and the writer as an individual while largely ignoring the social and cultural contexts in which writing takes place (Atkinson, 2003). Process-oriented pedagogy may also be culturally biased because it assumes a certain set of values and a particular kind of socialisation of its students (Delpit, 1988; Inghilleri, 1989). In fact, the process movement itself may be more of a Western approach to writing pedagogy as it may have bypassed many East Asian cultures (Casanave, 2003). Thus, the process model has been followed by the notion of 'post-process', which Atkinson (2003:10) defines as, 'including everything that follows, historically speaking, the period of L2 writing instruction and research that focused primarily on writing as a cognitive or internal, multi-staged process, and in which by far the major dynamic of learning was through doing, with the teacher taking (in some – sometimes imagined – senses) a background role'. While Atkinson (2003) himself admits this definition is problematic as it does not necessarily define a post-process approach, he suggests that the notion of post-process is an expansion of the current theoretical perspective on second language writing rather than a complete replacement of it. Thus, genre-based models, which consider the purposes of second language writing and the socio-cultural contexts in which they are embedded (Hyland, 2003) as well as the cognitive processes necessary in second language writing, would be one example of a post-process approach.

So, what do these theoretical perspectives mean for second language learners in independent contexts? How might they be guided or informed by these perspectives on second language writing? These models provide the framework on which second language writing may be discussed in general and can be used to provide independent language learners with specific tasks that can guide their development of second language writing skills. For example, Scott (1996) also offers two questionnaires that can easily be adapted and administered in distance and independent settings that help student writers focus on writing as a process by prompting them to consider their steps and habits when writing in both their first and second languages (see Tables 6.1 and 6.2 below).

We could add to Scott's list of questions, questions that might place the writing task either in a particular genre or in a particular social context. Additional questions might include: Do you seek and analyse models of similar pieces of writing in the target language? Do you consider the purpose of your writing? Do you consider the relationship between yourself and your intended audience? Asking students to take a moment to reflect on what they do while writing in a first and second language, through a simple questionnaire, such as those in Tables 6.1 and 6.2, can encourage the independent writer to focus on the writing purpose, process, and the social context in which it occurs.

Table 6.1 Writing process questionnaire

When writing in your native language ...
(1) Do you get your ideas more from thinking, reading, or discussing? Explain:
(2) Do your ideas take the shape of images or words? Explain:
(3) Do new and different ideas come to you before or during writing? Explain:
(4) Do you make a formal outline before beginning to write? Explain:
(5) Do you reread your work while writing? Explain:
(6) Do you imagine who your audience is? Explain:
(7) Do you revise or change your work? Explain:
(8) Do you prefer writing with pencil and paper or with a computer? Explain: (Scott, 1996: 46).

Table 6.2 Foreign language writing process questionnaire

When writing in a foreign language ...
(1) Do you write down your ideas in your first language or your second language? Explain:
(2) Do you use your textbook while you are writing? Explain:
(3) Do you use a grammar reference while you are writing? Explain:
(4) Do you use a dictionary while you are writing? Explain:
(5) Do you translate from your first language into the foreign language while you write? Explain:
(6) Do you revise and correct grammatical errors? Explain:
(7) Do you revise ideas and content? Explain: (Scott, 1996: 47).

Second Language Writing Strategies

In addition to moving the students' focus away from the form-focused product to the purposes, recursive processes, and social contexts of writing, students in general, and independent learners in particular, must be made aware of and armed with appropriate writing strategies specific to second language. Fortunately, we now have a substantial body of data on both general and specific writing strategies that second language learners use when producing a text in the target language (Manchón, 2001). Although very little research has been conducted specifically on writing strategies in ILL contexts, the research on strategy use and on the writing process can certainly be applied to ILL settings.

As Petrić and Czárl (2003) note, research on second language writing strategies, as defined by the second language acquisition perspective on language learning strategies (O'Malley & Chamot, 1990), is relatively scant. Research of this kind typically seeks to discover the effect of specific strategies or categories of strategies on either second language writing achievement (Olivares-Cuhat, 2002) or proficiency (Aziz, 1995). In her study of writing strategy use and achievement, as measured by composition grade, Olivares-Cuhat (2002) found that her students most frequently used cognitive strategies and that the use of cognitive and memory strategies could account for 44% of grade variability. She suggests that this finding supports the importance of cognitive strategies across all language skills. Likewise, Aziz (1995) emphasised the importance of cognitive strategies in her study of writing proficiency. However, she found that those students who used both cognitive and metacognitive strategies in their L2 writing were able to outperform those who used cognitive strategies alone, supporting the claim that learners with control over a wider range of strategies will be more successful (O'Malley & Chamot, 1990). These findings have clear implications for ILL contexts suggesting that support materials should be developed for independent language learners which provide training in a broad array of writing strategies.

McDonough (1999) notes that the majority of writing strategy research has been characterised as writing process research as it examines writers' strategic behaviour in the planning, translating, and reviewing stages (Flower & Hayes, 1981). Research in this area has focused on the strategic competence of inexperienced versus experienced writers (Cumming, 1989; Raimes, 1985, 1987; Sasaki, 2000; Zamel, 1983), writing behaviours of L2 writers in their L1 versus their L2 (Lally, 2000a; Raimes, 1987; Roca de Larios et al., 2001, 2006; Thorson, 2000), and the strategic use of the L1 in L2 writing (Chelala, 1982; Cumming, 1989; Friedlander, 1990; Lally, 2000b) to name just a few areas of inquiry. While a detailed review of this large body of research is outside the scope of this chapter, we can glean some important findings that are applicable to ILL contexts. Findings in this area may be best presented in the three stages of process writing. Research on pre-writing or writing planning has suggested that skilled writers have a tendency to spend more time planning (Sasaki, 2000, 2004; Zamel, 1983) and that the use of the L1 in pre-writing activities may facilitate the L2 writing process (Friedlander, 1990; Knutson, 2006; Lally, 2000b). In the writing stage, research has suggested that successful problem-solving strategies in writing may affect writing outcomes (Cumming, 1989; Bosher, 1998; Roca de Larios et al., 2006). Finally, during the revising stage, skilled L2 writers may revise more and may revise their writing at the discourse rather than surface level (Raimes, 1987; Sasaki, 2000, 2004; Zamel, 1983). All of these findings have implications for L2 writing instruction in general, but may be particularly useful in guiding L2 writers in ILL contexts.

Adapting Cognitive Strategies to Support Independent Language Learners

One of the difficulties with examining writing in ILL contexts is often defining the writing task, as the range of writing tasks in which independent L2 writers engage may be extremely broad. Tasks could include: writing via email for personal communication, drafting a letter for professional purposes, communicating in a synchronous online chat with tutors or teachers, composing an essay for academic purposes, and the list could go on. As many researchers suggest that strategy use and/or selection may be tied to the type of writing task the learner is engaged in (Cumming, 1989; Petrić & Czárl, 2003; Sasaki, 2000; Thorson, 2000), defining the writing task and the purpose of the writing task is extremely important for any discussion of L2 writing strategies. For the purpose of brevity, this chapter will not attempt to identify strategies for the myriad of potential writing tasks that may present themselves in ILL contexts; rather it will focus specifically on the composition process as it relates to creating formal written communication, essays, academic papers, and so on. This task was chosen owing to the amount of research on strategy use and the composing process (Bosher, 1998; Cohen & Brooks-Carson, 2001; Lally, 2000a; Leki, 1995; Olivares-Cuhat, 2002; Roca de Larios *et al.*, 2006; Sasaki, 2000, 2004) and the fact that computer mediated communication (another writing task common in ILL contexts) is typically investigated under the framework of communication strategies (see e.g. Biesenbach-Lucas, 2005; Peterson, 2006; Smith, 2003; Trenchs, 1996).

The suggestions made here constitute an attempt to merge two views of writing strategies based on two different theoretical backgrounds: O'Malley and Chamot's (1990) taxonomy of cognitive, metacognitive, and socio-affective strategies and Flower and Hayes' (1981) process approach of planning, translating, and reviewing. Thus, this presentation of strategies is much like Petrić and Czárl's (2003) writing strategy questionnaire as it addresses strategies within the stages of pre-writing, writing, and revising.

Pre-writing strategies

The pre-writing stage is generally defined by idea generation, shaping, refining, and organisation (Scarcella & Oxford, 1992). This stage may be characterised by many different activities including discussion, brainstorming or free-writing (Lally, 2000b). As the research suggests that skilled writers spend more time on planning their writing (Cumming, 1989; Sasaki, 2002; Zamel, 1983) and that planning time may affect the fluency, syntactic complexity and accuracy of L2 writing (Ellis & Yuan, 2004), independent language learners should be provided with specific strategies that they can use to support their pre-writing activities. As the language in which pre-writing activities are conducted may affect writing outcomes (Friedlander, 1990; Lally, 2000b; Knutson, 2006), independent learners may want to conduct the following pre-writing activities in their L1. Three cognitive strategies independent learners can use during this stage of writing are resourcing, elaboration and grouping.

Resourcing is an important strategy in ILL contexts as learners may be highly dependent on reference material and may have little or no access to a language tutor or teacher. Reference materials play an important role in many skill areas, but especially in writing. A good model of the writing task to be accomplished is perhaps one of the most useful resources for independent writers at the pre-writing stage. However, an unanalysed model of writing does the independent language learner little good (Hyland, 2003). Therefore, learning to seek out and analyse models of writing is a skill that can be extremely useful to second language writers

Table 6.3 Role-model writing analysis

(1) What is the purpose of this piece of writing? Does the author effectively achieve his/her purpose?
(2) How is the purpose or central theme of the piece presented? How is it supported by evidence or ideas?
(3) Who is the intended reader? What is the relationship between the author and the reader? Does the style appropriately reflect this relationship?
(4) How is the writing organised? Are there certain linguistic features that help to organise the text?
(5) What linguistic features typically appear in this piece of writing?
(6) Do you notice an absence of certain linguistic features?

(Swales & Feak, 2000). Independent learners may be prompted to analyse models of writing by asking the questions presented in Table 6.3. These questions may guide independent learners, especially at the intermediate and advanced levels, to attend to various aspects of a piece of writing including its ability to achieve its intended purpose, the interaction between the writer and the reader, and certain stylistic or linguistic features that are characteristic of a particular genre of writing. Analysing models of writing can be a successful pre-writing strategy; however, Leki (1995) warns that imitating models may be inappropriate for writing assignments designed for a specific teacher as the model might not match the teacher's expectations for the assignment. Therefore, distance learners may want to check the appropriateness of the models they analyse with their teachers.

O'Malley and Chamot (1990) define elaboration as a strategy of relating new information to prior knowledge. Elaboration may be an essential pre-writing strategy as it encourages learners to activate their background knowledge and apply it to the writing task at hand. One way that independent language learners can achieve both these objectives is by creating a K-W-L (know, want to know, learned) chart. Although originally developed for the reading context (Ogle, 1986), K-W-L charts can be applied to the writing context to help independent language learners activate their background knowledge and help in the planning process. This is a technique that independent writers at all proficiency levels can use. In the 'K' step, independent language learners write down everything that they know already about the topic of their writing and/or the writing style. In the 'W' step, learners write questions based on their background knowledge about what they still need to find out about the topic and/or the genre before they begin writing. This step helps guide their research process by creating clear objectives.

Finally, in the 'L' step, learners note what they learned from their research on the topic and/or style. Here they will answer the questions that they wrote in the 'W' step and also revise any of their background knowledge that they found to be erroneous or incomplete. Using this technique, independent language learners can activate their background knowledge, elaborate on that knowledge by asking appropriate questions that guide their research, and relate new information discovered in their research to their previous knowledge.

Another strategy useful in activating background knowledge and brainstorming is grouping. Grouping can include the processes of ordering, classifying, or labelling material based on common attributes (O'Malley & Chamot, 1990). One common grouping pre-writing strategy is the creation of a semantic map or concept map. A semantic map is a type of graphic organiser that depicts the mental connections that writers make when focusing on a major concept and making connections to sub-categories. Semantic maps are used as a second language pre-writing activity to help learners generate and organise their ideas (Webster, 1998), and research has suggested that they may aid learners' written production (Ojima, 2006). These maps can be used at all levels of proficiency, but they may be especially helpful for novice or less skilled writers (Zamel, 1983). Creating a semantic map is typically an individual endeavour and, therefore, this technique can easily be applied to ILL contexts. Angelo and Cross (1993) suggest the following steps to create a semantic map. First, the learner selects the target concept or topic. Second, he/she brainstorms for a few minutes, writing down terms and short phrases closely related to the stimulus. Third, the learner draws a semantic map based on the brainstorming outcomes, placing the stimulus at the centre and drawing lines to the other concepts. For example, a semantic map could resemble a wheel and its spokes, with the focus concept at the hub. Or, it could be based on a model of the solar system, with the stimulus in the sun's position. Fourth, the learner determines the ways in which the various concepts are related to each other and indicates these relationships on the lines connecting the concepts. Not only does the creation of this map allow writers to generate and group their ideas, but it also allows them to establish the relationship between various groups of ideas. Thus, this pre-writing activity may help individual language learners establish a tentative structure for their writing.

The three pre-writing techniques discussed here were presented in isolation, but the reader may note some overlap between the cognitive activities supported by each. As O'Malley and Chamot (1990: 139) note, some cognitive strategies are 'so closely related as to be inseparable at times'. Therefore, the independent language learner may choose one or more technique out of the three presented that best supports his or her learning and/or writing style.

Writing strategies

Although writing is viewed as a recursive process (Flower & Hayes, 1981) and the writing stage certainly involves planning and revising, here I consider several techniques that independent learners can use while in the process of composing a text. Research suggests that second language writers spend more time on certain types of problem-solving behaviour while composing in their L2 (Roca de Larios et al., 2006), and that some problem-solving strategies are more successful than others (Bosher, 1998; Cumming, 1989). Thus, perhaps the best way to support independent L2 writers is to help them develop cognitive strategies to support their problem-solving behaviour. Three cognitive strategies that could help support this activity in independent L2 writers at varying levels of proficiency are rereading, substitution and strategic use of the L1.

Time constraints often affect the resourcing and rereading strategies available for use during the writing stage in the second language classroom. Therefore, independent language learners may have an advantage over classroom language learners in this respect, as they may have more time to complete a particular writing task. Successful problem-solving behaviour often involves engaging in a search routine that could involve the text produced thus far as well as other resources (Bosher, 1998). For example, the second language learner may choose to return to his or her own text to reread a sentence, a paragraph, or an introduction. This process may encourage second language writers to consider the gist of their writing, their intention, or their discourse organisation. This rereading promotes the writer's attention to the content of his or her writing which is a characteristic of more skilled second language writers (Raimes, 1987; Sasaki, 2000).

Another use of rereading may lead independent writers to seek out other resources. For example, a writer may choose to reread some source material that he or she selected to support the writing task. This can be a successful strategy as it can help L2 writers attend again to the gist of their own writing, their discourse organisation, or perhaps even language use, by using the resource as a model of vocabulary use or sentence structure. Thus, writers in ILL contexts should be made aware of the benefits of rereading. This is a technique that should be encouraged to draw learners' attention to the discourse-level and content of their own writing rather than their language use or correctness.

Substitution is often a necessary strategy in L2 writing as it involves selecting a revised plan or alternative wording to solve a problem in writing (O'Malley & Chamot, 1990). Specifically, substitution is a cognitive strategy that can be used to support the generation and analysis of alternatives related to the content of a text or language issues, a successful problem-solving strategy (Bosher, 1998; Cumming, 1989). Therefore, when independent learners are faced with a problem in their own writing, whether idea- or language-related, they should be encouraged to develop alternatives. This can be accomplished in two ways. For issues related to the ideas presented, writers can create tentative semantic maps or outlines for their different ideas. Once these are written, learners can compare the different ideas with the purpose of their writing, their audience, and their main idea to see which idea most appropriately fits their writing task. For language related issues, learners can develop a list of different phrasings of the same idea. However, unlike the analysis of their ideas, learners can choose to revisit their alternatives during the revising stage rather than during the writing stage. Raising independent L2 writers' awareness of these strategies might aid their ability to solve problems that arise during the writing process.

The use of the L1 is a common strategy that L2 writers use to solve problems and manage the L2 writing process. The L1 may be used to translate key words or phrases (Lay, 1988; Sasaki, 2000) or to think through the L2 writing process (Cohen & Brooks-Carsen, 2001; Cumming, 1990). In general, research in this area has supported the use of the L1 in the pre-writing stage (Freidlander, 1990; Knutson, 2006; Lally, 2000b), but not necessarily for the writing stage. However, at least one study has suggested that the strategic use of the L1 may support some L2 writing tasks (Cohen & Brooks-Carson, 2001). One use of the L1 that independent L2 writers might consider is using an L1 word or phrase as a place holder in the text. This allows the writer to focus on the flow of ideas rather than their lexical and grammatical accuracy. The writer may come back to that phrase at a later time and use another cognitive strategy, such as a resource or the development of substitutes, to solve the language issue. Independent learners who are having difficulty with the local planning of their ideas while writing in the L2, might also benefit from generating alternative ideas in the L1, analysing them, and then returning to the L2 writing task. Although the use of the L1 during L2 composing may be helpful as a strategic tool, independent learners should be cautioned against overusing this strategy as research has suggested that relying too much on the L1 may have the undesirable side-effect of stilting L2 written fluency, organisation, clarity, syntactic complexity and vocabulary use (Chelala, 1982; Cohen & Brooks-Carson, 2001; Sasaki, 2000).

The strategies presented here are intended to guide independent L2 writers through the composition of an L2 text. They help by supporting their problem-solving processes, fluency of ideas, and local planning.

Revising strategies

As it has been suggested that self-assessment is an important aspect of learner autonomy (Hurd *et al.*, 2001), independent L2 writers may especially benefit from learning to assess their own writing through the revision process. Here I refer to revision as the rewriting, replacing or rearranging of components of an existing written product with the intention of improving the content and the linguistic accuracy (He, 2005). Revising strategies may be used at any point during the writing process. In fact, the substitution and rereading strategies presented above could also be used as revising strategies. The revising strategies presented in this section are to be used between drafts; that is, they assume that the writer has already completed a first draft of the written text. These strategies aim to help independent L2 writers at all proficiency levels focus on both the content and the linguistic accuracy of their texts. (See also Chapter 14 on self-correction strategies.)

As research suggests that successful writers spend more time revising the global components or content of their writing (He, 2005), providing independent L2 writers with a tool to help them assess their own writing could prove extremely valuable. The list of questions presented in Table 6.4 is meant to serve as a resource to help independent L2 learners focus on the ideas and organisation of their written texts. The questions can be used to help learners revise a wide variety of written tasks. By answering these questions, the learners can both identify problematic areas of their texts and begin to address them.

The revising process must also include attention to linguistic form. This may be especially challenging for learners in ILL contexts who may not have access to native speakers, peers, tutors, or teachers and who must rely on self-evaluation of their linguistic content. Here I present three cognitive strategies to support independent L2 writers' revision of linguistic form: guided proofreading, resourcing and recombining.

Table 6.4 Questions to guide the revision process

(1) What is the purpose of my writing? Do I achieve it?
(2) Is my main idea or thesis presented clearly?
(3) Who is my intended reader? What is my relationship with the reader? Does the style of my writing appropriately reflect our relationship?
(4) Is my writing interesting? Could I add anything to increase the reader's interest?
(5) Do I leave any questions unanswered? What are they and how can I address them?
(6) Are any of my ideas unclear? How can I clarify them?
(7) Do I provide too many details? Do I provide details that do not reflect my main idea or purpose?
(8) Is the text well organised? Does one idea flow logically to the next?
(9) Do I employ appropriate openings and closings?

Just as they may reread a text to resolve questions of content and organisation, independent learners can also benefit from rereading a draft for mechanical and grammatical issues. Writers in the ILL context may need a guide to help them know what to look for in their own writing. Thus, the checklist presented in Table 6.5 aims to provide independent L2 writers with a guided manner in which to proofread and edit their own writing. This is a general guide for proofreading as each target language may have specific linguistic features with which learners typically experience difficulty.

In order to solve some of the problems identified by proofreading, independent L2 writers may need to turn to various resources in order to access a model of L2 writing, an explanation of a grammatical rule, or information on vocabulary. However, the mere presence of resources does not guarantee learners will use them successfully. Independent learners need to develop the skills to evaluate the resources available to them and to use them effectively. The use of bilingual dictionaries to solve problems in orthography or with lexical items or to aid in translation tends to be a common revising strategy among L2 writers regardless of learning context (New, 1999; Petrić & Czárl, 2003). However, learners do not always use dictionaries effectively. L2 writing instructors are all too familiar with the dictionary use mistakes learners make such as selecting the wrong part of speech. There are several skills that independent learners can develop in order to more effectively use a bilingual dictionary. Barbe (2001) suggests that learners should first be warned against choosing the first lexical item listed as it does not guarantee it is the most appropriate for the writer's context. Learners should also familiarise themselves with the table of contents, the abbreviations used, and the structure of the entries of their dictionary (Barbe, 2001; Walz, 1990). Back translation is also a useful strategy in bilingual dictionary use, as the independent writers may either confirm or disconfirm the meaning of a lexical item.

Table 6.5 Proofreading checklist

☐ Do my subjects and verbs agree?
☐ Do I have verb tense inconsistencies?
☐ Do I have any incomplete sentences?
☐ Have I used any words I am unsure about?
☐ Do I overuse any words or phrases?
☐ Is my spelling accurate?
☐ Have I correctly used punctuation conventions? (Adapted partially from The Center for Advancement of Learning, 2007.)

Finally, learners should be aware that there may not be one-to-one equivalents between two languages, especially in the case of idiomatic expressions (Barbe, 2001). Thus, independent L2 writers equipped with the skills to use a bilingual dictionary may be more effective in their use of this resource.

Attending to grammatical accuracy is not the only way that learners may revise the linguistic form of their writing. Independent L2 writers at all proficiency levels may want to revise their writing to create longer and more syntactically complex sentences characteristic of skilled L2 writers. Recombining is a strategy that 'involves constructing a meaningful sentence or longer expression by putting together known elements in new ways' (Oxford, 1990: 74). Continued use and practice of this strategy may lead to greater syntactic complexity in L2 writing (Cooper & Morain, 1980). The first step to using this strategy is to identify conjunctions or phrases typically used in the target language to connect ideas. Ideally, these phrases would be collected by a materials writer or teacher/tutor and be available to the individual language learner; however, the learner could also analyse model texts in the target language to identify such lexical items. In the second step, the writer rereads his/her text and identifies areas that do not flow well or that could benefit from the use of connectors. Finally, the writer can experiment with the use of different connectors to combine sentences or to create new sentences thus adding to the grammatical complexity and flow of his/her writing.

The revising strategies suggested here are ones that independent L2 learners can use in-between drafts to help them focus on the content and organisation of their texts as well as the linguistic form their ideas take. Both of these areas are necessary for independent L2 writers to address as developing good editing and self-correction skills is vitally important for the successful independent L2 writer (Hurd *et al.*, 2001).

Conclusion

It is clear from the discussion presented here that writing in the ILL context may not necessarily be an entirely independent endeavour. The independent L2 writer needs to be constantly cognisant of the audience for his or her writing and constantly interfacing with other texts to support the writing process. Thus, writing may not necessarily be the solitary activity that Chastain (1988) suggests. Instead, like speaking, writing intertwines communicative purposes, cultural and social perspectives, and linguistic features. The aim of this chapter has been to help independent L2 writers gain control of these interrelated characteristics of L2 writing. The suggestions provided are based on research in L2 writing strategies and reflect the characteristics of good L2 writers who, according to Scott (1996), take sufficient time to plan what they are going to write, rescan, or pause frequently to reread while they are composing, and revise content as well as form.

The cognitive strategies presented here aim to guide the independent L2 writer through the writing process as well as to support metacognitive strategies, such as self-evaluation and planning, that may be vital in developing learner autonomy (Hurd, 2000). Weinstein and Mayer (1986) recommend that the independent learner activate four types of knowledge: (1) self-knowledge, including an understanding of one's own learning preferences, abilities, and cognitive style; (2) knowledge of the learning task; (3) knowledge of prior understanding; and (4) knowledge of strategies and techniques appropriate for the setting, the learner, and the task. These types of knowledge and strategies 'help make students more active participants in their own learning and [can] give them more control over their learning' (Angelo & Cross, 1993: 256). Equipped with the knowledge and insights produced by the techniques presented, the independent L2 writer can better understand, assess, and subsequently improve his or her learning and writing, and thus become a more successful autonomous second language learner.

References

Angelo, T.A. and Cross, K.P. (1993) *Classroom Assessment Techniques: A Handbook for College Teachers* (2nd edn). San Francisco, CA: Jossey-Bass.
Atkinson, D. (2003) L2 writing in the post-process era: Introduction. *Journal of Second Language Writing* 12 (1), 3–15.
Aziz, L. (1995) A model of paired cognitive and metacognitive strategies: Its effect on second language grammar and writing performance. Unpublished doctoral dissertation, University of San Francisco.
Barbe, K. (2001) Mit dem autoschwimmbad in die verkehrsmarmelade: Learning to use bilingual dictionaries successfully. *Unterrichtspraxis/Teaching German* 34 (1), 66–75.
Barnett, M. (1989) Writing as a process. *The French Review* 63 (1), 31–44.
Biesenbach-Lucas, S. (2005) Communication topics and strategies in e-mail consultation: Comparison between American and international university students. *Language Learning & Technology* 9 (2), 24–46.
Bosher, S. (1998) The composing process of three southeast Asian writers at the post-secondary level: An exploratory study. *Journal of Second Language Writing* 7 (2), 205–241.
Casanave, C.P. (2003) Looking ahead to more sociopolitically-oriented case study research in L2 writing scholarship (But should it be called 'post-process'?). *Journal of Second Language Writing* 12 (1), 85–102.
Center for Advancement of Learning (2007) *Proofreading checklist*. On WWW at http://www.muskingum.edu/~cal/database/general/writing.html#Checklist. Accessed 10.07.07.
Chastain, K. (1988) *Developing Second Language Skills: Theory and Practice*. Orlando: Harcourt, Brace and Jovanovich.
Chelala, S.I. (1982) The composing process of two Spanish speakers and the coherence of their texts: A case study. Unpublished doctoral dissertation, New York University, New York.

Cohen, A.D. and Brooks-Carson, A. (2001) Research on direct versus translated writing: Students' strategies and their results. *The Modern Language Journal* 85 (2), 169–188.

Cooper, T. and Morain, G. (1980) A study of sentence-combining techniques for developing written and oral fluency in French. *The French Review* 53 (3), 411–423.

Cumming, A. (1989) Writing expertise and second-language proficiency. *Language Learning* 39 (1), 81–135.

Cumming, A. (1990) Metalinguistic and ideational thinking in second language composing. *Written Communication* 7, 482–511.

Delpit, L. (1988) The silenced dialogue: Power and pedagogy in educating other people's children. *Harvard Educational Review* 58 (3), 280–298.

Ellis, R. and Yuan, F. (2004) The effects of planning on fluency, complexity, and accuracy in second language narrative writing. *Studies in Second Language Acquisition* 26 (1), 59–84.

Flower, L. and Hayes, R. (1981) A cognitive process theory of writing. *College Composition and Communication* 32, 365–387.

Friedlander, A. (1990) Composing in English: Effects of a first language on writing in English as a second language. In B. Kroll (ed.) *Second Language Writing: Research Insights for the Classroom* (pp. 109–125). Cambridge: Cambridge University Press.

He, T. (2005) Effects of mastery and performance goals on the composition strategy use of adult EFL writers. *The Canadian Modern Language Review* 61 (3), 407–431.

Hurd, S. (2000) Distance language learners and learner support: Beliefs, difficulties and use of strategies. *Links and Letters* 7, 61–80.

Hurd, S., Beaven, T. and Ortega, A. (2001) Developing autonomy in a distance language learning context: Issues and dilemmas for course writers. *System* 29, 341–355.

Hyland, K. (2003) Genre-based pedagogies: A social response to process. *Journal of Second Language Writing* 12 (1), 17–29.

Inghilleri, M. (1989) Learning to mean as a symbolic and social process: The story of ESL writers. *Discourse Processes* 12 (3), 291–411.

Knutson, E.M. (2006) Thinking in English, writing in French. *The French Review* 80 (1), 88–109.

Lally, C. (2000a) Writing across English and French: An examination of strategy use. *The French Review* 73 (3), 525–538.

Lally, C. (2000b) First language influences in second language composition: The effect of pre-writing. *Foreign Language Annals* 33 (4), 428–432.

Lay, N.D.S. (1988) The comforts of the first language in learning to write. *Kaleidoscope* 4, 15–18.

Leki, I. (1995) Coping strategies of ESL students in writing tasks across the curriculum. *TESOL Quarterly* 29 (2), 235–260.

Manchón, R.M. (2001) Trends in the conceptualisations of second language composing strategies: A critical analysis. *International Journal of English Language Studies* 1 (2), 47–70.

McDonough, S. (1999) Learner strategies. *Language Teaching* 32 (1), 1–18.

New, E. (1999) Computer-aided writing in French as a foreign language: A quantitative and qualitative look at the process of revision. *The Modern Language Journal* 83 (1), 80–97.

Ogle, D. (1986) K-W-L: A teaching model that develops active reading of expository text. *The Reading Teacher* 39, 564–571.

Ojima, M. (2006) Concept mapping as pre-task planning: A case study of three Japanese ESL writers. *System* 34 (4), 566–585.

Olivares-Cuhat, G. (2002) Learning strategies and achievement in the Spanish classroom: A case study. *Foreign Language Annals* 35 (5), 561–570.

O'Malley, J.M. and Chamot, A.U. (1990) *Learning Strategies in Second Language Acquisition.* Cambridge: Cambridge University Press.

Oxford, R.L. (1990) *Language Learning Strategies: What Every Teacher Should Know.* Boston: Heinle and Heinle.

Peterson, M. (2006) Learner interaction management in an avatar and chat-based virtual world. *Computer Assisted Language Learning* 19 (1), 79–103.

Petrić, B. and Czárl, B. (2003) Validating a writing strategy questionnaire. *System* 31 (2), 187–215.

Raimes, A. (1985) What unskilled ESL students do as they write: A classroom study of composing. *TESOL Quarterly* 19 (2), 229–258.

Raimes, A. (1987) Language proficiency, writing ability, and composing strategies: A study of ESL college student writers. *Language Learning* 37 (3), 439–468.

Roca de Larios, J., Manchón, R.M. and Murphy, L. (2006) Generating text in native and foreign language writing: A temporal analysis of problem-solving formulation processes. *The Modern Language Journal* 90 (1), 100–114.

Roca de Larios, J., Marín, J. and Murphy, L. (2001) A temporal analysis of formulation processes in L1 and L2 writing. *Language Learning* 51 (3), 497–538.

Sasaki, M. (2000) Toward an empirical model of EFL writing: An exploratory study. *Journal of Second Language Writing* 9 (3), 259–291.

Sasaki, M. (2002) Building an empirically-based model of EFL learners' writing processes. In S. Ransdell and M-L. Barbier (eds) *New Directions for Research in L2 Writing* (pp. 49–80). Amsterdam: Kluwer Academic.

Sasaki, M. (2004) A multiple-data analysis of the 3.5-year development of EFL student writers. *Language Learning* 54 (3), 525–582.

Scarcella, R. and Oxford, R. (1992) *The Tapestry of Language Learning: The Individual in the Communicative Classroom.* Boston: Heinle and Heinle.

Scott, V. (1996) *Rethinking Foreign Language Writing.* Boston, MA: Heinle and Heinle.

Smith, B. (2003) The use of communication strategies in computer-mediated communication. *System* 31 (1), 29–53.

Swales, J.M. and Feak, C.B. (2000) *English in Today's Research World.* Ann Arbor, MI: The University of Michigan Press.

Thorson, H. (2000) Using the computer to compare foreign and native language writing processes: A statistical and case study approach. *The Modern Language Journal* 84 (2), 155–169.

Trenchs, M. (1996) Writing strategies in a second language: Three case studies of learners using electronic mail. *Canadian Modern Language Review* 52, 464–497.

Valdés, G., Paz, H. and Echevarriarza, M.P. (1992) The development of writing abilities in a foreign language: Contributions toward a general theory of L2 writing. *Modern Language Journal* 76, 333–352.

Walz, J. (1990) The dictionary as a secondary source in language learning. *The French Review* 64 (1), 79–94.

Webster, J.P. (1998) Semantic maps. *TESOL Journal* 7 (5), 42–43.

Weinstein, C.E. and Mayer, D.K. (1986) The teaching of learning strategies. In M.C. Wittrock (ed.) *Handbook of Research on Teaching.* New York: Macmillan.

Zamel, V. (1983) The composing processes of advanced ESL students: Six case studies. *TESOL Quarterly* 17 (2), 165–187.

Chapter 7

Speaking Strategies for Independent Learning: A Focus on Pragmatic Performance

ANDREW D. COHEN

Introduction

This chapter looks at the issue of how to enhance L2[1] speaking skills in independent learning through the use of strategies to promote pragmatic ability. Pragmatics deals with how meaning is conveyed by speakers – and understood by their hearers – in actual conversational contexts. While independent learning may well be provided offline, new technological advances would suggest that the online study of L2 pragmatics could be beneficial to language learners, especially with the prospect of using virtual environments as a place to practise L2 pragmatic skills.

Pragmatic Ability

Within the realm of pragmatic ability, the ways in which people carry out specific *social functions* in speaking such as apologising, complaining, making requests, refusing things/invitations, or complimenting have been referred to as *speech acts*. Speech acts have (1) a basic meaning as conceived by the speaker ('Do you have a watch?' = do you possess a watch?), (2) an *intended illocutionary* meaning (e.g. 'Do you know what time it is?'), and (3) an actual illocutionary force on the hearer, referred to as the *uptake* (i.e. a request to know the time, and hence, a reply like 'It's 10:30 a.m. right now.'). In this instance, a young kid or a facetious adult might respond, 'Yes, I do.' If so, the uptake would not work for the speaker, who might then need to ask, 'What is the time, then?' While sometimes speech acts are accomplished by a single word like 'thanks,' at other times they involve complex and indirect speech over a series of conversational turns.

Many of these speech acts tend to follow regular and predictable patterns for members of the given speech community. In the case of 'greetings,' for example, an associate at work in the United States might say, 'How're you doing?' You are expected to say: 'Fine, thank you', rather than delving into a litany of woes, given that you have a bad knee and will be having surgery in a few weeks, and one of your kids just lost his job. To take the latter course would be unexpected. In fact, the person who asked how you were probably kept on walking and had no intention of engaging you in genuine conversation. Members of a given speech community generally know how to perform such greetings and how to interpret them as well.

For L2 learners of that language left to their own devices, however, the speech act of greeting and leave taking may be difficult to interpret and even more so to perform. On the performance end, in fact, L2 learners may simply translate what they would say in their native language in such a situation, rather than thinking how best to say it in a way that conforms with the largely predictable patterns for the target language and culture. So, the student's version of an apology may not be appropriate: 'Sorry, I couldn't make it because things came up ...', for example, might not work in a speech community where the addressee is expecting a more detailed explanation. By the same token, 'The reason I didn't come was that my kid got sick and I took him to the doctor and then ...' may be too detailed an explanation for the context.

Whereas early efforts at teaching speech acts, or language functions involved little more than providing learners with lists of those functions, usually in minimal contexts, current L2 instruction may now include curriculum informed by empirical research studies, sometimes involving natural data collected in corpora[2] (see, e.g. Golato, 2003; Holmes, 2003; Koester, 2002; Schauer & Adolphs, 2006). Cross-cultural research on apologies has found that there are a series of strategies that are specific to the performance of apologies in many different languages in a variety of speech communities (see Table 7.1). Preference for using one or more of these strategies in a given apology situation in a given language depends on the language and sociocultural situation. The following is an example of one such situation:

> You completely forget a crucial meeting at the office with your boss. An hour later you call him to apologise. The problem is that this is the second time you've forgotten such a meeting. Your boss gets on the line and asks: 'What happened to you?'

For Israeli Hebrew speakers, the apology would probably put emphasis on the strategy of *explanation* (more than an American would): e.g. 'Well, I had to take a sick kid to the doctor and then there was a problem with the plumbing ...' They would also probably avoid the strategy of *repair*, because research has shown that in the Israeli culture, the boss

Table 7.1 Strategies for apologising

(1) Expression of an apology:
• A word, expression, or sentence containing a verb such as 'sorry', 'excuse', 'forgive' or 'apologise'.
• In American English, 'I apologise …' is found more in writing than it is in oral language.
• An expression of an apology can be intensified – in American English, usually by adding intensifiers such as 'really' or 'very' – e.g. 'I'm really sorry'.
(2) Acknowledgment of responsibility – degree of recognition of fault:
• Accepts the blame: 'It's my fault'.
• Self-deficiency: 'I was confused/I didn't see/You are right'.
• Lack of intent: 'I didn't mean to'.
• Implicit expression of responsibility: 'I was sure I had given you the right directions'.
• Not accepting the blame/denying responsibility: 'It wasn't my fault', or even blaming of the hearer: 'It's your own fault'.
(3) Explanation or account: description of situation which led to the offence, serving as indirect way of apologising.
• Intended to set things right.
• In some cultures this may be a more acceptable way of apologising than in others.
• In cultures where public transportation is unreliable, coming late to a meeting and giving an explanation like, 'The bus was late', might be perfectly acceptable.
(4) Offer of repair: the apologiser makes a bid to carry out an action or provide payment for some kind of damage which resulted from his/her infraction.
• This strategy is situation specific and is only appropriate when actual damage has occurred.
(5) Promise of non recurrence: the apologiser commits him/herself to not having the offence happen again. Situation-specific and less frequent than the other strategies

Source: Based on Cohen and Olshtain, 1981.

determines the next step (Cohen & Olshtain, 1981). It would be an extra infraction for the employee to suggest what the next step would be, while an American might consider it imperative to offer repair as a way of righting the wrong.

In addition to the basic strategies associated with a speech act, there may also be modification according to the familiarity between the apologiser and the person being apologised to (intimate to very formal). Moreover, the intensity of the act could play a role – its gravity, seriousness or importance. For example, bumping into a stranger in a café and splashing hot coffee on the person, an American would be more likely to say 'I'm really sorry', indicating real regret, rather than 'I'm very sorry', which is more a sign of good etiquette, as in 'I'm very sorry to have to call an end to this meeting'.

A learner who is adept at L2 pragmatics has an ability to go beyond the literal meaning of what is said, in order to interpret the intended meanings, assumptions, purposes or goals, and the kinds of actions that are being performed (Yule, 1996: 3–4). Speakers and the hearers, therefore, need to collaborate to ensure that genuine communication takes place. In fact, pragmatics deals with meaning that is *co-constructed* and negotiated within a given sociocultural context (LoCastro, 2003; Thomas, 1995).

At present there is an ever-increasing body of printed and online materials that can serve in part as teachers' resource books on the teaching of pragmatics in an L2 (e.g. Bardovi-Harlig & Mahan-Taylor, 2003; Kasper & Rose, 2002; Rose & Kasper, 2001; Tatsuki, 2005). In the last two decades, researchers have conducted numerous empirical studies to collect data on such speech acts. They have also begun to validate the benefits of having teachers explicitly describe certain key speech acts as they appear within selected discourse contexts (see e.g. Bardovi-Harlig, 2001; Rose, 2005), rather than extracting them from their context for the purpose of teaching and learning.

But while there is increasing focus on the teaching of speech act sets,[3] it would appear that little attention has been given to how one might support learners in acquiring these complex speech forms. And a propitious way to support learners in this endeavour is through strategy instruction – hence the focus of a research and development project, which will be described in the next section of the paper. This paper will make the case that a convenient way to deliver this strategy instruction is through an online website which combines pragmatic content with a strategy 'overlay' so that students get both at the same time.

Defining and Classifying Language Learning Strategies

One important distinction is between *language learning* strategies (i.e. learning language material for the first time, such as a new word or phrase, or grammar structure) and *language use* strategies (i.e. using the material that has already been learned) (see Cohen, 2007). This distinction is played out in this chapter as we first consider strategies for *learning* L2 pragmatics and then strategies for *performing* the material that has been learned.

Strategies for Learning and Performing L2 Pragmatics

In an effort to fine-tune speaking strategies, by focusing on strategies for the learning and use of L2 pragmatics, a taxonomy was designed which included strategies (1) for the initial learning of speech acts, (2) for using the speech act material that has already been learned to some extent, and (3) for evaluating the effectiveness of their use, referred to as *metapragmatic strategies* (Cohen, 2005). Sources for strategies in this taxonomy include the general learner strategy literature, the speech act literature and insights from strategy research conducted to enhance college students' learning of Japanese L2 speech acts through a strategies-based online curriculum (Cohen & Ishihara, 2005) and from a language and culture study abroad project (Cohen *et al.*, 2005). For the most part, the strategies listed in the taxonomy are in need of empirical validation so they can be viewed as a series of hypotheses. A few examples from the taxonomy appear in Table 7.2.

Table 7.2 Sample strategies from a taxonomy of speech act strategies

Speech act learning strategies
• Taking practical steps to gain knowledge of how specific speech acts work, such as by identifying the L2 speech acts to focus on, using criteria such as:
(1) their frequency of use in common situations encountered by the L2 speaker in the given speech community (e.g. 'requesting', 'refusing', and 'thanking');
(2) their potentially high-stakes value in discourse (e.g. 'apologising' and 'complaining');
(3) their special role in the given community of practice within the speech community the society, such as in creating solidarity (e.g. the use of expletives).
• Asking native-speakers (instructors and non-instructors) to model performance of the speech acts as they might be realised under differing conditions, possibly to answer questions about their performance as well. A key goal of the learner would be to see if there is variation in the realisation of the speech act(s) according to:
(1) the magnitude or seriousness of the issue prompting the speech act (e.g. apologising for missing a meeting vs. spilling hot coffee on a friend);
(2) the relative age of the speaker and the addressee (e.g. making a request to a senior professor vs. making a request to a young child);
(3) the relative status of the speaker and the addressee (e.g. making a request to the senior vice president of a firm vs. one to a custodian);
(4) the relative roles in the speaker and the addressee in the relationship (e.g. making a request to the chair of the board meeting vs. to a waiter in a restaurant);

(Continued)

Table 7.2 *(Continued)*

Speech act learning strategies
(5) the length of acquaintance of the interlocutors (e.g. making a request to a stranger about switching seats upon boarding an airplane as opposed to making an appeal for assistance to a longtime friend over morning tea).
Speech act use strategies
• Practising those aspects of speech act performance that have been learned:
(1) Engaging in imaginary interactions, perhaps focusing on certain pragmalinguistic aspects of the speech act.
(2) Engaging in speech act role play with fellow learners of the L2 or with native speakers playing the other role.
(3) Engaging in 'real play', with native speakers in the speech community, where the native speakers perform their usual roles (e.g. lawyer, doctor, shop clerk, etc.) but with the added knowledge that the learners are simply practising speech acts and may say things that are contrary to fact (e.g. apologising for something that in reality they did not do).
(4) Engaging in interactions with native speakers without them being aware that the learner's purpose is actually to practise speech acts.
Metapragmatic considerations
• With regard to metacognitive strategies, the learner needs to determine how much pre-planning of the speech act to do beforehand, as well as the nature of the monitoring that will go on during its delivery and the evaluation that will go on afterwards. In an effort to avoid pragmatic failure, the learner may monitor for:
(1) the appropriateness of the chosen level of directness or indirectness in the delivery of the speech act (e.g. finding the right level of directness with an L2-speaking stranger on an airplane);
(2) the appropriateness of the selected term of address (e.g. referring in the L2 to Dr. Stephen Blake as 'Doc', 'Steve' or 'you' – either *tu* or *vous*);
(3) the appropriateness of the timing for a speech act in the given situation (e.g. whether to make an apology for a work-related incident to a colleague during a social event);
(4) the acceptability of how the discourse is organised (e.g. conveying the bottom-line message right at the start of the communication, gradually building up to it, or saving it for the last possible moment);
(5) the sociopragmatic appropriateness of the selected semantic formulas and the pragmalinguistic appropriateness of the linguistic material used to represent them (e.g. whether it is appropriate for a college student to give an outright refusal to the department chair's invitation to dinner and whether the refusal could include – even in jest – an informal phrase like 'No way!').

A revised taxonomy of strategies was implemented in the design and development of the later Spanish pragmatics website (Cohen & Sykes, 2006) which is described below.

In reality, strategies rarely function in isolation, but rather in sequences or clusters. In the case of clusters, the learner deploys the strategies simultaneously, in an overlapping manner. So, a strategy cluster deployed in requesting a raise could include at least the following learner strategies: retrieving from memory some possible language structures for making that request, choosing from that material forms that are at the level of politeness due to a boss, making sure that the request is sensitive to the norms for male-to-female talk in that speech community and situation, and using a monitoring strategy to see how well these two strategies are working.

From initial research to explore the strategies that L2 learners use in performing speech acts, it would appear that learners do make efforts to combine various strategies – perhaps some learners more than others (Cohen & Ishihara, 2005; Cohen & Olshtain, 1993; Robinson, 1992; Widjaja, 1997). However, given gaps in their knowledge about sociocultural and linguistic norms for the given speech community, speaking performance among L2 speakers is likely to reflect, at least in part, negative transfer from the norms that they use for speech act behaviour in their local L1 or other language community. According to the research evidence, it can take many years for L2 speakers' performance to reflect the norms of speech act behaviour for a given speech community (see Olshtain & Blum-Kulka, 1985; Barron, 2003).

Strategies for Independent Language Learning

To date the concern with regard to strategy applications for independent learning has focused on the capacity of learners for self-regulation based on their relationship with 'external' factors such as context, environment and materials, and related also to 'internal' factors such as personality and affect. Metacognitive strategies (particularly self-management strategies) have been reported to contribute notably to the development of autonomy among distance learners in particular (White, 1995), and have been found to provide the impetus for more effective distance learning experiences (White, 1999). Hurd (2000) noted in her study the importance of demonstrating the direct link between being more strategic in language learning and resulting language gain. While this link has been demonstrated through interventionist studies involving non-distance courses (see e.g. Cohen *et al.*, 1998; Macaro, 2001), according to Hurd the link remains to be studied in the distance learning context.

Language educators have called attention to the dilemma posed by the highly structured nature of distance language courses, such as those offered by the Open University (UK), in light of the need that learners have to develop autonomous approaches (Hurd *et al.*, 2001). Using examples from the Spanish Diploma, Hurd *et al.* have outlined ways in which autonomy can nevertheless be effectively promoted through careful attention to materials design. One such example that they provide is of how learners can work individually to learn about and self-evaluate both their formal and informal expression of politeness (Hurd *et al.*, 2001: 352–353). This and other strategies can be effectively applied to any independent language learning setting.

Many of the strategies related to both learning and spoken performance are generic to any speech act (following the taxonomy; Cohen, 2005). Others appear along with the content – for example, strategies for making a request in English, where the person making the request may well need to identify those language structures that make requests more polite such as the use of modal auxiliaries (e.g. 'Could you find the time . . . ?') and the use of the past progressive (e.g. 'I was wondering if . . .').

This now brings us to the issue of how we might enhance the learning of L2 pragmatics, through well-designed and targeted strategy instruction.

The Role of Technology in Independent Language Learning

Technology brings with it the promise of new venues for language learners: the rapid evolution of communication technologies has changed language pedagogy and language use, enabling new forms of discourse, new forms of authorship, and new ways to create and participate in communities (Kern, 2006). The use of computer-assisted language learning (CALL) allows for the creation of technologically-enhanced instructional materials focusing on pragmatics. CALL research has looked at the benefits of different technologies for pragmatic and cultural instruction: multimedia and authentic materials (Hoven, 1999; Kramsch & Andersen, 1999; LeLoup & Ponterio, 2001), asynchronous and synchronous computer-mediated communication (Biesenbach-Lucas, 2005; Sykes, 2005), and telecollaboration – whereby language learners engage in projects with students from other cultures through the use of on-line communication tools such as email and message boards (Belz, 2002, 2003, 2007; Furstenberg *et al.*, 2001).

There are now self-access websites for learners with material to support L2 pragmatic development. The Michigan State University Center for Language Education and Research (CLEAR, 2007), for example, provides short video clips in Arabic, Chinese, German, Korean, Russian and Vietnamese at the beginning, intermediate, and advanced levels, including a variety of speech acts, as well as culture notes and activities based on each clip. The Center for Advanced Research on Language Acquisition

(CARLA) at the University of Minnesota has three websites dedicated to L2 pragmatics, a general one, one focusing on Japanese (Cohen & Ishihara, 2005), and a third one focusing on Spanish (Cohen & Sykes, 2006).

However, the fact that these websites exist does not mean that they are entirely learner-friendly, since they may be lacking in social cues that learners have come to rely on (Thatcher, 2005). So, the challenge for website designers is to make sure that the technology is accompanied not only by content, but also by information about how to make use of the content strategically.

Website for teachers, curriculum writers, and learners

With funding from the Office of International Education to the Language Resource Center at CARLA, a project was initiated to provide self-access Internet sites for the learning and performance of L2 pragmatics. The first project involved the construction of a pragmatics website for teachers, curriculum writers and learners with detailed information about six speech acts (requests, refusals, apologies, complaints, compliments and thanking) in as many as 10 different languages: <http://www.carla.umn.edu/speechacts/descriptions.html> (accessed 17/8/2007). Strategies for teaching pragmatics and sample teaching materials are provided, along with an extensive annotated bibliography which includes information on numerous other speech acts.

Some six years later, after this website had been up for some time, a new project to construct a self-access website for learners of a less-commonly-taught language, Japanese, was initiated, followed three years later by the design and construction of a similar website for learners of a more-commonly-taught language, Spanish.

Website for learners of Japanese

The self-access website for learners of Japanese was constructed to include instructional units for five speech acts: requests, refusals, compliments, thanks, and apologies (see Cohen & Ishihara, 2005; Ishihara, 2007). It was intended to be used either on a stand-alone basis or as a supplement to an intermediate course in Japanese: <http://www.iles.umn.edu/introtospeechscts/> (accessed 17/8/2007). Strategies deemed supportive for the learning and performance of speech acts, and especially for speech acts in Japanese, were identified and built into the curriculum. The website materials include unscripted, audio-recorded pragmatic performance of native speakers to assist students in becoming more pragmatically adept at both receptive and productive skills, and at self-evaluation. The authenticity of the sample dialogues was evaluated by native speakers.

The following are a few sample strategies from the website. With regard to apologies, depending on the situation and the interlocutors, the following strategies may be appropriate: repeating the expression of apology (*sumimasen, gomennasai* or *moushiwake arimasen*) several times within a speech act set, speaking hesitantly so as to sound properly humble, leaving the sentence incomplete, and keeping any explanation or excuse brief and non-detailed. With regard to complementing someone of higher status, such as a professor on a lecture, instead of saying *lekuchawa yokata desu* 'your lecture was good', which would sound inappropriately evaluative, it would be more appropriate to use a Japanese equivalent of 'I learned a lot from your lecture' (e.g. *benkyoun narimashita:* 'it was informative to me' or *senseikara takusan naraimashita* 'I learned a lot from you'), a more humble approach.

The introductory section of the website makes it clear as learners encounter these strategies that it is up to them to determine just how native-speaker-like they want to sound. On the website, there is a link to communication strategies as a way for learners to get their message across using their own devices, rather than the normative ones. Raising learners' awareness about what native-speakers do gives them choices and enables them to decide to what extent they wish to act like native-speakers (see Ishihara, 2006).

Website for learners of Spanish

A more recent effort at pedagogical applications of pragmatic information involved the design, construction, and evaluation of the Spanish pragmatics website <//www.carla.umn.edu/speechacts/sp_pragmatics/home.html> (accessed 17/8/2007) (Cohen & Sykes, 2006), developed over 11 months and launched in August of 2006. It called for the following:

(1) the selection of empirically-based speech act material from naturalistic and elicited sources;
(2) efforts to accommodate conversational dynamics in the presentation of the material;
(3) attention to directness/indirectness and relative politeness;
(4) guidelines for enhancing strategies for learning and performing speech acts.

Unlike the Japanese site, the Spanish one includes unscripted video interchanges between speakers of various regional varieties of Spanish. Also, scaffolding is used for the purpose of addressing the learners' varying levels of language/pragmatic ability. Speech acts are dealt with sequentially – first as a core, then in interaction, and then as a naturally occurring sequence. The material is in many ways idealised for the sake of instructional purposes, and does not necessarily reflect the way pragmatic behaviour actually presents itself.

One of the strengths of both the Japanese and the Spanish pragmatics websites is the inclusion of the above-mentioned taxonomy of learner strategies to enhance pragmatic development (Cohen, 2005). The Spanish website has a far more developed strategy overlay than the Japanese website. Aside from an introductory unit, the website, 'Dancing with Words,' has the following speech act units or 'modules':

- Compliments
- Gratitude and leave taking
- Requests
- Apologies
- Invitations
- Service encounters
- Advice, suggestions, disagreements, complaints and reprimands
- Considerations for pragmatic performance

While the content within each module varies according to the empirical research available, all modules contain the following basic sections:

- Introduction
- Encountering the speech act
- Strategies for pragmatic performance:
- Sociopragmatic and pragmalinguistic strategies
- Important sociocultural factors
- Language varieties
- Summary

Although the model dialogues on the website are based on elicited interactions and not natural data, they are nonetheless unscripted and largely spontaneous, thus lending them some authenticity. The website also calls attention to the fact that the patterns vary (something that is all the more evident when using natural data). Thus, it is not only a matter of having 'the right' data, but also having an effective instructional approach as well. Other features of the website include a focus on varieties of Peninsular and Latin American Spanish, video clips to demonstrate conversational dynamics, coverage of directness/indirectness and relative politeness, guidelines for enhancing strategies for learning and performing speech acts, and extended exercises for learners to work their way through these strategy sections.

Suggestions are provided for ways to make use of the material in pragmatically appropriate ways. In the apology module, for example, learners are given strategies that are both hearer-oriented and speaker-oriented, with hearer-oriented ones focusing on the hearer as someone who can grant forgiveness (*Disculpe profesora, me perdí la hora,* 'I'm sorry, professor,

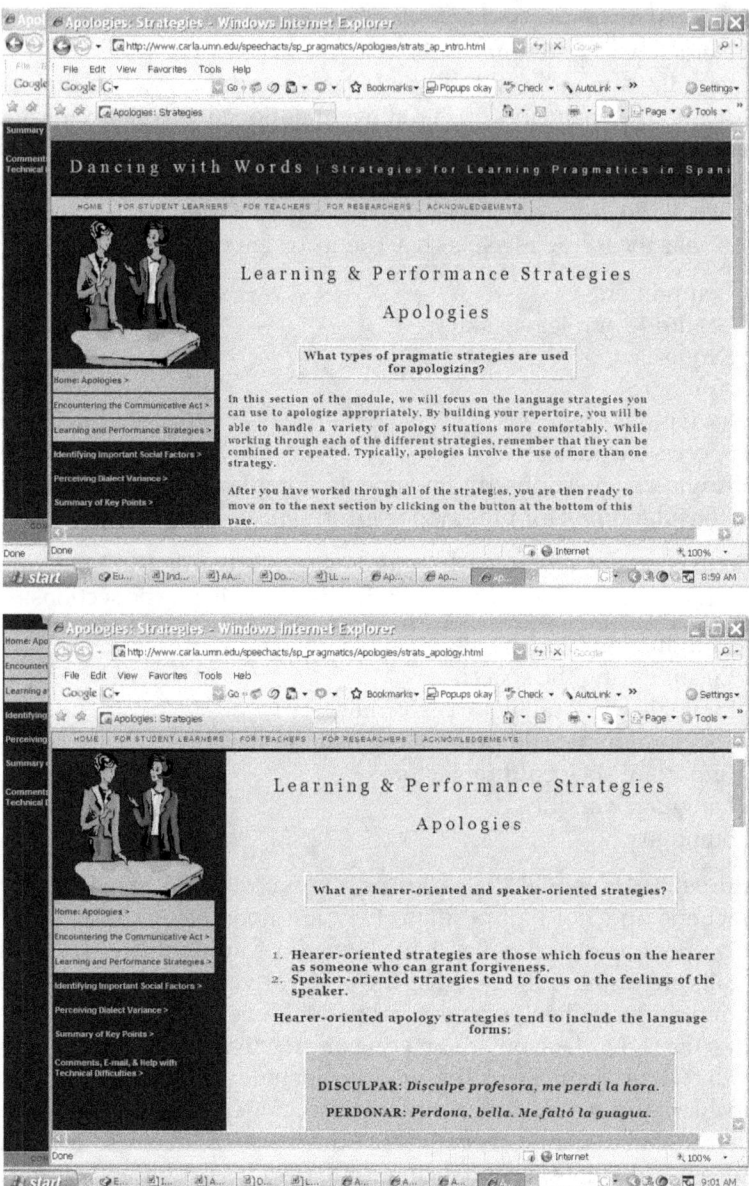

Figure 7.1 Strategies for learning and performing apologies

I lost track of the time') and speaker-oriented ones focusing on the feelings of the speaker (*Cuanto lamento haber causado este problema*, 'I'm so sorry I caused this problem') (see Figure 7.1). The strategy section also includes the suggestion to use native speakers as a resource, since a website cannot begin to cover the full range of material to accommodate age, gender, status and other distinctions in the given sociocultural context.

Adding a virtual environment to the learning of Spanish pragmatics

Using the Spanish pragmatics website 'Dancing with Words' as the core, the project has now been expanded to include a virtual online environment for the practice and assessment of speaking skills. This new venture has involved the creation of a Synthetic Immersive Environment (SIE) for L2 pragmatics, using computer software modelled on 'Second Life' <http://secondlife.com/> (accessed 17/8/2007) but on a more modest financial scale. This pragmatics work builds on experiences over the last decade with synchronous computer-mediated communication (SCMC) (Belz, 2004, 2005; Healy-Beauvois, 1992; Payne & Ross, 2005; Payne & Whitney, 2002; Sykes, 2005). The current work attempts to apply the positive features of SCMC to the design of virtual environments for learning and especially practising pragmatics (see Sykes, 2008, for further discussion of the relationship between SCMC and SIEs as related to learning L2 pragmatics).

The SIE used in conjunction with 'Dancing with Words' is an online virtual world named *Croquelandia* that was designed as part of a larger project financed by the University of Minnesota. The Spanish model is the first environment of its kind designed for language learners and is intended to serve as a model for similar SIEs in other languages. The space was developed to foster L2 pragmatic development by maximising the potential benefits of the new technological tools. At present, activities in the space give students an opportunity to interact with native speakers and use the speech act strategies that they have learned from 'Dancing with Words' in order to make requests, handle service encounters, and apologise. The plan is to eventually add the other five speech acts modules from the 'Dancing with Words' website, as listed on page 127.

The graphics in the space were created using photos from the Spanish-speaking world. These were then adapted and redesigned into the space by the graphic design and programming team. In the SIE, learners can collaborate and interact in three primary spaces – the study-abroad host family's house, a central plaza and market place, and a professor's office at the university. The players in the environment can collaborate with their group members or other players using voice or written chat and can interact with the environment by clicking on different items, walking around the space, and observing and talking with an *avatar* (i.e. a graphical image of a user) present in each of the spaces. In the future, SIE users will be able to create their own content and link to other areas outside the virtual space. (See Figures 7.2 and 7.3 for images of the SIE *Croquelandia*.)

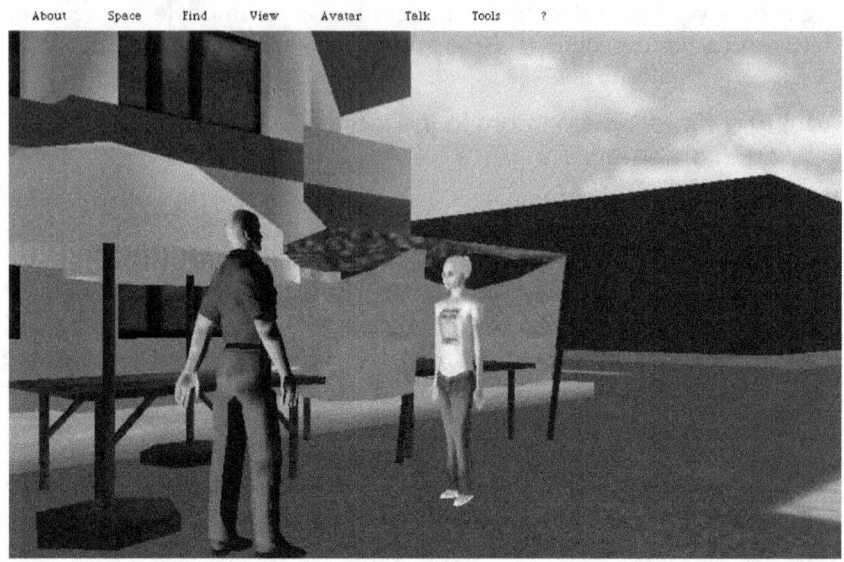

Figure 7.2 Sample of SIE *Croquelandia*

Figure 7.3 Sample house setting in SIE

A Small-Scale Study

Thanks to a grant from the University of Minnesota, a small-scale study was conducted in February 2007 with the following aims:

- To examine how learners use strategies-based materials on a website and a virtual, immersive environment for learning L2 pragmatics (e.g. strategies for the learning and performance of the material, time spent on videos, answers to questions posed, comparisons of learner approaches to the website).
- To examine the effect that using the website for learning Spanish pragmatics has on their ability to perform a subset of the speech acts on the website (i.e. requests, apologies, service encounters) during actual interaction.

We note that no effort was made to compare the use of the website and virtual environment with more traditional approaches to teaching pragmatics, such as the study of print materials and face-to-face interactions. Hence, the study was simply exploring the impact of these more recent vehicles for learning of L2 pragmatics.

Research design

The research design and available budget called for the recruitment of ten advanced learners of Spanish who received a technological orientation and were then asked to study the pragmatics modules appearing on the *Dancing with Words* website, and then to have that learning assessed in the SIE. All actions and oral language in the tasks that they performed on the computer were recorded using *Camtasia Studio* <www.techsmith.com/camtasia.asp> (accessed 17/8/2007). The pre-test required three role-plays in the SIE for assessment purposes: a request to borrow their study-abroad host sister's course notes, a service encounter with a street vendor (buying souvenirs), and apologising to their sister for spilling Coke on the notes in their backpack and ruining them. The students interacted with an avatar representing the host country sister and one representing the seller in the market place, both played by the Colombian native Spanish speaker. The pre-test also included a written multiple-rejoinder DCT, with five situations based on material from 'Dancing with Words'. Participants had to provide two requests, two apologies, and a service encounter (buying food at the market).

There was then a content orientation session, focusing on the taxonomy for L2 pragmatics, after which each of the participants completed three online modules from 'Dancing with Words', calling for requests, apologies, and service encounters (1–2 hours per module). After the completion of these modules, the participants took part in a reflective interview (10–20 minutes) which was recorded and transcribed. Next they took the immediate post-test also for assessment purposes, consisting of a virtual role-play with avatars as in the pre-test, but with a different request and apology. The students had to make a request to borrow money from the avatar representing their host sister, who only had a large *croquedo* bill which they needed to get changed and return the change. The service encounter was the same, but the apology was for losing the rest of the money. There was also a delayed post-test, which was the same as the pre-test.

The analysis of data called for comparing pre- and post-test results for both the oral role-plays and the written DCTs to determine the impact of the three modules from the *Dancing with Words* website on the subjects. Both quantitative and qualitative analyses were conducted to compare the frequency of speech act strategies and their nature (e.g. the use of speaker-oriented or hearer-oriented strategies), the complexity of interactions, and the number of turns taken before and after exposure to the material. In addition, the data from the interviews were analyzed for insights that students had in dealing with the website and SIE. For a more extensive study of this SIE, see Sykes (2008).

Selected findings

The following are initial results based on preliminary analysis of data. In the pre-test virtual interaction with the native Spanish-speaker playing the role of the avatar for the host country sister and the one for the vendor, students experienced some stumbling and difficulty with the tasks. They indicated that they had not had previous practice with this type of interaction, and, in fact, three of the subjects reported not having had any experience of talking to a native speaker outside of the language classroom. As for their strategies for using the pragmatics material from the online modules, there was notable individual variation. While all 10 students used the written transcripts provided along with the video clips, they were reportedly used for different purposes. Two students reported using them in order to answer questions and six said they used them to help comprehend the video clips. As regards the built-in feedback on the website, two reported using it as instructional input prior to completing the activities, while eight said they used it afterwards, just to check their answers. Since in piloting it was not clear whether the website provided more information than students would want, we were curious about students' reactions to the level of detail provided along with the online activities. While interest in details varied by module, learner, setting, and time of day, in general students were found to want even more details about the speech acts that they were interested in, as well as more practice and learning activities. There was only minimal difficulty with the technology itself – only one student indicated having trouble with the embedded videos.

The website's focus on strategies for learning, performing, and evaluating speech acts seemed to have produced the desired effect.

Participants demonstrated an increase in reported use of almost all strategies for the learning and use of pragmatics, with notable increases in awareness and consciousness-raising strategies, such as: *I pay attention to what native speakers do by noting what they say, how they say it, and their non-verbal behaviour*, and *I will identify the communicative act I need to focus on*. About half the students focused on the specific pragmalinguistic (i.e. language structure) strategies for performing a given speech act, saying things like, 'Now I can memorise what language to use in different situations.' The other half considered the general awareness of sociopragmatic (i.e. sociocultural) strategies associated with the given speech act, saying things like, 'I may not know exactly what to say, but I am more aware of what is going on ...'

Findings from the reflective interviews showed that the students had varying reactions to the features found in 'Dancing with Words' and in the virtual environments. Here are some examples:

Susana: [The website] kind of puts into written order what you kind of hear on your own, but you don't really know how to order it ... it helps to have it all written down and put together.

Henry: I'm kind of a fan of interactive things like if they were drop-down boxes.

Abril: I don't need like fancy stuff to help me learn, I guess.

So Susana appreciated having this information in one place, Henry felt that the way it was packaged made a difference, and the packaging of it was not important to Abril.

The following are a few student comments relating to their awareness of the impact of the *Dancing with Words* website on their own language, learning process, and social interaction:

Interviewer: Do you think you'll use the other modules?

Callie: I think so, yes. Spanish is a big part of my life ... I want not just to be able to know the words, but be able to use the same pragmatics as native people would.

Ronaldo: Before I would just ramble on, but now I would use the three steps that [I devised]. You can start on one and work on that. Once you get done with that, then move on to the next.

Interviewer: What did you like about the materials?

Veronica: The one on Ecuador stood out. That's where I want to go.

Students indicated that they were likely to continue working with the materials to improve their pragmatic skills (Cohen & Sykes, 2007). In a reflective interview, a student made the following observation:

> ... what you are getting at with the programme is really, really positive because I really don't think there is enough emphasis on real

world application ... what I am always super, super frustrated with is you always end up with a class full of people who can write A+ papers and perfect grammar, and they can't speak it to save their lives ... the fact that you're emphasising a lot more on real world situations than on grammar is something that the Spanish curriculum desperately needs.

As noted by this particular student, many advanced language learners are able to utilise complex linguistic systems, but are unable to express and interpret meaning in order to perform language functions (e.g. apologies, requests) appropriately. Even when pragmatic features are addressed in the classroom, the focus tends to remain on linguistic forms, rather than on the essential socio-cultural aspects of their use (Félix-Brasdefer, 2002).

Discussion and Conclusion

This chapter started by calling attention to the importance for language learners of having some control of L2 pragmatics, especially with regard to improving their speaking skills. The ability to make a request, refuse an invitation, complain, or apologise in high-stakes L2 situations may make or break a important relationship. Language learning strategies have a key role in enhancing pragmatic performance, both at the stage where the material is being learned for the first time and when what is learned needs to be accessed in order to perform it. Technology, as we have seen, can also play a major part in supporting the efforts of learners working on their own in various contexts. The three websites – a general one for teachers, curriculum writers, and learners; one dedicated to Japanese L2 pragmatics; and a third for Spanish L2 pragmatics – are all stages on the way to providing high quality state-of-the-art opportunities for students to develop spoken competence. A virtual environment for the learning of Spanish L2 pragmatics promises learners an effective and convenient way to practise their use of the language.

Finally, the small-scale study of the Spanish website and virtual environment would suggest that such efforts go a long way to enhance the learning of a language, covering areas that course work and even out-of-class experience do not cover. Findings from preliminary research with the Spanish pragmatics website indicate that learners utilise online content (i.e. videos, transcripts and feedback) in a variety of ways relevant to their own learning context. In addition, the learners in the Cohen and Sykes study (see Sykes & Cohen, forthcoming) displayed different characterisations of their online experience and tended to categorise their own focus on either pragmalinguistic or sociopragmatic factors relevant to each of the three speech acts being addressed. Perhaps the most encouraging finding was that the subjects of the study displayed a positive perception of the experience and indicated that they would continue to use the website materials in the future.

Notes

1. For the purposes of this paper, L2 refers to the learning of a foreign language both in a context where the language is spoken widely and where it is not. In principle, pragmatic development in an L2 will be faster in the former context than in the latter, but it depends largely on how the learner makes use of the available resources.
2. While corpora have been heralded as the true way to describe pragmatic behaviour, more complex speech acts than leave-taking, such as complaints or apologies, may be performed in indirect ways such that that a search of words and phrases in a corpus may be of limited value. In addition, complex speech acts may be performed over a series of turns, making them difficult to retrieve from a corpus.
3. A speech act set refers to a set of possible strategies, where one or more members of this set could constitute the speech act, depending on the situation.

References

Bardovi-Harlig, K. (2001) Evaluating the empirical evidence: Grounds for instruction in pragmatics? In K.R. Rose and G. Kasper (eds) *Pragmatics in Language Teaching* (pp. 13–32). Cambridge: Cambridge University Press.
Bardovi-Harlig, K. and Mahan-Taylor, R. (eds) (2003) *Teaching Pragmatics*. Washington, DC: US Department of State.
Barron, A. (2003) *Acquisition in Interlanguage Pragmatics: Learning How to Do Things with Words in a Study Abroad Context.* Amsterdam/Philadelphia: John Benjamins.
Belz, J.A. (2002) Social dimensions of telecollaborative foreign language study. *Language Learning and Technology* 6 (1), 60–81.
Belz, J.A. (2003) Linguistic perspectives on the development of intercultural competence in telecollaboration. *Language Learning and Technology* 7 (2), 68–99.
Belz, J.A. (2004) Learner corpus analysis and the development of foreign language proficiency. *System* 32 (4), 577–591.
Belz, J.A. (2005) Learner corpus analysis and the development of l2 pragmatic competence in networked intercultural language study: The case of German modal particles. *Canadian Modern Language Review* 62 (1), 17–48.
Belz, J.A. (2007) The role of computer mediation in the instruction and development of L2 pragmatic competence. *Annual Review of Applied Linguistic* 27, 45–75.
Biesenbach-Lucas, S. (2005) Communication topics and strategies in e-mail consultation: Comparison between American and international university students. *Language Learning and Technology* 9 (2), 24–46.
CLEAR (2007) Multimedia Interactive Modules for Education and Assessment (MIMEA) East Lansing, MI: Center for Language Education and Research, Michigan State University. On WWW at http://mimea.clear.msu.edu/. Accessed 17.08.07.
Cohen, A.D. (2005) Strategies for learning and performing L2 speech acts. *Intercultural Pragmatics* 2 (3), 275–301.

Cohen, A.D. (2007) Coming to terms with language learner strategies: Surveying the experts. In A.D. Cohen and E. Macaro (eds) *Language Learner Strategies: 30 Years of Research and Practice* (pp. 29–45). Oxford: Oxford University Press.

Cohen, A.D. and Ishihara, N. (2005) A web-based approach to strategic learning of speech acts. Minneapolis, MN: Center for Advanced Research on Language Acquisition (CARLA), University of Minnesota, 57 pp. On WWW at http://www.carla.umn.edu/speechacts/Japanese%20Speech%20Act%20Report%20Rev.%20June05.pdf. Accessed 17.08.07.

Cohen, A.D. and Olshtain, E. (1981) Developing a measure of socio-cultural competence: The case of apology. *Language Learning* 31 (1), 113–134.

Cohen, A.D. and Olshtain, E. (1993) The production of speech acts by EFL learners. *TESOL Quarterly* 27 (1), 33–56.

Cohen, A.D., Paige, R.M., Shively, R.L., Emert, H. and Hoff, J. (2005) *Maximising Study Abroad through Language and Culture Strategies: Research on Students, Study Abroad Program Professionals, and Language Instructors*. Final Report to the International Research and Studies Program, Office of International Education, DOE. Minneapolis, MN: Center for Advanced Research on Language Acquisition, University of Minnesota. On WWW at http://www.carla.umn.edu/maxsa/documents/MAXSAResearchReport_000.pdf. Accessed 17.08.07.

Cohen, A.D. and Sykes, J.M. (2006) *The Development and Evaluation of a Self-Access Website for Learning Spanish Speech Acts*. Paper presented at the Annual Joint AAAL-ACLA/CAAL Conference, Montreal, CN, 17 June 2006.

Cohen, A.D. and Sykes, J.M. (2007) *Strategies, CMC, and Learning Pragmatics*. Paper presented at the 17th International Conference on Pragmatics and Language Learning, Honolulu, HI, 26–28 March 2007.

Cohen, A.D., Weaver, S.J. and Li, T-Y. (1998) The impact of strategies-based instruction on speaking a foreign language. In A.D. Cohen (ed.) *Strategies in Learning and Using a Second Language* (pp. 107–156). Harlow: Longman.

Félix-Brasdefer, C. (2002) Refusals in Spanish and English: A cross-cultural study of politeness strategies among speakers of Mexican Spanish, American English, and American learners of Spanish as a foreign language. Unpublished doctoral dissertation, University of Minnesota, Minnesota.

Furstenberg, G., Levet, S., English, K. and Maillet, K. (2001) Giving a virtual voice to the silent language of culture: The *CULTURA* project. *Language Learning and Technology* 5 (1), 55–102.

Golato, A. (2003) Studying compliment responses: A comparison of DCTs and recordings of naturally occurring talk. *Applied Linguistics* 24 (1), 90–121.

Healy-Beauvois, M. (1992) Computer assisted classroom discussion in the foreign language classroom: Conversation in slow motion. *Foreign Language Annals* 25 (5), 455–464.

Holmes, J. (2003) Talk at work and 'fitting in': A socio-pragmatic perspective on workplace culture. In G. Wigglesworth (ed.) *Marking our Difference: Languages in Australia and New Zealand Universities. Proceedings of Conference on Language Education in Australian and New Zealand Universities* (pp. 95–115). Melbourne: University of Melbourne.

Hoven, D. (1999) A model for listening and viewing comprehension in multimedia environments. *Language Learning and Technology* 3 (1), 88–103.

Hurd, S. (2000) Distance language learners and learner support: Beliefs, difficulties and use of strategies. *Links and Letters* 7, 61–80.

Hurd, S., Beaven, T. and Ortega, A. (2001) Developing autonomy in a distance language learning context: Issues and dilemmas for course writers. *System* 29 (3), 341–355.

Ishihara, N. (2006) Centering second language (SL) speakers' experience: A study of SL speakers' resistance to pragmatic norms of the SL community. In *Subjectivity, Second/Foreign Language Pragmatic Use, and Instruction: Evidence of Accommodation and Resistance* (chap. 4, pp. 114–136). Unpublished doctoral dissertation, University of Minnesota, Minneapolis, MN.

Ishihara, N. (2007) Web-based curriculum for pragmatics Instruction in Japanese as a foreign language: An explicit awareness-raising approach. *Language Awareness* 16 (1), 21–40.

Kasper, G. and Rose, K.R. (2002) *Pragmatic Development in a Second Language.* Oxford, UK/Malden, MA: Blackwell.

Kern, R. (2006) Perspectives on technology in learning and teaching languages. *TESOL Quarterly* 40 (1), 183–210.

Koester, A.J. (2002) The performance of speech acts in workplace conversations and the teaching of communicative functions. *System* 30 (2), 167–184.

Kramsch, C. and Andersen, R.W. (1999) Teaching text and context through multimedia. *Language Learning and Technology* 2 (2), 31–42.

LeLoup, J.W. and Ponterio, R. (2001) ON THE NET: Interactive and multimedia techniques in online language lessons: A sampler. *Language Learning and Technology* 7 (3), 4–17.

LoCastro, V. (2003) *An Introduction to Pragmatics: Social Action for Language Teachers.* Ann Arbor, MI: The University of Michigan Press.

Macaro, E. (2001) *Learning Strategies in Foreign and Second Language Classrooms.* London: Continuum.

Olshtain, E. and Blum-Kulka, S. (1985) Degree of approximation: Nonnative reactions to native speech act behaviour. In S. Gass and C. Madden (eds) *Input in Second Language Acquisition* (pp. 303–325). Rowley, MA: Newbury House.

Payne, S. and Whitney, P.J. (2002) Developing L2 oral proficiency through synchronous CMC: output, working memory, and interlanguage development. *CALICO* 20 (1), 7–32.

Payne, J.S. and Ross, B. (2005) Working memory, synchronous CMC, and L2 oral proficiency development. *Language Learning and Technology* 9 (1), 35–54.

Robinson, M.A. (1992) Introspective methodology in interlanguage pragmatics research. In G. Kasper (ed.) *Pragmatics of Japanese as Native and Target Language* (Technical Report #3) (pp. 27–82). Honolulu, HI: Second Language Teaching and Curriculum Center, University of Hawaii.

Rose, K.R. (2005) On the effects of instruction in second language pragmatics. *System* 33 (3), 385–399.

Rose, K.R. and Kasper, G. (eds) (2001) *Pragmatics in Language Teaching.* Cambridge: Cambridge University Press.

Schauer, G.A. and Adolphs, S. (2006) Expressions of gratitude in corpus and DCT data: Vocabulary, formulaic sequences, and pedagogy. *System* 34 (1), 119–134.

Sykes, J.M. (2005) Synchronous CMC and pragmatic development: Effects of oral and written chat. *CALICO* 22 (3), 399–432.

Sykes, J.M. (2008) A dynamic approach to social interaction: Synthetic immersive environments and Spanish pragmatics. Unpublished doctoral dissertation, Hispanic Linguistics, University of Minnesota, Minneapolis.

Sykes, J.M. and Cohen, A.D. (forthcoming) Observed learner behavior, reported use, and evaluation of a website for learning Spanish pragmatics. In M. Bowles, R. Foote and S. Perpiñán (eds) *Second Language Aquisition and Research: Focus on Form and Function. Selected Proceedings of the 2007 Second Language Research Forum.* Somerville, MA: Cascadilla Press.

Tatsuki, D. (ed.) (2005) *Pragmatics in Language Learning, Theory, and Practice* (pp. 150–156). Tokyo: Pragmatics Special Interest Group of the Japan Association for Language Teaching.

Thatcher, B. (2005) Situating L2 writing in global communication technologies. *Computers and Composition* 22 (3), 279–295.

Thomas, J. (1995) *Meaning in Interaction: An Introduction to Pragmatics.* London: Longman.

White, C. (1995) Autonomy and strategy use in distance foreign language learning: Research writing. *System* 23 (2), 207–221.

White, C. (1999) The metacognitive knowledge of distance learners. *Open Learning* 14 (3), 37–47.

Widjaja, C.S. (1997) A study of date refusals: Taiwanese females vs. American females. *University of Hawai'i Working Papers in ESL* 15 (2), 1–43.

Yule, G. (1996) *Pragmatics.* Oxford: Oxford University Press.

Chapter 8
Bringing the Learner Back Into the Process: Identifying Learner Strategies for Grammatical Development in Independent Language Learning

ELSPETH BROADY and NICK DWYER

> *Some people seem to think we should learn a foreign language as adults the same way we learned our native language when we were children. But we have to learn languages more in the way we learn other things as adults, and there is more method and more system. We do have mental files and we do have indexes. Why deprive a person of these skills? Let them use them in language learning!*
> Derek in Stevick, 1989: 64

> *It's just rules ... that's all it is at this stage, it's not ... a whole lot of concepts that you've got to sort of unwind and unravel ... there are no great mysteries ... the mystery is – how the hell do I remember it all?*
> Harry in Cotterall, 2005: 111

Introduction

As the two citations above suggest, adult learners of second languages tend to express contrasting, and frequently ambivalent, views towards 'learning grammar'. This is hardly surprising since the term 'grammar' itself has a range of meanings, referring on the one hand to the syntactic and morphological systems of a target language, based on implicit knowledge not necessarily available to the learner as a conscious representation, or, on the other, to an explicit knowledge of grammatical rules which exist independently of their application (Ellis, 1994a). For some learners, like Stevick's Derek, explicit knowledge provides a metacognitive tool, a framework for organising sometimes dauntingly complex information, a tool which is accessible to conscious control and can therefore be reviewed and refined with a resulting sense of satisfaction. Various researchers have claimed that explicit knowledge and understanding of grammar can facilitate implicit language acquisition (see Ellis, 2005; Ellis, 2006 for overviews, and the section (below) on Current theoretical frameworks. Further, it may also play a facilitative role in language *use*, and a learner's developing literacy is likely to depend on some explicit sense of grammatical accuracy. Finally, it can help learners articulate their learning, thus facilitating the 'scaffolded learning' (Swain, 1998) or 'negotiation of input' that leads to learner 'noticing' (Basturkmen *et al.*, 2002). These views support Little's (1997: 103) argument that 'the means to reflect analytically on our target language as a rule-governed system' is important in the development of learner autonomy.

On the other hand, explicit grammar may be experienced by some learners as imposed from the outside and getting in the way of the expression of ideas; an area of infinite detail to be remembered, as was the case for Cotterall's learner, Harry, or of frustration, as Murphy's (2005) adult distance learners reported. 'Grammar' can be seen as detracting from the 'real' business of language learning, a view promoted by Krashen's (1981) well-known position that explicit knowledge of grammatical rules plays a very restricted role in second language proficiency. Anxieties and strong feelings about grammar are also reflected in teachers' discourse as studied by Borg (1999). Hanna, one of the teachers in Borg's study, highlights the same tension as Derek above, but from the opposite point of view, when she states: 'I'd prefer my students to pick up language as a skill rather than as something they have to continually analyse mentally' (Borg, 1999: 117).

Given the 'problem' of grammar, it is perhaps surprising that, compared with other areas of second language development, very little consideration has been given to learners' strategies in this area. While McDonough's (1999) and Wenden's (2005) reviews both devote sections to the acquisition of vocabulary and the four skills, neither makes any specific mention of strategies for acquiring or using L2 morphology and syntax. Similarly, the SLA literature on 'the grammar debate' focuses either on theoretical models of SLA which identify the cognitive processes involved in interlanguage development and the relative roles of explicit and implicit knowledge (see Ellis, 2005), or on related classroom-based pedagogic interventions (see Ellis, 2006). Grammatical development is rarely considered from the perspective of *learner* agency, making it difficult to identify grammatical strategies which might be used specifically by independent learners, that is, those who learn outside a formal classroom environment. However, the term 'independence' can also refer to the ability of the learner to take autonomous decisions in any learning context and the strategies that classroom learners use in order to develop their grammar may be of use for all learners.

In what follows, then, we review research relevant to the grammatical development of adult learners learning in a variety of contexts, but wherever possible highlight issues relating to learner agency and autonomy. First, we will review the early work on language learning strategies where key notions about strategies for grammatical learning were sketched; then we draw on qualitative studies based on learner accounts to try to highlight grammar-focused strategies in action; and finally we review current theoretical models of SLA and empirical research in order to draw out possible implications for the validity of conscious learner intervention in this area of learning.

The Good Language Learner: Generating and Testing Hypotheses

The early strategies researchers, Rubin (1975, 1981) and Naiman *et al.* (1978), clearly present grammar-focused strategies as significant in the repertoires of the 'good language learners' who informed their research. They characterise good language learners as able to combine attention to language both as communication and as a system. Good language learners are both inductive and deductive; they identify regularities from input and then use that knowledge to scout for more, adjusting their understanding based on feedback. These activities are portrayed by Rubin (1975: 47) as conscious strategies, enacting the key cognitive processes of second language learning. Naiman *et al.* (1978) group similar form-focused strategies under the two headings of 'Realisation of language as a system' and 'Monitoring of L2 performance', with the additional reference under the former to the strategy of 'referring back judiciously to the L1' and making 'effective cross-lingual comparisons'. Rubin's (1981) overview then presents strategies relevant to grammatical competence under four headings: 'Deductive Reasoning' (rule search, use and adjustment, including drawing on cross-linguistic comparisons); 'Monitoring' (self-correction and noting source of errors, observing others' language use for comparison); 'Clarification/Verification' (asking for a correct form, asking if a rule fits a particular case, or if a given form is explained by a previously learned rule, and looking up a structure in a grammar book) and 'Practice' which includes 'consciously applying grammatical rules when speaking' and practising corrected forms and then extending them to other contexts (Rubin, 1981: 124–125).

The strategies identified by Naiman *et al.* (1978) and Rubin (1981) are all *cognitive* strategies, 'specific actions which contribute *directly* to the learning process' (Rubin, 1981: 118). Further work by Wenden (1987) and O'Malley and Chamot (1990) began to emphasise the importance of *metacognitive* strategies, or 'higher order executive skills that may entail planning for, monitoring, or evaluating the success of a learning activity'

(O'Malley & Chamot, 1990: 44). Wenden's work (1987, 1998) provides a theoretical framework for metacognition, rooted in a learner's knowledge of themselves as a learner ('person' knowledge) and their understanding of the range of relevant tasks ('task' knowledge) and appropriate strategies ('strategic' knowledge), while O'Malley and Chamot (1990) present metacognitive strategies as essential to the development of effective target language skills, orienting their research towards the use of strategies in speaking, listening, reading and writing. Strategies are thus conceptualised as 'learning' strategies insofar as they support the learning of these skills rather than the development of L2 competence.

Insights from Language Learner Accounts: Juggling Meaning and Form

There is plenty of evidence, largely from qualitative studies of individual learners published since Rubin (1975, 1981) and Naiman *et al.* (1978), that language learners engage in a range of strategies to develop their command of target language grammar. There is also evidence of significant differences in learning styles or orientations in this endeavour. For example in Stevick's (1989) collection of adult learner case studies, Ann and Carla, respectively dubbed 'intuitive' and 'informal' learners, both feel they learn by absorbing phrases and repeating them in context, without any real need for conscious analysis. On the other hand, 'imaginative' Derek and 'self-aware' Gwen both talk about their need for representations of the target language system through tables, frameworks and overviews, either developed autonomously (Derek) or from published resources (Gwen). These tools, in their view, enable them to retain and use grammatical knowledge more quickly and effectively (Stevick, 1989: 58) Meanwhile, 'active' Ed aims to get an overview of structural patterns as early as possible so that he can get on to communicating in the language more quickly. He rejects the value of grammatical analysis using 'technical' terms, but memorises phrases ('formulas') and then actively tries to deconstruct them. He is metalinguistically aware, but without the need for metalinguistic terminology:

> I sometimes find it good to just learn something – memorise it or whatever – and only then to break it down, to look at it and find out what has happened: *How* has this been put together? *Why* has it been put together this way? To ask and answer questions like that, and then forget about it. (Stevick, 1989: 90)

Similar strategies are delineated in autobiographical diary studies of language learners (mostly university specialists in applied linguistics) such as Rivers (1981), Schmidt and Frota (1986), Jones (1994) and Carson and Longhini (2002). There are, for example, clear similarities with Derek's drive to master complex morphology through visual representation in the following extract from Joan Carson's diary:

> Anna, Ileana and I made a list of three paradigmatic forms ... Much overlap unfortunately. I was hoping for a common stem showing up everywhere but no such luck. Nevertheless, it's helpful to have them written down. I notice that I haven't actually referred to them yet (!!) I'm not into formal studying or memorising it appears. But it's helpful to me to have this organisation and some sense of systematicity in the language. (Carson & Longhini, 2002: 421)

Ed's strategy of deconstructing phrases or 'formulas' is evident in Schmidt and Frota (1986: 285), for example in Schmidt's account of analysing a Portuguese idiomatic formula from its instances *morrendo de calor* (dying from the heat) and *morrendo de fome* (dying of hunger) in order to generate *morrendo de cansa* (dying from exhaustion) and checking accuracy by monitoring the reactions of his interlocutors.

Gwen's strategy of consciously working particular grammatical constructions into real conversation is also mentioned frequently in Schmidt's diary, while Rivers also reports personalising formal pattern exercises in order to make them meaningful:

> I find practice exercises where one applied and reapplied new rules in variant situations to be useful and important to my learning. I do not find that they involve 'parroting'. Instead, they require active mental participation [...] I find myself definitely recreating [...] I add my own flourishes to the exercise sentences, thus creating my own meaning and even adding my own humour at times. (Rivers, 1981: 504)

Rivers (1981: 502), Bailey (1983: 40) Schmidt and Frota (1986: 244) and Jones (1994: 447–8) all express frustration at having to use language outside of a meaningful context. Jones, for example, recounts how he chose to ignore decontextualised drills in favour of practising 'personalised writing':

> Free to choose my own activities (...) I avoided grammar drills because message-based work – especially personalised ('my family', real-life letters, my learner diary, etc.) was simply more enjoyable. (Jones, 1994: 448)

He goes on to argue that his command of grammatical structure was stretched by this demanding writing activity since it engaged him in 'deep' semantic processing and 'repeated working-memory overload' – perhaps what Swain (1998) refers to as 'pushed output' – thus enhancing his acquisition.

The strategy of making otherwise decontextualised language 'meaningful' in some way appears to be particularly significant in independent language learning, judging by Rowsell and Libben's (1994) study of diaries from thirty independent learners in Canada. They concluded that what differentiated the more successful learners from the less successful (defined by whether they achieved their set goals or not) was not the amount, or even the type, of study they engaged in, but the former's strategy of inventing 'real' communication situations for their practice, imagining meaningful contexts and contents for decontextualised exercises. Somehow, successful independent learners seem to find ways to avoid the limited 'tunnel vision' approach to grammatical practice (i.e. focusing only on the mechanical transformation of a form, excluding all sense of meaning) which was highlighted by Hosenfeld (1979) in an early study of high school learners' language learning strategies and which seemed to characterise Vann and Abraham's (1990: 187) 'unsuccessful' adult learner, Mona, who experienced problems in cloze tests and composition because her strategies focused exclusively on formal 'local cues'.

More confident language learners, then, seem to adopt strategies to overcome the limitations of decontextualised grammatical practice. Several studies (Bialystok, 1981; Huang & Van Naerssen, 1985; Oxford, 1986 cited in Manghubai, 1991) appear to show that in a given learning group, more successful learners are distinguished from less successful ones, not by their use of formal practising strategies (doing grammar drills, learning rules, etc.), but by their engagement in functional practice (seeking out opportunities to read, listen, speak and write), although these findings might be restricted to the particular educational settings investigated. However, it is worth remembering that Jones (1994: 447), reflecting on his own highly successful language learning, does report that meaning-focused tasks alone did *not* enable him to acquire new grammatical forms. His approach was therefore to supplement his extensive meaning-focused 'real-text' reading and writing with the resource-focused strategy of consulting a target language grammar book and, in particular, selecting holophrastic expressions rather than using noun and verb tables to produce inflections. He sums up his preferred approach to independent grammatical learning thus:

> For grammar, explicit, well-indexed descriptions, backed up by opportunities for holophrastic input and real-message output, appear far more useful than the highly skippable controlled-practice exercises. (Jones, 1994: 452)

Assuming that Rivers, Jones, Schmidt and Carson can be considered 'successful language learners' (they were certainly highly informed, motivated and report a sense of achievement), their accounts appear to give support to Ellis's (1994b: 549) conclusion that 'the ability to switch to and fro in attending to meaning and form may be a crucial feature of successful language learning'. Vann and Abraham's (1990) two 'unsuccessful' learners appeared to be restricted to either one or the other. The language learning accounts we have reviewed here all reveal strategic decision-making to 'selectively attend' to grammatical form based on awareness of the trade-offs between form and meaning. 'Selective attention' is here demonstrably a metacognitive strategy, based on the learners' understanding of themselves as learners, of language learning and of possible strategies available to them.

Language learners, then, experience conflicts between the competing demands of focus on form and focus on meaning, as Van Patten (2002b: 757) argues:

> ... learners can only do so much in their working memory before attentional resources are depleted and working memory is forced to dump information to make room for more (incoming) information.

Van Patten's view is that learners' default approach is to prioritise meaning over form and that they will only process form that is not meaningful if they are 'able to process informational or communicative content at no (or little) cost to attention' (Van Patten, 2002b: 758). Adult learners, however, may choose to intentionally side-step these default processing strategies, but this may result in tensions or difficulties, as reported by Murphy (2005: 310) who studied the strategies and learning activities of adult students engaged in distance learning. These learners typically found it highly problematic to be both accurate and communicatively effective in recording their oral assessments, and some found this tension demotivating. Successful learners, though, do seem to find individual ways of resolving the problem of competing attentional demands, employing a range of strategies for developing both accuracy and fluency, while not neglecting either. Ioup *et al.*'s (1994) study of an exceptional naturalistic learner may shed interesting light on this. Their subject, Julie, prioritised communication in her interaction with Arabic but still seems to have acquired native-like grammatical competence. The authors suggest, confirming the good language learner research, that a key factor in her success was her active attention to grammatical form through strategies such as keeping a notebook of language items and observations, including reference to inflectional morphology, making a mental or written note of corrections, and reviewing her notebook entries on a regular basis. However, we should also note a second key factor that Ioup *et al.* believe supported Julie's success: they hypothesise that Julie may have possessed a particular talent for language learning based on 'atypical brain organisation' (Ioup *et al.*, 1994), enabling a more flexible and acute processing of L2 input. Julie may thus have achieved her native-like command through a combination of strategy and talent, this latter interpreted as greater processing capacity and therefore less susceptibility to the kind of form-meaning competition highlighted by Van Patten (2002b).

Ioup *et al.*'s (1994) hypothesis reminds us to be cautious in assuming that the learning strategies employed by demonstrably successful language learners can be used equally effectively by other learners. We may, however, make a tentative generalisation: the successful learners we have discussed in this review were all able to employ the cognitive strategies of rule-searching, note-taking and structuring, hypothesis testing and integrating feedback, firstly within an environment where opportunities for meaningful interaction existed or were created, and secondly, in the context of some probable cognitive advantage to deal with the processing demands of language learning. This cognitive advantage could be either a natural enhanced processing capacity as hypothesised in Julie's case, or, in the case of the applied-linguist-diarists, a learned strategic ability to manage processing demands based on enhanced metacognition. This speculation suggests an important role for metacognitive awareness in the area of grammar, in support of learners' choices – and particularly independent learners' choices – about when and how to focus on grammatical form. This then leads us to consider how researchers in SLA currently conceptualise what developing second language grammatical competence entails and how the balance between focus on form and focus on meaning functions most effectively.

Current Theoretical Frameworks: What Processes are Involved in Developing Second Language Grammar?

The literature on theoretical models of SLA quickly supplies a possible explanation for why little sustained research has been undertaken into grammar-focused learning strategies: it is simply that the process of second language grammatical development is still assumed to be largely beyond direct conscious control (Ellis, 2005: 306; Ellis, 2006: 95; Krashen, 1981: 1). L2 grammatical competence is seen as constituted essentially by implicit knowledge which is developed unconsciously as a result of interaction with meaningful L2 input through a process which Krashen (1981: 1) has dubbed 'acquisition', in opposition to 'learning'. Explicit knowledge that has been developed consciously (Krashen's 'learning') and in particular declarative knowledge of morphosyntactic rules, thus plays a limited role in the development of second language proficiency. Krashen's (1981) Monitor Model first gave prominence to this view, emphasising the separation or 'non-interface' of unconscious (or subconscious) acquisition and conscious learning, and arguing that the latter could only contribute to monitor output, rather than directly supporting spontaneous language use. This downplaying of the learner's conscious involvement clearly conflicts with the view of the effective language learner as consciously managing his or her learning. As O'Malley and Chamot (1990: 10) noted: '... the inescapable conclusion of this model is that conscious use of learning strategies will make little contribution to the development of language competence'.

O'Malley and Chamot's comment may, however, be something of an overstatement. While SLA models may imply that a learner's conscious strategies to control second language syntax and morphology have only limited effect, they imply nothing about the value or otherwise of the learner's metacognitive involvement. Nevertheless, it would be true to say that SLA as a discipline has primarily been focused on specifying internal cognitive *processes* with the learner seen as a mere locus for these processes, rather than as an agent in learning – a point made by researchers viewing SLA from a sociocultural perspective (e.g. Firth & Wagner, 1997; Lantolf & Pavlenko, 2001).

The key question in this debate, then, seems to be the extent to which internal cognitive processes can be consciously manipulated and managed by learners themselves; and if they can, then the extent to which this is facilitative for SLA. Back in 1985, Ellis (1985: 175) noted that the cognitive processes of generating and testing hypotheses about target language form were 'spontaneously activated by the learner while he is focused on some communicative purpose' and were 'typically subconscious procedures', but he also acknowledged that they could be 'conscious, i.e. deliberately activated by the learner with the intention of increasing his L2 knowledge' (Ellis, 1985: 175). Since 1985 there has been sustained challenging of Krashen's non-interface position, with different researchers positing different roles for explicit and implicit knowledge and different relationships between them, but there are few now who put the value of explicit knowledge in doubt (see Ellis, 2005; Ellis, 2006 for overviews) and a body of evidence has been built up to suggest that certainly with adult learners, more explicit pedagogic input can lead to increased learning gains, compared with less explicit input (Ellis, 2006; Ellis *et al.*, 2006; Norris & Ortega, 2000). Below we highlight three key 'interface' positions and draw implications for learners' conscious intervention in their grammatical learning.

Analysis and control

Bialystok (1982, 1983, 1991) has argued over the last 25 years that in the development of second language competence, implicit knowledge built up via induction needs to become gradually more explicit through a process of *analysis*, in order for it to be amenable for use in new and less predictable contexts. In this way, learners' conscious attempts to understand, shape and develop their grammatical competence can contribute significantly to their L2 use and their L2 development. At the same time, all knowledge – both implicit and explicit – needs to be proceduralised through practice in order for it to be accessed effectively in fluent performance; this is Bialystok's dimension of *control*. A similar distinction is drawn by Cummins (1984) between basic interpersonal skills (BICS), which equates to conversational fluency (similar to Bialystok's control) and cognitive academic language proficiency (CALP) which describes language use in decontextualised academic tasks, requiring a proficiency in the analysis of language and a substantially wider lexical range.

In this view, strategies of conscious reflection and personal structuring of language form seem to be significant for developing analysis. Bialystok (1991) also suggests that literacy instruction is important for developing analysis, and that the resulting metalinguistic knowledge has a facilitative effect on reading. This gives weight to arguments put forward to promote computer-mediated-communication (CMC) as a particularly useful environment for second language development. For instance, Salaberry (2000) conducted an experimental study in which a face-to-face oral task was compared to a text-based CMC task and found that first signs of change in developmental stages of grammatical development were more clearly identified in those engaged in the latter task, suggesting that CMC, which uses a written representation of conversational interaction (Salaberry, 2000: 9), may allow for enhanced analysis of grammatical information. However, Bialystok herself pinpoints some of the possible limitations of metalinguistic information:

> Learners who are in the process of explicating and organising linguistic knowledge may profit from forms of instruction which present rules and structures. The limitations of such instruction would be determined by the learner's spontaneous level of analysis, the applicability of the rule to a current problem in the learner's repertoire, and the comprehensibility of the rule as an organising principle for linguistic knowledge. The explicit rule, that is, must be close enough to the learner's emerging representational structure that it can be incorporated into that structure in a meaningful way. The gap between what the learner has spontaneously explicated and what can be provided to the learner as a meaningful principle may be similar to Vygotsky's (1962) 'zone of proximal development'. (Bialystok, 1991: 71)

This would confirm a role for learners to engage in consciously checking their understanding of grammatical rules, in reviewing their use in pair work and, in particular, for independent learners, for participating in the kind of form-focused discussion in a CMC environment that has been reported by Lamy (2006) and Lamy and Hassan (2003). It also confirms the need to encourage students to form their own rules explicitly and to develop skills of language analysis, using for example language corpora as suggested by McEnery *et al.*

> This can lead to students challenging reference works on the basis of their own observations; it is no exaggeration to say that exposure to corpus data turns the student into a researcher. (McEnery *et al.*, 1997)

However, not all learners feel confident about exploring for rules and regularities in this way, particularly not in independent contexts. In a small-scale questionnaire-based action research project, Fortune (1992) identified that in relation to self-study grammar exercises, the preference of a group of EFL students was for deductive exercises where a rule or regularity was identified at the start, and where practice was in the form of a gapped but meaningful text. Rule search or inductive exercises caused anxiety for some lower proficiency learners, although there was greater acceptance and enthusiasm among more advanced learners.

The value of grammatical metalanguage was questioned by Alderson et al.'s (1997) survey of UK university students which found no link between knowledge of metalanguage and ability to use it in analysis in both the L1 and the target language, and levels of target language proficiency among UK university students. However, other quantitative research studies focused on more specific tasks have highlighted a positive role. For instance, Green and Hecht's (1992) study with German university learners of English suggested that if students could state a grammatical rule, they were likely to be able to make accurate corrections. However, many accurate corrections also were made without rule knowledge. Roehr's (2006) study, this time with English university learners of German, found that those with metalinguistic knowledge, as assessed in retrospective verbal protocols, performed more consistently, more confidently and more accurately on a multiple-choice test of adjectival inflection; furthermore, the more complex and precise the metalinguistic knowledge, the more successful the learners were. However, there were a significant number (20%) of inaccurate responses co-occurring with a high level of metalinguistic knowledge. Roehr (2006: 195) concludes: 'high level metalinguistic knowledge may be useful in some circumstances and ineffective or possibly even unhelpful in others'. Nevertheless, work by Basturkmen et al. (2002) and Fortune (2005) suggests that the ability to use and understand grammatical metalanguage is significant in helping learners initiate queries and benefit from responses (change input into uptake), either from experts such as teachers or in the context of learner-to-learner dialogue. Thus, the role of grammatical metalanguage in enabling the strategies Rubin (1981) placed under 'Clarification/Verification' and which in Ellis (1985) enact the process of 'hypothesis testing', seems to have been confirmed by recent research.

The noticing hypothesis

A second position, known as the 'noticing hypothesis' has been developed by Schmidt (1990) triggered by his diary study of learning Portuguese (Schmidt & Frota, 1986: 281), referred to above. Schmidt offers an addition, rather than a complete challenge, to Krashen's Monitor Model by arguing that explicit knowledge can act as a spur to implicit acquisition, in particular in relation to features of the target language which might otherwise be neglected because of their lack of salience in the input or lack of communicative value. Perdue's (1993) study of the interlanguage development of immigrants within the European Community established that naturalistic learners typically develop a lexically-based 'Basic Variety' which lacks much morphology (Klein, 1998: 545), despite many years of exposure to the target language. The conclusion appears to be that implicit acquisition on its own is incapable of developing native-like mastery of such features as non-syllabic verb endings and determiners (see also discussion of Van Patten, 2002b above). Explicit knowledge is thus facilitative, but does not of itself contribute to the development of L2 competence. This position has been developed by Long (1991), who has emphasised that learners' attention should only be drawn to form in the context of meaning-focused activities, ideally through the 'negotiation of input' that occurs naturally in interaction when, for example, asking for clarification of meaning, repeating and recasting unclear or erroneous utterances. In contrast, focusing explicitly on form in a more sustained and decontextualised fashion does not, in Long's view, promote acquisition. One of the problems with Long's attempt to preserve the ecology of natural speech interaction from the pollution of distractions to form is that research suggests that interlocutors may not negotiate meaning in the course of target language interaction (see Foster, 1998 and discussion in Naughton, 2006), and even where they do, learners may not pay enhanced attention. This prompted Naughton (2006) to suggest that strategies for negotiating input may have to be taught to learners. Her study reports how she successfully trained her Spanish learners of English to actively request and give clarification in classroom conversations; it does not, however, give any evidence of whether this supported their language development of non-salient features. Nevertheless, such strategies could be useful devices even for independent learners, for example, in the context of CMC discussions.

According to this view, then, effective language learners actively negotiate meaning while continuing to engage in interaction. They prioritise meaning at all times, but acknowledge passing attention to form. Van Patten (2002a: 243) however specifically suggests that learners need to be helped to overcome their default processing strategy of prioritising meaning over form. Rather than leaving grammatical development to the vagaries of negotiation of input, Van Patten and his associates' experimental results (see Van Patten 2002a, 2002b for review) suggest that carefully structured input where the obvious lexical cues to understanding are removed (e.g. temporal adjectives) in order to trick learners into focusing on less salient morphological features (e.g. verb endings indicating tense) can provide an efficient and effective way of developing grammatical learning. But Van Patten's focus is very much on developing an effective training strategy and, in particular, one which would be suitable for computer-supported independent learning (Van Patten, 2002b: 768). However, it has little to say about the agency of the learner, or whether an independent learner might train *themselves* to overcome 'The Primacy of Meaning' principle.

Language learning as skill learning

The position taken by DeKeyser (1998) and Johnson (1996) is perhaps closest to a mainstream view of learning, that explicit knowledge can become automatised and proceduralised through practice, thus enabling the performance of the complex skill of using the target language. However, as DeKeyser points out, this process may work differentially for different grammatical structures:

> The degree to which structures are most easily learned explicitly through the gradual automatisation of conscious declarative knowledge – as opposed to completely implicitly – depends on the nature of the rule. (DeKeyser, 1998: 57)

Some rules, such as prototypical rules where application depends on a number of factors working together, may just be too complex to learn and use efficiently. In such cases, therefore, it may be better to trust to implicit acquisition. In the case of categorical rules which apply 'across the board', explicit learning and practice may be very effective; there is certainly experimental evidence to support the hypothesis that 'easy' rules can be learned explicitly while 'hard' rules cannot (DeKeyser, 1995; Ellis, 1993; Robinson, 1996). Effective language learners may therefore need to have some understanding of which techniques might work for which areas of language; certainly, such awareness might alleviate the demotivation that many learners experience when they find they cannot understand the rules as laid out in the grammar book, or cannot apply the rules they may have struggled long and hard to understand. This links back to Roehr's finding that metalinguistic knowledge may well help some areas of grammatical development, but not others.

An overview of current models

Finally, Ellis (2005) in his overview of current models of SLA and their underpinning in cognitive psychology research, recognises the psychological plausibility of the active, conscious involvement of the learner in the process of developing second language competence. He reaffirms the central paradox of SLA: 'most learning is implicit; the vast majority of our cognitive process is unconscious' but 'many aspects of a second language are unlearnable – or at best are acquired very slowly – from implicit processes alone' (Ellis, 2005: 306–307). So, adult second language acquisition in places – and morphology in particular seems to be one of those places – is a highly inefficient and ineffective process, unless there is conscious intervention from the teacher or the learner to deliberately direct attention onto non-salient features of the input. As Ellis puts it:

> The remedy is to bring the issue into the light of consciousness. In these situations, some type of explicit instruction or consciousness raising or form-focus can help the learner to notice the cue in the first place, consolidating an explicit construction linking the cue and its interpretation. Explicit instruction can also encourage subsequent use of this cue in processing. (Ellis, 2005: 324)

We then read in Ellis (2005: 329) one of the few portrayals in recent SLA theoretical debate of an active learner. It recalls the good language learner portrait from Rubin (1975, 1981) and Naiman *et al.* (1978) but is supported by renewed research on the value of explicit reflection:

> The more explicit the reasoning, the more likely it is to become productive and generalisable. Learners who observe their own thinking and are encouraged to think through and to give an account of why they consider one answer to be better or worse than another for a particular analogy problem learn better, make more accurate self-assessments of their understanding and use analogies more economically while solving problems. (Ellis, 2005: 329)

Ellis integrates here Bialystok's insistence on the significance of 'analysis', or the capacity to analyse and make explicit one's own reasoning and understanding, together with Schmidt's emphasis on the need to enhance noticing or the deployment of focal awareness in order to complement the processes of implicit induction. Ellis' perspective is that second language learning can be explained by mental processes that are not specific to language learning, but are engaged in all areas of human learning. This view challenges two key assumptions: firstly, that second language learning is necessarily unconscious and secondly, that second language competence is represented in the brain as a special set of rules. Along with DeKeyser (2003: 329), Ellis suggests we rethink our predilection for representing linguistic knowledge as rules. Implicit linguistic knowledge may be better represented by low-level associations between simple processing units organised in networks. Since it seems that many aspects of learning may be explained by simple associative theories within a connectionist model, it is perhaps unnecessary to invoke underlying rule-governed processes. Rules, in that case, are what we create *a posteriori* in order to understand phenomena that may not in fact be rule-governed: they are in other words metacognitive tools.

Conclusion: The Context for Future Research

With the gradual rehabilitation of explicit knowledge in SLA, the proliferation of research on the value of various pedagogic interventions in the area of grammar, and the suggestion that rules are better seen as a product or tool of learning rather than its object, the stage is now set for a renewed focus on learners' own interventions in this area. Work such as that of DeKeyser (2005) on what makes grammatical knowledge 'difficult', and work on learners' processing strategies such as Van Patten (2002a, 2002b) and Carroll (2005) might help us understand better where learners may need to explicitly intervene in their own learning and in what ways. This in turn can inform pedagogic intervention to help promote among learners the strategies they may require to function more effectively and independently in managing their learning in this highly complex area.

References

Alderson, J., Clapham, C. and Steel, D. (1997) Metalinguistic knowledge, language aptitude and language proficiency. *Language Teaching Research* 1, 93–121.

Bailey, K. (1983) Competitiveness and anxiety in adult second language learning: Looking *at* and *through* the diary studies. In H.W. Seliger and M.H. Long (eds) *Classroom Oriented Research in Second Language Acquisition* (pp. 67–103). Rowley, MA: Newbury House Publishers.

Basturkmen, H., Loewen, S. and Ellis, R. (2002) Metalanguage in focus on form in the communicative classroom. *Language Awareness* 11 (1), 1–13.

Bialystok, E. (1981) The role of conscious strategies in second language proficiency. *Modern Language Journal* 65 (1), 24–35.

Bialystok, E. (1982) On the relationship between knowing and using forms. *Applied Linguistics* 3, 181–206.

Bialystok, E. (1983) Inferencing: Testing the 'hypothesis-testing' hypothesis. In H.W. Seliger and M.H. Long (eds) *Classroom Oriented Research in Second Language Acquisition* (pp. 104–123). Rowley, MA: Newbury House Publishers.

Bialystok, E. (1991) Achieving proficiency in a second language: A processing description. In R. Phillipson, E. Kellerman, L. Selinker, M. Sharwood Smith and M. Swain (eds) *Foreign/Second Language Pedagogy Research* (pp. 63–78). Clevedon: Multilingual Matters.

Borg, S. (1999) The use of grammatical terminology in the second language classroom: A qualitative study of teachers' practices and cognitions. *Applied Linguistics* 20, 95–126.

Carroll, S.E. (2005) Input and SLA: Adults' sensitivity to different sorts of cues to French gender. In R. DeKeyser (ed.) *Grammatical Development in Language Learning* (pp. 79–138). Oxford: Blackwell Publishing.

Carson, J.G. and Longhini, A. (2002) Focusing on learning styles and strategies: A diary study in an immerson setting. *Language Learning* 52 (2), 401–438.

Cotterall, S. (2005) 'It's just rules ... that's all it is at this stage ...'. In P. Benson and D. Nunan (eds) *Learners' Stories: Difference and Diversity in Language Learning* (pp. 101–118). Cambridge: Cambridge University Press.

Cummins, J. (1984) *Bilingualism and Special Education*. Clevedon: Multilingual Matters.

DeKeyser, R. (1995) Learning second language grammar rules: An experiment with a miniature linguistic system. *Studies in Second Language Acquisition* 17 (3), 379–410.

DeKeyser, R. (1998) Beyond focus on form: Cognitive perspectives on learning and practising second language grammar. In C. Doughty and J. Williams (eds) *Focus on Form in Classroom SLA* (pp. 42–63). Cambridge: Cambridge University Press.

DeKeyser, R. (2003) Implicit and explicit learning. In C. Doughty and M.H. Long (eds) *The Handbook of Second Language Acquisition* (pp. 313–348). Oxford: Blackwell Publishing.

DeKeyser, R. (2005) What makes learning L2 grammar difficult?: A review of the issues. In R. DeKeyser (ed.) *Grammatical Development in Language Learning* (pp. 1–25). Oxford: Blackwell Publishing.

Ellis, N.C. (1993) Rules and instances in foreign language learning: Interactions of implicit and explicit knowledge. *European Journal of Cognitive Psychology* 5 (3), 289–319.

Ellis, N.C. (2005) At the interface: Dynamic interactions of explicit and implicit language knowledge. *Studies in Second Language Acquisition* 27, 305–352.

Ellis, R. (1985) *Understanding Second Language Acquisition*. Oxford: Oxford University Press.

Ellis, R. (1994a) A theory of instructed SLA. In N.C. Ellis (ed.) *Implicit and Explicit Learning of Languages* (pp. 79–114). London: Academic Press.

Ellis, R. (1994b) *The Study of Second Language Acquisition*. Oxford: Oxford University Press.

Ellis, R. (2006) Current issues in the teaching of grammar: An SLA perspective. *TESOL Quarterly* 40 (1), 83–107.

Ellis, R., Loewen, S. and Erlam, R. (2006) Implicit and explicit corrective feedback and the acquisition of L2 grammar. *Studies in Second Language Acquisition* 28, 339–368.

Firth, A. and Wagner, J. (1997) On discourse, communication, and (some) fundamental concepts in SLA research. *Modern Language Journal* 81 (3), 285–300.

Fortune, A. (1992) Self-study grammar practice: Learners' views and preferences. *English Language Teaching Journal* 46 (2), 160–171.

Fortune, A. (2005) Learners' use of metalanguage in collaborative form-focused L2 output. *Language Awareness* 14 (1), 265–282.

Foster, P. (1998) A classroom perspective on the negotiation of meaning. *Applied Linguistics* 19 (1), 1–23.

Green, P.S. and Hecht, K. (1992) Implicit and explicit grammar: An empirical study. *Applied Linguistics* 13, 168–184.

Hosenfeld, C. (1979) Cora's view of learning grammar. *Canadian Modern Language Review; La revue canadienne des langues modernes* 35 (4), 602–607.

Huang, X. and Van Naerssen, M. (1985) Learning strategies for oral communication. *Applied Linguistics* 6, 287–307.

Ioup, G., Boustangui, E., El Tigi, M. and Mosell, M. (1994) Re-examining the critical period hypothesis: A case study of success SLA in a naturalistic environment. *Studies in Second Language Acquisition* 16, 73–98.

Johnson, K. (1996) *Language Teaching and Skill Learning*. Oxford: Blackwell.

Jones, F.R. (1994) The lone language learner: A diary study. *System* 22 (4), 441–454.

Klein, W. (1998) The contribution of second language acquisition research. *Language Learning* 48, 527–550.

Krashen, S.D. (1981) *Second Language Acquisition and Second Language Learning*. Oxford: Pergamon.

Lamy, M-N. and Hassan, X. (2003) What influences reflective interaction in distance peer learning? Evidence from four long-term on-line learners of French. *Open Learning* 18 (1), 39–59.
Lamy, M-N. (2006) Interactive task design: Metachat and the whole learner. In P. Garcia Mayo (ed.) *Investigating Tasks in Formal Language Settings* (pp. 242–264). Clevedon: Multilingual Matters.
Lantolf, J.P. and Pavlenko, A. (2001) (S)econd (L)anguage (A)ctivity theory: Understanding second language learners as people. In M.P. Breen (ed.) *Learner Contributions to Language Learning: New Directions in Research* (pp. 141–158). London: Longman.
Little, D. (1997) Language awareness and the autonomous language learner. *Language Awareness* 6 (2&3), 93–105.
Long, M.H. (1991) Focus on form: A design feature in language teaching methodology. In K. de Bot, R. Ginsberg and C. Kramsch (eds) *Foreign Language Research in Cross-Cultural Perspective* (pp. 39–52). Amsterdam: John Benjamin.
Mangubhai, F. (1991) The processing behaviours of adult second language learners and their relationship to second language proficiency. *Applied Linguistics* 12 (3), 268–298.
McEnery, A.M., Wilson, A. and Barker, P. (1997) Teaching grammar again after twenty years: Corpus-based help for teaching grammar. *ReCALL* 9 (2), 8–16.
McDonough, S. (1999) Learner strategies. State-of-the-art article. *Language Teaching* 32, 1–18.
Murphy, L. (2005) Attending to form and meaning: The experience of adult distance learners of French, German and Spanish. *Language Teaching Research* 9 (3), 295–317.
Naiman, N., Frohlich, M., Stern, H. and Todesco, A. (1978) *The Good Language Learner*. Toronto: OISE Press.
Naughton, D. (2006) Cooperative strategy training and oral interaction: Enhancing small group communication in the language classroom. *The Modern Language Journal* 90 (2), 169–184.
Norris, J.M. and Ortega, L. (2000) Effectiveness of L2 instruction: A research synthesis and quantitative meta-analysis. *Language Learning* 50, 417–528.
O'Malley, M.J. and Chamot, A.U. (1990) *Learning Strategies in Second Language Acquisition*. Cambridge: Cambridge University Press.
Perdue, C. (ed.) (1993) *Adult Language Acquisition: Cross-linguistic Perspectives*. Cambridge: Cambridge University Press.
Rivers, W. (1981) Learning a sixth language: An adult learner's daily diary. In W.M. Rivers (ed.) *Teaching Foreign Language Skills* (pp. 500–516). Chicago: University of Chicago Press.
Robinson, P. (1996) Learning simple and complex second language rules under implicit, incidental, rule-search and instructed conditions. *Studies in Second Language Acquisition* 19 (2), 233–247.
Roehr, K. (2006) Metalinguistic knowledge in L2 task performance: A verbal protocol analysis. *Language Awareness* 15 (3), 180–198.
Rowsell, L.V. and Libben, G. (1994) The sound of one hand clapping: How to succeed in independent language learning. *Canadian Review of Modern Languages/ La Revue canadienne des langues vivantes* 50, 668–687.
Rubin, J. (1975) What the "Good Language Learner" can tell us. *TESOL Quarterly* 9 (1), 41–53.
Rubin, J. (1981) Study of cognitive processes in second language learning. *Applied Linguistics* 11 (2), 117–131.
Salaberry, M.R. (2000) L2 morphosyntactic development in text-based computer-mediated communication. *Computer Assisted Language Learning* 13 (1), 5–27.

Schmidt, R. (1990) The role of consciousness in second language learning. *Applied Linguistics* 11 (2), 129–158.

Schmidt, R. and Frota, S.N. (1986) Developing basic conversational ability in a second language: A case study of an adult learner of Portuguese. In R. Day (ed.) *Talking to Learn: Conversation in SLA* (pp. 237–327). Cambridge, MA: Newbury House.

Stevick, E.W. (1989) *Success with Foreign Languages*. Hemel Hempstead: Prentice Hall International.

Swain, M. (1998) Focus on form through conscious reflection. In C. Doughty and J. Williams (eds) *Focus on Form in Classroom SLA* (pp. 64–82). Cambridge: Cambridge University Press.

Vann, R.J. and Abraham, R.G. (1990) Strategies of unsuccessful language learners. *TESOL Quarterly* 24 (2), 177–197.

Van Patten, B. (2002a) Processing instruction, prior awareness and the nature of second language acquisition: A (partial) response to Batstone. *Language Awareness* 11 (4), 240–258.

Van Patten, B. (2002b) Processing instruction: An update. *Language Learning* 52, 755–803.

Vygotsky, L.S. (1962) *Thought and Language*. Cambridge, MA: MIT Press.

Wenden, A.L. (1987) Metacognition: An expanded view on the cognitive abilities of L2 learners. *Language Learning* 37 (4), 573–594.

Wenden, A.L. (1998) Metacognitive knowledge and language learning. *Applied Linguistics* 19 (4), 515–537.

Wenden, A.L. (2005) Language learning strategy instruction: Current issues and research. *Annual Review of Applied Linguistics* 25, 112–130.

Chapter 9
Deliberate and *Incidental:* Vocabulary Learning Strategies in Independent Second Language Learning

JOHN KLAPPER

Introduction

For a long time in the history of language education the development of grammatical knowledge took precedence over lexical knowledge, with many applied linguists believing the role of vocabulary was merely to provide context for the learning of structures. More recently, however, especially in L2 learning, vocabulary has come to the fore, with the development of lexical syllabuses and the recognition that vocabulary and grammar are inextricably linked, indeed that lexis takes precedence over sentence grammar in L2 learning (Lewis, 1993, 2002; Willis, 2003).

Of all the different aspects of language learning, vocabulary seems to be the one in which learners apply learning strategies most frequently; this is as true for school-age learners (Chamot, 1987) as it is for older learners (Ohly, 2007). This may be because learners place greatest store by vocabulary or simply because it is easier to apply specific strategies to learning vocabulary than, say, writing or listening.

While much investigative work has been undertaken into vocabulary learning strategies (VLS) in L2 learning in general, there has been surprisingly little research interest in specific aspects of strategy use in independent learning settings. Relevant questions here include the positive impact on VLS use of such factors as controlling one's own learning pace, private rehearsal and practice, and experimentation free from the performance anxiety often associated with the classroom. Conversely, one might ask what negative implications there are for vocabulary development in such features of the independent context as learners' inevitable isolation, the absence of immediate feedback, and the need for self-discipline and self-management. Research is as yet unable to answer such questions satisfactorily and so any discussion of VLS in independent contexts must inevitably draw on studies of strategy use in general L2 learning and interpret these in the light of the factors mentioned above.

After defining what precisely is meant by vocabulary knowledge, this chapter reviews research into vocabulary learning, in particular VLS, and considers its applicability to independent contexts. It describes approaches to categorising VLS, and elaborates explicit and implicit approaches to vocabulary learning, showing the relevance of *both* to the needs of the independent language learner.

'Knowing' a Word

Fundamental distinctions have long been made between 'active' and 'passive' vocabulary and the learning of vocabulary for 'receptive' and 'productive' purposes. Research (e.g. Waring, 1997a) suggests that receptive learning best serves receptive use of vocabulary, while productive learning is more effective for productive use. Nation (2001: 32) sees in these empirical findings evidence to refute the comprehensible input hypothesis, since they suggest that substantial listening and reading are not, on their own, enough to promote productive language use.

The active/passive and receptive/productive distinctions do not, however, tell the whole story about the nature of vocabulary learning since there are often intermediate developmental stages for certain items in our L2 lexical store (Melka Teichroew, 1982):

- some we may have instant access to and automatic use of;
- some we may have instant access to and use of, but we may not be fully aware of how they are used in different contexts;
- some we may have partial access to and slow use of;
- others we may have access to for comprehension but be able to produce the word ourselves only when prompted;
- still others we will only have access to for comprehension.

This suggests that for learners in all contexts, whether wholly independent, semi-independent or interdependent, we should conceive of lexical knowledge as a progressive scale rather than an either/or phenomenon. This is especially so in view of the fact that the whole of our vocabulary knowledge is subject to constant change: if we have learnt a word in only a superficial way, without investing any real effort in it, or if we fail to use or read/hear again a word which we have recently encountered, then the item is likely to move towards the recognition-only end of the memory scale.

Learning a word is thus most definitely not a one-off event. As Schmitt (1998) argues, there is no single moment when we can say we 'know' a word: gaining knowledge of vocabulary is a lengthy, cumulative process, depending on:

(1) knowing the form of the word: its spelling, pronunciation, its constituent parts;
(2) knowing its meaning: the basic concept it represents, its meaning in different contexts, its associations (e.g. other members of the word family);
(3) knowing its use: its grammar, collocations, register and variations or restrictions on use.

(For a readable discussion of these issues, see Taylor, 2003: 10.4).

The active–passive contrast is important in alerting independent learners to the fact that most of the vocabulary encountered in learner manuals at lower levels is intended for active use, but that as proficiency develops, large amounts of the vocabulary encountered will only be required for passive purposes. Without this insight, learners who lack the support of the classroom run the risk of using their learning time ineffectively by seeking deep knowledge of and ready access to low-frequency words.

Besides considering individual words, learners also need to pay attention to lexical 'chunks', multi-word units and collocations (Moon, 1997; Willis, 2003). Widespread use of computerised corpora and concordancing programmes have helped linguists establish patterns of lexical use involving such units and this has led to a variety of recommendations for learning and teaching (e.g. Lewis, 1997). The question of how learners can be helped to acquire these extended lexical items through incidental and intentional learning approaches, and the investigation of the efficacy of such approaches, remain major challenges to the world of pedagogy and language research respectively. This is a significant issue for independent learners whose natural inclination is to focus on discrete lexical units. Access to the types of learning material referred to in Lewis (2002), and exemplified in Lamy and Klarskov Mortensen (2007), along with guidance on their use, are therefore important.

Research into Vocabulary Acquisition

In reviewing research into vocabulary learning one must be careful not to make too strong a distinction between general L2 learning and the specific context of independent language learning. One of the reasons for the dearth of research specifically exploring the latter is that many basic insights apply to all contexts and several approaches to vocabulary learning in general (e.g. vocabulary book work, memorisation) already assume a substantial element of independent learning; a lot of vocabulary is, after all, learnt independently of the classroom.

There has been no shortage of research over the past 20–30 years. Nation's (2001) comprehensive study runs to over 470 pages with about 700 references, while an even greater wealth of references can be found at the following two locations: http://www.vuw.ac.nz/lals/staff/paulnation/vocrefs/index.aspx and www.swan.ac.uk/cals/calsres/varga/.

Implicit and explicit vocabulary learning

Based on research findings from L1 suggesting the primacy of learning from context (Nagy *et al.*, 1985; Swanborn & de Glopper, 1999), it was long assumed that L2 vocabulary learning should focus on repeated exposure and incidental learning rather than direct instruction. The predictable claim of Krashen (1989) for the superiority of incidental vocabulary 'acquisition' over intentional learning is based on the mistaken premise that the development of L2 vocabulary is the same as in L1 (he largely reviews studies relating to L1). This early research assumed that *implicit* learning through exposure to authentic texts and interaction in the target language, was the key factor in expanding vocabulary. It was also thought that *explicit* learning in the structured manner of the language lesson, or the independent learner's conscious focus on memorising word lists, was not possible owing to time constraints. More recent research findings indicate that explicit attention to particular words and the development of varied learner strategies are important complementary approaches to vocabulary acquisition and often lead to better results (Fan, 2003; Hulstijn, 2001; Nation, 2001).

This is in line with the view which has emerged in second language acquisition (SLA) more generally. Although meaning-based syllabuses expose learners to L2 input, they cannot guarantee that learners will actually attend to and *notice* this input. This has prompted an emphasis on 'consciousness-raising', on improving input to promote noticing strategies (Schmidt, 1990; Sharwood Smith, 1993), which is now seen as a prerequisite of acquisition, serving to turn input into 'intake' (Ellis, 1985). Similarly, implicit learning of vocabulary from context undoubtedly plays a role in developing depth of understanding of a lexical item, but the process of moving it along the continuum of knowledge is helped by bringing selective attention to bear on it. Inferring meaning serves an immediate need, it does not fix the word in the mind; this is more effectively achieved via noticing strategies and explicit, systematic learning.

The deliberate learning of vocabulary has thus moved more to centre stage in research since it has been found to promote rapid and durable learning of large numbers of words. However, deliberate learning on its own does not allow knowledge of other aspects of a word to develop: collocations, associated meanings and limitations on use are more effectively learnt through context and meaning-focused work. In summary, explicit and implicit approaches serve to complement each other.

A further important theory of SLA is relevant here. The claim that Krashen's 'comprehensible input' is a necessary but not sufficient condition for the acquisition of a second language (Long, 1981) is supported by Canadian immersion studies, in particular, which suggest that what is also needed is meaning-focused productive work in the form of sustained speaking and writing. The latter 'push' learners to produce 'comprehensible output' (Swain, 1985), giving them the chance to test hypotheses about language and to practise more varied and complex language. Applied to vocabulary, this means that speaking and writing help receptive knowledge of a word develop into more rounded, productive knowledge by increasing the learner's awareness of such features as the word's collocational associates and restrictions on its use. This clearly has implications for independent language learners: it is not enough to see vocabulary learning as a passive activity; to develop true knowledge of a word the independent learner must exploit every opportunity possible to use the item.

Vocabulary learning strategies research

VLS has become a significant area of research into vocabulary. All language learners need to develop and manage the use of appropriate techniques to help them access and learn new words. This is an especially important task for learners in independent settings who have fewer opportunities to benefit from the explicit teaching of vocabulary and limited exposure to teacher direction in strategy development.

Self-management and awareness of how one learns are indeed amongst the key characteristics of effective language learning, according to VLS research. Ahmed (1989), for example, examined the VLS of Sudanese learners of English and found that good learners employed a wider range of strategies than underachieving learners, appreciated the importance of learning words in context, were able to connect new words to those they already knew and used other learners as a resource for vocabulary. Sanaoui (1995) looked at the approaches to vocabulary learning of French L2 learners through a longitudinal case study design. She too found that effective vocabulary learners used various activities to promote learning, that they took responsibility for their work on vocabulary, showing considerable initiative in structuring their learning, seeking varied opportunities for learning and regularly going over and practising L2 words. Lawson and Hogben's (1996) very specific study of the learning of new L2 Italian words in an Australian university context, sought to investigate the relationship between learners' use of strategies and their ability to recall the meaning of the tested items. Once again, successful learners were shown to employ strategies more frequently than less effective ones and also to use a wider range of strategies.

Important questions for research are which strategies are most commonly used and which are likely to prove most effective. In the study just mentioned, Lawson and Hogben reported that the most common approaches were repetition strategies but that, by and large, these were not especially successful; elaboration strategies were more likely to promote successful recall. Ahmed (1989) found good learners tended to make effective use of both monolingual and bilingual dictionaries. Meanwhile, Schmitt (1997) discovered that adult learners were more likely to employ meaning-based strategies than their younger counterparts (schoolchildren) who relied on memorisation and consolidated learning by focusing almost exclusively on word form.

In their major study involving 850 learners, Gu and Johnson (1996) sought to correlate vocabulary size and L2 English proficiency with (reported) use of strategies. It was found that a focus on word form, on written repetition and on memorisation strategies generally, did not correlate well with either of the language measures used in the study. The authors found significant correlations, however, for the following strategy groupings:

- selective attention (knowing which words to focus on);
- self-initiation (i.e. seeking out vocabulary for oneself);
- contextual guessing;
- dictionary look-up;
- extended dictionary strategies (studying examples);
- meaning-oriented note-taking (noting down meanings, linking with synonyms);
- semantic encoding (making associations with known words);
- activation (using the vocabulary learned).

A fundamental notion of vocabulary research is that learning is most effective when it involves 'deep' processing (Craik & Lockhart, 1972), that is where learners have in some way to work at accessing the meaning of the item to be learnt. However, there is considerable evidence to suggest that, in certain circumstances, 'shallow' strategies such as learning by heart or list learning can also prove highly effective (Nation, 2001). Indeed, less proficient learners (see Gu & Johnson, 1996 above) may actually find shallow strategies of greater help since they do not feature distracting contextual material, whereas the context associated with many deep learning activities is often of benefit to more advanced learners.

This idea of strategy use developing over time figures prominently in Schmitt's (1997) study which found that learners' use of some strategies (e.g. written repetition, focus on spelling and the use of paired L2–L1 associate words recorded in lists and on cards) became less important with age, while imaging, association and analysis, that is, forms of deep processing, were used more frequently as learners matured (although it should be noted this was not a longitudinal but a cross-sectional study). Schmitt (1997: 225) hypothesises that 'some learning strategies are more beneficial at certain ages than others, and that learners naturally mature into using different strategies'. This offers clear pointers to future research which will be especially relevant to the needs of independent learners who, on average, tend to be more mature.

Strategy taxonomies

There have been different attempts to categorise VLS, including the aforementioned Gu and Johnson (1996) study, Nation (2001) and Schmitt (1997, 2000). The last of these is based on a large study of Japanese learners of English vocabulary and proposes an extensive taxonomy of 58 strategies, organised largely under Oxford's (1990) well-established general classifications with the addition of a major new category. Schmitt makes a fundamental discovery/consolidation distinction between:

(1) Strategies for the *discovery* of a new word's meaning: these include the categories 'determination' (i.e. discovering the meaning of a new word without reference to another person or authority) and 'social' (i.e. asking others for a definition, paraphrase, synonym or translation).
(2) Strategies for *consolidating* a word once it has been encountered: these include the following Oxford-inspired groupings: 'social'; 'memory' (linking words with known lexical items, employing groupings, images and other mnemonics); 'cognitive' (working directly on words and transforming them in some way to promote understanding and recall); and 'metacognitive' (managing one's vocabulary learning and thinking about how it can be improved, including directing attention, self-management, self-monitoring and self-evaluating).

A potential weakness in this broad division is that several strategies overlap and might be placed under either or both headings; this applies especially to discovery strategies such as analysing affixes and roots, checking for L1 cognates and using word lists, most of which one could also imagine some learners using to consolidate vocabulary. However, given the substantial and varied evidential base for most of his individual strategies (600 learners were surveyed across four distinct groups, including junior high school, high school, university and adult learners), Schmitt's inventory is perhaps the most helpful guide to work in this field.

Strategies for Explicit Vocabulary Learning

Since Schmitt's strategy taxonomy is based on such wide-ranging empirical findings and since it focuses on those conscious, deliberate approaches to both accessing unknown words and retaining learnt items, strategies with which independent learners need particular guidance, this section is structured around his classification. A subsequent section considers how learners can benefit from incidental vocabulary learning.

Determination strategies

Under this heading, two strategies, in particular, have attracted considerable interest: analysing the constituent parts of words and using dictionaries. Both have an important role to play in supporting the work of the independent language learner.

Analysing word parts

Although most work on VLS has focused on the English language, it is pertinent for learners and teachers of languages other than English to remember that English is, in many ways, a lexically atypical language. Its complex patchwork of Anglo-Saxon, Norman French, Latin and Greek means it consists of different 'layers of words' (Nation & Meara, 2002: 48); that is, semantically related words have entered the language at different times and developed distinct nuances and usages. While this is by no means an exclusively English phenomenon, it does seem to be a particular feature of English and it means EFL learners need to develop a variety of strategies to help tackle the large vocabulary that is required to function adequately in educated language use. By contrast, as Nation and Meara (2002: 49–50) point out, other, morphologically richer languages (e.g. German) can change the function of words by adding verbal or adjectival suffixes in a way English cannot, and they can also invent new words by recombining basic words into new compounds. It may be that understanding the way words are formed in such languages and being able to use these processes oneself are as important as having a large vocabulary. English-language approaches to learning large numbers of semantically related but physically dissimilar words may not constitute a perfect model for other languages.

Nation's (2001: 263–281) review of word parts, affixes, word stems and word building skills in English, thus needs to be interpreted carefully for the purposes of other L2s. His general principles for guiding work on these aspects of vocabulary learning are, however, transferable to most contexts:

- work on word parts is likely to be most effective once learners have already met a large number of complex words and learned them as unanalysed wholes;
- learning word parts is a long-term endeavour;

- it is best to work on one affix at a time to avoid interference between items that are similar in terms of either form or function;
- learners should approach receptive and productive work on word parts as a creative, problem-solving activity;
- in the interests of efficiency and productivity, learners should pay attention to only the most frequent stems and affixes;
- learners should learn as unanalysed wholes those complex words which are not based on frequent patterns.

Dictionary use

This is clearly a crucial area for independent language learners since, for many, the dictionary constitutes the principal linguistic authority and source of support. While it is important for all learners to know how best to exploit this resource, effective dictionary strategies are fundamental to learning beyond the classroom.

The past 15 years have seen many empirical studies of the use of lexica in L2 learning, including electronic and online aids (Hulstijn, 1993; Koren, 1997; Laufer & Hill, 2000; Laufer & Kimmel, 1997). This research has shown the old view of the superiority of guessing from context over using a dictionary to be false. In an interesting study, involving reading a text on computer with access to a computerised dictionary, Knight (1994) showed that vocabulary acquisition is best promoted through a combination of inferring word meaning from surrounding context and dictionary use. Given the time-consuming nature of consulting a dictionary, however, a key issue is the independent learner's ability to decide when it is worth looking up a word and when comprehension (and motivation to read further) might be better served by forming a temporary hypothesis based on contextual information. This ability is a much underrated metacognitive sub-strategy.

The question of whether to recommend monolingual or bilingual dictionaries to learners is a long-standing one. It has become conventional to assume that L2 learning should be supported by the near-exclusive use of monolingual lexica, since bilingual dictionaries lead learners to assume a precise word-level correspondence between languages, encourage translation and do not provide sufficient information on how words behave in context (see Baxter, 1980; Hayati, 2005).

However, there are theoretical grounds for thinking that at all levels of learning, including advanced ones, and in all learning contexts, the use of bilingual dictionaries should not be proscribed. The mother tongue has a key role to play in L2 learning (Dodson, 1967, 1985) as L2 learners inevitably use bilingual medium-oriented communication, which involves them contrasting, in private speech, utterances in the two languages and seeking L1 equivalents of L2 utterances they have not fully understood. Furthermore, an interesting finding in Hulstijn (1993) was that high verbal ability students look up a word even though they might have already successfully guessed its meaning from context. This desire to get the precise L1 equivalent of a word is the reason why any insistence on the *exclusive* use of monolingual dictionaries at advanced levels of L2 learning should be considered unsound: learners need to establish all the connotations and nuances of a new utterance, which cannot be done solely through L2 (Hiller, 1981). Since the independent learning context is often characterised by ambiguity and insecurity, one might add that the reassurance provided by a bilingual dictionary is especially important for both the socially and intellectually independent learner.

The development of so-called 'bilingualised' dictionaries in the EFL world, an attempt to link the contextual benefits of monolingual with the translations of bilingual dictionaries, has proved promising (Laufer & Hadar, 1997) but the practice has not spread very rapidly to other L2s. This is to be regretted since such hybrid lexica serve the needs of the independent learner especially well.

Memory strategies

Although not as prevalent amongst independent language learners as dictionary strategies, these deserve a prominent place in the learner's skills portfolio. The two techniques which have been the focus of most research are semantic association and the keyword technique.

Semantic associations

Here a learner might decide to group words by associated meanings: for example, the word 'fine' might be linked to and grouped with 'police', 'law', 'arrest', 'charge', 'court', 'accused', etc. This can lead to the systematic creation of word networks. Since, as schema theory suggests (Anderson *et al.*, 1978), we naturally tend to group words according to sense, semantic webs or networks are a good example of strategies working *with* rather than against the cognitive grain. This 'mind-map' strategy lends itself especially well to the consolidation of lexical items encountered in topic-based learning materials.

The organisation of vocabulary according to semantic interrelations has been encouraged by work on lexical semantics (e.g. Channell, 1988) and it has become a stock-in-trade of many study guide authors. There is not, however, a lot of research evidence to suggest the efficacy of such approaches. While some (e.g. Crow & Quigley, 1985) present a positive picture, others (Tinkham, 1997; Waring, 1997b) indicate potential pitfalls: when similar items are first taught together there is a danger of confusion or 'cross-association', whereby learners, although they may learn the new words' meaning and form, are unable to distinguish the items from each other. This appears to be especially true of opposites ('rough/smooth'), synonyms ('broad/wide') and groups linked by meaning (foods, colours, numbers, body parts).

This is, therefore, an area where the independent learner needs clear guidance since, often prompted by textbooks, many consider a focus on semantic interrelations to be a default learning approach and yet it does not appear to be supported by empirical findings.

Keyword technique

By contrast, this is a well-attested, 'deep' approach which links the form of a word to its meaning. A mother tongue word is chosen that sounds like the L2 item to be learnt and allows the learner to make an association between the two – the more frivolous the association, the better, since one is then more likely to remember it. (In order for the image to be memorable, it is important that the *learner* chooses it him- or herself.) For example, for French *fourmi* ('ant') one might imagine someone giving a Frenchman an ant as a present and him replying in a strong French accent: 'For me?!' (For further examples see the Linkword website, www.linkwordlanguages.com.)

The keyword method has been shown by research over the past thirty years to be superior to all other memory-based methods, including semantic approaches or rote learning (see Hulstijn, 1997; Pressley *et al.*, 1980; Sagarra & Alba, 2006). Studies suggest the method is quick and efficient and that results are typically 25% higher than for ordinary rote learning (Nation & Meara, 2002: 45); once the technique has been mastered, it represents an ideal form of individualised learning for the independent language student.

However, certain provisos need to be added. There are some doubts about long-term retention of words under this method (Wang & Thomas, 1995). The keyword method may also be especially suited to students with a visual learning style, to less-experienced language learners or to those with lower levels of proficiency (Van Hell & Candia Mahn, 1997). Certain areas of vocabulary, especially abstract items (Hall, 1988), do not lend themselves very well to such mnemonic devices as keyword technique. The method also seeks to develop L2–L1 word pairs, and yet retaining a new word in this way is merely the start of a gradual process of deeper familiarisation. Finally, keyword and similar mnemonic devices have proved very successful in learning L1 equivalents of L2 words but considerably less so in learning L2 items, for which simple rote repetition has been shown to be much more effective (Ellis & Beaton, 1993).

Cognitive strategies

The most intensively studied cognitive VLS are word cards, rote learning and rehearsal, and list learning. These strategies are especially relevant to independent learners such as distance learners who lack access to classroom vocabulary reviews and tests.

Word cards

This strategy involves writing an L2 word on one side of a small card and the L1 equivalent on the other. The learner collects a set of cards and looks through the L2 words trying to recall the meaning, turning the card over where this proves too difficult. Nation (2001: 306–308) suggests the quality of learning might be enhanced by such techniques as saying the words out loud to oneself, frequently changing the order of the cards in the pack and putting more difficult ones near the top. This is one of the easiest and most efficient ways for independent learners to become aware of vocabulary so that they notice the words concerned when they meet them subsequently in their listening and reading.

Rote learning and rehearsal

The frequent repetition of new words is an obvious strategy for learning large numbers of L2 words and is one many independent learners adopt almost without thinking. In the 1960s and 1970s, there were a lot of studies of vocabulary rehearsal (reviewed by Nation, 1982) but more recently the focus of research has shifted to deep learning of vocabulary. While one must, of course, note that memory, as a key individual learner difference, can vary from learner to learner, impressive results have been found for the ability to remember L2–L1 word pairs, with one study (Crothers & Suppes, 1967) claiming over 100 Russian–English word pairs were remembered after just seven repetitions. Another interesting finding has been that repeating words out loud is more effective than silent (Kelly, 1992) and written repetition (Gu & Johnson, 1996). As one would expect, retention of rote-learned vocabulary diminishes progressively over time, and periodic rehearsal is therefore paramount.

List learning

Research suggests this is not an especially useful strategy if the order of words on a list cannot be changed (Nation, 2001). In this case, learners would be better splitting a list into groups of four or five words, and learning and testing themselves on each group in turn.

Even though studying word pairs and lists may be strategies with varied success, one should note the 'reassurance' factor of rote learning for those learning largely on their own. Periodic rehearsal of vocabulary in private can serve to reduce the anxiety frequently felt by those learning at a distance.

Metacognitive strategies

Amongst these indirect approaches to vocabulary growth, a key one has been shown to be use of a vocabulary book.

Since learners tend to forget large numbers of words encountered in language work, a formal record which they periodically review seems instinctively to be desirable. Vocabulary books are a good way to promote learner independence and, for those who lack the support of a teacher who recycles vocabulary throughout a taught syllabus, it is a prime support strategy but one which requires discipline and systematicity. How words are recorded is especially important for independent learners who should ideally expand on the meaning of items recorded by supplementing the simple recording of L2–L1 pairs with some graphic representation of how the word is pronounced, information on collocations and semantic associations, and a short contextualising sentence containing the new word. Such elements all help encourage students to learn words in context (Schmitt & Schmitt, 1995).

Strategies for Implicit Learning from Context

In contrast to deliberate strategies, learning from context denotes the incidental learning of vocabulary from reading or listening, in which attention is focused primarily on the message of the text. It can include extensive and intensive reading, listening to stories, watching films or television and participating in conversations. Learning is not intentional and there is usually no conscious focus on language.

As suggested above, early L1-based vocabulary research posited the superiority of implicit learning. Most studies of incidental L2 vocabulary acquisition, however, provide a less positive or at least more ambiguous picture, suggesting considerably fewer gains for learning from context than in L1. While, in one major experiment, substantial lexical gains (76% mastery of the tested items) were found for contextual guessing (Saragi *et al.*, 1978), in a partial replication study, Pitts *et al.* (1989) found only a 7% gain in new items. Other studies (e.g. Haynes, 1993) point to the severe problems many L2 learners encounter when they try to access the meaning of unfamiliar lexical items in a text. Crucially, it also seems that guessing from context does not necessarily lead to long-term retention (Parry, 1993). In general, research indicates that deficient language skills reduce the effectiveness of L2 vocabulary learning from context and, since most studies to date have been conducted with intermediate to advanced L2 learners, this must apply *a fortiori* to lower-level learners. These findings need to inform advice to independent learners, firstly on how they prioritise their learning strategies and secondly on the way they approach reading in L2.

Reading

Despite the move in vocabulary research away from incidental learning, work specifically on L2 reading suggests that learners can gain vocabulary knowledge from meaning-focused encounters with appropriate texts and that learning from context still constitutes a major vocabulary learning strategy.

In addition to the evidence provided by the Saragi *et al.* (1978) and Pitts *et al.* (1989) studies, Day *et al.* (1991), who tested almost 500 EFL learners in Japan, showed that reading for pleasure in L2 improves learners' ability to recognise previously unknown words. Meanwhile Horst *et al.* (1998), in a study involving a graded reader text, found that about 20% of unknown words were learnt to some extent. Such findings are especially important for L2 learners in independent settings who often lack ready access to native speakers and for whom extensive reading is frequently the main source of naturalistic L2 exposure.

One important point concerns the amount of unknown vocabulary learners should be presented with in extensive reading. While in reading for fluency there should be little unknown vocabulary at all, in extensive reading aimed at lexical development, learners, if they are to be able to use contextual clues to guess meaning, need to be familiar with at least 95% and ideally 98% of the words in the text (Hu & Nation, 2000), that is, there should be fewer than one unknown word every two lines.

This highlights the need for a planned reading programme that emphasises controlled extensive reading (Day & Bamford, 1998). The best approach for most learners in independent settings is likely to be the use of graded readers, and Nation and Wang (1999) suggest that L2 learners should be reading at least one graded reader every one to two weeks to ensure exposure to a sufficient volume of vocabulary. The point is that, as several first language studies but also some second language studies (e.g. Fraser, 1999) have demonstrated, learning vocabulary from context is a *gradual* process in which words are not learned through a single encounter but in which repeated meetings with a word serve to build on initial familiarisation and help flesh out the different aspects of knowledge of a word. A well planned graded reader series which systematically recycles new vocabulary is the most effective means of achieving this, but it has to be seen as a long-term endeavour requiring a serious commitment to substantial extensive reading at a vocabulary level appropriate to the individual learner.

Besides engaging in graded reading which controls the number of unknown lexical items, independent learners also need to be reading texts containing concepts with which they are already familiar; in other words, they must have some prior knowledge of the text's subject matter (Huckin & Coady, 1999).

A major qualification of this ringing endorsement of the efficacy of extensive reading is that learners of an L2 with a different orthography (e.g. Russian, Arabic or Chinese) will inevitably find L2 reading more of a struggle, and this will limit their ability to learn from context. More generally, learning from context assumes learners possess a certain basic reading ability and this is clearly less likely to be the case with near beginners.

Getting the balance right

There is research evidence to indicate that incidental learning from context is inadequate on its own for the promotion of vocabulary development, and that it should be supplemented by selective attention to direct or decontextualised learning of vocabulary. Fraser (1999) suggests the ability to infer successfully from context is particularly enhanced by finding and noting an L1 equivalent or synonym and by consulting a dictionary as a follow-up to inferring – a strategy which led to an almost 100% improvement in retention (see also Hulstijn, 1993). Other studies too suggest that a combination of intentional and incidental learning, of direct and indirect approaches to vocabulary, is likely to yield better results than learning exclusively from context (Paribakht & Wesche, 1997; Nation, 2001) and that supplementing incidental work with glossing (Watanabe, 1997) and more demanding tasks such as re-narrating what has been read will increase the number of words learnt (Joe, 1998; Laufer & Hulstijn, 2001). Indeed, there is an increasing awareness that the choice and effectiveness of vocabulary learning strategies in general depend very much on a combination of task, learner and context (Gu, 2003).

Conclusion

Vocabulary is no longer the 'Cinderella' of language learning (Meara, 1980). Considerable research has been undertaken into the earlier assumption of the superiority of incidental learning from context. Work on good L2 learners' direct study of vocabulary in input-poor environments (Kouraogo, 1993) shows the added value of such an approach, increasing not just recognition but also retention and active vocabulary use. However, it is fair to say that extensive reading remains an essential co-requisite of a deliberate focus on determination, social, memory, cognitive and metacognitive vocabulary strategies.

This chapter has shown that the most effective learners of vocabulary tend to employ a range of strategies, often a mixture of direct and indirect ones, and it would be foolish to emphasise one type over the other. Nation's (2005: 585) championing of a four-strand approach of meaning-focused input, meaning-focused output, deliberate study and fluency-focused activity, thus seems a balanced and empirically justified prescription.

Research into VLS has started to respond in recent years to the growing acceptance that strategy use amongst learners is a dynamic process, with learners making varied metacognitive decisions, deploying different mnemonic, social and cognitive strategies in response to different tasks. However, it is clear that such decisions are heavily dependent on the learner and that strategy use is closely related to individual differences, such as age, motivation and proficiency levels, and to individual learning styles. Differing learning contexts (classroom, semi-independent, distance) are also likely to influence both the nature and effectiveness of strategy use (Gu, 2003). Now that empirical work on VLS has largely exhausted the subject of strategy *types*, this area of inquiry seems to be the key one for future research.

Arguably, by its very nature, much vocabulary learning is primarily an independent learning activity. Thus, although the absence to date of specific empirical studies into independent language learners' strategy use is regrettable, research on VLS in L2 learning in general has many relevant lessons for independent learners. In the light of this research, they are advised to sample as many different strategies as possible and in particular to balance the use of deliberate VLS with ample opportunities for incidental learning from context. Profiting from their experiences of using such strategies, learners need to decide which best suit their individual learning style and ensure they employ the resulting range of strategies consistently and methodically.

References

Ahmed, M.O. (1989) Vocabulary learning strategies. In P. Meara (ed.) *Beyond Words* (pp. 3–14). London: British Association for Applied Linguistics (BAAL) in association with The National Centre for Languages (CiLT).

Anderson, R.C., Spiro, R.J. and Anderson, H.C. (1978) Schemata as scaffolding for the representation of information in connected discourse. *American Educational Research Journal* 15, 433–440.

Baxter, J. (1980) The dictionary and vocabulary behavior: A single word or a handful? *TESOL Quarterly* 14, 325–336.

Chamot, A.U. (1987) The learning strategies of ESL students. In A. Wenden and J. Rubin (eds) *Learner Strategies in Language Learning* (pp. 71–83). Englewood Cliffs, NJ: Prentice Hall.

Channell, J. (1988) Psycholinguistic considerations in the study of L2 vocabulary acquisition. In R. Carter and M. McCarthy (eds) *Vocabulary and Language Teaching* (pp. 83–96). London: Longman.

Craik, F. and Lockhart, R. (1972) Levels of processing: A framework for memory research. *Journal of Verbal Learning and Verbal Behavior* 11, 671–684.

Crothers, E. and Suppes, P. (1967) *Experiments in Second-language Learning*. New York: Academic Press (cited in Gu, 2003).

Crow, J.T. and Quigley, J.R. (1985) A semantic field approach to passive vocabulary acquisition for reading comprehension. *TESOL Quarterly* 19, 497–513.

Day, R.R. and Bamford, J. (1998) *Extensive Reading in the Second Language Classroom*. Cambridge: Cambridge University Press.

Day, R.R., Omura, C. and Hiramatsu, M. (1991) Incidental EFL vocabulary learning and reading. *Reading in a Foreign Language* 7, 541–551.

Dodson, C.J. (1967) *Language Teaching and the Bilingual Method*. London: Pitman.

Dodson, C.J. (1985) Second language acquisition and bilingual development: A theoretical framework. *Journal of Multilingual and Multicultural Development* 6, 325–346.
Ellis, R. (1985) *Understanding Second Language Acquisition.* Oxford: Oxford University Press.
Ellis, N.C. and Beaton, A. (1993) Psycholinguistic determinants of foreign language vocabulary learning. *Language Learning* 43, 559–617.
Fan, M.Y. (2003) Frequency of use, perceived usefulness, and actual usefulness of second language vocabulary strategies: A study of Hong Kong learners. *Modern Language Journal* 87, 222–241.
Fraser, C.A. (1999) Lexical processing, strategy use and vocabulary learning through reading. *Studies in Second Language Acquisition* 21, 225–241.
Gu, Y. (2003) Vocabulary learning in a second language: Person, task, context and strategies. *TESL-EJ* 7, 1–26. On WWW at http://www-writing.berkely.edu/TESL-EJ/ej26/a4.html. Accessed 27.03.07.
Gu, Y. and Johnson, K. (1996) Vocabulary learning strategies and language learning outcomes. *Language Learning* 46, 643–679.
Hall, J.W. (1988) On the utility of the keyword mnemonic for vocabulary learning. *Journal of Educational Psychology* 80, 554–562.
Hayati, A.M. (2005) A comparative study of using bilingual and monolingual dictionaries in the reading comprehension of intermediate EFL students. *The Reading Matrix* 5, 61–66.
Haynes, M. (1993) Patterns and perils of guessing in second language reading. In T. Huckin, M. Haynes and J. Coady (eds) *Second Language Reading and Vocabulary Learning* (pp. 46–64). Norwood, NJ: Ablex Publishing Corporation.
Hiller, U. (1981) Der Semantisierungsprozeß im Zweitsprachenerwerb. *Neusprachliche Mitteilungen aus Wissenschaft und Praxis* 34, 144–152.
Horst, M., Cobb, T. and Meara, P. (1998) Beyond a clockwork orange: Acquiring second language vocabulary through reading. *Reading in a Foreign Language* 11, 207–223.
Hu, M. and Nation, I.S.P. (2000) Vocabulary density and reading comprehension. *Reading in a Foreign Language* 13, 403–430.
Huckin, T. and Coady, J. (1999) Incidental vocabulary acquisition in a second language: A review. *Studies in Second Language Acquisition* 21, 181–193.
Hulstijn, J.H. (1993) When do foreign-language readers look up the meaning of unfamiliar words?: The influence of task and learner variables. *Modern Language Journal* 77, 139–147.
Hulstijn, J.H. (1997) Mnemonic methods in foreign language vocabulary learning. In J. Coady and T. Huckin (eds) *Second Language Vocabulary Acquisition: A Rationale for Pedagogy* (pp. 203–224). Cambridge: Cambridge University Press.
Hulstijn, J.H. (2001) Intentional and incidental second language vocabulary learning: A reappraisal of elaboration, rehearsal, and automaticity. In P. Robinson (ed.) *Cognition and Second Language Instruction* (pp. 258–286). Cambridge: Cambridge University Press.
Joe, A. (1998) What effect do text-based tasks promoting generation have on incidental vocabulary acquisition? *Applied Linguistics* 19, 357–377.
Kelly, P. (1992) Does the ear assist the eye in the long-term retention of lexis? *IRAL* 30, 137–145.
Knight, S. (1994) Dictionary use while reading: The effects on comprehension and vocabulary acquisition for students of different verbal abilities. *Modern Language Journal* 78, 285–299.

Koren, S. (1997) Quality versus convenience: Comparison of modern dictionaries from the researcher's, teacher's and learner's points of view. *TESL-EJ* 2, 1–16.

Kouraogo, P. (1993) Language learning strategies in input-poor environments. *System* 21, 165–173.

Krashen, S. (1989) We acquire vocabulary and spelling by reading: Additional evidence for the input hypothesis. *The Modern Language Journal* 24, 237–270.

Lamy, M-N. and Klarskov Mortensen, H.J. (2007) *Using Concordance Programs in the Modern Foreign Languages Classroom*. ICT4LT module. On WWW at http://www.ict4lt.org/en/en_mod2-4.htm. Accessed 25.06.07.

Laufer, B. and Hadar, L. (1997) Assessing the effectiveness of monolingual, bilingual and 'bilingualised' dictionaries in the comprehension and production of new words. *The Modern Language Journal* 81, 189–196.

Laufer, B. and Hill, M. (2000) What lexical information do L2 learners select in a CALL dictionary and how does it affect word retention? *Language Learning and Technology* 3, 58–76.

Laufer, B. and Hulstijn, J. (2001) Incidental vocabulary acquisition in a second language: The construct of task-induced involvement. *Applied Linguistics* 22, 1–26.

Laufer, B. and Kimmel, M. (1997) Bilingualised dictionaries: How learners really use them. *System* 25, 361–369.

Lawson, M.J. and Hogben, D. (1996) The vocabulary-learning strategies of foreign-language students. *Language Learning* 46, 101–135.

Lewis, M. (1993) *The Lexical Approach*. Hove: Language Teaching Publications.

Lewis, M. (1997) Pedagogical implications of the lexical approach. In J. Coady and T. Huckin (eds) *Second Language Vocabulary Acquisition: A Rationale for Pedagogy* (pp. 255–270). Cambridge: Cambridge University Press.

Lewis, M. (2002) *Implementing the Lexical Approach: Putting Theory into Practice*. Boston, MA: Heinle.

Long, M. (1981) Input, interaction and second language acquisition. *Annals of the New York Academy of Sciences* 379, 259–278.

Meara. P. (1980) Vocabulary acquisition: A neglected aspect of language learning. *Language Teaching and Linguistics Abstracts* 13, 221–246.

Melka Teichroew, F.J. (1982) Receptive vs. productive vocabulary: A survey. *Interlanguage Studies Bulletin* (Utrecht) 6, 5–33 (cited in Nation, 2001).

Moon, R. (1997) Vocabulary connections: Multi-word items in English. In N. Schmitt and M. McCarthy (eds) *Vocabulary: Description, Acquisition and Pedagogy* (pp. 40–63). Cambridge: Cambridge University Press.

Nagy, W.E., Herman, P. and Anderson, R.C. (1985) Learning words from context. *Reading Research Quarterly* 20, 233–253.

Nation, I.S.P. (1982) Beginning to learn foreign vocabulary: A review of the research. *RELC Journal* 13, 14–36.

Nation, I.S.P. (2001) *Learning Vocabulary in Another Language*. Cambridge: Cambridge University Press.

Nation, I.S.P. (2005) Teaching and learning vocabulary. In E. Hinkel (ed.) *Handbook of Research in Second Language Teaching and Learning* (pp. 581–595). Mahwah, NJ: Lawrence Erlbaum Associates.

Nation, I.S.P. and Meara, P. (2002) Vocabulary. In N. Schmitt (ed.) *An Introduction to Applied Linguistics* (pp. 35–54). London: Arnold.

Nation, I.S.P. and Wang, K. (1999) Grade readers and vocabulary. *Reading in a Foreign Language* 12, 355–380.

Ohly, K. (2007) Language learning strategies: A study of older learners of German at the university of the third age. Unpublished PhD dissertation, The Open University.

Oxford, R. (1990) *Language Learning Strategies: What Every Teacher Should Know.* Boston, MA: Heinle and Heinle.

Paribakht, T.S. and Wesche, M. (1997) Vocabulary enhancement activities and reading for meaning in second language vocabulary acquisition. In J. Coady and T. Huckin (eds) *Second Language Vocabulary Acquisition: A Rationale for Pedagogy* (pp. 174–199). Cambridge: Cambridge University Press.

Parry, K. (1993) Too many words: Learning the vocabulary of an academic subject. In T. Huckin, M. Haynes and J. Coady (eds) *Second Language Reading and Vocabulary Learning* (pp. 109–129). Norwood, NJ: Ablex Publishing Corporation.

Pitts, M., White, H. and Krashen, S. (1989) Acquiring second language vocabulary through reading: A replication of the Clockwork Orange study using second language acquirers. *Reading in a Foreign Language* 5, 271–275.

Pressley, M., Levin, J., Hall, J., Miller, G. and Berry, J. (1980) The keyword method and foreign language acquisition. *Journal of Experimental Psychology: Human Learning and Memory* 6, 163–173.

Sagarra, N. and Alba, M. (2006) The key is in the keyword: L2 vocabulary learning methods with beginning learners of Spanish. *The Modern Language Journal* 90, 228–243.

Sanaoui, R. (1995) Adult learners' approaches to learning vocabulary in second languages. *Modern Language Journal* 79, 15–28.

Saragi, T., Nation, P. and Meister, G. (1978) Vocabulary learning and reading. *System* 6, 70–78.

Schmidt, R. (1990) The role of consciousness in second language learning. *Applied Linguistics* 11, 17–46.

Schmitt, N. (1997) Vocabulary learning strategies. In N. Schmitt and M. McCarthy (eds) *Vocabulary: Description, Acquisition and Pedagogy* (pp. 199–227). Cambridge: Cambridge University Press.

Schmitt, N. (1998) Tracking the incremental acquisition of second language vocabulary: A longitudinal study. *Language Learning* 48, 281–317.

Schmitt, N. (2000) *Vocabulary in Language Teaching.* Cambridge: Cambridge University Press.

Schmitt, N. and Schmitt, D. (1995) Vocabulary notebooks: Theoretical underpinnings and practical suggestions. *English Language Teaching Journal* 49, 133–143.

Sharwood Smith, M. (1993) Input enhancement in instructed SLA: Theoretical bases. *Studies in Second Language Acquisition* 15, 165–179.

Swain, M. (1985) Communicative competence: Some roles of comprehensible input and comprehensible output in its development. In S.M. Gass and C.G. Madden (eds) *Input in Second Language Acquisition* (pp. 235–253). Rowley, MA: Newbury House.

Swanborn, M. and de Glopper, K. (1999) Incidental word learning while reading: A meta-analysis. *Review of Educational Research* 69, 261–285.

Taylor, L. (2003) *Teaching Vocabulary.* DELPHI distance-learning module. On WWW at http://www.delphi.bham.ac.uk. Accessed 16.04.07.

Tinkham, T. (1997) The effects of semantic and thematic clustering on the learning of second language vocabulary. *Second Language Research* 13, 138–163.

Van Hell, J.G. and Candia Mahn, A. (1997) Keyword mnemonics versus rote rehearsal: Learning concrete and abstract foreign words by experienced and inexperienced learners. *Language Learning* 47, 507–546.

Wang, A.Y. and Thomas, M.H. (1995) Effect of keywords on long-term retention: Help or hindrance? *Journal of Educational Psychology* 87, 468–475.

Waring, R. (1997a) A comparison of the receptive and productive vocabulary sizes of some second language learners. *Immaculata (Notre Dame Seishin University, Okayama)* 1, 53–68 (cited in Nation, 2001).

Waring, R. (1997b) The negative effects of learning words in semantic sets: A replication. *System* 25, 261–274.

Watanabe, Y. (1997) Input, intake and retention: Effects of increasing processing on incidental learning of foreign vocabulary. *Studies in Second Language Acquisition* 19, 287–307.

Willis, D. (2003) *Rules, Patterns and Words: Grammar and Lexis in English Language Teaching.* Cambridge: Cambridge University Press.

Chapter 10
Strategies for Acquiring Intercultural Competence

INMA ÁLVAREZ, TITA BEAVEN and CECILIA GARRIDO

Introduction

In the past few decades, language and culture have been placed at the heart of foreign language education by many scholars (Damen, 1987; Galloway, 1999; Jones, 2000; Kramsch, 1998; Van Ek, 1986). Language learning has increasingly focused on the development of both linguistic and cultural fluency, as the one does not necessarily imply the other. It is possible for progress in foreign language proficiency to take place separately from knowledge and understanding of another culture. However, it is increasingly felt that to communicate effectively across cultures a speaker 'needs the right mix of linguistic, sociolinguistic, socio-cultural and strategic competences' (Álvarez & Garrido, 2001: 152). Despite this recognised critical intersection between language and culture, Cohen *et al.* (2005: 16) have pointed out that language students aim to acquire linguistic proficiency but still 'lack strategies for culture learning and do not have a coherent overall plan for learning the culture or developing intercultural communication skills'.

This situation is not surprising since there has been little guidance on the learning of strategies and development of skills for intercultural communication. The specification of intercultural objectives in language programmes, that is, those that aim to bridge gaps between the target culture and one's own culture, rarely include specific training in cultural and intercultural strategies and, much less so, explicit training in integrated language, cultural and intercultural strategy learning and use. As Willems (2002: 10) has described, interculturality is a complex 'moral-ethical' dimension of foreign language education that requires '*knowledge* (of cultural factors), *insight* (into what constitutes cultural identity), *readiness* (towards opening up to cultural differences) and *skills* (in negotiating "common territory" and identifying and bridging gaps)'. Moreover, the widely adopted formula 'intercultural communicative competence' (Byram, 1997) recognises the challenge of incorporating this dimension into language education. In addition to knowledge of other cultures, an open attitude towards others, together with skills for interpreting and relating and skills for discovery and interaction, learners need to develop a critical cultural awareness that helps them to reflect on their own values as well as those of others in the target culture(s). They also need to develop strategies to compensate for the linguistic or cultural gaps that may arise in intercultural exchanges. Research in this field so far has identified the different skills that will enable a language learner to become an effective intercultural speaker but has not explored to any great extent the strategies that learners need to acquire and use in the process of learning how to communicate competently across cultures. (See Chapter 7 on the use of strategies to develop pragmatic ability.)

This chapter highlights the dearth of research evidence in this field, and also explores two key areas: (1) general learning strategies which can help language learners acquire intercultural competence, and (2) the ways in which language learners can familiarise themselves with other cultures and, more importantly, establish an effective dialogue with them. In the second half, we discuss examples of strategies that can help language learners become more independent and exercise control over their intercultural development.

Culture and Language Learning

For well over a decade now, there has been an emphasis on incorporating an intercultural dimension into the general objectives of language programmes, but there has been less focus on skills development for learning about other cultures and communicating and interacting effectively with target language speakers. Moreover, language and cultural strategies have rarely been described as linked concepts, but rather as separate, as 'the conscious and semi-conscious thoughts and behaviours used by learners to improve their knowledge and use of a target language (TL) on the one hand, and their understanding and functional use of all that is culture on the other' (Cohen *et al.*, 2005: 17). The inclusion of the cultural dimension in language education clearly demands a complex strategies-based approach that acknowledges the integration of both in the process of becoming competent in learning and interacting effectively in the target language and culture.

Byram's (1997) definition of intercultural communicative competence in the context of language learning has been widely recognised and used. His model is based on the mastery of a set of factors that combine:

- knowledge (*savoir*);
- attitudes (*savoir être*);

- skills that allow the speakers to learn, discover and interpret the target culture (*savoir comprendre*), relate it to their own (*savoir apprendre*), interact with it (*savoir faire*), and at the same time develop critical cultural awareness (*savoir s'engager*).

Knowledge includes learning about social groups, products, practices and processes of interaction. Attitudes involve curiosity and openness towards the other as well as readiness to revise cultural values and beliefs, and to interact and engage with 'otherness'. Skills of interpreting and relating mean being able to identify and explain cultural perspectives and mediate between them. Skills of discovery and interaction refer to the ability to identify, understand and function in new cultural contexts. Intercultural competence also involves the ability to evaluate critically against explicit criteria. In brief, intercultural competence can be summed up as 'an ethical orientation in which certain morally "right" ways of being, thinking and acting are emphasised' (Jokikokko, 2005: 79). The development of intercultural (and not just linguistic) competence enables individuals to be better equipped to communicate successfully with other speakers.

One of the crucial impacts of the intercultural approach has been its criticism of the old model of language competence based on the approximation of the foreign language learner to the native speaker. It has exposed the difficulties that arise when trying to define a native speaker: are native speakers native by birthright or by adoption into a community, or by education? The intercultural trend in language education has proposed that language learners, instead of trying to imitate a native speaker, an ideal impossible to define and reach, should become 'intercultural speakers' (e.g. Byram, 1997; Kramsch, 1998). An intercultural speaker is an individual 'aware of a constant process of formation and transformation: culture is not a given but constituted in the everyday practices of groups and individuals' (Roberts *et al.*, 2001: 30). Most importantly, being an intercultural speaker 'must be accompanied by an increased sense of personal and individual responsibility' (Kramsch, 1998: 31).

From this perspective, language learning is not about trying to sound and be like a native speaker but rather about taking conscious steps to communicate efficiently in intercultural situations. Language learners need to understand that increasing their intercultural awareness and actively engaging with other cultures will gradually increase their intercultural communicative competence.

This shift of focus from the narrow aim of becoming language proficient to the wider goal of acquiring intercultural competence allows learners more freedom to shape their language identities in their own and other cultures. As Bateman (2002: 320) explains, 'the process of learning to understand one's own and other cultural viewpoints challenges learners' sense of self, their cultural identity, and their worldview. As a result, they may experience a lasting change in self-concept, attitudes, and behaviour, which ideally results in greater openness towards individuals of other cultures and an increased desire to interact with them'.

Training in intercultural strategies is a direct way to support that process and should include strategies which enable language learners to grow a 'cross-cultural mind' (Galloway, 1999), in other words, to develop intercultural communicative competence *and* become an effective autonomous intercultural speaker. Intercultural strategies range from those that focus on developing knowledge and understanding of one's own culture and that of others, to those that develop the capacity to interpret other cultural manifestations and assess their representation in one's own cultural repertoire. Autonomous intercultural speakers are confident negotiators and mediators as well as competent constructors of new language identities. The next section explores the extent to which existing models for learning strategies can accommodate the demands of the intercultural dimension.

Learning Strategies

There are a number of competing definitions and classifications of learning strategies, and there seems to be no consensus about how many strategies are available to learners when learning a foreign language (Hsiao & Oxford, 2002) or indeed about how to best define and classify these strategies, with different and often competing models being proposed (e.g. O'Malley & Chamot, 1990; Oxford, 1990; Rubin, 1981). The four categories of strategies more commonly used (Cohen *et al.*, 1996; O'Malley & Chamot, 1990; Oxford, 1990) are: cognitive, metacognitive, social and affective. A full account of these various groups of strategies and of their relative importance in independent language learning can be found in Chapters 1 and 3.

The taxonomy of strategies for acquiring intercultural competence is not as well researched and developed as that of the general language learning field, and the strategies identified do not always map clearly onto the four areas of cognitive, metacognitive, social and affective. There is a need for further research to be carried out on how to define what constitutes good intercultural strategies, and to ascertain whether some of the findings about language learning strategies are also relevant to the development of the skills needed for successful intercultural communication and mutual understanding.

Some of the questions that were asked in the early days of strategy research would need to be reviewed in this new context, for example: Do intercultural strategies aid language and culture learning? Can they be taught? Are there 'good' and 'bad' universal intercultural strategies? or, to paraphrase Cohen (1998), even if we cannot say that some strategies are inherently good or bad, how can they fulfil their potential of being used effectively? Does intercultural strategy training affect language and culture learning directly, or is it just a way of improving sensitivity and motivation? Similarly, it remains to be seen whether inappropriate learning strategy use can be useful in explaining poor language learning results, and whether this is also applicable to strategies for intercultural communication.

The next section focuses on the type of strategies that might specifically help students to develop intercultural competence.

Learning How to Learn about Other Cultures

Cross-cultural awareness in foreign language education entails an understanding of the nature of culture rather than a mere accumulation of cultural facts (Knutson, 2006). Traditional models of culture learning have tended to view culture as a body of knowledge to be learned (e.g. social practices, cultural institutions, habits, etc.), or as a set of culturally appropriate behaviours to be understood and mastered. As mentioned above, a more recent constructivist perspective (Roberts *et al.*, 2001) sees culture from a somewhat different viewpoint: culture, it is argued, is constructed by people in their everyday lives, and language is the chief instrument in this endeavour; it is therefore necessary for learners to be aware of the fact that they will not just *acquire* cultural knowledge but that they will also *construct* it. Therefore, it can be argued that it is more appropriate to focus on strategic approaches to culture learning rather than on specific cultural elements (Damen, 1987). So the issue here is not simply that of learning about unfamiliar cultures but also of learning to construct other cultural realities.

Two essential premises should be the basis of any cultural learning: on the one hand, the acceptance that there are different cultural realities and that one's own background has a very important role to play in finding out about the 'other' culture; on the other, that cultural patterns evolve with the passage of time.

Until fairly recently it was assumed that language learning brought the target cultures to the learner (Lixian & Cortazzi, 1998) without much consideration for the fact that learners also bring their own cultural input to the language interaction. Individuals have their own view of who they are and where they are located, their own 'constructed realities', that is they have 'ways of perceiving self and others, sets of assumptions and expectations, beliefs and values and meanings' (Galloway, 2001: 9), which they inevitably bring with them to any encounter with other languages and cultures. Moreover, it is argued that these realities are in flow, that 'cultural stance or disposition are not fixed, or even stable phenomena' (Knutson,

2006: 594); so our experiences with the language of the cultural other are in constant evolution. This adds to the challenge of becoming an intercultural speaker, but if strategies for intercultural communication are applied, each exchange should give rise to enhanced intercultural interaction.

The strategies that develop our capacity for cultural learning can be described as practices that aim at capturing, understanding, reflecting on, preserving and recalling cultural information. They are mostly of a cognitive and metacognitive nature, although social and affective strategies are inevitably involved. Their activation will contribute to the ability to construct culturally diverse worlds, which significantly affects how learners interact with others.

As we will see in the next section, in order to interact effectively, individuals need to be able to learn how to negotiate meaning (Bateman, 2002) as well as how to reflect critically on themselves (Byram, 1997), key practices that will help them to become true intercultural speakers.

Learning How to Engage with People from Other Cultures

In addition to culture *learning* strategies that raise self-awareness and help to overcome cultural difficulties and differences, learners also need *use* strategies that apply the acquired cultural knowledge, that is, learning techniques that facilitate interaction with those from a different culture. We refer here to the actions learners carry out as intercultural speakers drawing on their intercultural communicative competence (i.e. knowledge, skills and attitudes) in order to engage in a cross-cultural situation. The approaches below all point to learning strategies that move from the achievement of linguistic competence to a dialogue between cultures.

Galloway (2001: 32) has suggested that the focus should be on activities that help students 'activate their own cultural framework while at the same time becoming sensitised to the possibility that other cultures may have other preferences and other ways, arising from other perspectives'. But as Byram's *savoirs* imply, in order to learn to be strategic in their practice of intercultural communicative competence, students need to develop their attitudes beyond intercultural sensitivity, learn how to engage critically with otherness and have a successful dialogue with members of a foreign culture.

The Council of Europe's (2001: 25) *Common European Framework of Reference* (CEF), describes strategies as 'a hinge between the learner's resources (competences) and what he/she can do with them (communicative activities)'. The Framework highlights the importance of interaction strategies, grouping them into reception and production strategies on the one hand, and cognitive strategies and collaborative strategies (or discourse and cooperation strategies) on the other. Reception and production strategies support interaction through processes such as the identification and inference of contexts and relevant knowledge, rehearsing situations, making adjustments according to linguistic competence, etc.

However, it is not difficult to realise that it is collaboration during interaction where intercultural proficiency is best demonstrated since when we interact with each other we co-create meanings that can either bring us closer together or separate us.

According to the CEF (Council of Europe, 2001: 73), cognitive and collaborative strategies involve the management of co-operation and interaction. This process implies a framework that goes from the planning of the interaction, through to the evaluation and adjustments that need to be made to re-establish communication if it has been impeded for one reason or another. Table 10.1 summarises the strategies included in the process, as outlined in the CEF.

Table 10.1 Common European Framework of Reference (CEF) strategies

Planning	
Framing	Thinking of the probable exchanges
Identifying information/opinion gap	Considering how close, in communicative terms, the interlocutors are and what the likely differences/similarities of views may be
Judging what can be presupposed	
Planning moves	Deciding how to approach the different scenarios
Execution	
Taking the floor	Turntaking to obtain the discourse initiative
Cooperating	Collaborating to keep the discussion on course
Dealing with the unexpected and asking for help	So that there is a proactive attitude from the speaker to maintain the lines of communication open even in difficult exchanges
Evaluation	
Monitoring	Judging what is happening in relation to what was planned and how effective the strategy has been
Repair	
Asking or giving clarification	To avoid miscomprehension or ambiguity
Communication repair	Active intervention to re-establish communication and clear up misunderstandings

A similar approach with a different emphasis is offered by Savignon and Sysoyev (2002: 513), who refer to the need to train language learners in how to use sociocultural strategies which prepare them for 'interaction with unfamiliar cultures in unpredictable communicative situations' (e.g. seeking emergency health care, dealing with an impromptu offer of hospitality). Within these strategies they differentiate between strategies for establishing and maintaining intercultural contact and strategies for creating sociocultural portraits (of context and participants) in intercultural communication.

Finally, a crucial factor in cross-cultural communicative interaction is the ability to negotiate meaning, that is, to negotiate a 'place' in order to 'achieve more than either could achieve on their own' (Galloway, 2001: 55), an aspect that has been surprisingly neglected in studies focusing on strategy instruction in oral communication (Nakatani, 2005). More recently Littlemore (2003) has addressed the issue of strategies that enable the negotiation of meaning during social interaction. In her analysis of different types of communication strategies, Littlemore explains that these can be subdivided into two main categories: interactional and compensation strategies. On the one hand, interactional strategies involve the manipulation of conversations and negotiation of meaning (e.g. back channelling, subject manipulation, use of gestures) in communicative situations. Compensation strategies, on the other hand, are steps to compensate for the absence of linguistic knowledge (substitution and reconceptualisation strategies). In this respect we would like to argue that, whilst the literature on strategies has identified how learners compensate for inadequate communicative competence (including as well restructuring, circumlocution, asking for help) for the task in hand, inadequate intercultural competence is not necessarily something a learner would automatically know how to identify or be aware of, and therefore compensate for.

We can now return to the main questions raised in this chapter, namely how independent language learners can be encouraged to develop autonomy in the ways in which they learn about and interact with other cultures. In the next section we examine the strategies which can effectively support the acquisition of intercultural communicative competence and the development of independent language learners as intercultural speakers.

Strategy Training for Intercultural Purposes

Strategies have been characterised as conscious or unconscious according to the degree of attention and awareness from the learner (Schmidt, 1994). When they are conscious, a learner can adopt them systematically to enhance his or her learning. Studies emphasise the potential benefits of specific and explicit training which will lead to the development of a solid conscious repertoire of strategies (Cohen, 1998; Flaitz et al., 1995;

Macianskiene *et al.*, 2004; O'Malley, 1987), despite the fact that success is not easily predictable or measurable (e.g. Nakatani, 2005). Strategy training can take many forms, depending on different cultural approaches to learning (Oxford, 1996).

It is generally recommended that strategy training should be carried out in an explicit manner, either taught by teachers or simply supported by materials, and should ultimately aim to promote learner autonomy (Cohen, 1998; Harris, 2003; Hurd *et al.*, 2001; Juffer, 1993; Macianskiene *et al.*, 2004; Wenden & Rubin, 1987). It has also been highlighted as critical the fact that the training is better done in a contextualised fashion where strategies are presented along with the relevant materials rather than in isolation (Harris, 2003). The interest of both teachers and learners in strategy development is a critical factor in their successful implementation (Cohen, 1996; Oxford, 1996). If a key educational goal in independent language education is intercultural communicative competence, then learner training should include a range of strategies whose aim is to increase/promote/foster autonomous intercultural competence. If it is agreed that learners need a portfolio of strategies to enhance their linguistic skills and to put them in control of their learning, the same applies to the development of intercultural competence. Students need to be aware and competent in the use of approaches that will be conducive to successful intercultural interactions.

Like other strategy training, intercultural strategy instruction can take place in two main direct ways, through teacher guidance or via freestanding materials. In training students to develop and use their strategies teachers have been identified as having a key role (Cohen *et al.*, 2005; Galloway, 2001; Lessard-Clouston, 1997), although this may imply changing their own beliefs and attitudes towards the development of learner autonomy (Yang, 1998). So far, there have been only a few specific suggestions in the literature on how to conduct strategy training for language learners. Oxford (1999) proposes three possible types of training: awareness training, on-time strategy training, and long-term strategy training. Studies focusing in particular on instruction for awareness-raising have taken a number of similar steps. For example, with communicative objectives in mind, Cohen (1998) has proposed preparation, self-monitoring and self-evaluation strategies, and Vandergrift (2003) has suggested that teachers encourage learners to engage in self-evaluation and reflect on their use of listening strategies. (See also Chapter 5 on listening strategies.)

Savignon and Sysoyev (2002) suggest strategy training using a three-stage approach: explanation, exploration and expression. The first, the explanatory stage of explicit strategy training is theoretical: the teacher explains the role and importance of a specific strategy. The second stage involves practical application: learners study real life examples of the particular strategy in communication. Finally, in the third phase, learners practise the strategy via simulations, and reflect on their experiences. The point of the practice stage is that if in future learners encounter a situation in real-life, they will be able to draw on their experience of having modelled a similar situation. Jones's (2000) suggestion could be considered as complementary to this approach. He indicates that teachers should offer language learners opportunities to find their way in the other culture through a route of self-discovery while in contact with different realities and diverse points of view and, at the same time, facilitate and challenge their interaction with other cultures. This proposition emphasises a fundamental component of intercultural awareness: the incorporation of ourselves as one of the many perspectives in a bigger reality.

Strategy Inventories for Learning Culture

One of the most interesting and practical pieces of work on culture learning strategies is the *Culture-Learning Strategies Inventory and Index* by Paige *et al.* (2002). The purpose of the inventory is to enable learners to find out about themselves as 'culture learners' and to discover strategies that will help them 'adapt' to other cultures. The strategies are tailored specifically to students' periods of residence abroad, but they can easily be transferred to other language contexts. They are organised into pre-departure, in-country, and post-study abroad strategies, to reflect the stages of learning.

Pre-departure strategies are those which encourage learners to think about what strategies they might use when they are in culturally different environments from those they are used to. Although previous stays abroad may make learners more aware about some of these issues, those that have no prior experience of living abroad are encouraged to use this section as a way of reflecting on some of the issues they will encounter. The strategies under this heading include items such as:

- Consider ways in which different cultures might view things in different ways (e.g. how different cultures value 'alone time' or independence).
- Figure out what cultural values might be involved when I encounter a conflict or something goes wrong.
- Think about different cross-cultural perspectives to examine situations in which I seem to offend someone or do something wrong.
- Use generalisations instead of stereotypes when I make statements about people who are different from me.

In-country strategies are those which help the learner, for instance, to adjust to a new culture and cope with culture shock, deal with difficult times in the new culture, make judgments about another culture, communicate with people from another culture, and understand nonverbal communication in another culture. Under each type, the inventory provides a set of suggested strategies, including:

- Consider what my friends living in the host country say about people from my own culture, using what I know about cultural bias.
- Participate in sports and other activities while abroad.
- Refrain from making quick judgements about another culture.
- Build relations with local people by finding opportunities to spend time with them.
- Respect the way people from other cultures express their emotions.
- Examine how my own nonverbal communication is influenced by my culture.
- Share pictures of my own family with my homestay family.

Post-study-abroad strategies are those which help learners manage their re-entry into their own culture. They include the following:

- Find a group of people who have had similar study abroad experiences to talk to and share experiences.
- Share my feelings and experiences with friends and family, without expecting that they will relate to all that I say.
- Try to keep connected with friends I made while studying abroad.
- Give myself time to readjust to my own country.

The original inventory was subsequently revised as the *Strategies Inventory for Learning Culture* (SILC) (Paige *et al.*, 2004: 260), which consisted of 52 items 'conceptually organised into [...] nine culture learning categories: adapting to culturally different surroundings, culture shock/coping strategies, interpreting culture, communicating across cultures, communication styles, non-verbal communication, interacting with culturally different people, homestay strategies, and re-entry strategies'.

Studies of strategies emphasise the importance of explicit training and the potential of this awareness for using strategies in new situations. For instance, Cohen (1996: 16) argued that overt training in the use of strategies 'better enables students to consciously transfer specific strategies to new contexts'; Wenden (1998) emphasises how acquired strategies considered effective by the learner will motivate the transfer of such strategies to other learning situations. Oxford (1996) also points out that the conscious use of strategies is linked to students' language achievement and proficiency. One possible area for future research would be to determine the effect that explicitness, clarity of objectives and conscious use of intercultural strategies have on the development of intercultural competence, and the extent to which these strategies are transferable.

Regardless of the explicit or implicit nature of training, there are some difficulties in intercultural strategy instruction. For example, it is important for learners to understand that the acquisition and use of strategies will be easier in some cases than others. As Macianskiene *et al.* (2004: 7) have explained, 'some strategies will soon become automatic, "internalised" and will require little conscious thinking; some will need a long time of conscious thinking and repetition to be used automatically; others will require thorough planning, constant control, consistent work and a high level of learner self-concept'. In relation to this, learners need to be aware of the fact that they need to actively sustain their use of the learned strategies, and that they should not neglect strategy practice, which should be conceived as a life-long process. Interest and motivation are key factors in this process, as they contribute to the improvement and continuation of strategic approaches (Norvele, 2004). However, it should be remembered that both factors are conditioned by students' cultural backgrounds (Oxford, 1996) and by beliefs about language learning (Yang, 1998).

In particular, the degree of interest and motivation with respect to learning about another culture and communicating with members of that cultural community is, on the one hand, dependent on students' beliefs and attitudes towards them, and, on the other, related to the particularities of specific communicative contexts (e.g. classroom, foreign country, CMC, exchanges with friends, etc.). Effective intercultural strategy instruction should therefore aim at penetrating any cultural barriers, ensure an increase in motivation and transform positions. The ability of learners to reposition themselves successfully during cross-cultural interaction will demonstrate their intercultural autonomy, but it may also result in either positions of affinity or positions of resistance to different aspects of the target cultures.

Finally, it is worth mentioning two further points. First, that apart from the impact of formal education in language and culture learning strategies, informal settings might prompt learners to develop and use strategies as well. A comparison of the strategies learners deploy in different environments might also inform future educational practices (Oxford & Crookall, 1989). Second, and related to that, is the fact that teachers have often been reluctant to spend time in strategy instruction because of time pressures and high teacher-student ratios (Chamot, 1993; Flaitz *et al.*, 1995), and this is probably even more the case with intercultural strategies, since they are probably felt to be even more of a 'soft' issue.

Intercultural Strategies in an Independent Learning Setting

Language learning strategies have been generally recognised as important for the promotion of learner autonomy (Cohen, 1998; Council of Europe, 2001; Harris, 2003; Little, 1994; Wenden, 1991; Wharton, 2000).

Equally, strategies can be taught that enable learners 'to become independent cross-cultural learners' (Juffer, 1993: 202) as well as autonomous intercultural speakers. The key to this is providing training that teaches students both how they can learn about new cultures and how they can interact with them. The ability to discover and interpret significant facts and events, as well as developing new and different perspectives, will build independence, as individuals become more secure in their ability to 'read' the target culture. However, there is also a need for studies that could help firmly establish a clearer link between learners' use of strategies for intercultural development and those for successful autonomous intercultural communication.

There is some evidence that self-access materials can successfully contribute to independent strategy development (Cohen *et al.*, 2005; Harris, 2003). However, it has been argued that the literature on intercultural training, 'while excellent in introducing students to cultural concepts and the processes of cultural adjustment and adaptation, does not systematically identify, or prepare students to develop and use, culture learning strategies' (Cohen *et al.*, 2005: 16). Materials for all independent learners need to encourage analysis, reflection and self evaluation to trigger the development of intercultural strategies transferable to a variety of contexts. The expectation should be that the learning activities proposed create the framework so that students become aware of and interested in culture learning strategies. For instance, activities that further their ability to cope with possible misunderstandings when they arise and to interpret the cultural connections encompassed in their encounters, be it face to face or through the linguistic resources they are exposed to, or activities that put learners in different roles in the deconstruction of crucial events in the history of a community, or that encourage them to challenge traditional interpretations of such history, are likely to promote better understanding of the other culture (and probably of their own) and will develop the learner's ability to transfer the skills acquired to other contexts in real intercultural exchanges, independently and outside the learning environment.

Conclusion

This chapter has firstly considered the importance of the awareness and practice of intercultural strategies for language learners. Secondly, it has shown how general strategies for language learning can be adapted to include the development of intercultural competence and how they can have very practical applications as language learners discover other cultures and interact with them in the target language. Thirdly, it has highlighted the challenge of training learners in the use of such strategies and the lack of research that could help underpin the real impact of their use in becoming independent intercultural speakers.

We have specifically emphasised the interrelated nature of language and culture learning strategies and the importance of training that consciously works on the connections between them. This is best facilitated by the teacher and aims to involve a transformation in the learners that will lead eventually to the ability to make autonomous strategic decisions and take action. We have, however, acknowledged that language learning resources for independent learning also have an important role to play in promoting the development of intercultural strategies that can help learners manage their cultural interactions. In the absence of the teacher's voice, such resources must enable students to develop an understanding of cultural strategies and their use that involves in-depth processing. In other words, the success of intercultural interaction should not just be left to chance.

An awareness of the relevant strategies should empower students to make successful choices as far as intercultural interactions are concerned. They should feel as competent, if not more, to exercise such choices effectively as when deciding, for instance, which particular verb tense it is more appropriate to use in a particular utterance. After all, linguistic inaccuracy can be easily forgiven, but intercultural incompetence has more adverse effects in the communication process among speakers of different languages.

We should not, however, ignore the role that culture plays in our choice, use, assessment and instruction of strategies competence (Oxford, 1996), nor should we forget the role played by our individual beliefs and personalities and the influence of other characteristics such as gender, age, motivation and prior language experience on the strategic choices that we make (Schmeck, 1988; Wharton, 2000). Strategy training, including intercultural strategies, should, therefore, consider the extent to which particular strategies are appropriate to each context and to each individual learner.

More than 30 years ago, Naiman *et al.* (1976) noted that 'good' language learners differed from 'poor' language learners in that they used a larger and more varied range of strategies, although many researchers subsequently exposed this premise as biased towards a specific ethnocentric perspective (Wharton, 2000). If, as the research points out, a good language learner is one who is 'a mentally active learner, monitors language comprehension and production, practices communicating in the language, makes use of prior linguistic and general knowledge, uses various memorisation techniques and asks questions for clarification' (Chamot, 2005: 115), then what would a good intercultural learner be? Perhaps he or she is represented in Phipps and González' (2004: 29) concept of the 'intercultural being' who engages 'with the whole social world', and carries out 'reflective engagement with self and other'.

References

Álvarez, I. and Garrido, C. (2001) Strategies for the development of multicultural competence in language learning. In J.A. Coleman, D. Ferney, D. Head and R. Rix (eds) *Language Learning Futures* (pp. 150–163). London: The National Centre for Languages (CiLT).

Bateman, B.E. (2002) Promoting openness toward culture learning: Ethnographic interviews for students of Spanish. *The Modern Language Journal* 86 (3), 318–331.

Byram, M. (1997) *Teaching and Assessing Intercultural Communicative Competence.* Clevedon: Multilingual Matters.

Chamot, A.U. (1993) Student responses to learning strategy instruction in the foreign language classroom. *Foreign Language Annals*, 26 (3) 308–321.

Chamot, A.U. (2005) Language learning strategy instruction: Current issues and research. *Annual Review of Applied Linguistics* 25, 112–130.

Cohen, A.D. (1996) *Second Language Learning and Use Strategies: Clarifying the Issues.* Unpublished manuscript, Mineapolis.

Cohen, A.D. (1998) *Strategies in Learning and Using a Second Language.* London: Longman.

Cohen, A.D., Weaver, S.J. and Li, T-Y. (1996) *The Impact of Strategies-based Instruction on Speaking a Foreign Language.* Minneapolis: Center for Advanced Research on Language Acquisition, University of Minesota.

Cohen, A.D., Paige, R.M., Shively, R.L., Emert, H.A. and Hoff, J.G. (2005) *Maximising Study Abroad through Language and Culture Strategies: Research on Students, Study Abroad Program Professionals, and Language Instructors.* Minneapolis: Center for Advanced Research on Language Acquisition, University of Minesota.

Council of Europe (2001) *Common European Framework of Reference for Languages: Learning, Teaching, Assessment.* Cambridge: Cambridge University Press.

Damen, L. (1987) *Culture Learning: The Fifth Dimension in the Language Classroom.* Reading: Addison-Wesley.

Donato, R. and MacCormick, D. (1994) A sociocultural perspective on language learning strategies: The role of mediation. *The Modern Language Journal* 78 (4), 453–464.

Flaitz, J., Feyten, C., Fox, S. and Mukherjee, K. (1995) Raising general awareness of language learning strategies: A bit goes a long way. *Hispania* 78 (2), 337–348.

Galloway, V. (1999) Bridges and boundaries: Growing the cross-cultural mind. *Language Learners of Tomorrow: Process and Promise* (pp. 151–187). Lincolnwood: National Textbook.

Galloway, V. (2001) Giving dimension to Mappaemundi: The matter of perspective. In V. Galloway (ed.) *Teaching Cultures of the Hispanic World: Product and Practices in Perspective.* Ohio: Thomson Learning Custom Publishing.

Harris, V. (2003) Adapting classroom-based strategy instruction to a distance learning context. *TESL-EJ* 7 (2). On WWW at http://www-writing.berkeley.edu/tesl-ej/ej26/a1.html. Accessed 09.04.08.

Hsiao, T. and Oxford, R. (2002) Comparing theories of language learning strategies: A confirmatory factor analysis. *The Modern Language Journal* 86 (3), 368–383.

Hurd, S., Beaven, T. and Ortega, A. (2001) Developing autonomy in a distance language learning context: Issues and dilemmas for course writers. *System* 29 (3), 341–355.

Jokikokko, J. (2005) Interculturally trained Finnish teachers' conceptions of diversity and intercultural competence. *Intercultural Education* 16, 69–83.

Jones, B. (2000) Developing cultural awareness. In K. Field (ed.) *Issues in Modern Foreign Languages Teaching* (pp. 158–170). London and New York: Routledge.

Juffer, K.A. (1993) The first step in cross-cultural orientation: Defining the problem. In R.M. and R.M. Paige (eds), *Education for the Intercultural Experience* (2nd edn) (pp. 201–218). Yarmouth: Intercultural Press.

Knutson, E.M. (2006) Cross-cultural awareness for second/foreign language learners. *The Canadian Modern Language Review* 62 (4), 591–610.

Kramsch, C. (1998) The privilege of the intercultural speaker. In M. Byram and M. Fleming (eds) *Language Learning in Intercultural Perspective* (2nd edn) (pp. 16–31). Cambridge: Cambridge University Press.

Lessard-Clouston, M. (1997) *Language Learning Strategies: An Overview for L2 Teachers*. The Internet TESL Journal III (12). On WWW at http://iteslj.org/Articles/Lessard-Clouston-Strategy.html. Accessed 09.04.08.

Little, D. (1994) Autonomy in language learning: Some theoretical and practical considerations. In A. Swarbrick (ed.) *Teaching Modern Languages*. London: Routledge in association with the Open University.

Littlemore, J. (2003) The communicative effectiveness of different types of communication strategy. *System* 31, 331–347.

Lixian, J. and Cortazzi, M. (1998) Relationship between language learning strategies and Israeli vs. Russian cultural-educational factors. In R. Oxford (ed.) *Language Learning Strategies around the World: Cross-cultural Perspectives*. Manoa: University of Hawaii Press.

Macianskiene, N., Tuomaite, V. and Magnus, V. (2004) *Learning Strategies in Foreign Language Teacher Professional Development*. On WWW at http://www.ut.ee/teacher/springuniv/articles/Macianskiene.pdf. Accessed 09.04.08.

Naiman, N., Frohlich, M., Stern, H.H. and Todesco, A. (1976) *The Good Language Learner* (Vol. 7). Toronto: The Ontario Institute for Studies in Education.

Nakatani, Y. (2005) The effects of awareness-raising training on oral communication strategy use. *The Modern Language Journal* 89, 76–91.

Norvele, I. (2004) *Developing Learner Strategies in English as a Foreign Language Distance Learning Courses*. On WWW at http://www.ut.ee/teacher/springuniv/articles/Norvele.pdf. Accessed 09.04.08.

O'Malley, J.M. (1987) The effects of training in the use of learning strategies on learning English as a second language. In A. Wenden and J. Rubin (eds) *Learner Strategies in Language Learning*. Englewood, NJ: Prentice-Hall.

O'Malley, J.M. and Chamot, A.U. (1990) *Language Learning Strategies in Second Language Acquisition*. Cambridge: Cambridge University Press.

Oxford, R. (1990) *Language Learning Strategies: What Every Teacher Should Know*. New York: Newbury House Publishers.

Oxford, R. (ed.) (1996) *Language Learning Strategies around the World: Cross-cultural Perspectives*. Manoa: University of Hawaii Press.

Oxford, R. (1999) Anxiety and the language learner: New insights. In J. Arnold (ed.) *Affect in Language Learning* (pp. 58–67). Cambridge: Cambridge University Press.

Oxford, R. and Crookall, D. (1989) Research on language learning strategies: methods, findings and instructional issues. *Modern Language Journal* 73 (4), 404–419.

Paige, R.M., Cohen, A.D., Kappler, B., Chi, J.C. and Lassegard, J.P. (2002) *Maximising Study Abroad. A Student's Guide to Strategies for Language and Culture Learning and Use*. Minneapolis: Center for Advanced Research on Language Acquisition.

Paige, R.M., Cohen, A.D. and Shively, R.L. (2004) Assessing the impact of a strategies-based curriculum on language and culture learning abroad. *Frontiers: The Interdisciplinary Journal of Study Abroad* X, 253–276.

Phipps, A. and González, M. (2004) *Modern Languages: Learning and Teaching in an Intercultural Field*. London: Sage.

Roberts, C., Byram, M., Barro, A., Jordan, S. and Street, B. (2001) *Language Learners as Ethnographers*. Clevedon: Multilingual Matters.

Rubin, J. (1981) Study of cognitive processes in second language learning. *Applied Linguistics* II (2), 117–131.

Savignon, S.J. and Sysoyev, P.V. (2002) Sociocultural strategies for a dialogue of cultures. *The Modern Language Journal* 86 (4), 508–524.

Schmeck, R. (1988) Individual differences and learning strategies. In C. Weinstein, E. Goetz and P. Alexander (eds) *Learning and Study Strategies* (pp. 171–191). New York: Academic Press.

Schmidt, R. (1994) Deconstructing consciousness in search of useful definitions for applied linguistics. *AILA Review* 11, 11–16.

Vandergrift, L. (2003) Orchestrating strategy use: Toward a model of the skilled second language listener. *Language Learning* 53 (3), 463–496.

Van Ek, J. (1986) *Objectives for Foreign Language Learning*. Strasbourg: Council of Europe.

Wenden, A. and Rubin J. (1987) *Learner Strategies in Language Learning*. Englewood NJ: Prentice-Hall.

Wenden, A. (1991) *Learner Strategies for Learner Autonomy: Planning and Implementing Learner Training for Adult Learners*. Englewood, NJ: Prentice-Hall.

Wenden, A. (1998) Metacognitive knowledge and language learning. *Applied Linguistics* 19, 515–537.

Wharton, G. (2000) Language learning strategy use of bilingual foreign language learners in Singapore. *Language Learning* 50 (2), 203–243.

Willems, G.M. (2002) Language teacher education policy promoting linguistic diversity and intercultural communication. *Language Policy Division: Guide for the Development of Language Education Policies in Europe – from Linguistic Diversity to Plurilingual Education*. Strasburg: Council of Europe. On WWW at http://www.coe.int/t/dg4/linguistic/Source/WillemsENG.pdf. Accessed 09.04.08.

Yang, N-D. (1998) Exploring the new role for teachers: Promoting learner autonomy. *System* 26, 127–135.

Part 3
Strategies for Learner Self-Management

Chapter 11

Learning Logs and Strategy Development for Distance and Other Independent Language Learners

LINDA MURPHY

Introduction

Learning logs can be used in a variety of ways to support the development of language learning strategies as well as being deployed as a strategy in their own right. This chapter first outlines what the term 'learning log' may cover, before examining the theoretical basis for their use and some of the potential difficulties for learners. The rest of the chapter presents examples of how keeping a learning log can be a useful strategy to encourage reflection, enhance planning, monitoring and evaluation of progress and develop specific language skills in independent learning settings.

What is a Learning Log?

The term 'learning log' is generally used to refer to a regular record of language learning or learning-related activity which is kept by the learner, together with some form of review of that activity in order to inform future action. The terms learner diary, reflective journal and learner portfolio are sometimes used interchangeably with learning logs, though distinctions have been drawn between these concepts. For example, Riley (2005) sees learning logs as a closely structured description of language study, often involving completion of a table, whereas in a learning diary the content is left entirely up to the student. It may be more like a personal diary, although it can be similar to a learning log. The emphasis is on a spontaneous record of the student's experiences, feelings and reactions to their learning. Riley describes learning journals as a combination of log and diary but, as the examples below show, such distinctions may be hard to maintain in practice. Portfolios tend to include a record of language learning activity, along with examples of the student's work which reflect achievements in specific areas. The European Language Portfolio is an example which is being used increasingly in language programmes, including distance learning and in support provided for independent language learning (CiLT, online).

The learning log record can be oral or written, formal or informal, with frequent or occasional entries depending on the learning context. It can be very personal, kept by an individual in response to their own needs and circumstances, or it may be required as part of the learning programme and even form part of the assessment. It may be a private document or shared with a tutor or fellow learners, and it can be a collaborative activity. It can be kept in the target language, or in the student's preferred language. Each of these choices raise issues which will be explored in the next section. In all cases, simply recording activity undertaken is not enough. The crucial element is the review of activity in order to learn from the experience and shape the next phase of learning. In other words, learning logs are based on the concept of reflection and its role in learning.

Reflection in Learning and Language Learning

The relationship between theories of learning and learning logs

Critical reflection is central to a number of influential conceptions of learning. From the experiential perspective, Kolb (1984: 38) defined learning as 'the process whereby knowledge is created through the transformation of experience'. He presented a model of a learning 'cycle' or 'spiral' to explain how this transformation takes place. In this cycle, concrete experience is subjected to reflective observation which leads to abstract conceptualisation and active experimentation, producing a new concrete experience and so on. This has been summarised and interpreted for learners as 'do it', 'review it', 'conclude from it', 'plan it'. Boud et al. (1985) attempted to clarify the nature of 'reflective observation'. They suggest two main stages, that is, 'returning to the experience' and 'attending to feelings', before 're-evaluating the experience'. They argue that the original experience is often given too little attention as learners rush to decide what action is needed next. They emphasise the importance of recognising and accepting feelings generated by the experience before further learning can take place. By working through the learning cycle/spiral, conceptual understanding is developed and existing ideas and assumptions are adapted or challenged and replaced by new ways of looking at the world, new knowledge and understanding. The learning cycle/spiral has been adopted widely as a tool to enhance the effectiveness of personal learning through activities such as learning logs in particular.

Critical reflection is also central to cognitive conceptions of learning where it underpins metacognitive strategies: planning, goal-setting, reviewing, self-monitoring and self-evaluation. Although the terminology is different and stems from a different view of learning, metacognitive strategies broadly correspond to stages proposed in the experiential learning cycle/spiral and can also be seen to underpin the development of a variety of learner training resources (e.g. Ellis & Sinclair, 1989) and tools such as learning logs, personal learning plans and learner portfolios. Cotterall (1995) highlights the significance of the capacities for self-monitoring and self-assessment for successful autonomous language learning. Burton and Carroll (2001: 3) argue that reflection via learning journals can encourage learner autonomy by moving responsibility from teacher to student for defining learning needs and planning strategies to meet these needs. Learning logs offer independent learners a structure for the development of metacognitive strategies as the examples later in this chapter demonstrate.

From social constructivist perspectives, learning and the development of internal cognitive processes, including critical reflection and self-direction, derive from the internalisation of meaning during social interaction which provides repeated exposure to language use by others within a 'zone of proximal development' (Vygotsky, 1986). Little (2001: 32) sees learning as the result of a complex interplay between social and reflective processes where both are equally important for cognitive development and autonomy. Through reflection, experience of language during social interaction is transformed into knowledge of the language for future use or used to 'notice gaps' which need to be filled (Long, 1996 in Ellis, 2001: 10). Reflection on the experience of interaction through a learning log can help learners to make explicit what they have 'noticed' through use of 'selective attention' to items made salient for them via course or other learning resources.

From each of these three theoretical perspectives, the term 'reflection' is used to denote processes of which the individual is consciously aware, as opposed to intuitive thought. Schön (1983) talks of two different kinds of thinking involved in reflection: 'reflexiveness', that is, 'the mind's conversation with itself' (Thorpe, 2000: 82), the purpose of which is to become aware of one's existing knowledge, skills, attitudes and assumptions, and 'critical analysis' where assumptions, judgements, application of models and theories are questioned. Such questioning is essential if awareness is to lead to learning. Learning logs are a tool which can enable learners to engage in such conscious, critical reflection.

The challenges and barriers

Although learning theories highlight the importance of reflection, learners may experience a number of potential challenges or barriers.

Developing the capacity for critical reflection

Researchers (e.g. Van Kleek, 1982 in Ridley, 1997: 45; Boud *et al.*, 1985: 19) have noted that the capacity of individuals to reflect may differ considerably and so we cannot assume they will know how to keep and use a learning log or diary without guidance. A number of factors affect development of the capacity to reflect. Learners may find it time-consuming and difficult, challenging their previous experience of what learning involves (Dewar *et al.*, 1994: 254; Thorpe, 2000: 91). Matsumoto (1996: 147) notes that language learners tend to just 'go forward, not backward', that is, learners do not usually reflect upon their second language learning experiences. As noted above, structured learning logs can provide a framework to help learners develop the capacity for critical reflection deployed in metacognitive strategies to enhance language learning.

The context for reflection

Absence of an environment conducive to reflection can be a serious barrier. Moon (1999: 166–170) gives a detailed description of the conditions required if deliberate, conscious reflection is to be encouraged. Learners need time and space for reflection, together with a clear explanation of its purpose and likely outcomes, support or strategies to guide them in the process and a sense that reflection is a valued part of learning. To be taken seriously by learners, and really enhance learning, learning logs need to be an integral part of distance or other independent learning programmes, contributing to the achievement of the intended learning outcomes and perhaps also to assessment. On the other hand, if learning logs or diaries are examined or corrected by teachers, learners may feel inhibited and unable to express their feelings as advocated by Boud *et al.* (1985). Moreover, there is a danger that detailed guidance or closely prescribed structures may lead to mechanical 'recipe following' (Boud & Walker, 1993: 85), producing what the teacher wants to hear or what seems to be required for assessment purposes rather than actually fostering learning. This situation may be exacerbated by what Barnett (2000: 261) highlights as a tendency away from self-monitoring relying on internal and reflexive capacities towards self-monitoring as 'performative' in character where students are asked to use learning logs 'to demonstrate publicly their powers of self-monitoring'. In other words, assessment of learning logs and their reflective element may have the opposite effect to that intended if not designed carefully to enhance learning.

The framework for reflection

For some learners, the format or style of the learning log may prove to be a barrier in itself. Newton (1996) describes her difficulties in using a reflective journal on her own. She found that she was able to overcome the barriers by reflecting with colleagues. Convery (1998) suggests that it is difficult for individuals to stand back and take a critical view of their experience and actions. A number of researchers have noted the dangers in experiential or cognitive perspectives on learning as these seem to imply that reflection is an individual, solitary activity (e.g. Brookfield, 1987; Brockbank & McGill, 1998). They argue the need for dialogue in order to avoid reflection being limited to individual insights, self-confirmation or self-deception. The development of collaborative online learning logs, blogs or wikis may be a way to overcome isolation for independent learners. Petersen *et al.* (2006), for example, describe the use of mobile community blogs by Norwegian students of French during a semester in France to record and share experience, but Newton's example also highlights the importance of finding a log format which suits the individual learner.

The language for reflection

For some learners, the choice of language to be used in the learning log may present a challenge or potential barrier to reflection. Arguments in favour of using the target language centre on the development of self-expression. Quirke (2001) argues that the practice of regular journal writing can be a powerful language learning activity. Riley (2005) points out that learners may produce more spontaneous writing in unstructured diaries and journals than they are likely to do otherwise. The need for such practice opportunities is highlighted by Murphy (2005) in a study which found that distance learners engage in little or no spontaneous writing practice, even when they have identified this as a development priority. However, if learning logs are being used as a strategy to develop reflection, learners may find it difficult enough to put their feelings into words in their first language, let alone in another. Learners may not have the linguistic repertoire to reflect in the target language (Butzkamm, 2003).

Learning Logs in Practice

Using reflective learning logs to develop metacognitive strategies

This section presents some examples of the ways in which learning logs, learner diaries, reflective journals and portfolios have been used to enhance the capacity for reflection deployed through the metacognitive strategies of planning, goal-setting, monitoring, self-assessment and self-evaluation.

Monitoring, self-assessment and planning

Nunan *et al.* (1999) report on a programme which aimed to increase the ability of Hong Kong undergraduate arts students to reflect on and monitor their own learning processes. These learners were studying English to support their English medium arts undergraduate programme. They were invited to complete a guided reflective journal each week for 12 weeks on a voluntary basis. The guidance provided took the form of a number of statements for learners to complete (see Table 11.1).

Table 11.1 Nunan *et al.* (1999: 72) Framework for reflective journal

This week:
I studied …
I learned …
I used my English in these places …
I spoke English with these people …
I made these mistakes …
My difficulties are …
I would like to know …
I would like help with …
My learning and practising plans for next week are …

Learners who opted to keep the journal had regular opportunities for self-monitoring, self-assessment and planning. Nunan *et al.* noted a shift in behaviour among these learners away from a linguistic focus towards a more communicative focus, their approach became more process-orientated than product-orientated and they showed greater control of their learning processes. They had begun to see the value of the English course for their subject study and to look for opportunities to use the language.

This example was taken from a classroom setting, but the framework could work equally well in an independent language learning context. Riley (2005) suggests a more open set of headings that could be used to guide learner diaries:

- thoughts about activities and tasks;
- annoying mistakes;
- difficulties;
- achievements;
- objectives/plans;
- views and opinions.

The guidance provided in these examples prompts students to reflect and encourages 'critical analysis' rather than simply 'reflexiveness' (Schön, 1983).

Planning, goal-setting, monitoring and self-assessment
The European, Socrates-funded project *Opening the Door to Language Learning* (OdLL Project Partners, 2005) explored ways in which higher education institutions could offer flexible pathways to language learning for adults. A number of open learning models, including distance learning, were trialled and evaluated with groups of non-traditional, non-specialist, lifelong learners from seven European countries learning a variety of languages. Project findings recommend the use of learning logs or diaries to encourage learners to reflect on and monitor their study activity once they have considered their reasons for learning the language and established a number of short

and longer-term language learning goals or targets. The project report suggests that learners keep a written record of weekly learning tasks in an E-log which includes space for reflection and review, probably guided in the form of responses to a set of reflective questions. For example the UK strand of the project, *Reactivate your language learning*, which focused on independent language learners, provided the framework in Table 11.2.

In this UK study, students worked independently, but study sessions could involve a visit to a language centre. Learners were encouraged to identify their learning goals and break these down into achievable targets. As one of the programme organisers participating in this study, Manchester University Language Centre's independent language learning support service provides structured guidance on needs analysis, goal setting, action planning, recording and monitoring of learning within the framework of a learning journal, which is then developed into a portfolio (University of Manchester, online).

The OdLL report suggests that learning logs or journals should be mailed to tutors, programme organisers or a discussion list each week so that tutors keep in contact with learners and monitor their progress, but also as a means for learners to keep in touch with each other. They can share information about useful language learning resources or ways of using their language locally, give each other support over problems faced, and provide mutual encouragement, as shown by the following quotation from a UK-based learner: 'We learned from each other too, because maybe some words we know, the others don't know ... this is really great to have people of different levels together' (Dickens, online: 6).

Some learners felt that the need to submit these weekly records provided motivation 'because I have no willpower that weekly goal to sort of give you a prod was very useful' (Learner OdLL, 2005: 34). However, the interim report on the UK study also indicates experience of resistance to formal methods of monitoring from one programme organiser 'with many learners considering the task of writing about their progress to be a time-consuming activity which distracted them from their language learning' (Davis, online: 4).

Table 11.2 Keep track of your progress (adapted from *Reactivate pack*, online: 9)

Date	Your plans for this session	Your goal/ target number	What did you do?	How did it go?	What next?
10 May	work on perf/ imperf	2	exercises on forms and use; wrote own examples;	got answers right! produced 10 of each and 10 mixed	collect examples when reading;

This experience illustrates some of the challenges identified in the previous section, the importance of learners understanding the purpose and benefits of keeping logs and the barriers that may be caused by formal external requirements.

Planning, goal-setting, monitoring, self and peer-assessment

Walker (2003) provides another example of a structured learner diary to support the development of autonomous language learning between Tandem partners. Brammerts (2003: 28) defines Tandem partnerships as 'two people with different mother tongues working together in order to learn from each other'. Each aims to improve their ability to communicate in their partner's mother tongue, while getting to know their partner and his or her cultural background and benefiting from their knowledge and experience in areas of mutual interest. Tandem learners may meet face-to-face, but increasingly, Tandem partners work via email or synchronous audio-graphic conferencing. The Tandem Learner Diary developed at the University of Sheffield is structured to help both partners achieve their own goals through this reciprocal relationship. Learners are guided through an analysis of what they want or need to be able do in the language, considering areas such as vocabulary extension, sentence structure, language accuracy, pronunciation and intonation, listening and cultural knowledge, before being asked to prioritise their needs and complete a goal-setting table by answering the following questions:

- What do I want to be able to do?
- By when?
- What means am I going to use? How often?
- Where?
- Day and Time? (Walker, 2003: 133)

The main part of the diary consists of recording individual Tandem sessions and reflecting on each one, in order to plan for the next or identify other work to be done, as shown in Figure 11.1. It was recognised that learners may have difficulty with reflecting on their learning, and that detailed advice and guidance is needed to enable learners to complete their diary entries. Harris (2003) emphasises the need for very clear guidance and support to avoid limited and unreflective diary entries. The examples in Figure 11.1 show how learners are initially helped to 'return to the experience' and 'attend to feelings' before re-evaluating the experience and drawing up plans for the future.

At Sheffield University, Tandem learning has been an assessed module for some years (although this is not the case in many Tandem learning programmes), and the final part of the diary guides learners towards reviewing their experience overall and producing an assessment of language proficiency in which both learner and partner assess the

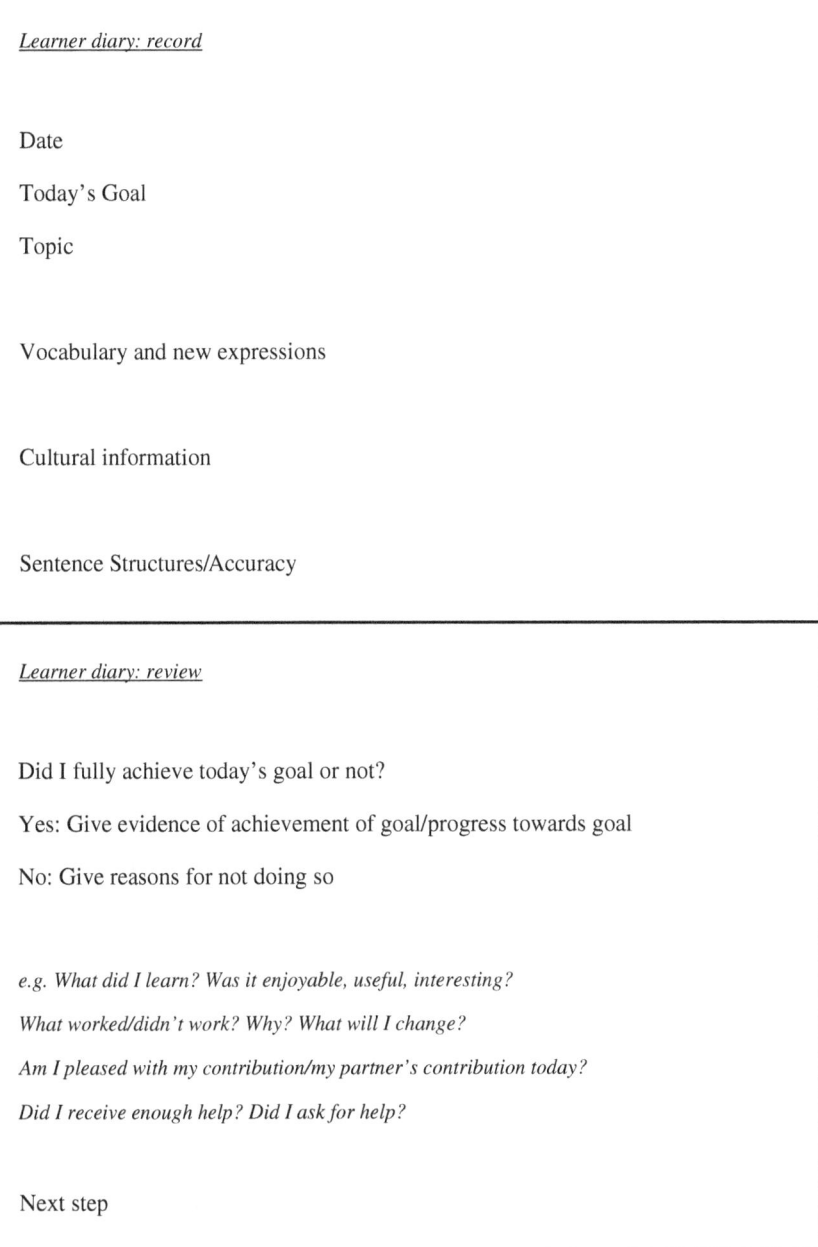

Figure 11.1 Learner diary recording and review sheets (Walker, 2003: 134–136).

e.g.

1 Consolidation

e.g. learn new material (vocabulary/cultural information)

Re-use grammar and constructions

Where, when and how do I plan to do this?

2 Monitor progress

What do I know now that I didn't know before this session?

Ask for partner's help in checking new learning

3 Planning

Need further practice on e.g. grammar point/producing correct sound?

Next session

Can I move on or do I need to spend more time to achieve this goal?

Find suitable material and tell partner in advance what we will be discussing

Individual preparation: gather vocabulary/prepare grammar/listen to same topic material

Observation of self and partner

e.g. Am I copying partner's use of grammatical structures correctly? Am I modelling my pronunciation on my partner's? Am I re-using the vocabulary and structures I have acquired?

Figure 11.1 *Continued*

standard and progress made. Morley and Truscott (2006) describe how this assessment process has developed. (For more on Tandem learning, see Chapter 13: Collaborative learning strategies.)

Awareness of learning and self-evaluation through reflective audio journals

Dantas-Whitney (2002) describes using taped audio journals, rather than written logs, with students enrolled on an advanced, content-based ESL course, with a focus on communication skills, listening and note-taking, in the United States. Her study was undertaken from a social constructivist perspective and aimed to encourage learners to engage in critical reflection. She argues that content-based methodologies assume that 'people do not learn languages and then use them, but learn languages by using them' (Eskey, 1997: 133 in Dantas-Whitney, 2002: 544) and the audio journals were used as a means of helping students to make essential connections between the subject-matter and their individual experiences. Students were asked to prepare reflective audio journals at the end of each content unit. First of all, they were to summarise the information they had learned about the topics, whether from the textbook, radio interviews, videos, outside speakers or classmates' presentations and discussions, then they were to present a general overview before focusing on one topic which they found particularly interesting. For the second part of the task, they were asked to talk about their personal perspectives on the topic, for example: giving their opinions, relating the information to their personal experience, comparing what they had learned to the situation in their own country, talking about how they might use the information in future or any other related issues that were of interest (Dantas-Whitney, 2002: 554). The teacher listened to the journals and provided some feedback, mainly in the form of comment on the content.

The results of the study showed that students had increasingly engaged in critical reflection both on the content and on their own oral performance. Working on the audio journals provided students with an opportunity to revisit course content, attend to their feelings and review what they had experienced in order to draw conclusions for the future. Their reflections on topics in the light of past experience showed a high degree of interest and engagement as well as demonstrating intercultural learning by 'analysing any cultural practices and meanings they encounter' (Byram, 1997: 19). For example, students examined and compared family relationships in their country and the United States following study of a topic on aging and family relationships.

Students reported that the journals provided additional opportunities for oral language practice, particularly presentation skills. They also provided a significant opportunity for self-evaluation. Half the participants in the study listened to their recordings after finishing the journal items and one described re-recording many times over to eradicate grammar mistakes. One student commented on the value of hearing her own speech and being able to evaluate her pronunciation for the first time; another transcribed her own journal items, creating further opportunities for listening and note-taking practice. None of these language-focused activities had been required by the journal task guidelines. Dantas-Whitney concludes that the audio journals encouraged self-direction and self-awareness.

> As students became responsible for building explicit connections between the course content and their personal experiences, they made conscious choices about the areas of the curriculum which they wished to explore further and about the strategies they would use to monitor and evaluate their learning. (Dantas-Whitney, 2002: 553)

Although this study was carried out with a group of class-based learners, the journal entries were created outside the classroom. Instead of using audio-tape, it is now possible for distance learners to record such journals via their computer and to email them to their tutor, or post them to an online conference or shared website for fellow learners to listen to and comment on. It may be that making the journal public, whether to tutors or peers, provides the incentive to monitor performance more closely, although as already noted, it could have an inhibiting effect. Inhibition may be more of an issue for an oral log or journal given the literature on language anxiety and public performance (see e.g. MacIntyre, 2002: 66–67) but it may also be reduced in contexts where learners do not have face-to-face contact and perhaps can more easily construct a new language learner identity. Roed (2003, quoted in Ward, 2004: 4–5) refers to the term 'disinhibition' to describe how the perceived anonymity of communicating via computer can benefit the language learner by reducing anxiety and helping to develop confidence.

Dantas-Whitney's study highlights the potential use of reflective learning logs or journals as a way of developing both metacognitive strategies and specific language skills. Although she did not set out to demonstrate that critical reflection via spoken journals enhances oral language acquisition, participants perceived that it did. The next section considers some examples of the use of learning logs and journals as a strategy for the development of specific language skills, although as is already apparent, there is not always a clear dividing line.

Using Learning Logs as a Strategy to Develop Specific Language Skills

Focus on listening skills

Goh (1997) describes using a 'listening diary' with a group of Chinese learners of English at the National Institute of Education in Singapore.

They were asked to keep a record of the occasions when they listened to English and what they did in order to understand better. They were also asked to record their thoughts and feelings about learning to listen and any activity they engaged in to practise or develop this skill. Goh found that having to keep a listening diary and to think explicitly about their listening raised awareness and prompted the learners to verbalise their thought processes while listening, together with factors they believed could enhance or impair their listening comprehension. They described an extensive range of strategies, both for assisting comprehension and developing their listening, using a mix of top-down and bottom-up processing. By focusing explicitly on their listening in this way, learners began to take more account of the factors that assisted comprehension and to try to create better conditions for their listening. Goh (1997) suggests that to exploit the benefits of listening diaries fully, learners should be encouraged to share the thoughts and ideas which they have noted down, 'since by finding out what other students are doing, learners can evaluate and improve their own learning practices' (Goh, 1997: 367).

Nunan *et al.* (1999), also working with Chinese learners of English, but this time in Hong Kong, encouraged learners to keep a listening journal by keeping a record of everything they listened to in English. The structure of the journal directed learners' attention to

- selection of listening materials
- setting of learning objectives;
- identification of listening problems;
- development of listening strategies;
- self-assessment of learning outcomes. (Nunan *et al.*, 1999: 74)

They found that over time, learners began to select a wider range of materials for practising their listening skills. They showed enhanced ability to set themselves appropriate learning objectives for specific listening resources and greater precision in defining their listening problems and the corresponding strategies for dealing with them. They also engaged in more in-depth self-assessment of their listening skills.

These examples show how learning logs can be used as a strategy to develop language skills by encouraging conscious, critical reflection. They are taken from classroom settings, involving learners of English, but the approach can be adapted to independent or distance learning of any language. In each case, the listening diaries and journals were kept by learners outside the classroom. Advances in communications technology allow learners to access a variety of broadcast or podcast material in many languages through the Internet and to keep an electronic log of sources, content of interest, personal reactions to the content or style of delivery, and listening strategies which can be shared with fellow learners, particularly in the context of an open or distance learning programme.

Focus on reading skills

Ikeda and Takeuchi (2006) used a structured portfolio to encourage the practical use of specific reading strategies taught to groups of higher and lower proficiency Japanese learners of English at intermediate level. The learners were asked to find their own example of an English passage which appeared to lend itself to the application of the strategy taught in the previous class. They then read the passage, used the strategy in question and wrote a retrospective account of how they had used this strategy and their thoughts or opinions on using it. The strategies included, for example, breaking sentences into sense units by slashes (/) between them; guessing unfamiliar words from context; identifying and skimming the topic sentence in each paragraph to understand the outline of a passage; and paying attention to discourse markers (e.g. however, while, then, first) to aid comprehension. Learners completed the portfolio entries in their first language, Japanese, for the sake of ease but also so that they could give an accurate picture of their strategy use. Researchers were aware that, otherwise, the task could require a linguistic repertoire not available to the learners.

Researchers such as Cohen (1998), Matsumoto (1996) and Ridley (1997) point out that simply raising awareness of strategies is not enough. Learners need opportunities to try them out and become confident in using them in order to be able to apply them effectively in appropriate contexts. Ikeda and Takeuchi found that higher proficiency learners were able to describe their strategy use in far greater detail in their portfolio entries, showing that they had understood the purpose of the strategy, how it helped their reading comprehension and when it could be used most effectively. They also showed evidence of using combinations of reading strategies as the course progressed. Lower proficiency learners, on the other hand, showed little evidence of having understood the purpose of the strategy or ability to deploy it appropriately. They appeared to need far more concrete examples and models. Ikeda and Takeuchi suggest that the portfolios of higher proficiency learners could be the source of such examples.

Moving away from a focus on reading strategies for decoding and understanding shorter texts, many language teachers suggest learners develop the habit of extensive reading. This is promoted as a strategy to consolidate and increase vocabulary, to provide examples in context of the language being studied (opportunities for 'noticing'), to increase reading comprehension and above all to show the language as a source of enjoyment and interest, through focusing on meaning rather than form. Leung (2002) describes her own use of a reading diary as a tool to encourage and analyse her use of extensive reading from the perspective of an independent beginner learner of Japanese. Although her prime interest is in researching the impact of extensive reading on vocabulary acquisition, reading comprehension, attitude to reading and the challenges of extensive reading for a beginner, this qualitative case study highlights how a reading diary may be used as a strategy to prompt more reading and encourage reflection on the reading process. As a beginner, she chose to keep the diary in Chinese (her first language) since she had been writing a personal journal in this language for some years. Entries focused on her experience and the progress she felt that she had made.

Leung's study shows the possibilities of a reading diary even at beginner level. She records the excitement she felt: 'it's amazing to see how much more I can understand. [...] It is very exciting' (Leung, 2002: 9). The study also highlights her realisation of the importance of reading material at her level: 'where I can find books at my level of proficiency it sure makes me feel good and increases my desire to read more' (Leung, 2002: 9), and therefore the way in which such a diary could help beginner learners engage in conscious, critical reflection on the factors that enhance their enjoyment of reading.

The examples above focus primarily on individual activity. Yen-Ren (1996) outlines the possibilities of a Group Reading Diary. In this case, groups of advanced learners agree a selection of books, short stories or other types of reading material. One member of the group writes a diary entry giving an opinion on the item which they have read. The next member responds and adds their views and so on, perhaps developing a debate before moving on to the next item. This approach lends itself to asynchronous electronic conferencing, blogs or wikis and can be more or less structured. For example, learners can be guided to summarise what they feel are key points in what they have read, give their reactions and opinions and then respond to others. A time-frame can be agreed for entries on a particular item before moving on to the next, but learners could come back to previous items at any time. Yen-Ren points out that contributing to a reading diary which is shared with others who may have read the same item, but have very different opinions about it may encourage closer reading, attention to content and form: '... they may adapt the way they read because they know that focusing on surface level comprehension will not be enough to generate and convey ideas [...] defending their own opinions' (Yen-Ren, 1996: 62–63).

Focus on oral and writing skills

The examples above focus on receptive language skills, but learning logs can be used in similar strategic ways to develop productive skills. As noted earlier, target language learning logs and journals can provide an impetus for spontaneous writing and encourage learners to engage in more writing than they might otherwise do. Many independent distance learners expend considerable time and effort on finding ways to listen to and speak the target language in order to practise what they are learning and they find successful communication greatly boosts their confidence and desire to learn more (Murphy, 2005). They pay less attention to writing, perhaps because learners feel that is 'easier' to do in isolation compared with developing oral communication skills which are often the prime motivation for learning the language in the first place. Writing entries for a learning log or journal can greatly increase the amount of target language writing which learners engage in and when the logs are shared or part of a collaborative effort, learners have a real audience and purpose for their writing as well as a possible source of correction and advice from their peers or a tutor.

Holmes and Moulton (1997) found adult learners of English in the United States were very positive about writing 'dialogue journals'. They felt their writing became more fluent and spontaneous as a result of more frequent writing. They felt motivated to write because they had an audience (in this case their teacher) and were assured that the focus was on meaning, not grammatical accuracy. However, they also felt that they learned a lot from modelling of forms by the teacher. Holmes and Moulton suggest similar outcomes might be achieved by encouraging learners to share and comment on each others' journals, rather than relying on dialogue with the teacher. Goettsch (2001) reports putting this into practice via an on-line journal with an advanced ESL composition class in the United States. Students again reported improved fluency, they sought advice on form from more proficient students, perceived an enhanced sense of community and valued the opportunity to exchange and increase their skills in critical argument and analysis in preparation for writing course assignments.

Although many independent learners may put more effort into developing their oral communication skills, there are plenty more who feel isolated and lack access to other speakers of the language. They may feel inhibited and find it difficult to join in discussions or conversations whether face-to-face or in audiographic conferencing environments. Such learners may benefit from keeping an 'audio log' or diary, along the lines of that developed by Dantas-Whitney, as a way of providing regular impetus for spontaneous speech. The language benefits of sharing this kind of audio log with peers perhaps as a podcast, have already been noted. For learners who find it difficult to take part in discussions or conversations, a log can be used in conjunction with an action plan which sets goals for oral interaction. For example, a learner might log the times when they contribute to a conversation or group discussion, how they contribute and how they feel. A different approach is used in the Open University beginners' Spanish course, *Portales*. Here students are encouraged to keep a 'diario hablando', personal recordings of speaking tasks which they have worked on, for example, talking about themselves and their family, or describing where they live. Students are then able to review their performance over time and use the collection to help measure their progress in terms of, for example, pronunciation, fluency or confidence.

Conclusion

The examples in this chapter show a variety of ways in which learning logs can be used strategically to develop the capacity for critical reflection on learning. They help learners to deploy this capacity through the use of metacognitive strategies, which facilitate a more independent approach. At the same time, conscious, critical reflection through a learning log can be a valuable strategy in the development of specific language skills. In either case, the key to successful and effective use of learning logs is clarity of purpose, clear guidelines and their explicit integration within a learning programme.

References

Barnett, R. (2000) Supercomplexity and the curriculum. *Studies in Higher Education* 25 (3), 255–265.

Boud, D., Keogh R. and Walker, D. (1985) Promoting reflection in learning: A model. In D. Boud, R. Keogh and D. Walker (eds) *Reflection, Turning Experience into Learning* (pp. 18–40). London: Kogan Page.

Boud, D. and Walker, D. (1993) Barriers to reflection on experience. In D. Boud, R. Cohen and D. Walker (eds) *Using Experience for Learning* (pp. 73–86). Buckingham: Open University Press.

Brammerts, H. (2003) Autonomous language learning in tandem: The development of a concept. In T. Lewis and L. Walker (eds) *Autonomous Language Learning in Tandem* (pp. 27–36). Sheffield: Academy Electronic Publications Ltd.

Brockbank, A. and McGill, I. (1998) *Facilitating Reflective Learning in Higher Education*. Buckingham: Society for Research into Higher Education and Open University Press.

Brookfield, S. (1987) *Developing Critical Thinking: Challenging Adults to Explore Alternative Ways of Thinking and Acting*. San Francisco, CA: Jossey Bass.

Burton, J. and Carroll, M. (2001) Journal writing as an aid to self-awareness, autonomy and collaborative learning. In J. Burton and M. Carroll (eds) *Journal Writing* (pp. 1–7). Alexandria, VA: TESOL.

Butzkamm, W. (2003) We only learn a language once. The role of the mother tongue in FL classrooms: Death of a dogma. *Language Learning Journal* 28, 29–39.

Byram, M. (1997) *Teaching and Assessing Intercultural Communicative Competence*. Clevedon: Multilingual Matters.

CiLT – The National Centre for Languages, *European Language Portfolio for Adult and Vocational Language Learners*. On WWW at http://www.cilt.org.uk/qualifications/elp/adultelp.htm. Accessed 30.09.06.

Cohen, A.D. (1998) *Strategies in Learning and Using a Second Language*. Harlow: Longman.

Convery, A. (1998) A teacher's response to reflection in action. *Cambridge Journal of Education* 28 (2), 197–205.

Cotterall, S. (1995) Readiness for autonomy: Investigating learner beliefs. *System* 23 (2), 195–205.

Dantas-Whitney, M. (2002) Critical reflection in the second language classroom through audiotaped journals. *System* 30, 543–555.

Davis, P. *Opening the Door to Language Learning: Bringing Language Learning to the Wider Community*. Subject Centre for Languages, Linguistics and Area Studies, University of Southampton. *UK project phase 1 report*. On WWW at http://opendoor2languages.net/Resources/EN/UK%20phase%201%20report_rev.pdf. Accessed 30.09.06.

Dewar, K., Hill, Y. and Macgregor, J. (1994) Continuing education for nurses: Orientating practitioners towards learning. *Adults Learning* 5 (10), 253–254.

Dickens, A. *Opening the Door to Language Learning: Bringing Language Learning to the Wider Community*. Subject Centre for Languages, Linguistics and Area Studies, University of Southampton. *OdLL Project Report*. On WWW at http://www.opendoor2languages.net/Resources/EN/OdLLReport_pd_amends.doc. Accessed 30.09.06.

Ellis, G. and Sinclair, B. (1989) *Learning to Learn English: A Course in Learner Training*. Cambridge: Cambridge University Press.

Ellis, R. (2001) Introduction: Investigating form-focused instruction. *Language Learning* 51 (1), 1–46.

Goettsch, K. (2001) On-line journals: Creating community and competency in writing. In J. Burton and M. Carroll (eds) *Journal Writing* (pp. 1–7). Alexandria, VA: TESOL.

Goh, C. (1997) Metacognitive awareness and second language listeners. *ELT Journal* 51 (4), 361–373.

Harris, V. (2003) Adapting classroom-based strategy instruction to a distance learning context. *TESL-EJ* 7 (2), 1–16. On WWW at http://tesl-ej.org/ej26/a1.html. Accessed 06.10.06.

Holmes, V.L. and Moulton, M.R. (1997) Dialogue journals as an ESL learning strategy. *Journal of Adolescent and Adult Literacy* 40 (8), 616–621.

Ikeda, M. and Takeuchi, O. (2006) Clarifying the differences in learning EFL reading strategies. *System* 34 (3), 384–398.

Kolb, D.A. (1984) *Experiential Learning: Experience as the Source of Learning and Development*. New Jersey: Prentice Hall.

Leung, C.Y. (2002) Extensive reading and language learning: A diary study of a beginning learner of Japanese. *Reading in a Foreign Language* 14 (1), 1–15. Accessed 06.10.06.

Little, D. (2001) How independent can language learning really be? In J. Coleman, D. Fearney, D. Head and R. Rix (eds) *Language Learning Futures: Issues and Strategies for Modern Languages Provision in Higher Education* (pp. 30–43). London: The National Centre for Languages (CiLT).

MacIntyre, P.D. (2002) Motivation, anxiety and emotion in second language acquisition. In P. Robinson (ed.) *Individual Differences in Second Language Acquisition* (pp. 45–68). Amsterdam: John Benjamins.

Matsumoto, K. (1996) Helping L2 learners reflect on classroom learning. *ELT Journal* 50 (2), 143–149.

Moon, J.A. (1999) *Reflection in Learning and Professional Development*. London: Kogan Page.

Morley, J. and Truscott, S. (2006) Incorporating peer assessment into tandem learning. *Language Learning Journal* 33, 53–58.

Murphy, L. (2005) Critical reflection and autonomy: A study of distance learners of French, German and Spanish. In B. Holmberg, M. Shelley and C. White (eds) *Distance Education and Languages: Evolution and Change* (pp. 20–39). Clevedon: Multilingual Matters.

Newton, R. (1996) *Getting to Grips with Barriers to Reflection*. Paper presented at 26th Annual SCUTREA Conference, School of Continuing Education, University of Leeds.

Nunan, D., Lai, J. and Koebke, K. (1999) Towards autonomous language learning: Strategies, reflection and navigation. In S. Cotterall and D. Crabbe (eds) *Learner Autonomy in Language Learning: Defining the Field and Effecting Change* (pp. 69–77). Frankfurt am Main: Peter Lang.

OdLL Project Partners (2005) *Opening the Door to Language Learning: Bringing Language Learning to the Wider Community*. Antwerp: Drukkerij De Beurs. OdLL Project, *Opening the Door to Language Learning: Bringing Language Learning to the Wider Community: Reactivate Pack*. On WWW at http://www.opendoor2languages.net/Resources/EN/Pack6.pdf. Accessed 30.09.06.

Petersen, S.A., Chabert, G. and Divitini, M. (2006) Supporting language learning communities using mobile blogs. In *Proceedings of IADIS Mobile Learning '06*, Dublin, Ireland, 14–16 July.

Quirke, P. (2001) Maximising student writing, minimising teacher correction. In J. Burton and M. Carroll (eds) *Journal Writing* (pp. 11–22). Alexandria, VA: TESOL.

Ridley, J. (1997) *Reflection and Strategies in Language Learning*. Frankfurt am Main: Peter Lang GmbH.

Riley, K. (2005) *Independent Language Learning*. School of International Studies, University of Trento. On WWW at http://people.lett.unitn.it/riley/ILL.htm. Accessed 26.09.06.

Schön, D.A. (1983) *The Reflective Practitioner*. London: Temple Smith.

The Open University (2003) L194 *Portales*. Milton Keynes: The Open University.

Thorpe, M. (2000) Encouraging students to reflect as part of the assignment process: Student responses and tutor feedback. *Active Learning* 1 (1), 72–92.

University of Manchester Language Centre. *Independent Language Learning*. On WWW at http://www.langcent.manchester.ac.uk/learningresources/languagesupport/learningguide/independentlanguagelearning/. Accessed 07.10.06.

Vygotsky, L. (1986) *Thought and Language*. Cambridge, MA: MIT Press.

Walker, L. (2003) The role of the tandem learner diary in supporting and developing learner autonomy. In T. Lewis and L. Walker (eds) *Autonomous Language Learning in Tandem* (pp. 131–143). Sheffield: Academy Electronic Publications Ltd.

Ward, J.M. (2004) Blog Assisted Language Learning (BALL): Push button publishing for the pupils. *TEFL Web Journal* 3 (1), 1–16.

Yen-Ren, T. (1996) Group reading diary. *Forum China* 34 (3), 63–69.

Chapter 12
Affect and Strategy Use in Independent Language Learning

STELLA HURD

Introduction

Affect is about emotions and feelings, moods and attitudes, anxiety, tolerance of ambiguity and motivation. For some it is also connected with dispositions and preferences (Oatley & Jenkins, 1996). It is generally accepted that the affective domain encompasses a wide range of elements which reflect the human side of being, and play a part in conditioning behaviour and influencing learning. We are becoming more knowledgeable about the importance of attention to affective factors, but there is still a huge gap in terms of our knowledge of the affective strategies that students use or could use to promote more effective language learning. Moreover, the research that has been carried out into affect over several years has largely concentrated on language learning in the classroom (Arnold, 1999; Ehrman, 1996; MacIntyre, 1999; Young, 1999) with very few studies devoted to independent learning settings. Independent language learners, whether learning through self-access, distance or other modes, are a fast-growing group, and we need to know more about them, in particular the ways in which their affective needs differ from those of classroom learners (Harris, 2003; Hurd, 2002; White, 2003).

This chapter investigates affect and strategy use in independent settings. It looks first at the concept of affect and its interrelationships with other domains, continues with an exploration of strategy definitions and classification schemes in relation to affect, and concludes with a study carried out with a small group of distance language learners using think-aloud verbal protocols.

Affect and Cognition: Interrelationships

The cognitive and metacognitive domains of language learning have been a dominating force on the second language acquisition (SLA) research agenda for at least three decades (Flavell, 1976; Victori & Lockhart, 1995; Wenden, 1998, 2001), while affective considerations have attracted less interest. Inspired by the work of Gardner and Lambert (1972), Gardner and MacIntyre (1993), Horwitz *et al.* (1986), and others, the 1990s, however, witnessed a growing interest in affect which has continued to gather momentum. In her seminal book on language learning strategies, Oxford (1990: 140) asserts that 'the affective side of the learner is probably one of the very biggest influences on language learning success or failure'. She adds that '... negative feelings can stunt progress, even for the rare learner who fully understands all the technical aspects of how to learn a language. On the other hand, positive emotions and attitudes can make language learning far more effective and enjoyable'. Elaborating on this, Ehrman (1996: 137) focuses on learner identity and self-concept: 'Every imaginable feeling accompanies learning, especially learning that can be as closely related to who we are, as language learning is'. Others talk of learning a new language as an unsettling or uncomfortable experience (Guiora, 1983; Horwitz, 2001). In sum, there is an emerging consensus on the primacy of affect in learning and that language learning is greatly enhanced by attention to affective aspects (Arnold, 1999; MacIntyre, 2002; Rossiter, 2003).

With regard to one important independent setting, distance language learning, Hurd (2005: 7) suggests that, of all the individual differences, 'for the distance language learner it is perhaps affective variables – in particular motivation and anxiety – that are of greater relevance, because their effect on learning may be intensified in an independent context, and because of their capacity for modification and change'. White (2003: 117–118) identifies as a 'further critical dimension' for distance learners, 'the circumstances in which they pursue their learning, including learning sites, life roles, and support structures within their learning environment'. These circumstances can 'impact on affective experiences' by requiring learners to focus on managing their own feelings more so than in the classroom, in order to compensate for the lack of peer support and the physical absence of a teacher. Harris (1995: 48) talks of 'affective inhibition' in the distance language learning context, which can 'arise from academic or practical problems, or from the unsatisfying emotional experience of attempting solitary study' and may lead to 'loss of impetus, confidence and study lapses'.

Affect and cognition are increasingly seen as multidimensional overlapping and interdependent constructs. As Arnold (1999: 1) points out: 'Neither the cognitive nor the affective has the last word, and, indeed, neither can be separated from the other'. Arnold and Brown (1999: 8) contend that 'the way we feel about ourselves and our capabilities can either facilitate or impede our learning ...' and underline the 'difficulty of isolating the cognitive, for at many points affect inevitably enters the picture' (Arnold & Brown, 1999: 16). Arnold (1999) emphasises the need to treat students as whole persons, referring to the complex relationship between affect, learning and memory, and the inseparability of emotion and cognition in the workings of the human brain. Stevick (1999: 47) too, contends that 'affect is encoded to various degrees in the cognitive schemata of memory' and that 'affect participates in the process of learning ... by *interfering* with it' (Stevick, 1999: 50). The theme of 'interference' is also emphasised by Ehrman (1996: 138): '... the affective dimension affects how efficiently students can use what they have. For example, strong motivation tends to help students marshal their assets and skills, whereas low motivation or intense anxiety interferes with their ability to use their skills and abilities'. These findings are strengthened by those working in the field of cognitive neuro-science (Damasio, 1994; Schumann, 1999). Neural scientist LeDoux (1996, quoted in Arnold & Brown, 1999: 1) sees emotion and cognition as 'partners in the mind', a view backed up Ramnani (2006) who considers that 'reason and emotion work in concert' and that 'we use our emotions to guide our reasoning, to encode and retrieve our memories and to bias our responses'.

The integral relationship between cognition and affect is a sound basis for arguing that affective strategies are as strongly implicated in successful language learning as cognitive and metacognitive strategies. The next section discusses the place of affect within the field of language learning strategies, and suggests a re-think of current classifications.

Affect and Strategies

The definition of language learning strategies has been variously described in the literature as 'elusive' (Wenden & Rubin, 1987: 7) 'fuzzy' (Ellis, 1994: 529) and 'fluid' (Gu, 2003a: 15) and a variety of classification schemes have been proposed during the last two decades (Kondo & Ying-Ling, 2004; O'Malley & Chamot, 1990; Oxford, 1990; Wenden, 1991; Wenden & Rubin, 1987). In her Strategy Inventory for Language Learning (SILL), Oxford (1990: 17) stated that there was 'no complete agreement on exactly what strategies are; how many strategies exist; how they should be defined, demarcated and categorised ...' and that 'classification conflicts were inevitable'. Oxford (1993) later drew attention to the predominance of cognitive and metacognitive strategies in the literature and the lack of attention to affective strategies.

This lack of attention is manifest in some classification schemes. Rubin (1981), for example, did not recognise affective strategies as a category in their own right. O'Malley and Chamot (1990) combined social and affective strategies to produce socio-affective strategies, while Hsiao and Oxford (2002) concluded from their study using factor analysis that they should be separated. Oxford's (1990) SILL remains the most comprehensive inventory of affective strategies and covers:

- anxiety reduction (using progressive relaxation and deep breathing exercises, music and laughter);

- self-encouragement (making positive statements, taking risks wisely, and rewarding yourself);
- monitoring emotions (listening to your body, using a checklist, writing a language learning diary, and discussing feelings with others).

Despite the increasingly accepted view of the critical role of affect in successful language learning (Dörnyei, 2001; Griffiths, 2004; Nunan & Lamb, 1996; Oxford & Shearin, 1994; Ushioda, 1996), findings from studies demonstrate that affective strategies are the least frequently used by students (Hong-Nam & Leavell, 2006; Oxford, 1990; Wharton, 2000). Moreover, it is often the case that those who need them most are least likely to be using them. As Oxford (1993: 177) says: '… some of the best learners use *affective* and *social* strategies to control their emotional state, to keep themselves motivated and on-task, and to get help when they need it', yet many students are unaware of the potential of such strategies, and affective strategies in particular are 'woefully underused' (Oxford, 1990: 143). Oxford (1993: 179) considers that a possible reason for this is that learners are 'not familiar with paying attention to their own feelings and social relationships as part of the L2 learning process'.

A further dimension to the strategies debate is the suggestion of overlap between cognitive and metacognitive strategies (O'Malley & Chamot, 1990; Oxford, 1990; Phakiti, 2003) and between affective and metacognitive strategies (Macaro, 2006). This is a reflection of the interrelationships of affect and cognition, discussed earlier, and prompts a closer look at what precisely affective strategies are and whether it is useful to keep them as a separate category. Kondo and Ying-Ling's (2004) typology of 70 strategies grouped according to five main categories – preparation, relaxation, positive thinking, peer seeking and resignation – contain a mix of cognitive, metacognitive and affective strategies that can be used to deal with anxiety.

Studies of this kind beg the question as to whether we should be talking in terms of *affective states* and strategies to deal with them, rather than affective strategies. In other words, it might be more useful to abandon the traditional separation of strategies that are more emotion-focused from those that involve mental processes. In this scenario, strategies would be classified according to their intended goal, for example: taking a break (a metacognitive strategy to deal with frustration, anger, disappointment), re-reading a section of text (a cognitive strategy to deal with anxiety caused by incomplete comprehension), planning and prioritising (a metacognitive strategy to combat anxiety caused by overload), rehearsal and repetition (a cognitive strategy to cope with nervousness about speaking aloud), deep breathing (an affective strategy to address the stress of spoken interaction), and many more.

Macaro (2006: 328) proposes that 'metacognitive strategies subsume affective strategies … because the latter require knowledge of oneself as a learner through recurrent monitoring of one's learning'. The link between affective control, metacognitive self-knowledge and learner self-regulation would lend support for this view. When faced with a particular language task, asking certain questions, for example 'How do I feel about this?' and 'Is there anything I could do to make the task more pleasant and less stressful?' (Rubin, 2001: 28) involves both metacognitive knowledge of self and the use of affective strategies, for example:

- using a checklist to monitor emotions;
- doing some relaxation exercises to reduce anxiety;
- positive talk for self-encouragement;
- promising a treat as a reward for completing a task.

Others, however, might have strong arguments for keeping the traditional distinctions in place. Blurring or removing the boundaries between affective and metacognitive strategies might risk affect losing visibility and being consigned to its customary low status, at a time when there is a growing awareness of its importance, not just for learning enjoyment but also as explicitly implicated in success or failure. These issues clearly need further investigation.

In the last few years there has been a noticeable shift in focus among some researchers (Dörnyei, 2005; Tseng et al., 2006) away from *product* (strategies) towards *process* (self-regulatory and self-management processes and the learner capacity underlying them), and to recognise strategies as 'integral components of processing theory' (Macaro, 2006: 332). A focus on self-regulation has relevance for affective strategies which are used by learners to 'manage' their emotions, feelings and motivational states.

The link between affective strategies and self-regulation has been made by Rossiter (2003: 4) who considers that affective strategies lie in a spectrum from teacher to learner control: 'For example, the use of humour, music, visualisation and relaxation in the classroom would likely be initiated by the teacher, whereas self-talk, risk-taking, and monitoring are more student-regulated strategies.' Self-regulated strategies are of special importance to language learners in independent settings, given the need for these learners to take control in a situation in which teacher and peers are physically absent for most or all of the time.

While some researchers struggle to reach a consensus on important theoretical considerations concerning language learning strategies such as definitions, interrelationships and shifts in focus, others also push forward the practical agenda which includes concentrating on the learning context (Chamot, 2005; Cohen, 1998; Gu, 2003b; Hsiao & Oxford, 2002), encouraging learners to talk about their learning experience (Harris, 1995; Hurd, 2006, 2007a; White, 2005) and attempting to make sense of all this within a cognitive-affective framework. The following sections discuss ways in which learners cope with their affective states, in particular language anxiety and motivation, and the role of learner support.

Managing Affect in Independent Learning Settings

All learners, whatever their mode of learning, bring their own 'baggage' to the learning process and this encompasses a wide spectrum of individual differences that influence and are influenced by the learning process. For Gu (2003b: 3): 'Person, task, context, and strategy are interrelated and work together to form the chemistry of learning'. Griffiths (2004: 14) cites 'gender, psychological type, motivation, culture' as factors influencing strategy choice. While a strong correlation between metacognitive strategies and effective language learning has been found in a number of research studies (Griffiths, 2004; Hurd, 2000; O'Malley & Chamot, 1990), Ehrman *et al.* (2003: 319) contend that 'it is at least as important to manage feelings as it is to use more cognitive strategies, since negative feelings reduce the effectiveness of most learning activities'. For learners in independent contexts, affective considerations, as we saw earlier, are likely to be more pressing than in classroom settings. Other factors which illustrate the particular situation of SLA at a distance are the 'lack of fit between an inherently social discipline such as language learning and the distance context whose main characterising feature is physical remoteness from others' (Hurd, 2006: 299); and the fact that languages are considered to be more difficult to learn in distance mode than other subjects (Sussex, 1991).

Language anxiety and motivation are both considered to be highly influential in facilitating or inhibiting SLA, and have become central to any examination of factors contributing to the learning process and learner achievement (Dörnyei, 2001, 2005; Ellis, 1994; Horwitz, 2000, 2001; Horwitz *et al.*, 1986; MacIntyre, 1995, 1999; Matsuda & Gobel, 2004; Oxford, 1999; Young, 1999). A longitudinal study of affect carried out with distance language learners investigated both anxiety (Hurd, 2007b) and motivation (Hurd, 2006). After four months of study, 21.3% of participants said they were more anxious learning in distance mode and 51.7% felt that there was no difference in terms of anxiety between learning at a distance and learning face-to-face. Among the strategies used for coping with anxiety were risk-taking, self-encouragement, relaxation techniques, sharing worries with tutor and other students, ticking off completed tasks, revision and repetition to build confidence, joining a French self-help group, and engaging in leisure activities such as gardening. The 27% who claimed that the distance factor made them less anxious gave the following reasons: opportunity to work at your own pace and be more in control; absence of exposure to public criticism; lack of competition and peer pressure; and the chance to practise and make mistakes in private, and to try things out.

Motivation is the factor most frequently cited as critical to successful learning by distance learners themselves (Hurd, 2000, 2006; White, 1999, 2003). Its close link with autonomy (Dickinson, 1995; Ushioda, 1996) is further evidence of its critical role in independent contexts, As Hurd (2005: 9) states: 'Maintaining motivation levels is a particular challenge at a distance. The demands of self-instruction, together with the shift of control from teacher to learner can be overwhelming for many students'. The strand of her study investigating motivation (Hurd, 2006: 304) found that this 'was clearly signalled as the most important factor in distance language learning by an overwhelming majority of students'. The main strategies students used for keeping motivated were positive self-talk, followed by setting goals and keeping in touch with French native speakers. Using a rewards system and talking to peers were also popular. Their advice to new learners, using the yoked-subject technique in which students are asked to imagine that they are talking about their strategy use to another person who is about to embark on similar tasks (White, 1994), included good preparation, developing self-knowledge, pacing, risk-taking, making the most of support, patience, organisation and time management, a positive and realistic approach, and taking advantage of all language practice opportunities.

Developments brought about by the rapid advance of technology, including blended learning and blended tuition through the use of synchronous and asynchronous tools way well have a beneficial effect on the learner by offering a different kind of support and complementing a particular advantage of distance language learning: the opportunity to work at your own pace and control output according to individual preference and need. There is already evidence that computer-mediated communication can help to minimise anxiety and increase motivation (Debski, 1997; Hampel *et al.*, 2005; Hauck & Hurd, 2005; Lamy & Hampel, 2007; Roed, 2003). Virtual learning environments available 24/7 can provide an ideal opportunity, particularly for independent language learners, to work together, to discuss and reflect on learning, to give and receive support, and thus gradually overcome their inhibitions. Referring to online learning, Macdonald (2003: 378) cites the 'interplay between competence and affective factors such as growing confidence, motivation and group dynamics' and 'the importance of the affective aspects of collaborative working – group cohesion and the evolution of mutual trust'. Creating and maximising opportunities for online interaction through the use of blogs, wikis, discussion forums and other tools is having an increasingly important role in addressing the affective challenges of a distance language context, although they are relatively untested in language learning, and the risk of new forms of anxiety arising from their use should not be underestimated. (For a full discussion of strategies for online environments, see Chapter 15.)

Finally, the role of the tutor in distance and other independent learning contexts is of crucial importance for 'developing a palpable sense of belonging' (White, 2007: 104) and supporting learners in managing their learning. As the only contact with the tutor for some students is through assignments, clear, detailed feedback in a sensitive framework that addresses learners' concerns is essential for building confidence which can lead to better outcomes. Highlighting progress made and giving value to experimentation with language in a structured environment can encourage learners to take risks, which will extend their range and ultimately improve proficiency. Recognising affective differences, providing reassurance and encouragement, and giving advice in the use of appropriate strategies can minimise negative feelings as well as building on more positive emotions and attitudes.

Investigating Affect and Strategy Use Among Distance Language Learners Using Think-Aloud Protocols: A Pilot Study

The acknowledged power of affective factors to influence language learning prompted the longitudinal study investigating motivation (Hurd, 2006) and anxiety (Hurd, 2007b) referred to earlier. As part of this main study, a small-scale pilot, presented in the next section, was set up using audio-recorded think-aloud protocols (TAPs) with distance learners of French at lower-intermediate level. This mini-study aimed to raise awareness of the feelings and emotions experienced by distance learners, and the strategies they use to manage them.

Think-aloud protocols have been used extensively in classroom contexts but less widely with students learning in independent language settings. To date, none have been found which investigate affect and strategy use with distance language learners. Based on the principles of information processing (Ericsson & Simon, 1984, 1993; Newell & Simon, 1972), TAPs record information that is present in *short-term memory* and *concurrent with actual thinking*, while a task is being performed. The small lapse of time between the thought and its articulation render them potentially more accurate and less subject to 'embellishment or decay of information' (Pressley & Afflerbach, 1995) than other more structured self-report methods, such as questionnaires. They are also said to have a human quality, in that they give the data, 'a unique soul' (Smagorinsky, 1994) which can enhance our understanding of human cognitive processing. Moreover, they have the potential to yield information on context and strategy use, in addition to cognitive and affective processes (Afflerbach, 2000).

The main methodological criticisms directed at TAPs are automaticity (Singhal, 2001), defined as fluent performance without the conscious deployment of attention, that is there is no thinking going on; reactivity

(Matsumoto, 1993; Nielson *et al.*, 2002) which refers to the extra load placed on students who are having to carry out a task and talk about the process at the same time; and incompleteness, in that students do not always finish their sentences or even construct whole sentences. In response to the automaticity concerns, Ericsson and Simon (1980) point out that researchers can counter this potential problem by selecting tasks that are complex and difficult for the learner, as these are less likely to involve processes that are engaged in automatically. With regard to reactivity, Leow and Morgan-Short (2004: 42) find no evidence in TAPs studies that internal processes are altered and that 'the only evidence of reactivity in studies to date is the amount of time required to complete the task'. McDonough (1995: 12) finds the charge of incompleteness 'no more a criticism of verbal protocol research than of any kind of research where data is necessarily limited: if anything, verbal reports suffer from the opposite, being too rich'.

Despite possible weaknesses, Oxford and Burry-Stock (1995: 2) contend that: 'Think-aloud protocols offer the most detailed information of all because the student describes strategies while doing a language task'. These factors were persuasive in the selection of TAPs as a research tool to try out with distance language learners. It was hoped that the unmediated data might usefully add to our understanding of the ways in which distance language learners approach and work through language tasks. The fact that they could be carried out in private at a time and in a place of the individual student's choice was an additional advantage.

Participants, procedure and methods

Three areas were investigated for this pilot study using TAPs: (1) the nature and prevalence of positive and negative affective factors among distance language learners; (2) learners' awareness of themselves as learners, and of the context of their learning; (3) the strategies language learners use to cope with the demands of distance learning.

The four participating students were all female volunteers studying the Open University, UK lower-intermediate French course *Ouverture*. Two were in their early 40s and two in their early 60s. The older two had a first degree or equivalent professional qualification, while those in their forties had acquired basic qualifications from school in four or five subjects.

The two tasks for the study both involved the use of the imperfect tense in French and were chosen from the end of the first unit of Book 3 of their course which was the book they would be starting at the time the TAPs were scheduled to take place:

- a reading task – a passage of around 200 words in French with three comprehension questions;
- a writing task – a short essay of 100–150 words.

Detailed information was sent out to all participants which explained what TAPs were and the rationale for their use. Students were also given full instructions on how to proceed, including the need to 'record everything that is going through your mind *as you work through each step of the two activities*', to 'keep talking' and 'to record your thoughts *as they come to mind and not after having had time to reflect*'. It was also suggested that they do a practice run with an earlier activity to get used to talking to themselves, and contact the researcher if there were any problems. The absence of queries and the quality of their protocols is evidence that they fully understood what they were required to do. This was undoubtedly linked to their maturity as adult learners.

Data analysis

The data were analysed with the help of QSR N6, a qualitative software tool which allows the researcher to organise the data into main categories ('tree-nodes') subdivided into further sub-categories ('sub-nodes'), to allow for a more detailed analysis. For example, the tree-node 'Positive affect' contained the sub-nodes 'pleasure', 'satisfaction', 'relief', 'laughter' and 'excitement', while the tree-node 'Negative effect' was the umbrella for the sub-nodes 'frustration', 'boredom', 'disappointment', 'uncertainty', 'confusion' and 'embarrassment'. The other main categories included self-confidence, anxiety, affective strategies, positive and negative self-evaluation and feelings. The N6 software made it possible to see the coding of an entire transcript in one document, and to access all utterances from all participants that were coded to any particular node.

Findings

The transcripts of the TAPs amounted to over 12,000 words, providing data that was immensely rich and varied. Selected extracts follow which illustrate the areas investigated.

Affective factors

Positive utterances included enjoyment of certain French words, occasional lighheartedness about grammar, and satisfaction or even excitement when students found they could do an activity: 'That's easy!'; 'Oh yeah, that's obvious!'; 'I know, I know this, I know I've read it already!'; 'I understood the first question, no problem ... I'm sure I'll understand the other ones, except ... ah yes I do!'

All four students gave evidence of reasonably high levels of confidence. This category included being decisive, having a clear plan of action and focusing on the 'can do':

> I can recognise the imperfect tense, that's not a problem to me.

I think I probably understand when to use expressions that go with it, it's fairly obvious.

However, difficulty, uncertainty and some frustration were evident in a number of utterances, for example:

> I do find this kind of question difficult. It's a question of ... er ... using the language that you have ... er ... but also trying to think about something that you can write about realistically ... er ...

> This is a bit annoying 'cos I keep going backwards and forwards on the page, which is a bit frustrating.

> I don't know whether I should be writing just the verb or the subject of the verb as well ... I haven't understood what they're on about. I can't think of anything to write.

Written accuracy caused concern for some:

> ... I always worry that I am not being accurate in how I put things down, so that is one of my concerns.

One student felt particularly inadequate when faced with sample answers to open-ended writing tasks:

> When they are not precise answers, it can be a little bit intimidating because you look at what's given in the suggested answer and my answers are nowhere near as formal or as accurate or as interesting.

Another student's anxiety focused on the content of the writing activity, which evoked strong feelings:

> ... There's been a lot in this course ... 'cos it's a way of teaching you to use the past tenses ... about talking about the past and your childhood, and then of course there was the thing you had to do about Christmas, ... I found that very hard to do because ... my parents died when I was young, and it's hard for me to talk about that. So it's ... you know ... there's lots of people have difficulty talking about the past for lots of different reasons ... and I can't be the only person who feels that way, but it does sort of add a little extra emotional blanket on to everything when I have to do that ... it makes it sometimes hard to think straight.

Awareness of self and context

Awareness of self in terms was illustrated by the following:

> I do have trouble sometimes quite getting exactly what's wanted, not in terms of the words 'cos I know it doesn't matter if they're not exactly the same words, but the gist of what they want in the answer.

> I think this is half the problem: I sometimes look at the *Corrigés* to see what I am supposed to do, and then it's like cheating – you've looked

at the answers first, then you find there's no point in doing it again 'cos you know what it is now.

However much practice I have, I still need more practice on all of it really, because I understand it when I'm doing it, but if I waited until I could just do it without thinking or without looking, I'd be here forever.

Students were also very forthcoming about their own ability and performance. Examples of positive self-evaluations were:

I've used the right endings on everything.

So I've got all those right, and one they missed, which is satisfying.

Other evaluations were a little more tentative:

... well I can do that, not necessarily good though, not easily, not fluently, not without thinking, but I know when and how to use it ...

Negative self-evaluations revealed that learners often took personal blame for lack of understanding or poor performance, rather than attributing this to factors outside their control such as the type of activity, the time allowed, or the clarity of explanation. Examples were:

My conclusion is bad compared to that ... ooooh, looks bad!

Yeah, I just really misunderstood that completely.

I didn't pick up any of that.

Awareness of the advantages and disadvantages of learning at a distance expressed in the TAPs were particularly valuable. Advantages were the fact that you could prepare, practise and rehearse in private and 'no-one knows what you actually put, not even your tutor'. However, the long interval between tutorials was seen as a distinct disadvantage when you had a query:

This is part of the problem of working remotely: by the time I see anybody, I'll have forgotten it.

Strategies

All four students used a range of strategies to manage their affective states, although the frequency of use overall was low. Self-encouragement, skipping bits of text, re-reading text, keeping going regardless, consulting the *Corrigés* (answer keys) when worried, not dwelling on problems, taking a break, and checking back for reassurance were among the strategies employed. Examples of strategies (underlined) included:

If I have trouble with an activity, I sometimes, if I'm really anxious, if it's become a block, I will just <u>mark it with a post-it note,</u> and <u>come</u>

> back to it another time. I try to keep going, because I think it's easy to get hung up ...
>
> Sometimes when I'm not sure or anxious, I have given in to the temptation to look at the *Corrigés* there and then, because otherwise I'm going to waste my time ... so if I'm really unhappy and unsure, I do sometimes do that.
>
> I've now decided I am just going to write whatever comes to mind and not worry about the spelling of the words, and if I can't think of the words, I'll just blag it, and then look them up in the dictionary afterwards.

Evaluation of TAPs as an Ethnographic Research Tool for Investigating Affect

This small-scale pilot study aimed to give preliminary insights into positive and negative affective factors, awareness and strategy use, as demonstrated by language learners engaged in a reading and writing task in a distance environment.

A particular advantage of the TAPs methodology was the opportunity to get a sense of the diversity of learners, the range of affective factors that characterise individual learners and which are intricately connected with learning capacity and learning success. A comment from one student also indicated the potential of TAPs as a useful learning tool for raising self-awareness:

> I think in a way doing this project has concentrated me and focused me on my own study skills and made me think about what I should be doing and not doing ...

Although students were asked to record their thoughts as they came to mind and not after having had time to reflect, there was nevertheless some evidence of reflective thinking in their protocols. As Graham (1997) points out, it is in practice very difficult to separate out the concurrent thoughts of TAPs from other introspective and retrospective thoughts, as the categories tend to overlap. One task is likely to generate all three activities in a very short space of time: externalising thoughts as they occur (concurrent), making inferences or analysing the processes or strategies involved in completing the task (introspective) and finally commenting on those processes and strategies (retrospective). Think-aloud comments from her own study were an 'amalgam of thinking aloud, introspection proper and retrospection after a few seconds' (Graham, 1997: 44). In this study, had the reported findings been confined to concurrent thoughts only, much of the richness of the data relating to affective factors would have been lost. The problem is one of terminology and clearly raises important questions for investigations of this kind. What is certain is that findings from TAPs must be considered as exploratory and not conclusive and that

TAPs investigations need to be supplemented by data from other research (Smagorinsky, 1994; Young, 2005).

For independent language learning settings, where gathering qualitative data is problematic, the opportunities TAPs offer to gain insights into what students really think and feel about their learning make them a particularly valuable research tool. TAPs cannot offer outcomes that can be measured with certainty, but they can 'reveal aspects of language learning previously inaccessible to investigation' (Gillette, 1987: 269).

Implications of the Study for Strategy Research and Learner Support

Robinson (2002: 63) reminds us that 'researchers in the field of language learning have not paid sufficient attention to emotional phenomena'. The purpose of the study was, therefore, to provide a starting point for developing a better understanding of the affective factors that facilitate or inhibit learning at a distance and the ways in which learners deal with them.

Participants exercised affective control by using a variety of strategies, of which only 'self-encouragement' comes into the category of affective strategy. Yet, learners clearly found that certain cognitive and metacognitive strategies, for example skipping or re-reading text, keeping going regardless, consulting the *Corrigés* or a dictionary, making notes, taking a break when in difficulty, and checking back for reassurance, helped them to manage their emotions, underlining the integral link between cognition and affect, and lending support for the need to review current classifications or abandon them, and concentrate more on intended goals and underlying processes.

The results from this pilot, although limited by the small sample and the fact that it was entirely female, provided useful insights and information which give food for thought about how distance language educators might better support their learners. Larger, more representative samples are needed in follow-up studies. Both Block (1986) and McDonough (1995) emphasise the importance of hearing what students have to say, in order to inform the ways in which their tutors are trained. Equally important is how those learner stories can be used to improve learning materials. The protocols provided a valuable starting point for a reappraisal of certain aspects of distance language courses, for example clarity of instructions, the design of open-ended writing tasks, and learner support. Findings indicated that students without support do manage to find ways of coping, but would benefit from explicit guidance in affective strategy development which would take more account of the range of personality characteristics; anticipating sensitivities and offering strategies that are practical and appropriate for adult learners.

According to Robinson (2002: 8) 'motivation and anxiety can clearly often be changed and shaped through teacher intervention in learning'. For independent learners, this intervention has to happen within the learning materials. If cognitive and metacognitive strategies in addition to affective strategies are useful for dealing with affective problems, an explicit focus on these in learning materials would clarify and validate their importance in this respect, and give concrete advice to learners whose negative emotions are impeding their learning. Of equal importance is the need to focus on positive emotions and attitudes and build in strategies in the materials that can help students to maintain a positive outlook.

Finally, given that reflecting on experience is an important pre-requisite for taking control of feelings and emotions, the potential of TAPs as an awareness-raising tool could be maximised for independent learners as a way of developing the 'reflective and analytic capacity that is central to autonomy' (Hurd, 2005: 2).

Conclusion

Affect is a 'complex phenomenon in language learning' (White, 2003: 117) and needs careful consideration because of the extent to which it is implicated in effective language learning. Dörnyei (2005: 219) calls for 'the integration of linguistic and psychological approaches in a balanced and complementary manner'. This chapter attempts to bring the affective domain into sharper focus and to underline the special place affect has in SLA in independent settings.

Learner support is critical for helping learners adjust to the demands of independent learning, for encouraging self-motivation, for providing high quality feedback, and for addressing as far as possible any difficulties that may arise, in particular, language anxiety. It is important to remember that learning is a dynamic process and that 'as the locus of control moves from one to the other, students increase their metacognitive awareness and skills; perceptions and behaviours evolve and change (Hurd, 2006: 301). Teachers, writers and researchers need to be constantly aware of changing support needs, and to be prepared to adopt a flexible approach. The challenge is to re-conceptualise language learning strategies to include the social and affective sides of learning as well as the more intellectual and 'executive-managerial' sides. As Oxford and Burry-Stock (1995: 18) affirm: 'Language learning, more than almost any other discipline, is an adventure of the whole person, not just a cognitive or metacognitive exercise'.

References

Afflerbach, P. (2000) Verbal reports and protocol analysis. In M.L. Kamil, P.D. Mosenthal and R. Barr (eds) *Handbook of Reading Research* 3 (pp. 163–179). Mawwah, NJ: Lawrence Erlbaum.
Arnold, J. (ed.) (1999) *Affect in Language Learning*. Cambridge: Cambridge University Press.
Arnold, J. and Brown, H.D. (1999) A map of the terrain. In J. Arnold (ed.) *Affect in Language Learning* (pp. 1–24). Cambridge: Cambridge University Press.

Block, E. (1986) The comprehension strategies of second language readers. *TESOL Quarterly* 20 (3), 463–494.

Chamot, A.U. (2005) Language learning strategy instruction: Current issues and research. *Annual Review of Applied Linguistics* 25, 112–130.

Cohen, A.D. (1998) *Strategies in Learning and Using a Second Language.* New York: Addison Wesley Longman.

Damasio, A. (1994) *Descartes' Error: Emotion, Reason and the Human Brain.* New York: Avon.

Debski, R. (1997) Support of creativity and collaboration in the language classroom: A new role for technology. In R. Debski, J. Gassin and M. Smith (eds) *Language Learning Through Social Computing* (pp. 39–65). Melbourne: University of Melbourne.

Dickinson, L. (1995) Autonomy and motivation: A literature review. *System* 23 (2), 165–174.

Dörnyei, Z. (2001) *Teaching and Researching Motivation.* Harlow: Pearson Education Ltd.

Dörnyei, Z. (2005) *The Psychology of the Language Learner.* Mahwah, NJ: Lawrence Erlbaum Associates.

Ehrman, M.E. (1996) *Understanding Second Language Learning Difficulties.* California: Sage Publications.

Ehrman, M.E., Leaver, B.L. and Oxford, R.L. (2003) A brief overview of individual differences in second language learning. *System* 31, 313–330.

Ellis, R. (1994) *The Study of Second Language Acquisition.* Oxford: Oxford University Press.

Ericsson, K.A. and Simon, H.A. 1980: Verbal reports as data. *Psychological Review* 87 (3), 215–251.

Ericsson, K.A. and Simon, H.A. (1984) *Protocol Analysis: Verbal Reports as Data.* Cambridge, MA: MIT Press.

Ericsson, K.A. and Simon, H.A. (1993) *Protocol Analysis: Verbal Reports as Data* (2nd edn). Cambridge, MA: MIT Press.

Flavell, J. (1976) Metacognitive aspects of problem solving. In B. Resnick (ed.) *The Nature of Intelligence* (pp. 231–236). Hillsdale, NJ: Lawrence Erlbaum.

Gardner, R.C. and Lambert, W. (1972) *Attitudes and Motivation in Second Language learning.* Rowley, MA: Newbury House.

Gardner, R.C. and MacIntyre, P.D. (1993) A student's contributions to second-language learning. Part II: Affective variables. *Language Teaching* 26, 1–11. Cambridge: Cambridge University Press.

Gillette, B. (1987) Two successful language learners: An introspective approach. In C. Faerch and G. Kasper (eds) *Introspection in Second Language Research* (pp. 268–279). Clevedon: Multilingual Matters.

Graham, S. (1997) *Effective Language Learning.* Clevedon: Multilingual Matters.

Griffiths, C. (2004) Language learning strategies: Theory and research. Occasional Paper 1. Auckland: School of Foundation Studies, AIS St Helens. On WWW at http://www.crie.org.nz/research_paper/c_griffiths_op1.pdf. Accessed 10.04.08.

Gu, P.Y. (2003a) Learning strategies: Prototypical core and dimensions of variation. National Institute of Education. Unpublished manuscript.

Gu, P.Y. (2003b) Vocabulary learning in a second language: Person, task, context and strategies. *TESL-EJ* 7 (2). On WWW at http://www-writing.berkeley.edu/TESL-EJ/ej26/a4.html. Accessed 10.04.08.

Guiora, A.Z. (1983) The dialectic of language acquisition. *Language Learning* 33, 3–12.

Hampel, R., Felix, U., Hauck, M. and Coleman, J. (2005) Complexities of learning and teaching languages in a real-time audiographic environment. *GFL-German as a foreign language* 3, 1–30. On WWW at http://www.gfl-journal.de/3–2005/hampel_felix_hauck_coleman.html. Accessed 10.04.08.

Harris, C. (1995) What do the learners think?: A study of how *It's over to you* learners define successful learning at a distance. In S. Gollins (ed.) *Language in Distance Education: How Far Can We Go?* Proceedings of the NCELTR Conference, NCELTR, Sydney.

Harris, V. (2003) Adapting classroom-based strategy instruction to a distance learning context. *TESL-EJ* 7 (2). On WWW at http://writing.berkeley.edu/TESL-EJ/ej26/a1.html. Accessed 10.04.08.

Hauck, M. and Hurd, S. (2005) Exploring the link between language anxiety and learner self-management in face-to-face and virtual language learning contexts. *European Journal of Open, Distance and E-Learning*. On WWW at http://www.eurodl.org/materials/contrib/2005/Mirjam_Hauck.htm. Accessed 10.04.08.

Hong-Nam, K. and Leavell, A.G. (2006) Language learning strategy use of ESL students in an intensive English learning context. *System* 34, 399–415.

Horwitz, E.K. (2000) It ain't over 'til it's over: On foreign language anxiety, first language deficits and the confounding of variables. *The Modern Language Journal* 84, 256–259.

Horwitz, E.K. (2001) Language anxiety and achievement. *Annual Review of Applied Linguistics* 21, 112–126.

Horwitz, E.K., Horwitz, B. and Cope, J. (1986) Foreign language classroom anxiety. *The Modern Language Journal* 70 (2), 125–132.

Hsiao, T. and Oxford, R.L. (2002) Comparing theories of language learning strategies: A confirmatory factor analysis. *The Modern Language Journal* 86 (3), 368–383.

Hurd, S. (2000) Helping learners to help themselves: The role of metacognitive skills and strategies in independent language learning. In M. Fay and D. Ferney (eds) *Current Trends in Modern Language Provision for Non-specialist Linguists* (pp. 36–52). London: The National Centre for Languages (CiLT) in association with Anglia Polytechnic University (APU).

Hurd, S. (2002) Taking account of individual learner differences in the planning and delivery of language courses for open, distance and independent learning. CiLT, University of Manchester, 24–26 June 2002. Web conference proceedings. On WWW at http://www.lang.ltsn.ac.uk/resources/conferenceitem.aspx?resourceid=1315. Accessed 10.04.08.

Hurd, S. (2005) Autonomy and the Distance Language Learner. In B. Holmberg, M. Shelley and C. White (eds) *Languages and Distance Education: Evolution and Change* (pp. 1–19). Clevedon: Multilingual Matters.

Hurd, S. (2006) Towards a better understanding of the dynamic role of the distance language learner: Learner perceptions of personality, motivation, roles and approaches. *Distance Education* 27 (3), 299–325.

Hurd, S. (2007a) Distant voices; Learners' stories about the affective side of learning a language at a distance. *Innovation in Language Learning and Teaching*, Learners' Voices Special issue 1 (2), 142–159.

Hurd, S. (2007b) Anxiety and non-anxiety in a distance learning environment: The distance factor as a modifying influence. *System* 35 (4), 487–508.

Kondo, D.S. and Ying-Ling, Y. (2004) Strategies for coping with language anxiety: The case of students of English in Japan. *ELT Journal* 58 (3), 258–265.

Lamy, M-N. and Hampel, R. (2007) *Online Communication in Language Learning and Teaching*. Basingstoke: Palgrave.

LeDoux, J.E. (1996) *The Emotional Brain*. New York: Simon and Schuster.

Leow, R.P. and Morgan-Short, K. (2004) To think aloud or not to think aloud: The issue of reactivity in SLA research methodology. *Studies in Second Language Acquisition* 26, 35–57.

Macaro, E. (2006) Strategies for language learning and for language use: Revising the theoretical framework. *The Modern Language Journal* 90 (3), 320–337.

Macdonald, J. (2003) Assessing online collaborative learning: Process and product. *Computers & Education* 40, 377–391.

MacIntyre, P.D. (1995) How does anxiety affect second language learning?: A reply to Sparks and Ganschow. MLJ Response Article. *The Modern Language Journal* 79 (1), 90–99.

MacIntyre, P.D. (1999) Language anxiety: A review of the research for language teachers. In D. Young (ed.) *Affect in Foreign Language and Second Language Learning: A Practical Guide to Creating a Low-Anxiety Classroom Atmosphere.* USA: McGraw-Hill College.

MacIntyre, P.D. (2002) Motivation, anxiety and emotion in second language acquisition. In P. Robinson (ed.) *Individual Differences and Instructed Language Learning* (pp. 45–68). Amsterdam/Philadelphia: John Benjamins B.V.

Matsuda, S. and Gobel, P. (2004) Anxiety and predictors of performance in the foreign language classroom. *System* 32, 21–36.

Matsumoto, K. (1993) Verbal-report data and introspective methods in second language research: State of the art. *RELC Journal* 24 (1), 32–60.

McDonough, S.M. (1995) *Strategy and Skill in Learning a Foreign Language.* London: Edward Arnold.

Newell, A. and Simon, H.A. (1972) *Human Problem Solving.* Englewood Cliffs, NJ: Prentice-Hall.

Nielson, J., Clemmensen, T. and Yssing, C. (2002) *Getting Access to What Goes in People's Heads? Reflections on the Think-Aloud Technique.* Denmark, Århus: NordiCHI 10/02.

Nunan, D. and Lamb, C. (1996) *The Self-Directed Teacher: Managing the Learning Process.* Cambridge: Cambridge University Press.

Oatley, K. and Jenkins, J. (1996) *Understanding Emotions.* Cambridge, MA: Blackwell.

O'Malley, J. and Chamot, A.U. (1990) *Learning Strategies in Second Language Acquisition.* Cambridge: Cambridge University Press.

Oxford, R.L. (1990) *Language Learning Strategies: What Every Teacher Should Know.* Boston, MA: Heinle & Heinle.

Oxford, R.L. (1993) Research on second language learning strategies. *Annual Review of Applied Linguistics* 13, 175–187.

Oxford, R.L. (1999) Anxiety and the language learner: New insights. In J. Arnold (ed.) *Affect in Language Learning* (pp. 58–67). Cambridge: Cambridge University Press.

Oxford, R.L. and Burry-Stock, J.A. (1995) Assessing the use of language learning strategies worldwide with the ESL/EFL version of the strategy inventory for language learning (SILL). *System* 23 (1), 1–23.

Oxford, R.L. and Shearin, J. (1994) Language learning motivation: Expanding the theoretical framework. *The Modern Language Journal* 78 (1), 12–28.

Phakiti, A. (2003) A closer look at gender and strategy use in L2 reading. *Language Learning* 53 (4), 649–702.

Pressley, M. and Afflerbach, P. (1995) *Verbal Protocols of Reading: The Nature of Constructively Responsive Reading.* Hillsdale, NJ: Lawrence Erlbaum.

Ramnani, N. (2006) Interview BBC Radio 4 Today, 1 August 2006.

Robinson, P. (ed.) (2002) *Individual Differences and Instructed Language Learning.* Amsterdam/Philadelphia: John Benjamins.

Roed, J. (2003) Language learner behaviour in a virtual environment. *Computer Assisted Language Learning* 16 (2–3), 155–172.

Rossiter, M.J. (2003) The effects of affective strategy training in the ESL classroom. *TESL-EJ* 7 (2). On WWW at http://writing.berkeley.edu/TESL-EJ/ej26/a2.html. Accessed 10.04.08.

Rubin, J. (1981) Study of cognitive processes in second language learning. *Applied Linguistics* 2, 117–131.

Rubin, J. (2001) Language learner self-management. *Journal of Asian Pacific Communication* 11 (1), 25–37.

Schumann, J.H. (1999) A neurobiological perspective on affect. In J. Arnold (ed.) *Affect in Language Learning* (pp. 28–42). Cambridge: Cambridge University Press.

Singhal, M. (2001) Reading proficiency, reading strategies, metacognitive awareness and L2 readers. *The Reading Matrix* 1 (1), 1–8.

Smagorinsky, P. (ed.) (1994) *Speaking about Writing*. London: Sage Publications.

Stern, H.H. (1975) What can we learn from the good language learner? *Canadian Modern Language Review* 31, 304–318.

Stevick, E. (1999) Affect in learning and memory: From alchemy to chemistry. In J. Arnold (ed.) *Affect in Language Learning* (pp. 43–57). Cambridge: Cambridge University Press.

Sussex, R. (1991) Current issues in distance language education and open learning: An overview and an Australian perspective. In G.L. Ervin (ed.) *International Perspectives on Foreign Language Education* (pp. 177–193). Lincolnwood, IL: National Textbook Company.

The Open University (1995/2002) *L120 Ouverture*. Milton Keynes: The Open University.

Tseng, W-T., Dörnyei, Z. and Schmitt, N. (2006) A new approach to assessing strategic learning: The case of self-regulation in vocabulary acquisition. *Applied Linguistics* 27 (1), 78–102.

Ushioda, E. (1996) The role of motivation. *Learner Autonomy 5*. Dublin: Authentik.

Victori, M. and Lockhart, W. (1995) Enhancing metacognition in self-directed language learning. *System* 23, 223–234.

Wenden, A.L. (1991) *Learner Strategies for Learner Autonomy*. Hemel Hempstead: Prentice Hall Europe.

Wenden, A.L. (1998) Metacognitive knowledge and language learning. *Applied Linguistics* 18 (4), 515–537.

Wenden, A.L. (2001) Metacognitive knowledge in SLA: The neglected variable. In M.P. Breen (ed.) *Learner Contributions to Language Learning: New Directions in Research* (pp. 44–64). Harlow: Pearson Education.

Wenden, A.L. (1991) *Learner Strategies for Learner Autonomy*. London: Prentice Hall.

Wenden, A.L. and Rubin, J. (eds) (1987) *Learner Strategies in Language Learning*. London: Prentice Hall.

Wharton, G. (2000) Language learning strategy use of bilingual foreign language learners in Singapore. *Language Learning* 50 (2), 203–243.

White, C. (1994) Language learning strategy research in distance education: The yoked subject technique. *Research in Distance Education* 3, 10–20.

White, C. (1999) Expectations and emergent beliefs of self-instructed language learners. *System* 27, 443–457.

White, C. (2003) *Language Learning in Distance Education*. Cambridge: Cambridge University Press.

White, C. (2005) Contribution of distance education to the development of individual learners. *Distance Education* 26 (2), 165–181.

White, C. (2007) Innovation and identity in distance language learning and teaching. *Innovation in Language Learning and Teaching* 1 (1), 97–110.

Young, D. (1999) *Affect in Foreign Language and Second Language Learning: A Practical Guide to Creating a Low-Anxiety Classroom Atmosphere*. USA: McGraw-Hill College.

Young, K.A. (2005) Direct from the source: The value of 'think-aloud' data in understanding learning. *Journal of Educational Enquiry* 6 (1), 19–33.

Chapter 13
Collaborative Language Learning Strategies in an Email Tandem Exchange

URSULA STICKLER and TIM LEWIS

Introduction

The most widespread form of collaborative language learning in Europe today is Tandem learning. The practice of working in partnership is probably as old as foreign language learning itself, but Tandem was first established as a formal pedagogic concept in the late 1960s, in courses organised by the German-French youth exchange organisation, the *Deutsch-Französisches Jugendwerk*.[1] In Adult Education, one of the early experiments in the field, initiated by the *Volkshochschule München* in 1973, brought together skilled workers from the Turkish community and German social workers and teachers.[2] Pioneers of Tandem learning in Higher Education have included the *Sprachinstitut Tübingen*, which has been running German/French Tandem courses for students of social work since 1973 and the *Institut für Deutsche Sprache* of the bilingual University of Fribourg (Switzerland), which has arranged more than 100 German/French Tandem partnerships per year since 1982–1983.[3] Finally, Intensive German/Spanish Tandem courses were organised in the Universities of Bochum and Oviedo from 1986 onwards (see Herfurth, 1993: 73–97).

Among the first English-speaking beneficiaries of Tandem learning were personnel from a British military base in Bielefeld (*Nordrhein-Westfalen*) where a German/English Tandem programme, running from 1991, paired members of the base (aged 18–54) with German secondary school pupils in their 9th year of study at the local *Realschule*. The military personnel were beginners, who received an initial four-week intensive course in German. Thereafter, the programme involved two whole-day sessions, held first on the army base, then – one week later – in the school. Participants learnt to talk about their partners, the town or region they came from and their place of study or employment. They also took part in role-plays based on common everyday activities (see Herfurth, 1993: 253

for details). In the UK itself, intensive courses in English and Spanish, structured according to Tandem principles, were organised from 1993 by Michael Calvert of the University of Sheffield, while from 1994 onwards, the Modern Languages Teaching Centre of the University of Sheffield mounted intensive and extensive programmes of Tandem learning, which, for the first time in UK, were accredited as an integral element of the University's modular undergraduate language programme (see Lewis & Walker, 2003).

It was the advent of the Internet in the early 1990s, however, which gave collaborative learning a new lease of life. It was no longer necessary for pairs of learners to be physically proximate. Time differences permitting, partners from anywhere in the world could for the first time work together in virtual space to learn each other's languages and cultures. This potential was perhaps most fully realised by the EU-funded International Email Tandem Network, whose moving spirit was Helmut Brammerts of the *Seminar für Sprachlehrforschung* of *Ruhr-Universität Bochum*. Email Tandem learning was a significant departure, offering the learner entirely new challenges. While Face-to-Face Tandem focuses on the spoken language, the email variant involves two different language skills, reading and writing. In face-to-face spoken communication, prosodic and paralinguistic information facilitate understanding by giving crucial information about speakers' attitudes. In an online written partnership, however, strategic sophistication and a high level of motivation are both required to sustain an exchange with someone you may never have met in person. Comprehension checking, the negotiation of meaning, agreeing on learning goals, the correction of errors, are all likely to be more laborious in the electronic written medium, since they require greater explicitness, whether in the use of language itself or in recourse to such devices as 'emoticons' e.g. ☺. On the other hand, online learners do benefit from access to written texts, from longer processing times and from the ability to use reference tools in deciphering their partner's messages and composing their own.

Tandem Learning: Main Features

Tandem learning takes place when members of two different language communities form a collaborative partnership with the aims of: (1) learning each other's mother tongue; (2) learning about each other; and (3) learning more about the culture to which each of them belongs. When working in Tandem, both partners alternate between learning a second language and acting not as teachers but as expert informants on their own language and culture. One of the underlying assumptions of Tandem learning is that this twofold experience stimulates learners to reflect on the nature of language and of the learning process and enables them to learn more effectively and to exercise a greater degree of autonomy.

Autonomy is one of the two key principles of Tandem learning. Autonomy has a range of meanings, but it is not a synonym – except in the most exceptional circumstances – for learning on one's own, without any form of assistance or support. Though it may imply a degree of independence in the learner, it does not imply isolation. In the words of Little:

> The various freedoms that autonomy implies are always conditional and constrained, never absolute. As social beings, our independence is always balanced by dependence, our essential condition is one of interdependence; total detachment is a principal determining feature not of autonomy but of autism. (Little, 1990: 7)

In embracing interdependence, autonomy embraces collaboration and partnership, which are central to Tandem learning. What autonomy means, in the context of Tandem, is that partners are encouraged to take responsibility – individually and collectively – for their learning. They are expected to develop a reflective capacity, which will enable them to appraise their strengths and weaknesses, to acquire self-management skills, such as the ability to set their own goals and objectives, and to identify the most effective means of attaining them. Finally they are expected to develop the capacity for assessing the extent to which they and their partners have achieved their objectives, and for evaluating the quality of their learning experience. They are also required to correct their partners' errors and to agree with their partner appropriate ways of having their own errors corrected. Autonomy, as it relates to Tandem learning, is oriented not towards individualism, but towards collaboration.

The second founding principle of Tandem learning is that of *reciprocity*. This dictates that each partner should benefit equally from the exchange. At its most basic, this can mean simply that an equal amount of time is spent working in each language. On a more sophisticated level, however, it means that learning objectives, and the means of achieving them, are negotiated between partners, so that each feels that he or she is deriving full benefit from the partnership. It helps, though this is not absolutely indispensable, if both partners have approximately the same level of proficiency in each other's language, if they are roughly the same age and if they have a common interest.

Success in email Tandem learning implies the skilled application of a range of partnership-building strategies. It is to be expected that these will be predominantly social. Other strategies deployed are specific, either to the online environment, or to Tandem learning itself. Collaborative strategies, for example, enable learners to pursue quite disparate objectives as individuals, yet to feel that each is contributing equally to the fulfilment of the partnership's aims, that is, taking part in a 'fair deal exchange'. It is these that form the centrepiece of this chapter.

The German/English Tandem Project

From February 2003, students enrolled on the Open University's higher intermediate German course, *Motive*, were offered the opportunity to participate in voluntary email Tandem exchanges. In the first year, 25 students were paired with German partners via the International Tandem Network based in Bochum and received individual emails from their Tandem partners. Because the Tandem project was from the start envisaged as a research and evaluation project as well as an enhancement of students' normal learning opportunities, participants were asked to collect copies of their own and their partners' emails and to share them with the researchers. Students also filled in a short questionnaire about their previous learning experiences and computer skills.

In the second year of the project, a German partner institution, the *Volkshochschule Ostkreis Hannover* joined the project. A *Volkshochschule* (*VHS*) is an adult education institution originally founded on the principle of continuing education for the 'working classes'. Traditionally, learners at the *VHS* are mature and of varying educational background, which fits well with the profile of Open University students. (For factors influencing the set-up of collaborative projects between institutions, see O'Dowd & Ritter, 2006.) A slight difference in ICT experience and the way in which the courses were set-up was accepted in order to prioritise shared interests and common background experience among the learners. Students at the Open University, who are used to the distance learning context, had only virtual (email) contact with their learning advisor and Tandem organiser. Students at the *VHS* had regular face-to-face English classes and worked on their Tandem email partnerships in addition to that. Some advice on writing emails was also given by their tutor during class time. Volunteers from both institutions joined the Tandem project and exchanged emails over a timescale of approximately five months. After that initial phase of 'virtual contact' with their partners, students were offered the opportunity to meet face-to-face during the Open University's Residential School held in the month of August in Jena, Germany. This set-up has proved successful and has subsequently been adapted and extended.

In 2004, 15 English students were paired with German learners, although only two German partners could actually participate in the face-to-face meetings. In 2005, 14 English students had partners from the *VHS*, and four students found partners through alternative means. In 2006, the *VHS Ostkreis Hannover* offered the very successful Tandem scheme as a full course for the first time. Students enrolled in a Tandem course, received information and were supported mainly electronically, with the reinforcement of five face-to-face meetings. The students at the Open University continued to work voluntarily and were supported only electronically. Thirteen pairs participated in this Tandem course.

Based on this successful collaboration between our institutions, the Department of Languages at the OU and the *VHS* applied for a European funded Grundtvig 2 Learning partnership project together with other institutions in Germany, Italy and Poland. Since August 2006, the Tandem learning project has been running as the LITERALIA project with exchanges between learners, facilitators and organisers of all institutions and a dedicated website (www.literalia.eu).

The data for this chapter has been selected from copies of emails sent to the authors by volunteer learners. The voluntary nature of contributions means that the actual number of emails collected is limited, as is the completeness of the exchanges. From the data available to them, the authors selected three fairly typical Tandem exchanges. One they evaluated as 'a very successful Tandem partnership', one from the category of 'successful partnerships' and one was a 'short' or 'truncated' partnership, where either an incomplete set of emails was available or the partnership itself had stopped after one or two initial email exchanges.

Learning Strategies

To examine the use of learning strategies by typical participants in the German/English Tandem project, we based our categories on Oxford's seminal account of the strategies[4] used by language learners. She lists two main classes of strategies, direct and indirect. Direct strategies fall into three main groups: memory strategies, cognitive strategies and compensation strategies. Indirect strategies are further subdivided into three groups: metacognitive strategies, affective strategies and social strategies. These categories were devised for a classroom setting. For the purpose of this investigation we needed to adapt them slightly, to fit the online, collaborative, written context (see Appendix B for the adapted version). In terms of methodology, our approach differs from many previous attempts to investigate strategies, which have tended to employ self-reports by language learners, or have asked them to identify from a given list the strategies they employ or employ most frequently (see e.g. Griffiths, 2003; Jimenez Catalán, 2003). We have chosen instead to analyse a corpus of actual email messages for direct evidence of strategy use. This has consequences. We can assume, for example, that our students use some kinds of memory strategies for their learning, but there is little evidence in the written projects to allow us to conjecture about what these are. However, given the evidence of the use of other strategy groups in the emails we analysed, we felt able to refine individual strategies, or even to add further strategies which were not covered by Oxford's schema. Some of these we felt would be generic, some would relate to any online independent learning environment, while others were judged to be more specific to the circumstances of a collaborative language learning partnership (i.e. Tandem learning).

We redefined the cognitive strategy of 'repeating' as 're-use of corrected language', and modified for our own use the cognitive strategy of 'using resources', which became 'using resources (for recording and sending messages)'.

One of the compensation strategies defined by Oxford is 'switching to the mother tongue to overcome limitations in speaking and writing'. There is evidence in the emails of switching to the mother tongue. However, in some instances, when two partners have negotiated the alternate use of both target languages in their emails, switching to the mother tongue becomes a co-operative social strategy. Rather than resorting to a compensation strategy, to overcome their linguistic limitations, the pair are simply following the Tandem convention they have espoused. These occurrences are analysed in terms of the use of L1 or L2 and not as compensation strategies.

In the case of metacognitive strategies we redefined some strategies to fit our context. We found it difficult to judge if our students were using the strategy of 'delaying speech (or rather writing in the email context) to focus on listening (reading)' and noted no examples of its usage. In a Tandem exchange, success in 'setting goals and objectives' is dependent on cooperation from one's partner. The partner has to agree on what to discuss, has to be informed and persuaded; his/her interests and limitations need to be taken into account. This is expressed in the Tandem-specific strategy of 'negotiating'. Nonetheless, the original strategy also remains in the metacognitive category since it can be practised both by an individual and on a reciprocal basis.

Many of the affective strategies identified by Oxford are impossible to detect in this context without directly asking the students, for example, 'using progressive relaxation', 'using music'. However instances of the 'use of laughter' – laughing at one's own mistakes, trying to make jokes with the email partner – soon became evident. 'Using a checklist' was amended to 'using a checklist or an email planning sheet', since an email planning sheet – enabling learners to organise, record and evaluate their work – was offered to participants.

As anticipated, Oxford's last, and smallest, category, social strategies, emerged as one of the most important ones for the purpose of our study. In fact, Oxford's proposed repertoire of six social strategies proved too limited to cope with the sheer range of invention found in this supremely social form of learning. We therefore added to her list the strategy of 'asking personal questions', 'offering information unsolicited' and also the social strategy of 'asking for feedback from a proficient user'. In all we looked for evidence of 10 memory strategies, 15 cognitive strategies, 10 compensation strategies, 12 metacognitive strategies, 10 affective strategies and 11 social strategies (see Appendix B). In addition to these, we explored six generic online strategies, which we felt might be used in any e-learning environment and seven collaborative strategies which we identified as specific to the Tandem method. Both the last two categories emerged from the data in the process of analysis. The following two tables show an overview of the 13 new strategies with examples and quotes taken from the email exchanges. Tandem learners have been coded as German (D1, D2, D3) or English (E1, E2, E3).

Online-specific strategies (Table 13.1)

Table 13.1 Online-specific strategies (overview)

No.	Name of child node	Example
7.1	Copying previous message	Copying the partner's previous email to highlight mistakes or offer corrections
	Quote D1: 'I have got a suggestion for you. You make a proof-correction in red; and send me back the correction-scrip corrected text.'	
7.2	Greetings and social niceties	Start and ending similar to letter writing conventions
	Quote D2: 'I'm waiting joyful of your answer. Much greetings.'	
7.3	Planning for next Email	Announcing time, date or content of next message
	Quote D2: 'In der nächste Email werde ich ein bißchen mehr über mein Haus schreiben, auch über Haustiere und Hobbys. Haben Sie die Tandemprojekt Arbeitsblätter? Natürlich können wir über diese Themen schreiben.'	
	['I will write more about my house in the next email, also about pets and hobbies. Do you have any Tandem worksheets? Of course, we can write about those topics.']	
7.4	Signposting in the Email	Announcing that the next part will contain correction; Announcing switch of language.
	Quote E3: 'Jetzt machen wir die Verbesserungen auf Englisch.'*	
	*(Only two Tandem learners used this strategy extensively.)	
	['Now we'll do the corrections in English.']	
7.5	Using symbols for correction	Making use of electronic communication affordances to highlight, underline or colour words for corrections
	Quote D1: 'Ganz spannend. (Dieser kurze Satz ist zwar umgangssprachlich in Ordnung; ich würde aber schreiben: Die Bücher sind ganz spannend.)'**	

(Continued)

Table 13.1 (Continued)

No.	Name of child node	Example
	**(Note use of colour in original: underline = red font, italics = blue font)	
	['How exciting. *(This short phrase is alright in colloquial language but I would rather say: The books are really exciting)*']	
7.6	**Using attachments**	e.g. pictures attached to email
	D1 to E1:	
	'Bevor das Kammerfach erfunden wurde, hat die Bauernfamilie im Flettbereich in diesen Schlafbutzen geschlafen, so wie es die beigefügte Zeichnung zeigt.'	
	['Before the invention of separate sleeping areas, the farmers' family slept in the old kitchen area in these sleeping alcoves, as shown in the attached drawing.']	

Tandem-specific strategies (Table 13.2)

Table 13.2 Tandem-specific strategies (overview)

No.	Name of child node	Example
8.1	**Offering or giving corrections**	
	Quote E3 to D3: 'The weather gets better and much work in our garden is waiting for me' is better expressed as 'The weather is getting better and there is much work awaiting me in our garden' or 'There's a great deal of work to be done in our garden.'	
	Quote D1 to E1: 'Ich finde Ihren Vorschlag gut mit dem Korrigieren. Momentan bin ich leider etwas gestresst, aber ich schreibe (wieder) in den nächsten Tagen wieder zurück mit Ihrem (korrigiertem) korrigierten Text.'*	
	*(Note use of colour in original: underline = red font)	
	['I like your suggestion for corrections. Unfortunately, I'm a little stressed at the moment but I will write (again) back to you over the next few days with your (correct) corrected text.']	
8.2	**Evaluating partner**[7]	Explicitly evaluating or grading partner's L2 performance
	Quote: D1 to E1: 'Ich glaube, dass einige Fehler nur Flüchtigkeitsfehler sind.'	
	['I believe that some of the mistakes are just slips of the pen.']	

(Continued)

Table 13.2 *(Continued)*

No.	Name of child node	Example
8.3	Encouraging partner	Giving positive feedback to partner or explicitly suggesting positive attitude
	Quote: E3 to D3: 'These are mostly just little points – I hope that you find them helpful. I'm very impressed by the standard your English!'	
8.4	Offering a fair deal exchange	
	Quote: E2: 'I hope that these things are helpful. Please do the same to my email!'	
8.5	Answering explicit questions	Responding to partner's direct questions in previous emails or referring directly back to partner's statements
	Quote: E3 to D3: 'Auf deine Frage hin, im Moment studiere ich nur Deutsch, und es gefällt mir gut. Ich habe aber schon Französisch mit der Open Universität studiert – das was toll. Im Moment lese ich übrigens "Harry Potter und der Stein der Weisen", um das Deutsch zu verbessern. Vielleicht soll ich etwas geistig Anspruchsvolleres lesen, aber Harry Potter gefällt mir sehr gut!'	
	['In response to your question: at the moment I'm only studying German and I like it. I've also done French with the Open University – that was great. At the moment, I'm reading "Harry Potter and the Philosopher's Stone" – in German – to improve my German. Maybe I should read something more demanding but I really like Harry Potter.']	
8.6	Planning face-to-face meeting	Negotiating time and place for meeting partner face-to-face
	Quote: E1 to D1: 'I now know that I will be in Jena for the summer school as part of my course from 12 to 18 August. I was told that it might be possible for us to meet in Jena. Do you know about this? Will it be possible for us to meet during that time?'	
8.7	Negotiating	
	Quote: E3 to D3: 'Wir sollen, soviel ich weiß, ungefähr 50% auf Deusch und 50% auf Englisch schreiben. Ich würde mich sehr freuen, wenn Sie meine Fehler korrigieren können. Sie werden sicher sehr beschäftigt sein! Sollen wir "du" oder "Sie" brauchen, wenn wir uns schreiben? Ich persönlich hätte lieber "du".'	
	['As far as I know, we should write about 50% in German and 50% in English. I would really appreciate it if you could correct my mistakes. You are probably very busy. Should we use "du" (informal) or "Sie" (formal address) in writing? I personally would prefer "du".']	
	Quote:	
	D1 to E1: 'Bad news is: I don't no, whether I became holiday on Wednesday and Thursday for the trip to Jena. I am afraid that is not possible. What can we do?'	

Data Analysis

Quantity of language

Six Tandem learners' exchanges were investigated: three German native speakers and three English native speakers forming three Tandem pairs. They exchanged emails over a period of up to seven months.

Successful Tandem pairs exchanged at least two emails per month. The overall number of emails exchanged between these Tandem pairs is 34; the highest number in evidence is of Tandem pair 1 (23 emails). The word count for all emails amounts to 16,175; 11,233 of which were in the Tandem learners' respective mother tongue (L1); the rest, 4942 words, were written in the target language (L2).

The discrepancy between L1 and L2 use is due largely to one student's decision to send two essays he had written in his mother tongue as part of (or attachment to) the Tandem mails. Without these essays of 5702 words total, the distribution would be more balanced with 5531 words (or 53%) written in L1 and 4942 words (or 47%) in the target language (see Figure 13.1).

Learning strategies

In this investigation, evidence of Tandem exchanges (copies of written emails) are analysed by two researchers, tagging strategy use where they can see evidence for it; either by explicitly reporting a particular strategy or by using the strategy implicitly. All emails were copied into MSWord and transferred into NVivo7 which was used as qualitative analysis software.

A node tree of eight main nodes (memory strategies, cognitive, compensation, metacognitive, affective, social, online-specific and tandem-specific

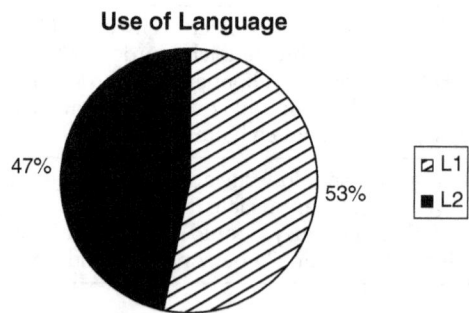

Figure 13.1 Use of language (L1 vs. L2)

Collaborative Language Learning Strategies 247

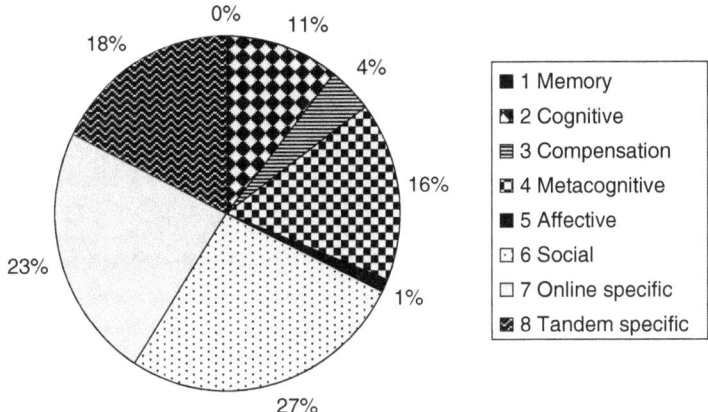

Figure 13.2 Distribution of strategies according to categories (main nodes; Memory = 0%)

strategies) was applied, taking as its point of departure the language learning strategy groups identified by Oxford, adapted to our data (see Oxford, 1990: 15–21). All main nodes had sub-nodes (corresponding to more specific groups of strategies: for example, guessing intelligently) and child nodes (corresponding to individual strategies: for example, using linguistic clues; using other clues). In all there were 18 sub-nodes and 81 child nodes. Of Oxford's six original strategy groups, not all were evident in email Tandem exchanges. There is no evidence of any memory strategies being employed or referred to (see Figure 13.2).

Affective strategies were used very infrequently (a total number of six tags referring to 'using music', 'making positive statements', 'discussing feelings with others' and 'listening to one's body' could be found). This may be due to the fact that affective strategies, such as enhanced self-talk and self-management, tend to be directed towards the self rather than other people (see Figure 13.3).

Compensation strategies were also little in evidence: 23 instances overall, and, apart from the strategy 'getting help' which was used by all Tandem learners at least once, only two learners had recourse to compensation strategies such as 'switching to the mother tongue' (13 times), 'coining words' twice) and 'using a circumlocution or synonym'(twice). The nature of written tasks and asynchronous communication can in part be held responsible for this low number: learners could use dictionaries or other resources to find appropriate words, and did (in some cases evidenced by mistranslations) make use of these.

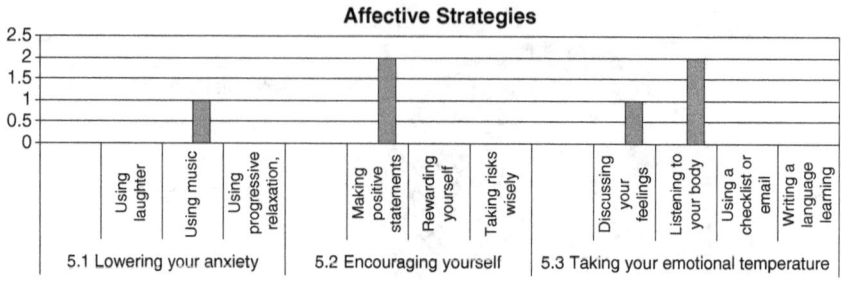

Figure 13.3 Affective strategies

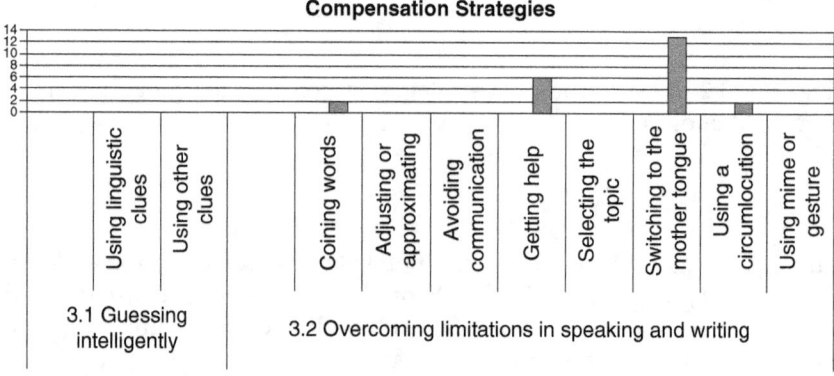

Figure 13.4 Compensation strategies

This is one of the few examples of the use of the compensation strategy of circumlocution or synonym (see Figure 13.4):

E1 to D1:

'Hauptsächlich Pollack (mit Kabeljau verwandt) aber auch Makrel.'

['Mainly pollock (related to cod) but also mackerel.']

Cognitive strategies were employed a total number of 58 times, the most obvious one, 'practising naturalistically' (27 times), was used for tagging emails where learners used the L2.[5] Other cognitive strategies that could be identified from the evidence were: 'recognising and using formulas and patterns' (16 times – e.g. obvious chunks or formulaic use of the L2), 'translating' (three times), 'creating structure for input and output' (three times), 'highlighting' (seven times), and 'summarising' (once). Surprisingly, 'repeating and/or re-use of corrected language' (a strategy that seems ideal for Tandem exchanges) was only used once (see Figure 13.5).

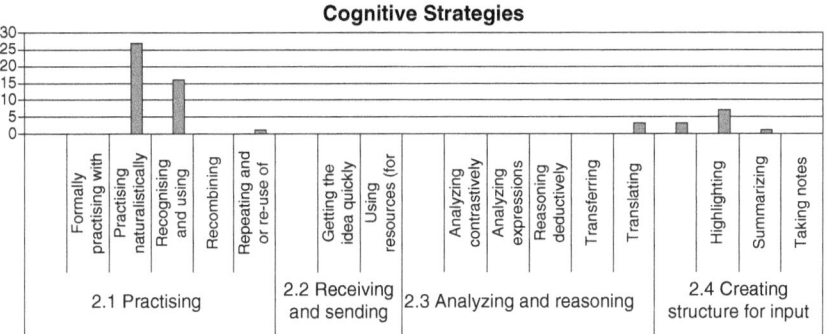

Figure 13.5 Cognitive strategies

A high number of metacognitive strategies were in evidence, 91 in total, showing that learners needed to discuss organisation and planning explicitly with their Tandem partner. Also, most of the metacognitive strategies investigated were used at least once, with the exception of 'paying attention' (cannot be shown) and 'finding out about language learning' (which is often used with a teacher rather than with a peer/co-learner).

The most frequent metacognitive strategies used were: 'organising' (26 times, for example, referring explicitly to organising one's own language learning or suggesting/describing organisation for the Tandem learning); 'planning for a language task' (20 times, for example inviting comments on a particular topic of interest, planning to read up or expand on one's language learning with reference to a particular topic or area).[6] Self-evaluation and self-monitoring were also frequently employed (13 and 14 times, respectively). Other metacognitive strategies used were: 'identifying the purpose of a language task' (once), 'seeking practice opportunities' (four times) and 'setting goals and objectives' (once).

The metacognitive strategy 'overviewing and linking: intercultural comparison' was devised by adapting an existing one to the Tandem context. Here is an example of it in use:

E1 to D1:

> Ich habe nichts dagegen wenn wir uns mit Vornamen ansprechen (wie's in England üblich ist). Aber für meine erste Email werde ich Sie noch siezen bis ich weiss, dass Sie auch mit dem Duzen einverstanden sind. Ich kenne ja die Sitten in Deutschland gut.

> [I have nothing against us using each others' first names (it's normal in English). But in my first email I'm going to call you 'Sie', until I'm sure that you're happy with me calling you 'Du'. I know how you're expected to behave in Germany.]

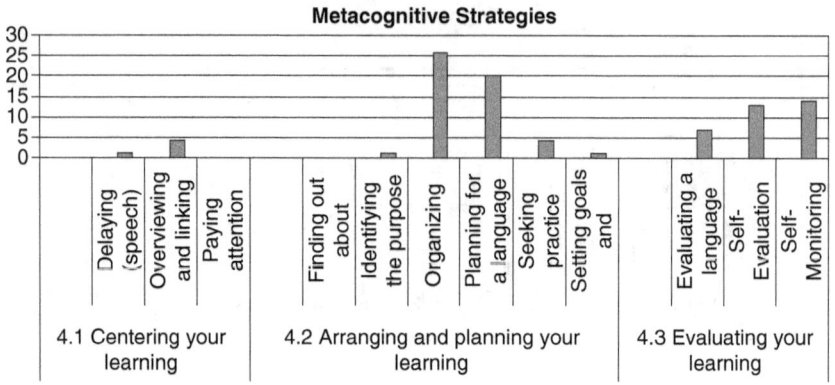

Figure 13.6 Metacognitive strategies

A further strategy had to be added to distinguish it from other evaluating strategies. It is that of 'evaluating a language task'. It was explicitly used by one Tandem student on no fewer than seven occasions (see Figure 13.6). For example:

E3 to D3:

'I think it's a good idea to read German books to get the feeling for the language.'

The highest number of incidences were, not surprisingly, in the category 'social strategies' with a total number of 142 tags; more than any of the other original categories.

Although, in theory, all Tandem exchanges could also be tagged as 'co-operating with peers', the researchers chose the more specific sister-strategy 'co-operating with proficient users of the new language' since it fits better the distinctive method of Tandem learning. This strategy was used 10 times in all.

The strategy used most frequently was 'giving personal information' (57 times), a strategy aimed at social cohesion and establishing a working relationship; it becomes particularly obvious in asynchronous online exchanges where the visual and other external cues that help to appraise a conversation partner are absent and have to be replaced by explicit written information. Thanking and apologising, which could also be seen as a part of the 'social niceties' category, were used 25 times overall. The next most frequent category was 'offering information unsolicited' (20 times), a category that can be closely related to 'giving personal information' but was only used where the information presented was not of a personal nature.

Other social strategies employed by email Tandem learners were 'empathising with others' (twice), a sub-node category only used where

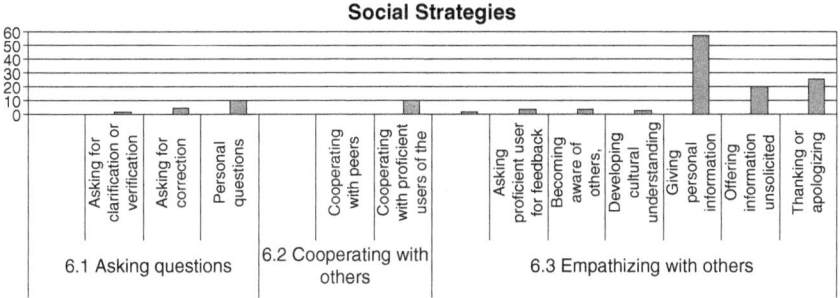

Figure 13.7 Social strategies

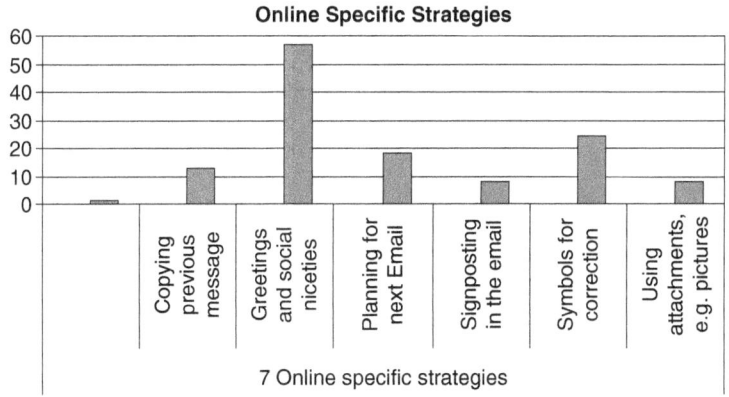

Figure 13.8 Online-specific strategies

learners refer back to their partner's email in a very general way; 'asking proficient user for feedback or evaluation' (four times), 'becoming aware of others' thoughts and feelings' (four times) and 'developing cultural understanding' (three times).

All nodes in the sub-node 'asking questions' were used (see Figure 13.7). 'Asking for clarification or verification' was used twice; 'asking for correction' five times. A new node had to be introduced, referring specifically to 'personal questions', as this appears quite often (10 times overall) in email Tandem exchanges.

The new category of 'online specific strategies' appeared 129 times in all (see Figure 13.8). Most frequently the strategy of 'offering greetings and social niceties' was employed (57 times), and nearly every Tandem exchange included at least one exemplification of this strategy. 'Using symbols for correction' was used 24 times overall, and 'planning for next

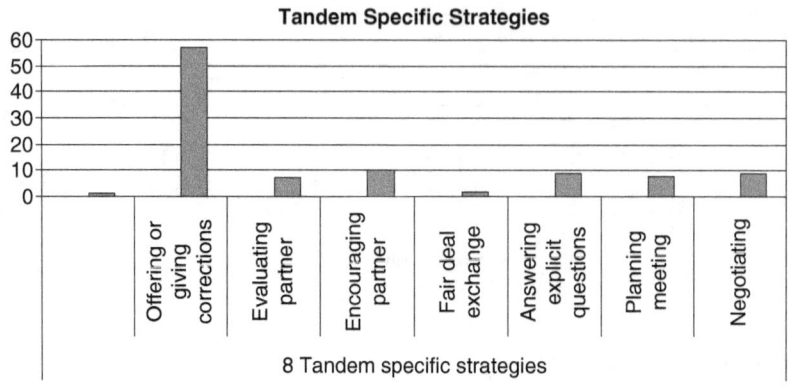

Figure 13.9 Tandem-specific strategies

email' could be coded 18 times. Three other new strategies: 'copying previous message', 'signposting in the email' and 'using attachments' were used less frequently (13, eight and eight times, respectively).

Tandem specific strategies were in evidence 103 times overall. The most frequently used strategy was 'offering or giving corrections' (57 times). This strategy is encouraged by the Tandem method where reciprocity and language learning are fore-grounded and some instructions (including our own brief introduction to Tandem learning) explicitly mention 'correcting the partner's utterances' as part of the learning method. Two other strategies that can be linked conceptually to this strategy are 'encouraging, supporting a partner' – this was used 10 times – and 'evaluating partner' (seven times).

Other strategies used were 'negotiating' and 'answering explicit questions' (nine times each) and 'planning meeting', where arrangements for a face-to-face meeting were negotiated, (eight times) (see Figure 13.9). The remaining tags consisted of two references to a 'fair deal exchange', and one general reference to Tandem learning, coded to the generic main-node.

Conclusion

Our data offers a picture of email Tandem learning as a highly social form of language learning. Of the conventional language learning strategies which can be observed in our data, social strategies are by some margin the most used. And of these 'giving personal information', 'thanking or apologising' and 'offering information unsolicited' are the most important. With regard to online strategies – the next most significant group to be used – by far the most frequently found strategy is 'greetings and social niceties'.

This is not altogether surprising, given that Tandem is based on a one-to-one exchange between individuals. It is likely, that those with well-developed online interpersonal skills will perform better than those who lack them. But this is some way from the still all too common image of the online learner as rather solitary and perhaps socially maladroit.

For all their sociability, successful email Tandem learners are not easily diverted from the task in hand: that of learning each other's language. They use the Tandem-specific strategy of 'offering or giving corrections' just as frequently as the top-ranking social and online strategies (respectively 'giving personal information' and 'greetings and social niceties'). This is borne out by the presence of 'using symbols for correction' as their second most favoured online strategy.

However, too much correction can ruin a partnership. In our present corpus, E3 devotes 24.52% of her production to offering correction. She grows tired of doing so, however, and ultimately abandons this incomplete exchange. Contrast this with the flourishing exchange between E1 and D1, where just 3.78% of the former's and 1.72% of the latter's production is devoted to correction.

What the data also tells us is that success in email Tandem learning is a matter of employing a distinctive set of language learning strategies. Though some of what Tandem learners do is common to all successful language learners (seeking practice opportunities, communicating with native speakers or proficient speakers), approximately 41% of their strategy use is specific either to the online environment or to the Tandem learning method itself.

Online specific strategies play a prominent role in the Tandem exchanges, accounting for 23% of overall strategy use. They show that our learners are, for the most part, confident users of the online environment who can use creative means (e.g. colour coding, copying, etc.) to help their learning partners or structure their own emails.

New strategies, specific to Tandem learning, were also identified in the data (making up 18% of the total). These were not simply a response to the initial guidance learners will have received – as, for example, offering and giving corrections, might be. Some also developed out of the actual practice of Tandem learning itself, for example, the focus on 'planning a face-to-face meeting'. All the Tandem specific strategies are by their nature social strategies (as they involve a learning partner); however, they are different enough from conventional classroom based strategies to merit their own category. Encouraging or evaluating a partner takes on a new dimension if this partner is in the same role (as expert in his or her own language) and can offer the same support in the next exchange. Negotiating procedures, tasks and content of future Tandem exchanges is made a more realistic task, as the Tandem partnerships operate for the most part as pairs of learners with the ability to manage their own learning.

A final word on one of the limitations of our study. It may be that our learners made use of memory strategies and affective (self-regulating) strategies, as well as the observable strategies in Oxford's other groups. To investigate this would require the use of a self-report methodology, rather than the corpus-based one used here. A combination of the two would enable us to gain a picture of both the inner and the outer worlds of email Tandem learners.

Notes

1. For a brief history of early initiatives in Tandem Learning, see Herfurth (1993): 243–245).
2. This exchange was run in collaboration with a Turkish immigrants self-help organisation, the *Anatolischer Solidaritätsverein*. The courses were held on Sundays, took up a whole day, and lasted two months. They ran from 1973 to 1983. Herfurth ascribes their eventual demise to a lack of interest from would-be German participants; the different social and educational backgrounds of putative partners, and the relatively large distance between the speech systems of German and Turkish. (See Herfurth, 1993: 244–255.)
3. For details of the Tübingen Tandem course see Herfurth (1993: 75–97). For some references to Fribourg, see Herfurth (1993: 247–249).
4. For a detailed list of strategies, see Appendix A, which is based on Oxford (1990: 18–21).
5. This means that seven out of the overall 34 emails were written exclusively in the L1.
6. This strategy is very closely related to Strategy 7.3 'Planning for next Email' which was used a total of 18 times.
7. As native speakers, Tandem learners act as expert informants where their partner's L2 language production is concerned and are therefore in a position to offer information, corrections and evaluation to their partner, in a relationship of trust.

References

Griffiths, C. (2003) Patterns of language learning strategy use. *System* 31, 367–383.
Herfurth, H-E. (1993) *Möglichkeiten und Grenzen des Fremdsprachenerwerbs in Begegnungssituationen: zu einer Didaktik des Fremdsprachenlernens im Tandem*. München: Iudicium.
International Tandem Network. On WWW at http://www.shef.ac.uk/mirrors/tandem/learning/idxeng11.html. Accessed 09.04.08.
Jimenez Catalán, R.M. (2003) Sex differences in L2 vocabulary learning strategies. *International Journal of Applied Linguistics* 13 (1), 54–77.
Lewis, T. and Walker, L. (eds) (2003) *Autonomous Language Learning in Tandem*. Sheffield: Academy.
Literalia Project. On WWW at http://www.literalia.eu/. Accessed 09.04.08.
Little, D. (1990) Autonomy in language learning: Some theoretical and practical considerations. In I. Gathercole (ed.) *Autonomy in Language Learning* (pp. 7–16). London: The National Centre for Languages (CiLT).
O'Dowd, R. and Ritter, M. (2006) Understanding and working with 'failed communication' in telecollaborative exchanges. *CALICO Journal* 23 (3), 623–642.
Oxford, R.L. (1990) *Language Learning Strategies: What Every Teacher Should Know*. Boston, MA: Heinle & Heinle.

Appendix A: Language Learning Strategies According to Oxford (1990: 16-21)

Category		*Individual strategy*
MEMORY		
Creating mental linkages	1	Grouping
	2	Associating/elaborating
	3	Placing new words into a context
Applying images and sound	4	Using imagery
	5	Semantic mapping
	6	Using keywords
	7	Representing sounds in memory
Reviewing well	8	Structured reviewing
Employing action	9	Using physical response or sensation
	10	Using mechanical techniques
COGNITIVE		
Practising	1	Repeating
	2	Formally practising with sounds and writing systems
	3	Recognising and using formulas and patterns
	4	Recombining
	5	Practising naturalistically
Receiving and sending messages	6	Getting the idea quickly
	7	Using resources
Analysing and reasoning	8	Reasoning deductively
	9	Analysing expressions
	10	Analysing contrastively (across languages)
	11	Translating
	12	Transferring

Category		Individual strategy
Creating structure for input and output	13	Taking notes
	14	Summarising
	15	Highlighting
COMPENSATION		
Guessing intelligently	1	Using linguistic clues
	2	Using other clues
Overcoming limitations in speaking and writing	3	Switching to the mother tongue
	4	Getting help
	5	Using mime or gesture
	6	Avoiding communication partially or totally
	7	Selecting the topic
	8	Adjusting or approximating the message
	9	Coining words
	10	Using a circumlocution or synonym
METACOGNITIVE		
Centring your learning	1	Overviewing and linking with already known material
	2	Paying attention
	3	Delaying speech production to focus on listening
Arranging and planning your learning	4	Finding out about language learning
	5	Organising
	6	Setting goals and objectives
	7	Identifying the purpose of a language task (purposeful listening/read/speak/writ.)

Category		Individual strategy
	8	Planning for a language task
	9	Seeking practice opportunities
Evaluating your learning	10	Self-monitoring
	11	Self-evaluation
AFFECTIVE		
Lowering your anxiety	1	Using progressive relaxation, deep breathing or meditation
	2	Using music
	3	Using laughter
Encouraging yourself	4	Making positive statements
	5	Taking risks wisely
	6	Rewarding yourself
Taking your emotional temperature	7	Listening to your body
	8	Using a checklist
	9	Writing a language learning diary
	10	Discussing your feelings with someone else
SOCIAL		
Asking questions	1	Asking for clarification or verification
	2	Asking for correction
Cooperating with others	3	Cooperating with peers
	4	Cooperating with proficient users of the new language
Empathising with others	5	Developing cultural understanding
	6	Becoming aware of others' thoughts and feelings

Appendix B: Language Learning Strategies – Adapted and New

Sub-node	Childnode
1 Memory	
1.1 Creating mental linkages	
	Associating or elaborating
	Grouping
	Placing new words into a context
1.2 Applying images and sound	
	Representing sounds in memory
	Semantic mapping
	Using imagery
	Using keywords
1.3 Reviewing well	
	Structured reviewing
1.4 Employing action	
	Using mechanical techniques
	Using physical response or sensation
2 Cognitive	
2.1 Practising	
	Formally practising with sounds and writing systems
	Practising naturalistically
	Recognising and using formulas and patterns
	Recombining
	Repeating and or re-use of corrected language
2.2 Receiving and sending messages	
	Getting the idea quickly
	Using resources (for recording and sending messages)
2.3 Analysing and reasoning	
	Analysing contrastively

Sub-node	Childnode
	Analysing expressions
	Reasoning deductively
	Transferring
	Translating
2.4 Creating structure for input and output	
	Highlighting
	Summarising
	Taking notes
3 Compensation	
3.1 Guessing intelligently	
	Using linguistic clues
	Using other clues
3.2 Overcoming limitations in speaking and writing	
	Coining words
	Adjusting or approximating the message
	Avoiding communication partially or totally
	Getting help
	Selecting the topic
	Switching to the mother tongue
	Using a circumlocution or synonym
	Using mime or gesture
4 Metacognitive	
4.1 Centering your learning	
	Delaying (speech) production to focus on listening or reading
	Overviewing and linking
	Paying attention

Sub-node	Childnode
4.2 Arranging and planning your learning	
	Finding out about language learning
	Identifying the purpose of a language task
	Organising
	Planning for a language task
	Seeking practice opportunities
	Setting goals and objectives
4.3 Evaluating your learning	
	Evaluating a language task
	Self-Evaluation
	Self-Monitoring
5 Affective	
5.1 Lowering your anxiety	
	Using laughter
	Using music
	Using progressive relaxation, deep breathing or meditation
5.2 Encouraging yourself	
	Making positive statements
	Rewarding yourself
	Taking risks wisely
5.3 Taking your emotional temperature	
	Discussing your feelings with someone else
	Listening to your body
	Using a checklist or email planning sheet
	Writing a language learning diary
6 Social	

Sub-node	Childnode
6.1 Asking questions	
	Asking for clarification or verification
	Asking for correction
	Personal questions
6.2 Cooperating with others	
	Cooperating with peers
	Cooperating with proficient users of the new language
6.3 Empathising with others	
	Asking proficient users for feedback or evaluation
	Becoming aware of others' thoughts and feelings
	Developing cultural understanding
	Giving personal information
	Offering information unsolicited
	Thanking or apologising
7 Online specific	
	Copying previous message
	Greetings and social niceties
	Planning for next email
	Signposting in the email
	Using symbols for correction
	Using attachments, e.g. pictures
8 Tandem specific	
	Offering or giving corrections
	Evaluating partner
	Encouraging, supporting a partner
	Offering a fair deal exchange
	Answering explicit questions
	Planning meeting
	Negotiating

Chapter 14
Self-correction Strategies in Distance Language Learning

MIKE TRUMAN

Introduction

One view of self-correction is that it makes a virtue out of necessity: independent learners, having chosen to forego opportunities for assessing progress and correcting linguistic faults[1] through classroom interaction (Chaudron, 1983; White, 1994, 1997), simply have to accept their misfortune, monitor their own progress without grumbling and quickly develop the ability to self-correct. However, as Hurd (2001) observes, the 'teaching voice' is present in the learning materials, which constitute the link between teacher and learner. In independent contexts, learners are accustomed to engaging with the materials without constant mediation by a tutor. Indeed, Little (1995) argues that even when there appears to be no social interaction, such as when a learner uses a textbook, the psychological process involved nevertheless includes a covert, internalised version of it.

Accordingly, an understanding of interaction and its associated cognitive processes can reveal much about second language acquisition (SLA) in these contexts. For instance, although classroom-based, the work of Aljaafreh and Lantolf (1994), who were among the first to investigate the fault correction/ learning interface from within a theoretical, rather than a phenomenological stance, is highly relevant. Exploring the implications for learners of Vygotsky's 'zone of proximal development' (ZPD) (the distance between learners' actual and potential development levels), a concept widely discussed in research into teacher-learner interaction, this study investigated the effect of negative feedback given to students on their linguistic faults. Learning was found to improve when tutor-learner dialogue was increased, especially when intervention was graduated and contingent, and the help provided was 'designed to discover the novice's ZPD in order to offer the appropriate level of assistance and to encourage the learner to function at his or her potential level of ability' (Aljaafreh & Lantolf, 1994: 468).

Self-instructional activities usually require students to engage in some form of guided self-correction, such as checking their answers in the Key, or comparing what they have written or recorded with a model version. Well designed, guided self-correction can help to increase students' confidence in their own judgement and deepen their understanding of the learning process. Self-correction is therefore woven into the fabric of independent learning and provides an important channel for the teaching voice, facilitating the covert interaction described by Little, as well as being a vital skill underpinning effective learning in such contexts (Powell, 2001). Furthermore, it plays a key role in self-directed learning schemes (Gremmo & Riley, 1995) through processes such as self-monitoring: when learners judge their own short-term performance against explicit or implicit standards (Dickinson, 1992); and in more global ones, such as self-assessment and self-management: when learners assume responsibility for planning, monitoring and evaluating their own learning (Holec, 1987); or self-regulation: the practical steps taken by learners to manage their own learning (Hurd, 2005). Finally, self-correction can be observed in conversation (repair strategies), in the drafting and redrafting of written work, and in interaction with tutors or language advisers.

Independent learners must necessarily assume a large share of the responsibility for their learning. However, self-correction has frequently been product rather than process-orientated, often being seen simply as a quality control mechanism designed to gauge whether students are able to proceed to the next stage of learning. In other words, the emphasis is on the student's answer (did I get it right?), rather than the process (how did I get it right, and how can I reflect on the experience to become a more effective learner?). This product-process tension is not unique to independent learning. Bailey quotes an experienced English language teacher:

> [...] [W]hen I put a 'wrong' sentence on the board, most of the students can tell me what's wrong with it, but they make the same mistakes [...] all the time. It's hard to say exactly what is going on here that makes them able to spot mistakes but not avoid them [...]. (Bailey, 1998: 84)

Her comment raises questions for researchers and teachers: what are the relationships between the cognitive processes underlying second language acquisition (SLA), self-regulation and the development of learner autonomy, and how can such relationships be influenced so that they benefit the learner? These issues will be considered in the following sections.

Some Pedagogical and Research Perspectives

Focus on form

Traditionally, the supervision of the learning process and the correction of linguistic faults have been seen as two of the teacher's main functions, at least in the early stages of learning (Billows, 1961). More recently, however, interest has shifted towards learner-centred approaches, in which students assume responsibility for their own learning by working together to achieve individual and common goals (Williams, 2001: 305). More specifically, *co-operative learning* aims to enhance cognitive and social skills via a set of known techniques; the teacher acts as a facilitator, but the group, to which the individual is accountable and vice-versa, is of primary importance. In *collaborative learning*, learners are acculturated into knowledge communities through engagement with 'more capable others' (teachers, advanced peers, etc.), who provide assistance and guidance. It encompasses concepts such as the ZPD (see Introduction) and 'scaffolding' (see 'Learner attitudes and beliefs' below). *Interaction*, the broadest of these terms, refers to learners and teachers engaging with each other in meaningful ways (Oxford, 1997: 444). Numerous studies of teacher-learner interaction have been concerned with focus on form, or form-focused instruction, defined by Ellis (2001: 1–2) as 'any planned or incidental instructional activity that is intended to induce language learners to pay attention to linguistic form'. Such interaction would, at first sight, appear to be of only limited relevance to independent learning contexts. However, many independent learners do have some tutor support and opportunities for interaction. It would also seem sensible to look closely at any research findings and evaluate their significance for independent learners, given that form-focused instruction is claimed to be pedagogically effective (Doughty, 2001: 206–207), so let us consider its methodological implications.

For Ellis, focus on form involves drawing students' attention to linguistic elements as they arise in lessons which have an overriding focus on meaning or communication. This differs from the traditional approach to grammar teaching (i.e. 'focus on *forms*'), in which language is presented as an 'object' to be studied, and which casts the learner in the role of a *student* rather than a *user* of the language (Ellis, 2001: 14). Focus on form entails learners participating in problem-solving tasks, and may be 'learner-centred' or 'teacher-centred', but Leow (1998: 51) argues that the former, characterised by the relative absence of teacher intervention and involving the completion of tasks promoting individual learners' activation of prior knowledge, may be more beneficial than the latter. Interestingly, Williams (2001) found that beginners were less likely to focus on form than more advanced students, although she acknowledged that neither group did so spontaneously with any degree of frequency or consistency.

Focus on form may be incidental or central to pedagogical interaction. Indeed, in meaning-focused lessons it is often invoked as a response to learners' specific problems with comprehension or production, obliging them to attend briefly and simultaneously to form, meaning and use during one cognitive event. This kind of joint processing may help to facilitate the cognitive mapping among forms, meaning and use that is fundamental to SLA (Doughty, 2001: 210–211). Underlying this is the assumption that learners are predisposed to systematisation, which involves an expectation for meaning and function, and that the latter should be mapped onto forms in some organised fashion (Doughty, 2001: 219). In SLA research this is reflected in the continuing interest in the study of learners' language, or 'interlanguage' as a system in its own right (Selinker, 1992: 247), rather than as an imperfect version of the L2 (Stern, 1983: 125).

Noticing and attention

There is broad agreement that SLA is, in the words of Schmidt (2001: 3–4), 'largely driven by what learners pay attention to and notice in target language input and what they understand the significance of noticed input to be'. He emphasises the importance of 'input salience', which can be internally derived (i.e. input becomes noticeable to the learner because of internal cognitive changes and processes) or externally derived (when input becomes more noticeable because the manner of exposure is changed) (Schmidt, 2001: 10). By changing expectations, explicit instruction can help to focus attention on forms and meanings in the input, a prerequisite for subsequent processing. Task requirements, task instructions and input enhancement techniques can therefore affect what is attended to and noticed (Schmidt, 2001: 10), although this does not preclude learners from making choices about what they need to focus on, or when they should do so (Williams, 2001: 310). The phenomenon whereby learners become aware of differences, either between their own linguistic production in the target language (TL) and that of more competent users, or between the language they can produce and that which they need in order to express their intentions, but are unable to produce, has been referred to as 'noticing the gap' by many researchers. Cognitive comparison – noticing mismatches between their interlanguage and the TL (Doughty, 2001: 225) – is thought to be an essential step in the learning process. Comprehension difficulties or 'instances of non-understanding' can serve to focus learners' attention on potentially troublesome parts of their discourse, which in turn leads them to make modifications to their interlanguage (Gass *et al.*, 1998: 301). We will now consider some of the implications of these processes.

Dealing with slips, mistakes and errors

James (1998: 83), building on Corder's (1967) earlier distinction between errors and mistakes, classified linguistic faults in terms of the actions learners need to perform in order to remedy them: *slips* can be detected and self-corrected, *mistakes* can be self-corrected once they are pointed out and *errors* can only be self-corrected once they have been pointed out and learners have undertaken further learning. In other words, slips and mistakes reflect the current stage of the learner's interlanguage development, whereas errors lie beyond it. He relates each type of fault to the most appropriate form of correction or remedial action (James, 1998: 236–237). Ros i Solé and Truman (2005a: 80) have suggested that in supported distance learning, each type of fault should be treated differently by tutors. The various processes involved are drawn together in Table 14.1.

Crucial in all these approaches is the tutor's assessment of the learner's ZPD, which determines the type and level of assistance needed 'to encourage the learner to function at his or her potential level of ability' (Aljaafreh & Lantolf, 1994: 468) and modify his or her interlanguage accordingly.

The definition of what constitutes a slip, mistake or error is therefore not fixed, but contingent on the learning that has taken place: for example, what for advanced learners might be a slip, which they could self-correct with only minimal tutor intervention, might from a beginner's perspective be an error, necessitating considerable remediation from the tutor before any attempt at self-correction would be feasible. The parameters governing the choices surrounding self-correction are not static, but dynamic, being determined not only by learners' knowledge and level of competence, but also by their ability to deploy self-monitoring and self-regulation skills and strategies.

Learner attitudes and beliefs

Learner attitudes and beliefs are also important. White (1999: 453) has observed that some distance learners, when faced with uncertainty – for instance, doubts about the meaning of a word or a point of grammar – find it difficult to resolve the problem themselves, and wait for some external resolution. Thus, the learner-context interface becomes crucially important (White, 1999: 449), together with two key issues: 'locus of control' (the learner's orientation towards what determines success or failure for him or her) (White, 1999: 452) and 'tolerance of ambiguity' (the learner's response to feelings of uncertainty and confusion, whereby the uncertainty is accommodated so that it does not obstruct progress) (White, 1999: 451).

Self-correction, by allowing learners a degree of control over the learning process, can reinforce their belief in their own ability to shape events and, through activities that focus on self-monitoring and self-evaluation, has the potential to help them to perceive the locus of control not as fixed, and forever external to them, but dynamic, and capable of being internalised (White, 1999: 456). Self-correction focusing on the learning *process* rather than the *product* is likely to increase students' tolerance of

Self-correction Strategies in Distance Language Learning

Table 14.1 Linguistic faults, interlanguage development and self-correction

Fault Type	Interlanguage development	Remedial action[5]	Tutor approach/self-correction	Cognitive processes
Slip	Learner is capable of noticing interlanguage/TL mismatch and modifying TL accordingly.	<u>Feedback</u>: inform learner of fault, but leave him/her to identify and correct it.	Indicate that learner's language contains faults, but encourage self-repair. Tutor and learner are confident that latter can assume entire responsibility for self-correction.	Cognitive comparison undertaken by learner, although process may be tutor-initiated; mainly learner-centred exposure to form, with learner activating prior knowledge and assuming responsibility for overall cognitive mapping process.
Mistake	Learner may need some assistance in noticing interlanguage/TL mismatch and modifying TL.	<u>Correction</u>: provide treatment or information that helps learner revise or correct specific instance of fault without necessarily aiming to prevent later recurrences.	Point out learner's faults where necessary. Tutor may have to initiate or complete repair, but any help provided is graduated and contingent, being aimed at encouraging as much self-repair as possible. Tutor is not confident of learner's ability to notice, so aims to develop learner's selective attention capacity. Tutor performs most corrective actions, but	Cognitive comparison may require some tutor intervention; exposure to form largely teacher-centred, but aimed at activating learner's prior knowledge, where this is complete, providing additional information or treatment as necessary; learner completes cognitive mapping process with tutor support.

(*Continued*)

Table 14.1 *(Continued)*

Fault Type	Interlanguage development	Remedial action[5]	Tutor approach/Self-correction	Cognitive processes
			learner is encouraged to assume some responsibility by using Key, transcript, grammars, dictionaries etc.	
Error	Learner is unable to notice interlanguage/TL mismatch; necessary modifications are beyond current interlanguage development.	Remediation: provide learner with information that helps him/her to revise or reject wrong rule he/she was operating, inducing revised mental representation of the rule and obviating recurrences of the fault.	Tutor has to indicate faults, initiating and completing most of the repair, while supporting learner's attempts to notice; self-correction only possible once learner has extended or revised existing knowledge.	Cognitive comparison process dependent on learner acquiring further knowledge; exposure to form is teacher-centred; completion of cognitive mapping process dependent on revision of knowledge by learner.

ambiguity; for example, by making them aware that there is not always a single correct solution, but a range of possible ones. In learning materials, the Key should provide certainty when this is what is required, or help and guidance when the activity encourages reflection and awareness of the learning that is occurring.

One common pedagogical practice is the provision of 'scaffolding', defined by Ridley (1997: 70) as 'the process whereby teachers give guided support to individual learners who need assistance in learning tasks, until they get to the stage where they can perform the tasks independently'. In the classroom, the teacher facilitates this process by asking questions, or giving hints (e.g. recasting, which is discussed in the following section), but in independent learning materials scaffolding is usually provided in both the activities themselves and through the Key. Ridley (1997: 70–71) relates scaffolding to the ZPD, and considers whether it could be transferred to adult learners who, with their cognitive maturity and previous learning experience, may prefer to work on demanding tasks by themselves in their own time. It is precisely in such circumstances that scaffolding provided by self-correction activities can contribute to the development of the learner-context interface described by White (2005).

Self-correction may not come naturally to all learners, so some form of training may be needed, but a 'one size fits all' approach may be counterproductive. Ehrman and Oxford (1990), in their study of adult language learning styles and strategies, emphasised that psychological type influences learners' use of strategies and their progress in language learning, so training programmes should ideally take these factors into account. Self-correction can also challenge students, who may be uneasy at having to take on new responsibilities. This is highlighted by Carter (2005: 466), who reports on one learner's reaction when she was asked to self-correct a piece of written work: 'I had to correct my composition today? I think that headache should be for the teacher!'. Nevertheless, self-correction is becoming an ever more familiar part of the language learning landscape as elements of self-directed learning (Gremmo & Riley, 1995: 156–161; Hurd, 2000: 36–37) are incorporated into traditional face-to-face provision and financial cutbacks drive initiatives to make more efficient use of resources (Hansson & Wennö, 2005: 292).

Learner reactions to tutor interventions and automated feedback

The other side of the coin – how learners respond to tutor interventions – also has a bearing on this discussion. Let us first consider oral production. Lyster and Ranta (1997) studied form-focused corrective feedback (used in a generic sense rather than with the specific meaning given to it in the previous section) and learner uptake (i.e. responses to it) in interaction in six French immersion classrooms. Four uptake strategies were identified:[2]

(1) Repetition (probable context = conversation about football; student [S] repeats teacher's [T] feedback [FB] when the latter includes the correct form).
S: *Là, je veux, là je vas[3] le faire à pied.* [Error – lexical]
(There, I want ... I'm going to do it on foot.)
T: *... avec mon pied.* [FB – recast]
(... with my foot.)
S: *... avec mon pied.* [Repair – repetition]
(... with my foot.)

(2) Incorporation (probable context = conversation about weekend; student repeats the correct form provided by the teacher and then incorporates this into a longer utterance).
S: *Mais, mais, elle nous a appellés le matin pis uhm dimanche Diana et son frère ils ont venu chez moi.* [Error – grammatical]
(But ... but she called us in the morning ... um, er, on Sunday Diana and her brother came *[incorrect auxiliary verb]* to my place.)
T: *Sont venus.* [FB – recast]
(Came *[correct auxiliary verb]*)
S: *Sont venus chez moi pour jouer.* [Repair – incorporation]
(Came *[correct auxiliary verb]* to my place to play.)

(3) Self-repair (probable context = conversation about animals in a picture; student produces a self-correction in response to the teacher's feedback when the latter does not already provide the correct form).
S: *La marmotte c'est pas celui en haut?* [Error – gender]
(Isn't the marmot the one *[incorrect gender]* at the top?)
T: *Pardon?* [FB – clarification]
(Sorry?)
S: *La marmotte c'est pas celle en haut?* [Repair – self]
(Isn't the marmot the one *[correct gender]* at the top?)

(4) Peer-repair (probable context = conversation about party; peer correction provided by a student [S2], other than the one who made the initial error [S1], in response to the teacher's feedback).
S1: *J'ai apporté du pita bread. Le pita, c'est le même chose.* [Error – multiple]
(I took some pitta bread. Pitta, that's the same thing.)
T: *Oké, mais pita bread, comment tu pourrais dire ça tu penses?* [FB – elicitation]
(OK, but how do you think you could say 'pitta bread'?)
S2: *Le pain pita.* [Repair – peer]
(*Le pain pita.*)
(Adapted from Lyster & Ranta, 1997: 50)

Recasts (reformulations of all or part of the student's utterance, minus the linguistic fault), were least effective in fostering self-correction by students; the most effective strategies were elicitation, metalinguistic feedback, clarification requests and repetition, with the first two being particularly successful (Lyster & Ranta, 1997: 56–57). This suggests that teachers should deploy a range of intervention strategies, rather than over-relying on recasting, and that they should match their interventions to learners' needs, taking their interlanguage and ZPD into account.

Not all uptake results from teacher interventions, however. Lee (2005) studied interaction via collaborative online exchanges and found that computer-mediated communication (CMC) supports linguistic scaffolding, which can foster improvements in students' oral skills through the ZPD. She quotes an example of a weak student (S1) who was supported by a stronger one (S2):

S1: *Mi mamá trabajé muchas horas durante la semana.*
(My Mum worked *[first person verb form instead of third person]* many hours during the week.)
S2: *¿Tu madre trabajó mucho?*
(Your Mum worked a lot?)
S1: *Sí, ella trabajó mucho. Lo siento.*
(Yes, she worked *[verb form corrected to third person]* a lot. I'm sorry.)
(Adapted from Lee, 2005: 151)

Here, S2 helped S1 to modify her interlanguage and self-correct the person/verb form with the help of co-constructed knowledge through scaffolding (Lee, 2005: 151).

Similar conclusions can be drawn from Hedgcock and Lefkowitz's (1996: 299) study of student response to expert feedback on their writing. Learners expressed preferences for more control over the type of commentaries provided and for feedback consonant with their proficiency level and degree of readiness. From the above it is clear that effective self-correction and learner uptake are to some extent dependent on the nature of the feedback; the more closely it is tailored to students' needs and preferences, the more likely they are to be able to move towards self-regulation.

Until recently the analysis of student response in independent learning contexts has posed difficulties for researchers, given the dispersion and geographical isolation of potential informants. However, CMC has ended this isolation by providing opportunities for autonomous language learning and self-assessment via the Web (Chapelle, 2001: 23; see also Chapter 13 on Collaborative strategies); it has also made life easier for researchers by facilitating the tasks of administering surveys and gathering data.

Interest has grown in the potential of computer applications to provide 'intelligent', automated feedback that can be used to develop students' self-correction abilities. Nagata (1993) found that in this respect the help offered by 'traditional' computer-assisted language instruction (CALI) programmes was limited because learners simply matched their responses with a target language model stored in the computer's memory that showed the correct answer, but not how or why the student's input failed to match it. Typically, such programmes involve mechanistic activities that focus on word-level processing, so her study considered whether an intelligent CALI programme, based on an artificial intelligence approach – Natural Language Processing – would facilitate more sophisticated feedback for the more complex kinds of learning involved in the elimination of sentence-level faults. Her findings confirmed that intelligent programmes enabled learners to identify these types of faults, understand why they had occurred and correct them more effectively.

A constantly re-emerging theme in subsequent studies is the use of self-correction activities, combined with intelligent form and content-focused feedback. Pujolà (2001) examined the behaviour of users of ImPRESSions, a Web-based multimedia self-study package which encourages self-correction, giving learners some choice over the nature and extent of the help provided. He found that most learners opted for detailed explanations of wrong answers, with some using the software to pinpoint problem areas (Pujolà, 2001: 88–89). Heift (2001) studied learners' responses to metalinguistic feedback and their fault correction strategies in a Web-based Intelligent Language Tutoring System (ILTS) for German. ILTS analyses student input and gives fault-specific feedback, matching feedback messages to learner expertise and providing remedial exercises. Interestingly, she found that although students could access the correct answers at any time, they preferred instead to attend to the feedback and correct their output accordingly (Heift, 2001: 108). Brandl (1995), who studied learners' use of computerised grammar exercises, found that the different options provided for feedback engaged students in the learning process and allowed them to control their own learning experience (Brandl, 1995: 208). In these three studies learners tailored feedback to their needs; their preference for detailed feedback also suggests that they were more process than product-orientated. This theme is taken up by Chan and Kim (2004), who report on 'e-daf', an electronic self-access system for German as a Foreign Language which aims to increase learners' awareness of cognitive processing. It offers learners metacognitive strategy tips (see following section) on how to complete tasks, reflect on and exercise greater control over their learning by consciously analysing and planning the task, as well as monitoring and evaluating their task processing (Chan & Kim, 2004: 104–105).

Self-correction and Learner Autonomy

There is widespread – although by no means universal[4] – acknowledgement that autonomous learners possess skills and capacities that are important not only for learning, but also in life beyond the classroom (Dam, 1995: 3–4; Little, 1995: 175). Little (1991: 4) sees autonomy as 'a *capacity* – for detachment, critical reflection, decision-making, and independent action', whereas for Littlewood (1996: 430) learners' ability and willingness to make choices are at its core. From the student's perspective, Wenden (1987: 12) and Dickinson (1992: 61–62) both stress two different prerequisites: the acquisition by learners of independent learning techniques or strategies and changes in their attitude or consciousness. Dam, on the other hand, offers a practical definition of learner autonomy:

> [...] [A] readiness to take charge of one's own learning in the service of one's needs and purposes. This entails a capacity and willingness to act independently and in co-operation with others, as a socially responsible person. (Bergen, 1990 in Dam, 1995: 1)

Learner autonomy, then, is as much about the individual's attitudes as it is about his or her capacity to learn autonomously. This is also reflected in this description of the autonomous learner, taken from the same source:

> [...] [A]n active participant in the social processes of learning, but also an active interpreter of new information in terms of what she/he already and uniquely knows. It is essential that an autonomous learner is stimulated to evolve an awareness of the aims and processes of learning and is capable of the critical reflection which syllabuses and curricula frequently require but traditional pedagogical measures rarely achieve. An autonomous learner knows how to learn and can use this knowledge in any learning situation she/he may encounter at any stage in her/his life. (Bergen, 1990 in Dam, 1995: 1–2)

In other words, successful autonomous learners are protagonists in the learning process, rather than passive recipients of knowledge, reflecting critically on what and how they learn. They are also aware that the skills, knowledge and capabilities they have acquired are lifelong and transferable.

In language learning many other factors can also influence success, including cognitive style and abilities, aptitude, motivation, extroversion/introversion, willingness to take risks, and so on (Skehan, 1989), some of which are susceptible to manipulation. As Little (1995: 176) points out, learners need help in accepting responsibility for their learning, and critical reflection on the learning process is impossible without the appropriate tools and practice in using them. This raises the question of whether explicit instruction in the strategies used by successful autonomous language learners can be of general benefit. Chamot (2004: 19) claims that there is broad agreement in favour of such instruction, especially when it involves the development of students' awareness of strategy use, teacher modelling of strategic thinking, practice with new strategies, self-evaluation of strategies used and practice in transferring strategies to new tasks.

Metacognitive knowledge and strategies are crucial to the management of learning (Rubin, 1987: 23) and are therefore especially relevant to independent settings (Hurd, 2000: 42), where there is evidence that successful distance learners, for example, use them effectively (White, 1995). Wenden (1999: 437) affirms that the relationship between metacognitive knowledge and beliefs and self-regulation is of special relevance, influencing task analysis (involving the identification of the problem, comparison with potentially similar ones already encountered, together with the consideration of how to approach it and marshal the necessary knowledge and skills) and monitoring (the regulatory skill that oversees the learning process which follows the initial planning). She emphasises the key role played by metacognitive knowledge in monitoring, which provides learners with the basis for determining how they are progressing, and internal feedback, the state of awareness which lets them know that they have encountered a problem. These processes are akin to those in which students engage in self-correction; for instance, in repair strategies in conversation or the production of multiple drafts of written work.

Autonomy also involves changing attitudes and confidence-building. Murphy (2005) describes a study in which distance learners worked through materials designed to promote autonomy through critical reflection skills and the associated metacognitive strategies. Self-evaluation activities were included. Participants' capacity to cope psychologically with setbacks (e.g. disappointing marks for assessed work) appeared to improve, and they seemed better equipped to make realistic judgements on their ability. To sum up, learners' self-knowledge and self-awareness can be enhanced through learner training and, in particular, through appropriate metacognitive skill development, but their development also depends on the 'internal change of consciousness' to which Wenden (1987) refers.

A Wider View of Self-correction

Little (1995: 176) reminds us that learner autonomy has two dimensions, one pedagogical and the other communicative. Although the former precedes the latter (learners may practise pedagogical autonomy from their first language lesson, but it will be some time before they can function as autonomous language users in the TL community), language learning and language use engage the same psycholinguistic mechanisms. It could be argued that the same applies to self-correction: it, too, has a pedagogical dimension (for instance, as a metacognitive skill, taught explicitly or implicitly) as well as a communicative one (in the form of self-repair strategies in speech, for example). The three examples that follow illustrate both dimensions of self-correction and their interrelationship. The first shows how self-instructional materials can help independent learners acquire metacognitive skills underpinning autonomy.

Example 1

This example, which focuses on a sequence of learning activities, is taken from the Open University, UK's third level Spanish course (Book 6, L314 *A buen Puerto*). In it students are invited to consider the conflicts of interests emerging from international trade. The first activity (2.13) presents two newspaper article extracts about a trade war between the USA and the EU over the latter's decision to give privileged access to its markets to banana producers in countries in Africa and the Caribbean, where the EU has preferential agreements. This activity, with the aid of comprehension questions, encourages students to pay selective attention to key linguistic features in the texts, as well as presenting ideas and concepts that they must understand in order to complete 2.14, which is divided into two parts. In Part 1, learners have to listen to a recorded interview with a spokesman for banana producers on the Canary Islands and use the flow chart below to analyse his arguments. Figure 14.1 provides a structure for the analysis of the content, as well as clues to aid comprehension.

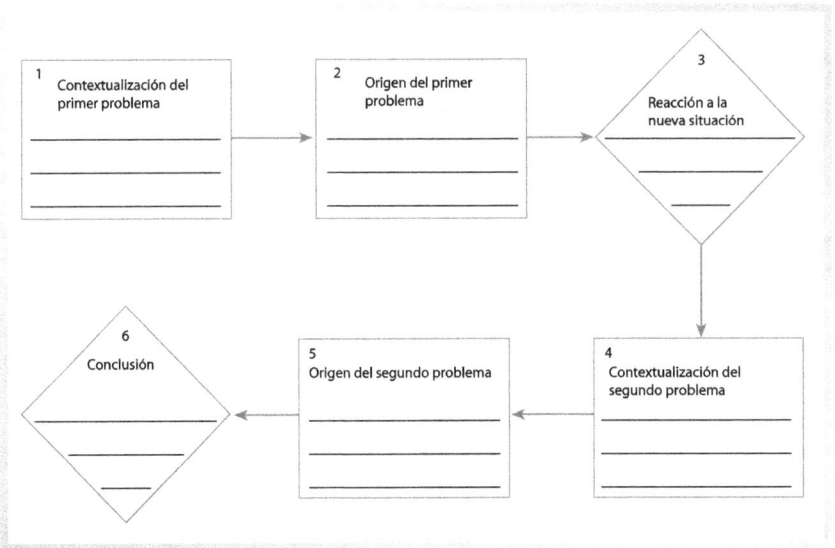

Figure 14.1 Extract from Activity 2.14, L314, *A buen puerto*, Book 6: 37 © The Open University, 2001

In Part 2 they are asked to listen again to the recording, note the phrases and expressions he uses to explain the problem, and compare them with the examples given in the accompanying teaching text. In activity 2.15 they are asked to match the components of an argument relating to a second problem (the relationship between producers of raw materials and manufacturers) to the structure of the argument presented in the recording used in 2.14 and propose a solution. Activity 2.16 encourages them to consider the features of a successful oral presentation, and the final activity, 2.17, draws all the threads together by asking them to give a short oral presentation on this second problem and possible solutions. As a preparatory step, they have to complete another flow chart which resembles the one in 2.14, but contains examples and illustrations relevant to the second problem. A recording of a model presentation is given in the Key to 2.17.

Embedded in the sequence are the rehearsal and development of a wide range of learning strategies, as can be seen in Table 14.2 (*cf.* O'Malley & Chamot, 1990: 137–139).

As is evident from the table, the metacognitive strategies of directed/selective attention and problem identification (or task analysis, to use Wenden's terminology) figure prominently, and are linked to the cognitive ones of deduction/induction, summarisation and, above all, transfer. Practice in other metacognitive strategies (self-management, self-monitoring and self-evaluation) linked to self-correction intensifies towards the end of the sequence. The Key also encourages critical reflection on the learning process. Although self-correction is related to metacognitive strategies in a pedagogical dimension, students are also encouraged to see their relevance to the communicative dimension – an important step as they progress towards learner autonomy.

The second example shows how the pedagogical and communicative dimensions of self-correction are intertwined.

Example 2

Buckwalter (2001), in a study of repair sequences in Spanish L2 spoken interaction, gives the following example taken from classroom pair work. 'Repair' (attempts by speakers to correct mishearings or misunderstandings) is a common phenomenon in conversation (see Levinson, 1983: 339–342 for a fuller explanation). However, it can also occur in the classroom, providing insights into the metacognitive processes surrounding self-correction.

Joey: *gritó? ella gritó no is that gritó or gritaba?*
(screamed? she screamed no is that screamed *[Preterite]* or screamed *[Imperfect]*?)
Joey: (unintelligible English)

Table 14.2 Learning strategy development (Activities 2.13–2.17, L314, *A buen puerto*, Book 6: 37, © The Open University, 2001)

Learning strategies	2.13	2.14(1)	2.14(2)	2.15(1)	2.15(2)	2.16(1)	2.16(2)	2.17(1)	2.17(2)	2.17(3)
Metacognitive										
Planning	✓			✓	✓				✓	
Directed and selective attention		✓	✓	✓	✓		✓	✓		
Self-management									✓	
Self-monitoring						✓			✓	✓
Problem identification						✓			✓	
Self-evaluation										✓
Cognitive										
Resourcing						✓			✓	
Grouping										
Note-taking		✓	✓		✓		✓	✓	✓	
Deduction/induction	✓	✓		✓		✓	✓	✓	✓	
Substitution				✓						
Elaboration					✓					
Summarisation	✓	✓		✓		✓	✓	✓	✓	
Transfer								✓	✓	✓
Affective										
Self-reinforcement										✓

Mick: (unintelligible, but provides help for Joey)
Joey: *so ella gritaba feliz nuevo año ...*
(so she screamed Happy New Year ...)
(Adapted from Buckwalter, 2001: 390)

Joey, uncertain about his choice of tense, sought other-regulation. The interaction provides a window into the metacognitive processing underway as he spoke; he knew he did not have complete control over the uses of the preterite and imperfect, and used this knowledge to inhibit and evaluate his linguistic output (Buckwalter, 2001: 390). In other words, he was deploying self-monitoring strategies by recognising his lack of knowledge and attempting to self-correct after seeking help from his partner. Joey's request in English and Mick's response were both made in a low voice because the teacher had asked the students to use only the TL for communication (Buckwalter, 2001: 390).

In the third example a student demonstrates his communicative autonomy within a pedagogical environment.

Example 3

Milton (2006: 126–129) describes how EFL learners were encouraged to use Check My Words (http://webtools.ust.hk/mmw/downloadcmw/), a program which installs as a word processor toolbar from which they can open dialogue boxes to access language in online resources as they

Table 14.3 Communicative autonomy in a pedagogical environment

Step 1	The student highlighted the expression 'You both have the same age' in Microsoft Word.
Step 2	The student selected Google Search from the options in the Check My Words drop-down menu.
	Check My Words generated a dialogue.
Step 3	In the dialogue, the student selected the query text, then clicked Search.
	Check My Words generated the appropriate search syntax: '*You both* * *the same age*,' then Google Search displayed the results.
	The first three highlighted results were
	You both are about the same age
	... even though you look the same age
	... you both have boys the same age

Source: Adapted from Milton, 2006: 128 in Hyland and Hyland (eds) *Feedback in Second Language Writing: Contexts and Issues* © Cambridge University Press, 2006, reproduced with permission.

compose and proof-read. One student used this toolbar to self-correct a sentence he had written ('You both have the same age') by querying Google Search. Table 14.3 shows the steps he took.

The student embarked on a simple self-correction exercise, but – without prompting – deployed a number of metacognitive strategies (selective attention, self-management, self-monitoring, problem identification and self-evaluation), thereby successfully taking charge of his own learning.

Conclusion

There is widespread recognition that self-correction is an important skill for language learners, especially in independent contexts. Despite this, it has been the subject of comparatively few studies, most of which have been classroom-based. The links between self-correction and over-arching metacognitive strategies and skills such as self-management are well understood, but its underlying mechanisms and learners' and teachers' perceptions of it have yet to be fully and systematically investigated. One reason for this may be that self-correction is seen as a solitary, introspective activity which does not easily lend itself to scrutiny by others. Nevertheless, a theme emerging from much of the literature is self-correction as interaction: in the pedagogical domain, for instance, this might be with learning materials; in the communicative domain, interaction stimulates self-correction as learners 'notice the gap' between their interlanguage and the TL and modify the former accordingly. In the collaborative approaches described earlier, self-correction can reinforce the cognitive and autonomous learning that feedback from tutors or learning materials can stimulate (Ros i Solé & Truman, 2005b: 303). As pedagogy places ever greater emphasis on learning and the learner (Kumaravadivelu, 2003: 25–27), the significance of self-correction in the learning process has been emphasised. Self-correction has also figured prominently in research into the strategies of good distance language learners (Hurd, 2000; White, 1994, 1995) and in technology-based individualised, intelligent feedback. Reflective and innovative approaches to self-correction may offer one way of fostering 'dialogic activity collaboratively constructed' (Aljaafreh & Lantolf, 1994: 467) while helping us to re-evaluate its nature and purpose in independent learning contexts.

Notes

1. From this point on the generic term 'fault' will be used to refer to unacceptable deviations from the expected norm. This term is preferred to 'mistake', 'error', etc. because the latter have been used at different times to denote specific types of deviations.
2. The English translations in these examples were provided by the author of this chapter. In these and subsequent examples the relevant faults have been

underlined by this author, who has also provided explanations in italics in square brackets where necessary. Other explanations in square brackets were provided by the author(s) of the source materials.
3. This should of course be *vais*, but is reproduced as in the original. However, the error that is highlighted in this example is *à pied*.
4. For the case against autonomy as an educational aim, see Hand (2006).
5. James, 1998: 236–237.

References

Aljaafreh, A. and Lantolf, J.P. (1994) Negative feedback and regulation and second language learning in the Zone of Proximal Development. *The Modern Language Journal* 78 (iv), 465–483.

Bailey, K.M. (1998) *Learning about Language Assessment: Dilemmas, Decisions and Directions*. Cambridge, MA: Heinle & Heinle.

Billows, F.L. (1961) *The Techniques of Language Teaching*. London: Longman.

Brandl, K.K. (1995) Strong and weak students' preferences for error feedback options and responses. *The Modern Language Journal* 79 (2), 194–211.

Buckwalter, P. (2001) Repair sequences in Spanish L2 dyadic discourse: A descriptive study. *The Modern Language Journal* 85 (iii), 380–397.

Carter, B-A. (2005) Reconceptualising roles and responsibilities in language learning in higher education. *Teaching in Higher Education* 10 (4), 461–473.

Chamot, A.U. (2004) Issues in language learning strategy research and teaching. *Electronic Journal of Foreign Language Teaching* 1 (1), 14–26.

Chan, W.M. and Kim, D.H. (2004) Towards greater individualisation and process-oriented learning through electronic self-access: Project "e-daf". *Computer Assisted Language Learning* 17 (1), 83–108.

Chapelle, C.A. (2001) *Computer Applications in Second Language Acquisition. Foundations for Teaching, Testing and Research*. Cambridge: Cambridge University Press.

Chaudron, C. (1983) A descriptive model of discourse in the corrective treatment of learners' errors. *Language Learning* 27 (1), 29–46.

Corder, S.P. (1967) The significance of learner's errors. *IRAL* 5 (4), 161–170.

Dam, L. (1995) *Learner Autonomy 3: From Theory to Classroom Practice*. Dublin: Authentik.

Dickinson, L. (1992) *Learner Autonomy 2: Learner Training for Language Learning*. Dublin: Authentik.

Doughty, C. (2001) Cognitive underpinnings of focus on form. In P. Robinson (ed.) *Cognition and Second Language Instruction* (pp. 206–257). Cambridge: Cambridge University Press.

Ehrman, M. and Oxford, R. (1990) Adult language learning styles and strategies in an intensive training setting. *The Modern Language Journal* 74 (3), 311–327.

Ellis, R. (2001) Introduction: Investigating form-focused instruction. *Language Learning* 51 (1), 1–46.

Gass, S.M., Mackey, A. and Pica, T. (1998) The role of input and interaction in second language acquisition. Introduction to the special issue. *The Modern Language Journal* 82, 299–307.

Gremmo, M-J. and Riley, P. (1995) Autonomy, self-direction and self-access in language teaching and learning: The history of an idea. *System* 23 (2), 151–164.

Hand, M. (2006) Against autonomy as an educational aim. *Oxford Review of Education* 32 (4), 535–550.

Hansson, H. and Wennö, E. (2005) Closing the distance: Compensatory strategies in distance language education. In B. Holmberg, M. Shelley and C. White (eds) *Distance Education and Languages: Evolution and Change* (pp. 278–294). Clevedon: Multilingual Matters.

Hedgcock, J. and Lefkowitz, N. (1996) Some input on input: Two analyses of student response to expert feedback in L2 writing. *The Modern Language Journal* 80 (3), 287–308.

Heift, T. (2001) Error-specific and individualised feedback in a Web-based language tutoring system: Do they read it? *ReCALL* 13 (1), 99–109.

Holec, H. (1987) The learner as manager: Managing learning or managing to learn? In A. Wenden and J. Rubin (eds) *Learner Strategies in Language Learning* (pp. 145–157). Hemel Hempstead: Prentice Hall International.

Hurd, S. (2000) Helping learners to help themselves: The role of metacognitive skills and strategies in independent language learning. In M. Fay and D. Ferney (eds) *Current Trends in Modern Languages Provision for Non-Specialist Linguists* (pp. 36–52). London: The National Centre for Languages (CiLT) in association with Anglia Polytechnic University (APU).

Hurd, S. (2001) Managing and supporting language learners in open and distance learning environments. In M. Mozzon-McPherson and R. Vismans (eds) *Beyond Language Teaching towards Language Advising* (pp. 135–148). London: The National Centre for Languages (CiLT) in association with the University of Hull.

Hurd, S. (2005) Autonomy and the distance language learner. In B. Holmberg, M. Shelley and C. White (eds) *Distance Education and Languages: Evolution and Change* (pp. 1–19). Clevedon: Multilingual Matters.

James, C. (1998) *Errors in Language Learning and Use: Exploring Error Analysis*. Harlow: Addison Wesley Longman.

Kumaravadivelu, B. (2003) *Beyond Methods: Macrostrategies for Language Teaching*. New Haven/London: Yale University Press.

Lee, L. (2005) Using Web-based instruction to promote active learning: Learners' perspectives. *CALICO Journal* 23 (1), 139–156.

Leow, R.P. (1998) The effects of amount and type of exposure on adult learners' L2 development in SLA. *The Modern Language Journal* 82 (1), 49–68.

Levinson, S.C. (1983) *Pragmatics*. Cambridge: Cambridge University Press.

Little, D. (1991) *Learner Autonomy 1: Definitions, Issues and Problems*. Dublin: Authentik.

Little, D. (1995) Learning as dialogue: The dependence of learner autonomy on teacher autonomy. *System* 23 (2), 175–181.

Littlewood, W. (1996) "Autonomy": An anatomy and a framework. *System* 24 (4), 427–435.

Lyster, R. and Ranta, L. (1997) Corrective feedback and learner uptake. Negotiation of form in communicative classrooms. *Studies in Second Language Acquisition* 19, 37–66.

Milton, J. (2006) Resource-rich Web-based feedback: Helping learners become independent writers. In K. Hyland and F. Hyland (eds) *Feedback in Second Language Writing: Contexts and Issues* (pp. 123–139). New York: Cambridge University Press.

Murphy, L. (2005) Critical reflection and autonomy: A study of distance learners of French and Spanish. In B. Holmberg, M. Shelley and C. White (eds) *Distance Education and Languages: Evolution and Change* (pp. 20–39). Clevedon: Multilingual Matters.

Nagata, N. (1993) Intelligent computer feedback for second language instruction. *The Modern Language Journal* 77 (3), 330–339.

O'Malley, J.M. and Chamot, A.U. (1990) *Learning Strategies in Second Language Acquisition*. Cambridge: Cambridge University Press.

Oxford, R. (1997) Co-operative learning, collaborative learning, and interaction: Three communicative strands in the language classroom. *The Modern Language Journal* 81 (4), 443–456.

Powell, B. (2001) Understanding errors and mistakes. In L. Arthur and S. Hurd (eds) *Supporting Lifelong Language Learning: Theoretical and Practical Approaches* (pp. 139–151). London: The National Centre for Languages (CiLT) in association with the Open University.

Pujolà, J-T. (2001) Did CALL feedback feed back?: Researching learners' use of feedback. *ReCALL* 13 (1), 79–98.

Ridley, J. (1997) *Learner Autonomy 6: Developing Learners' Thinking Skills*. Dublin: Authentik.

Ros i Solé, C. and Truman, M. (2005a) Feedback in distance language learning: Current practices and new directions. In B. Holmberg, M. Shelley and C. White (eds) *Distance Education and Languages: Evolution and Change* (pp. 72–91). Clevedon: Multilingual Matters.

Ros i Solé, C. and Truman, M. (2005b) Feedback in distance learning programmes in languages: Attitudes to linguistic faults and implications for the learning process. *Distance Education* 26 (3), 299–323.

Rubin, J. (1987) Learner strategies: Theoretical assumptions, research history and typology. In A. Wenden and J. Rubin (eds) *Learner Strategies in Language Learning* (pp. 15–30). Hemel Hempstead: Prentice Hall International.

Schmidt, R. (2001) Attention. In P. Robinson (ed.) *Cognition and Second Language Instruction* (pp. 3–32). Cambridge: Cambridge University Press.

Selinker, L. (1992) *Rediscovering Interlanguage*. Harlow: Longman.

Skehan, P. (1989) *Individual Differences in Second-language Learning*. Sevenoaks: Edward Arnold.

Stern, H.H. (1983) *Fundamental Concepts of Language Teaching*. Oxford: Oxford University Press.

The Open University (2001) L314 *A buen puerto*. Milton Keynes: The Open University.

Wenden, A.L. (1987) Conceptual background and utility. In A. Wenden and J. Rubin (eds) *Learner Strategies in Language Learning* (pp. 3–13). Hemel Hempstead: Prentice Hall International.

Wenden, A.L. (1999) An introduction to metacognitive knowledge and beliefs in language learning: Beyond the basics. *System* 27, 435–441.

White, C. (1994) Language learning strategy research in distance education: The yoked subject technique. In T. Evans and D. Murphy (eds) *Research in Distance education 3: Revised Papers from the Third Research in Distance Education Conference* (pp. 10–20). Geelong, Victoria: Deakin University Press.

White, C. (1995) Autonomy and strategy use in distance foreign language learning: research findings. *System* 23 (2), 207–221.

White, C. (1997) Effects of mode of study on foreign language learning. *Distance Education* 18 (1), 178–196.

White, C. (1999) Expectations and emergent beliefs of self-instructed language learners. *System* 27, 443–457.

White, C. (2005) Towards a learner-based theory of distance language learning: The concept of the learner-context interface. In B. Holmberg, M. Shelley and C. White (eds) *Distance Education and Languages: Evolution and Change* (pp. 55–71). Clevedon: Multilingual Matters.

Williams, J. (2001) Learner-generated attention to form. *Language Learning* 51 (1), 303–346.

Chapter 15
Strategies for Online Learning Environments

MIRJAM HAUCK and REGINE HAMPEL

Introduction

Online learners, like language learners in traditional classrooms, employ strategies that relate to the self-regulation of mental processes, and communicative or language use strategies. As Debski (1997: 42) argues, 'a fuller integration of contemporary computer technology and foreign language education is most likely to take place in learning environments in which students can easily […] combine learning a language with reflection about language learning strategies.' In more traditional language learning settings the importance of such strategies has been evidenced by research. Skehan's (1989) review of studies exploring the techniques used by proficient language learners in face-to-face settings, for example, suggests an interrelationship between the range and frequency of strategies they employ and their performance in the target language compared to competence levels achieved by less successful peers. Similarly, Chamot (2001) reports that more effective learners can be distinguished from less effective learners by the number and range of strategies they use, by the way they apply them, and by the appropriateness of those strategies chosen. She found that 'good language learners demonstrated adeptness at matching strategies to the task they were working on, while the less successful language learners seemed to lack the meta-cognitive knowledge about task requirements needed to select appropriate strategies' (Chamot, 2001: 32).

Informed strategy use seems particularly important in the context of online language learning, where learner interaction often takes place in environments that students are either less familiar with or that they use socially for communicating with their peers rather than for educational purposes. Thus the following challenges can arise (see also Lamy & Hampel, 2007):

- profusion of material;
- cognitive overload;

- need for technoliteracy;
- different time structures (asynchronous and synchronous environments) and impact on interaction;
- new spatial/visual devices (e.g. structural functions, avatars);
- unequal participation patterns (e.g. 'lurking');
- anonymity of the environment;
- need for netiquette;
- need for teacher involvement and support.

Some researchers (e.g. Chapelle & Jamieson, 1986, 1989, 1991; Chapelle, 1990, 1995) have long suggested that investigations of computer assisted language learning should incorporate areas central to second language acquisition (SLA). Learning strategies constitute one such area, yet – apart from an emerging interest in metacognitive strategies (Hauck, 2005; Hauck & Hurd, 2005) – research into strategy use in online settings has, to the authors' knowledge, as yet been scant. As a result, we still know little about how exactly learners deploy strategies when learning a language online and how they develop strategic competence, that is, 'the competence required to make effective use of [their] linguistic and pragmatic resources' (Ellis, 2003: 76).

In this chapter we will focus on affective and social online skills and explore how the fact that communication is mediated via the computer impacts on language learners' strategy use. Our observations are based on learner interactions in the context of an internet-mediated intercultural foreign language exchange, namely a telecollaboration with participants from three different countries – France, the UK and the United States. The following question is at the centre of our investigations: How do online language learners cope with challenges that arise from the geographical distance that separates them, particularly with the 'loss of embodiment' (Kress & van Leeuwen, 2001), which can be perceived as anonymity or depersonalisation (Lecourt, 1999)? We are particularly interested in what learners do to get to know one another and to successfully work together in a virtual learning environment and the effect of this environment on group dynamics.

The overview of the theoretical background for our considerations is followed by an investigation of online language learning strategies with a particular focus on social and affective issues. We propose to take an existing framework for language learning strategies as a starting point and to examine whether it can be applied to computer-mediated language learning contexts. The next section is dedicated to the description of the aforementioned intercultural online exchange, outlining its structure, the participants, methodological procedures, and the tools used. The final section discusses the findings and shows that a new set of strategies which we have termed 'socio-environmental strategies' plays a vital role in successful online learning of languages and cultures. We then draw some preliminary conclusions and point to areas which warrant further investigation.

Theoretical Background

Jones and Issroff (2005) argue for the importance of considering affective and social factors when using technologies for learning. They consider how these issues have been approached in developmental psychology, since many learning theories that are influential in research on learning technologies, theories such as constructivism have their origins in this field. It is also a discipline that traditionally has made a clear distinction between cognitive, social and emotional areas. With the so called 'social turn' in social sciences (e.g. Lea & Nicoll, 2002), however, it has become acknowledged that cognitive, social and emotional development are not only linked but that cognition is a social phenomenon (Resnick et al., 1991). As a result, the emphasis has shifted from an individual approach to learning to a much more socially and culturally based approach, which is particularly well illustrated in Wenger's (1998) view of the social learner as part of a community of practice. In line with this theoretical shift, research on learning has increasingly paid attention to social and affective aspects. Yet we still know much less about these than we do about cognitive factors.

The developments in psychology have exercised a vital influence on language learning theories; Block (2003: 4), for example, talks about a 'social turn' in SLA, arguing 'for a broader, socially informed and more sociolinguistically oriented SLA that does not exclude the more mainstream psycholinguistic one, but instead takes on board the complexity of context, the multi-layered nature of language and an expanded view of what acquisition entails'. This approach to SLA 'can account for some of the less easily defined characteristics of communication', including social and affective factors, whose link with other learner variables have as yet not been systematically addressed. For a full discussion of affective strategies, see Chapter 12.

Computer-mediated communication (CMC) has developed alongside the change in view of learning as a socially based activity. In the context of language learning we first saw computer-assisted language learning (CALL) materials complementing face-to-face teaching and conventional course materials (books, video, and audio); more recently we have witnessed a further move to embrace the new internet-based technologies through CMC. While CALL programmes model aspects of the tutor role (such as providing input and feedback), in CMC the computer is used as a tool, allowing the learner to communicate with other learners and the tutor. CALL is therefore often informed by a more cognitive, instructivist approach to language learning, whereas CMC can more easily reflect sociocultural theories, with a strong focus on language learning *in* interaction (Warschauer & Kern, 2000). However, in the area of online language learning little research has been carried out on the skills required for communicating successfully in computer-mediated environments, and social and affective issues remain particularly under-researched.

The only area where some insights are available is self-management of online language learners. Expanding O'Malley and Chamot's (1990) and White's (1995) complementary definitions of self-management in face-to-face and distance language learning contexts, Hauck (2005: 73) calls for a more comprehensive view of self-management. She argues that for self-directed language learners in virtual spaces 'self-management involves both understanding the conditions that help one successfully accomplish language learning tasks in independent and virtual learning contexts and arranging for the presence of those conditions in such contexts'. Furthermore, her studies suggest that the level of self-awareness of online language learners and their awareness of the affordances of the learning environment is related to the control and flexibility they exercise in their use of metacognitive strategies such as self-management and thus autonomy.

Language Learning Strategies and CMC

According to Wenden and Rubin (1987), affective and social strategies (alongside metacognitive strategies) contribute to learning indirectly since – in contrast to memory, cognitive and compensation strategies – they do not lead to the obtaining, storing, retrieving and using of language directly. Both direct and indirect strategies have been explored in detail in the context of conventional face-to-face language learning; in online learning situations, however, little systematic research has been carried out. We therefore start out with a taxonomy of affective and social strategies as they apply to face-to-face classroom situations and examine whether and how these apply to online learning, using data collected during the telecollaborative exchange. This will also allow us to assess whether these strategies are sufficient or whether new environments also require new approaches to language learning in terms of strategy use.

We have taken Oxford's (1990) detailed framework of learning strategies together with Ellis's (1994: 537–538) examples from conventional learning situations. Table 15.1 illustrates in what ways affective and social strategies are relevant in CMC environments. This table shows that those strategies that learners employ in the context of traditional language learning are potentially also crucial in online language learning contexts. In addition, if the learning process takes place at a distance (rather than in a setting that combines online interaction with conventional face-to-face sessions) other social and affective strategies may be required to deal with

Strategies for Online Learning Environments

Table 15.1 Language learning strategies and their relevance for CMC

Strategies	CMC tools and environments	Functions of strategies
Affective strategies		
Lowering your anxiety (using relaxation exercises, music, laughter)	Complex multimodal environments, including some with affectively-oriented functionalities ('applauding' icons, emoticons, photo galleries, sound files, automatic individualised 'signatures')	Enhancing the experience through expression and sharing of emotion
Encouraging yourself (making positive statements, taking risks wisely, rewarding yourself)	Environments without video	Using the fact that people can't see you to encourage yourself while communicating. Using asynchronous conferencing for calculated risks
Taking your emotional temperature (listening to your body, using a checklist, writing a language learning diary, discussing your feelings with someone else)	All environments and tools, particularly asynchronous ones for point-of-need communication with others and voice-over-Internet ones for access to human voices	Motivational but requires social skills, some specific to management of self in CMC contexts
Social strategies		
Asking questions (for clarification or verification)	Asynchronous environments for point-of-need communication with others and synchronous ones for access to immediate responses.	Immediate or near-immediate availability of assistance in the form of repetition, clarification and other explanatory input from others
Cooperating with others (peers or proficient users of the L2)	Environments with shared workspaces	Working with one or more peers to obtain feedback, pool information, or model a language activity
Empathising with others (developing cultural understanding; becoming aware of others' thoughts and feelings)	All environments	Interacting with native speakers to develop cultural understanding. Using frequent communication to find out more about others

the challenges outlined above, such as getting to know one's virtual peers and building and sustaining a virtual community of practice.

In the next section we describe the online project at the heart of this chapter, which involved three different institutions with students collaborating across three countries on two continents, a telecollaborative encounter which by its very nature posed a number of social and affective challenges. Some of the data gathered gives us the opportunity to test whether the strategies outlined in Table 15.1 were actually used by the participants and, whether they employed any additional strategies.

The Project

Description and methodological procedures

The project was based on an online intercultural exchange which took place in 2005. In such telecollaborative exchanges – which are considered to be one of the main pillars of online language learning – 'internationally-dispersed learners in parallel language classes use internet communication tools such as e-mail, synchronous chat, threaded discussion, and MOOs (as well as other forms of electronically mediated communication), in order to support social interaction, dialogue, debate, and intercultural exchange' (Belz, 2003: 1). The project brought together learners of French from the Open University (UK) and Carnegie Mellon University (USA) with French native speakers from the Université de Franche-Comté (France), and provided an opportunity to investigate how students tackled the affective and social issues raised in the previous section.

The participants belonged to one of the following four groups:

- seven tutor-researchers from all three institutions (three native French speakers and four non-native speakers of French);
- five UK students, all volunteers, advanced learners of French (in the gap period between two Open University courses);
- ten American students following an advanced beginners French course at Carnegie Mellon University, Pittsburgh;
- ten French native speakers studying at the Université de Franche-Comté, Besançon, to become distance education tutors[1] and keen on using the opportunity to practice their English (eight of whom provided data used in this chapter).

The project belongs to a type of telecollaboration which links up groups following different types of courses and which O'Dowd and Ritter describe as follows:

> One group might be enrolled in a class for cultural studies and intend to focus on cultural themes, another group of teacher trainees is primarily expected to investigate the educational potential of online

interaction at a metalevel, while yet another group envisages the collaboration essentially as a means of authentic language practice. (O'Dowd & Ritter, 2006: 633)

Thus the participants from the United States were following a language class with some focus on cultural input/knowledge gain, the UK students were mainly interested in practising their French outside their formal studies, and the learners from France were involved in a master's programme in distance education. Over a 10-week period between October and December 2005, they took part in a structured exchange exploring the benefits of synchronous and asynchronous learning environments for partnership language learning. Based in their respective homes/universities in the UK, the United States and France, the students met online to carry out collaborative tasks. Following the principle of tandem language learning (Brammerts, 2003; Little & Brammerts, 1996) where the same amount of time is dedicated to each of the languages involved, participants were expected to use French and English equally. The venture was partly modelled on a previous study carried out at the British Open University which had linked German students from the UK and Australia with native language informants from a German university and which had yielded important insights into the factors that influence success and failure in synchronous online language learning (see Hampel et al., 2005).

Pedagogically, the aim of this project was to break away from the standard pattern of an intercultural exchange between two groups of learners, a pattern which can lead to confrontation between the groups, with stereotypes being reinforced as a consequence (see e.g. Belz, 2003; O'Dowd & Ritter, 2006). It was hoped that a more complex mix of participants would create a more dynamic intercultural encounter.

Two initial tutor-led meetings in the synchronous environment were organised by each of the three institutions focusing on technical training, in order to give all participants the opportunity to 'play' with the various tools in the audiographic conferencing system chosen for the exchange and to get a 'feel' for their affordances (Hampel et al., 2005). At the same time, cross-institutional groups were formed, consisting of three or four students, and password-protected blogs were instituted for each of those groups. There was no training provided for familiarisation with this asynchronous environment, as it offers a comprehensive 'help' function on its website (http://www.blogger.com). All students were encouraged to use the basic blog functionalities (simple written entries, written entries inviting feedback in the form of entry-specific comments, pictures with text or captions) in order to introduce themselves and to get to know each other at the beginning of the project.

During the main project phase the learners carried out a series of collaborative tasks based on comparisons of their immediate setting (room, apartment, house, street, neighbourhood) and their wider environment (town, places for leisure activities, places of cultural relevance, etc.) and the significance of each of these for them. They used the synchronous environment for five scheduled fortnightly sessions as well as some informal meetings, and the blogs to prepare and further negotiate their tasks or to simply engage in exchanges of a more social nature in between the official meetings.

In the last week of the project all participants were invited to post a brief evaluation of the project which they could write either jointly with their partners or individually. A final synchronous session was scheduled for a debriefing based on a discussion of these evaluations.

The study based on this project combines quantitative and qualitative methods of analysis. Besides audio and screen recordings of the scheduled meetings using the audiographic conferencing application, the students' work in the blogs was recorded, pre- and post-questionnaires were administered and some students took part in post-treatment semi-structured interviews. The French participants also kept learner diaries in the form of 'interaction logs', which provided us with the data for this chapter.

Online tools: Audiographic conferencing and blogging

The application used for the synchronous sessions of this telecollaborative exchange was a conferencing system (called *Lyceum*), combining shared graphics with real-time spoken and written discussion tools. Such a system lends itself for use in language tutorials which require high levels of spoken student–student and tutor–student interaction across geographical space. The screenshot in Appendix A shows the voice conferencing facility, the onscreen whiteboard and the text-chat embedded in the application.

Synchronous sessions were complemented by the use of freely-available blogs, a form of online diary which also allows for comments. In our project each smaller group of telecollaborative partners managed its own blog. This was based on the idea that having a blog not only facilitates self-publishing of project work but can also encourage ownership and responsibility on the part of the participants. The screenshot in Appendix B shows an extract from one of the blogs created for the project.

Table 15.2 gives an overview of the main functionalities that the two environments used in this project offer (for a more detailed description of the tools in *Lyceum* see Hampel *et al.*, 2005). These features determine how audiographic conferencing and blogging can be used for online learning of languages and which strategies participants need to draw on in order to successfully take part in the learning process.

Strategies for Online Learning Environments 291

Table 15.2 Functionalities of audiographic conferencing and blogging

	Audiographic conferencing (Lyceum)	*Blogging (www.blogger.com)*
Temporal aspect	Synchronous communication	Asynchronous communication
Modes of representation	Written and spoken language, images	Written language, images, audio
Production and manipulation of resources	Individual and joint production and manipulation of text and images	Individual production of text
Use of other sources/media	Possible to download material from PC and World Wide Web (text and images)	Possible to download material from PC (text and images) and from telephone (audio messages transformed into MP3 files)
Other features	Paralinguistic features (e.g. 'raised hand' icon, 'away' icon, voting buttons, 'gather' button) to compensate for lack of body language; sub-conferences for pair and group work activities	Comment feature
Addressees of communication	Users present in the same conference	Group of learners; potentially everybody using the Internet
Logging of resources	Text and images can be saved	Archiving of published text, comments, images and sound files

Learners' Online Strategies

The French participants' evaluation of the project and their interactions with their telecollaborative partners is documented in individual learner diaries ranging from simple notes and chronological day-to-day schedules in table format to comprehensive narratives. As a result, they vary in length and detail as well as in depth of analysis, with one consisting mainly of verbatim copies of messages posted to the project blog while other learners provide detailed comments on their interactions. When analysing strategy use in the students' account of their online experience, we found examples of most of the affective and social strategies proposed by Oxford. Table 15.3 shows how the French partners (S1–S8) coped with affective and social challenges.

Table 15.3 Indirect strategies identified in the telecollaborative exchange

Strategies	Concrete manifestation
Affective strategies	
Lowering your anxiety	• Holding back on speaking in *Lyceum* (feels too shy) [S5]
Encouraging yourself	• Making a conscious effort to keep the momentum going by preparing her oral contributions in *Lyceum* [S5] • Making a conscious effort to keep the momentum going by regularly posting contributions to the blog [S5]
Taking your emotional temperature	• Contacting fellow French student to discuss ways of stimulating more active participation of Anglophone exchange partners [S1] • Having doubts whether 'investment' into the project is worth her while; at the same time, considering whether she might be too 'strict' [S1] • Keeping a project diary [all]
Social strategies	
Asking questions	• Posting questions in the blog in order to motivate her partners to participate [S6]
Empathising with others	• Using the blog to clear up misunderstandings [S1] • Not commenting on a missed (privately scheduled) meeting because of diplomacy [S1] • Using the asynchronous environment to apologise for failed communication in the synchronous session [S1]
Getting to know others	• Using a picture to introduce herself and suggesting this to others (here: her telecollaborative partners) [S1] • Joining the virtual pub/café sessions in *Lyceum* and the 'blog for all' [S2] • Posting a picture, her e-mail address and the URL of her private website to the blog [S5] • Publishing a photo of her favourite room in the blog [S5]
Facilitating interaction	• Addressing partners directly by name [S1] • Encouraging others to take part in the project more actively [S1] • Encouraging partners to comment by leaving an open ended message [S1] • Suggesting (regular) meetings (outside the scheduled events) in *Lyceum* [S1; S2] • Leaving reminders (e.g. of next scheduled synchronous meeting) in the blog [S1] • Posting pictures and humorous comments in the blog in order to motivate his partners [S3; S6]

(Continued)

Table 15.3 (*Continued*)

Strategies	Concrete manifestation
	• Deliberately choosing interesting and unusual elements for her presentation in *Lyceum* in order to motivate and inspire others [S4] • Approaching the tasks overall in a humorous fashion [S6] • Speaking less in order to let others have a go in *Lyceum* [S6] • Attempting to stimulate interactions [S6] • Using a humorous approach to presentations in *Lyceum* presentation [S8]

In order to deal with issues related to affect, that is, emotions, mood, attitude and value (Oatley & Nundy, 1996: 258) in the context of the online exchanges, students used a number of different strategies. Most striking are the approaches they chose to come to terms with what is commonly called 'language anxiety' and has been described as 'a distinct complex of self-perceptions, beliefs, feelings, and behaviors [...] arising from the uniqueness of the language learning process' (Horwitz *et al.*, 1986: 128). It is particularly obvious in 'communication apprehension' (Gregersen & Horwitz, 2002), that is, the uneasiness felt by an individual when talking in front of other learners, or, even worse, when native speakers are present. Such anxiety has inter alia been held responsible for deficits in listening comprehension and reduced word production (Gardner *et al.*, 1997).

One learner decided to compensate for infrequent oral contributions during the synchronous sessions in *Lyceum* by being more pro-active in the blog. This allowed her to use the written mode which suited her better, consciously trading the advantage of receiving immediate feedback for the opportunity to reflect before posting her messages. So the asynchronous environment enabled her to scaffold her online interactions by using the blog as a platform for rehearsing her oral input in *Lyceum*-based meetings, thus potentially lowering her speaking anxieties (for using asynchronous environments as a rehearsal for speaking, see e.g. Payne & Whitney, 2002: 25; Roed, 2003: 170; Weininger & Shield, 2003: 346). Another student dealt with speaking anxiety by preparing her oral contributions for the synchronous sessions in advance. She also used self-encouragement techniques by regularly publishing a message or a comment on someone else's posting in her project blog.

The extensive use of social strategies by the students confirms that compared to face-to-face settings online environments require different ways of making and maintaining contact, finding out about common interests and developing an identity as a group. The strategies used reflect various ways of coping with the 'pitfalls' (Kreijns *et al.*, 2003) of using virtual learning environments for community building and (tele-)collaborative work, namely the assumption that social interaction can be taken for granted, and disregarding the socio-psychological dimension of social interaction.

While paralinguistic elements such as body language are one of the main modes of communication in face-to-face interaction, neither audiographic conferencing nor the resources for representation offered in a blog allow for gestures and facial expressions to contribute to the process of meaning making. Through this 'loss of embodiment' virtual spaces can be perceived as 'depersonalising, fragmentary and lacking the humanity and intimacy that the face-to-face environment affords' (Hurd, 2005: 15). Moreover, the asynchronicity of the communication in the blog which on the one hand allows online learners to overcome time and distance constraints means on the other hand that they hardly ever receive spontaneous replies to their postings. This can be de-motivating, particularly for learners in telecollaborative ventures who work together across cultural boundaries. Consequently, the participants in this project had to work hard to get to know one another by posting pictures of themselves or joining social spaces such as the virtual pub/café and the blog for all. One participant – she emerged as the most active strategy user overall – also used empathising skills and cleared up several instances of failed communication in the synchronous online environment which had been caused by technological difficulties and/or linguistic challenges.

We also found a cluster of strategies which we have called 'facilitating interaction' and which consisted of different ways of encouraging others to continue to communicate. Some American students spent less time on the project, a behaviour which some of their French counterparts interpreted as a lack of commitment or, as the following reaction of a French participant to a posting of her American blog partner shows, as the intention to contribute just the minimum necessary to the exchange:

> '... Son intervention est très neutre et distante comme si elle publiait un message par obligation.'
> (Her contribution is very neutral and distant, as if she were writing a message as a matter of duty.)

In line with Belz's (2003) findings, such behaviour can either be seen as a result of institutional factors (e.g. less emphasis on the language exchange within the programme) or individual factors (e.g. a lack of proficiency in the target language and resulting language anxiety[2]). This can lead to students writing shorter messages than their partners – a behaviour that can be perceived as a lack of openness and friendliness and can eventually lead to failed communication in telecollaboration (Hauck, 2007; O'Dowd & Ritter, 2006). To counteract this, the French students in this project developed a range of strategies to try to motivate their English and American partners. They posted messages on their own blogs to simply thank their telecollaborative counterparts for a blog posting; to acknowledge that they had read their partners' latest contribution; to confirm that they found it thought provoking; and/or to signal that they were looking forward to the next message or comment.

The students also reminded the other participants of the next synchronous event (scheduled or private), or invited them to it, explicitly encouraged them to contribute to the blogs, and occasionally even solicited their feedback. Making humorous comments or observations to improve the interaction with individual partners and the group as a whole was also identified by several students as a motivating factor. When asked to prepare presentations about their immediate environment and its characteristic features for the second set of scheduled *Lyceum* sessions, one learner displayed photos of the king's chamber and the gardens in Versailles and talked about this as if he were living there himself. In this particular instance the use of humour in the learner's approach to the task – which was well received by his partners – could probably be categorised as 'empathising with others'. It originated from his impression that despite the initial familiarisation sessions, some of his peers still felt uncomfortable in the synchronous online environment and were therefore exposed to techno-stress and cognitive overload.

It also became clear that students developed other strategies which – although directly related to social strategies – can be grouped together as 'socio-environmental strategies'. These relate to how students made use of particular functionalities of the online learning environments, that is, the available modes and their affordances, in order to improve social relations. Table 15.4 gives an overview of these strategic approaches, which reflect the students' perception of the learning spaces (i.e. *Lyceum* and the blogs) and of their affordances. As the telecollaborative experience progressed, participants recognised that communication in the audiographic conferencing environment is of a different nature to face-to-face interaction. They developed strategies to cope with the lack of spontaneity by, for example, using the text chat tool, showing photos or by not over-preparing for a synchronous session. One student stated that communication improved once she was able to accept silences in *Lyceum*. Learners also developed the skill of using the strengths of one online environment in order to deal with the limitations of the other. Thus the asynchronous nature of the blog made it an ideal tool for sending out messages inviting others to the next synchronous session in *Lyceum*, and several students used the blog to that effect. Another participant posted summarising notes on the scheduled events to the blog to motivate her partner. Yet another student – who felt anxious in *Lyceum* – used the asynchronous and written nature of the blog to contribute more actively to the project.

Table 15.4 Socio-environmental strategies

Socio-environmental strategies	Concrete manifestation
Using the tools and modes available to improve communication and interaction	• Posting summarising notes on synchronous meetings to the blog as an encouragement for the partner to add comments and observations [S1] • Using text chat to compensate for the lack of spontaneity (silences) of *Lyceum* [S1] • Starting work on a collaborative task as if the learning partners were present (posting open ended comments and a series of questions to the project blog) [S3] • Accepting silences in *Lyceum* [S3] • Sending a welcome message to the blog just before a scheduled *Lyceum* session [S4] • Showing photos (previously not published in the blog) to invite more spontaneous contributions in a *Lyceum* session [S4] • Not over-preparing in order to leave room for improvisation in first scheduled *Lyceum* session [S5] • Contributing more actively to the blog (which is perceived as a more private online setting) [S5]

Most of the identified strategies ultimately contributed to forming a sense of community among the project partners – a necessary first step for collaborative learning in general and telecollaborative learning of languages and cultures in particular.

Preliminary Conclusions

When considering the conclusions that can be drawn from the findings presented here it is important to bear the following limitations in mind:

- The eight learners who documented the ways in which they participated in the telecollaboration project constitute a relatively small sample and the comprehensiveness of their records varies greatly. Moreover, they had not been asked to specifically list the strategies they used or comment on them. Any generalisations based on their self-observations must therefore be handled with caution.
- The French telecollaboration partners who provided the data for the present chapter are very likely to have joined the project with a

comparatively higher degree of strategic awareness than their peers from the United States or the UK. As a group of teacher trainees interested in investigating the educational potential of online interaction at a meta-level they were potentially more reflective and motivated in their approach than more conventional language learners.

Nonetheless, this study has given us a useful first insight into what kinds of strategies are important in CMC-based language learning. The strategic behaviour noted and reflected upon in the French participants' diaries strongly suggests that affective and social skills cannot simply be transferred from face-to-face language learning settings but need to be tailored to virtual learning environments. Unsurprisingly, some studies have even suggested that online communication is so different to face-to-face interaction that socialisation into online learning is required and that students need to learn how to build social relationships. Nicol *et al.* (2003: 272), for example, suggest a face-to-face induction 'to provide enough social information with which to build a mental picture of other learners or tutors'. In telecollaborative exchanges, however, where CMC tools are used to bring together globally dispersed language learners for the development of collaborative project work and intercultural exchange, this is clearly not possible. Yet neither online language learners in general nor exchange partners in virtual situations can be expected to be competent users of the new media and to develop appropriate interaction strategies on their own. This is especially true for socio-environmental strategies which allow learners to draw maximum benefit from the modes and functionalities available in a given online environment.

For tutors and learners expected to operate in virtual environments, training in the use of CMC tools complemented by continuous support in developing and reflecting on approaches to online language learning and teaching – i.e. strategy training – would be an important step in the right direction. Cohen's (1998) and Chamot's (2004) work on strategy instruction in the context of conventional language learning and Hauck's (2005) investigations of metacognitive strategy training for online language learners could be a useful starting-point. Hauck's findings indicate that – at least at beginners' level – direct, interventionist and de-contextualised methods are most apt to systematically foster learner reflection and to enhance learner self-management. This approach 'which gradually moves along the de-contextualised–contextualised continuum as learners' linguistic competence increases' (Hauck & Hurd, 2005) needs to be looked at more closely as it will eventually allow learners to 'develop their learning strategy repertoires while learning the target language at the same time' (Cohen, 1998: 80). Thus investigations of online strategies need to be expanded and diversified and should include the CMC specific strategies highlighted in this chapter in order to provide more targeted support to those who need it.

Notes

1. Masters FOAD: Formation Ouverte et A Distance.
2. The linguistic competence of the Anglophone students ranged from advanced beginners in the US (A2 in the Common European Framework of Reference for Languages, CEF) to advanced level French in the UK (C1 in the CEF).

References

Belz, J.A. (2003) From the special issue editor. *Language Learning & Technology* 7 (2), 2–5.
Block, D. (2003) *The Social Turn in Second Language Acquisition*. Edinburgh: Edinburgh University Press.
Brammerts, H. (2003) Autonomous language learning in tandem: The development of a concept. In T. Lewis and L. Walker (eds) *Autonomous Language Learning in Tandem*. Sheffield: Academy Electronic Publications.
Chamot, A.U. (2001) The role of learning strategies in second language acquisition. In M.P. Breen (ed.) *Learner Contributions to Language Learning: New Directions in Research* (pp. 25–42). Harlow: Longman.
Chamot, A.U. (2004) Issues in language learning strategy research and teaching. *Electronic Journal of Foreign language Teaching* 1 (1), 12–25.
Chapelle, C.A. (1990) The discourse of computer-assisted language learning: Toward a context for descriptive research. *TESOL Quarterly* 24, 199–225.
Chapelle, C.A. (1995) A framework for the investigation of CALL as a context for SLA. *CALL Journal* 6 (3), 2–8.
Chapelle, C.A. and Jamieson, J. (1986) Computer-assisted language learning as a predictor of success in acquiring English as a second language. *TESOL Quarterly* 20, 27–46.
Chapelle, C.A. and Jamieson, J. (1989) Research trends in computer-assisted language learning. In M. Pennington (ed.) *Teaching Languages with Computers: The State of the Art* (pp. 47–59). La Jolla: Athelstan.
Chapelle, C. and Jamieson, J. (1991) Internal and external validity issues in research on CALL effectiveness. In P. Dunkel (ed.) *Computer Assisted Language Learning and Testing: Research Issues and Practice* (pp. 37–59). New York: Harper & Row – Newbury House.
Cohen, A.D. (1998) *Strategies in Learning and Using a Second Language*. Harlow: Addison Wesley Longman Ltd.
Debski, R. (1997) Support of creativity and collaboration in the language classroom: A new role for technology. In R. Debski, J. Gassin and M. Smith (eds) *Language Learning through Social Computing* (pp. 36–65). Parkville, Australia: Applied Linguistics Association.
Ellis, R. (1994) *The Study of Second Language Acquisition*. Oxford: Oxford University Press.
Ellis, R. (2003) *Task-based Language Learning and Teaching*. Oxford: Oxford University Press.
Gardner, R., Tremblay, P. and Masgoret, A-M. (1997) Towards a full model of second language learning: An empirical investigation. *The Modern Language Journal* 81 (3), 344–362.

Gregersen, T. and Horwitz, E.K. (2002) Language learning perfection: Anxious and non-anxious learners' reactions to their own oral performance. *The Modern Language Journal* 86, 562–570.

Hampel, R., Felix, U., Hauck, M. and Coleman, J.A. (2005) Complexities of learning and teaching languages in a real-time audiographic environment. *German as a Foreign Language* 3, 1–30. On WWW at http://www.gfl-journal.de/3-2005/hampel_felix_hauck_coleman.html. Accessed 26.07.07.

Hauck, M. (2005) Metacognitive knowledge, metacognitive strategies, and CALL. In J. Egbert and G. Petrie (eds) *CALL Research Perspectives* (pp. 65–86). New Jersey: Lawrence Erlbaum.

Hauck, M. (2007) Critical success factors in a TRIDEM exchange. *ReCALL* 19 (2), 202–223.

Hauck, M. and Hurd, S. (2005) Exploring the link between language anxiety and learner self-management in open language learning contexts. *European Journal of Open, Distance and E-learning* 2005/II, n.p. On WWW at http://www.eurodl.org/materials/contrib/2005/Mirjam_Hauck.htm. Accessed 26.07.07.

Horwitz, E.K., Horwitz, B. and Cope, J. (1986) Foreign language classroom anxiety. *The Modern Language Journal* 70 (ii), 125–132.

Hurd, S. (2005) Autonomy and the distance language learner. In B. Holmberg, M. Shelley and C. White (eds) *Languages and Distance Education: Evolution and Change* (pp. 1–19). Clevedon: Multilingual Matters.

Jones, A. and Issroff, E. (2005) Learning technologies: Affective and social issues in computer supported collaborative learning. *Computers and Education* 44 (4), 395–408.

Kreijns, K., Kirschner, P.A. and Jochems, W. (2003) Identifying the pitfalls for social interaction in computer-supported collaborative learning environments: A review of the research. *Computers in Human Behaviour* 19 (3), 335–353.

Kress, G. and Van Leeuwen, T. (2001) *Multimodal Discourse. The Modes and Media of Contemporary Communication*. London: Arnold.

Lamy, M-N. and Hampel, R. (2007) *Online Communication in Language Learning and Teaching*. Houndmills: Palgrave Macmillan.

Lea, M. and Nicoll, K. (eds) (2002) *Distributed Learning: Social and Cultural Approaches to Practice*. London: Routledge.

Lecourt, D. (1999) The ideological consequences of technology and education: The case for critical pedagogy. In M. Selinger and J. Pearson (eds) *Telematics in Education: Trends and Issues* (pp. 51–75). Amsterdam: Pergamon.

Little, D. and Brammerts, H. (eds) (1996) *A Guide to Language Learning in Tandem via the Internet* (Occasional Paper No. 46). Dublin: Centre for Language and Communication Studies.

Nicol, D.J., Minty, I. and Sinclair, C. (2003) The social dimensions of online learning. *Innovations in Education and Teaching International* 40 (3), 270–180. On WWW at http://taylorandfrancis.metapress.com/link.asp?id=kkeux0vjh0rc427y. Accessed 26.07.07.

O'Dowd, R. and Ritter, M. (2006) Understanding and working with 'failed communication' in telecollaborative exchanges. *CALICO Journal* 23 (3), 623–642.

O'Malley, J.M. and Chamot, A.U. (1990) *Learning Strategies in Second Language Acquisition*. Cambridge: Cambridge University Press.

Oatley, K. and Nundy, S. (1996) Rethinking the role of emotions in education. In D. Olson and N. Torrance (eds) *Handbook of Education and Human Development: New Models of Learning, Teaching and Schooling* (pp. 257–274). Cambridge, MA: Blackwell.

Payne, J.S. and Whitney, P.J. (2002) Developing L2 oral proficiency through synchronous CMC: Output, working memory, and interlanguage development. *CALICO Journal* 20 (1), 7–32.

Resnick, L.B., Levine, J.M. and Teasley, S.D. (eds) (1991) *Perspectives on Socially Shared Cognition*. Washington, DC: American Psychological Association.

Roed, J. (2003) Language learner behaviour in a virtual environment. *Computer Assisted Language Learning* 16 (2–3), 155–172.

Skehan, P. (1989) *Individual Differences in Second-language Learning*. London: Edward Arnold.

Warschauer, M. and Kern, R. (eds) (2000) *Network-based Language Teaching: Concepts and Practice*. New York: Cambridge University Press.

Weininger, M. and Shield, L. (2003) Promoting oral production in a written channel: An investigation of learner language in a MOO. *Computer Assisted Language Learning* 16 (4), 329–349.

Wenden, A. and Rubin, J. (1987) *Learner Strategies in Language Learning*. London: Prentice-Hall International.

Wenger, E. (1998) *Communities of Practice: Learning, Meaning and Identity*. Cambridge: Cambridge University Press.

White, C.J. (1995) Autonomy and strategy use in distance foreign language learning: Research findings. *System* 23 (2), 207–221.

Appendix A: Lyceum

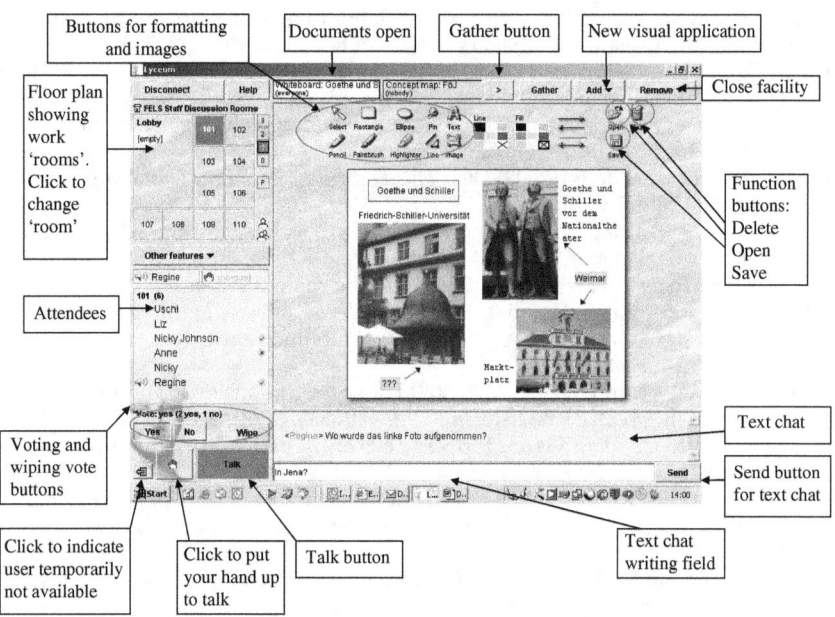

Source: Lyceum Screenshot © The Open University. Photos reproduced by kind permission of Regine Hampel.

Appendix B: Project Blog

PREVIOUS POSTS

- Le Mardi 1st Novembre
- La toussaint
- Le lundi le 31 octobre c'est Halloween. Traditionn...
- Lyceum 1st November
- From tridem 5,
- Ma pièce de favori.
- picture of my favourite room
- séance mardi 25 octobre
- J'ai appris beaucoup d'information culturel apres...
- Pour *S1*

Translation:

- Tuesday 1 November
- All Saints' Day
- Monday 31 October is Halloween, tradition ...
- Lyceum 1 November
- From tridem 5
- My favorite room
- (picture of my favorite room)
- Session Tuesday 25 October
- I have learned a lot of cultural information after ...
- For *S1*

SUNDAY, OCTOBER 30, 2005

Bonjour *British student* et *S5*!

Je suis vraiment désolé pour ne pas répondre plus tôt et Je n'ai pas communiquer sur le blog. J'ai été parti en beaucoup des voyages. Je fais partie d'une sororité à mon école, qui est une organisation des femmes aidant dans la communauté. Notre organisation favorise la conscience de Breast Cancer Awareness, ainsi la semaine passée j'avais voyagé à différents états qu'aider favorisent la conscience de Breast Cancer Awareness. Mais j'espère continuer à communiquer avec vous plus souvent. Mais en réponse à votre blog précédent, en Amérique, pour Halloween, les enfants habituellement portant vers le haut dans un costume et circulent aux maisons d'autres demandant la sucrerie. Et ils disent "trick or treat". Ces vacances sont plus vers des enfants, mais personnes plus âgées portant vers le haut dans des costumes d'amusement aussi. *British student*, je trouve au sujet de l'aspect religieux de Halloween en Angleterre tres intéressante. Il est très intéressant de savoir. Voici une image des personnes portant un costume typique pour halloween.

Translation:

Hi *British student* and *S5*,

I am really sorry I didn't reply earlier. I haven't contributed anything to the blog. I've been travelling a lot recently. I'm a member of a sorority, which is an organisation of women in my college who help in the community. We work in particular to promote breast cancer awareness. Last week I went to several States that help to raise awareness of breast cancer. But now I hope I can communicate with you more often. But to answer your previous blog, here in the US, for Hallowe'en, children dress up and go from door to door asking for sweets. And they say: 'trick or treat'. This holiday is more for children, but there are also adults who enjoy wearing funny costumes. Anna, I find the religious aspect of Hallowe'en in England very interesting. It is very interesting to find out about it. Here are a few photos of people wearing typical Hallowe'en costumes. *(In the original blog this text posting was followed by two pictures of children and adults wearing Hallowe'en costumes and the following two picture of pets in costumes.)* Et Voici quelques costumes d'animal de compagnie ...

Translation:

And here are a few costumes for pets ...

1 Comments:
S5 said...

Hi *American student*,
I'm very glad you've join us in our blog!
you pictures showing Halloween's day are very nice and funny as well!

Chapter 16
Integrating Strategy Instruction into Learning Materials

LINDA MURPHY

Introduction

The chapters in Part 2 of this book explore a variety of cognitive strategies for the development of specific language skills and in Part 3, the focus is on strategies for learner self-management. Each chapter has concentrated on an individual skill or strategic approach. However, there has been a lively debate in the research community (e.g. McDonough, 1995, 1999, 2005; O'Malley & Chamot, 1995; Oxford & Cohen, 1992) about the relative merits of 'learner training' and whether separate instruction about strategies is an effective approach, or whether it is more effective to integrate strategy instruction into language learning materials and if so, how it can best be achieved. This chapter examines the arguments surrounding strategy instruction and the issues involved in integrating such instruction in materials for independent and distance learning, before looking at some examples of integration in practice.

Strategy Instruction: Background to the Debate

Language learning researchers became interested in the notion of learning strategies from the 1970s when a number of studies explored the behaviour that made some learners more successful than others in second language acquisition (e.g. Naiman *et al.*, 1978; Rubin, 1975; Stern, 1975). Early results indicated that 'the good language learner' did not simply have aptitude and motivation, but drew on these characteristics to devise and apply their own strategies, actively engaging in the learning process. A substantial amount of further research followed to identify and categorise the strategies which assist effective language learning. The case for raising awareness of language learning strategies was strengthened by researchers who examined how unsuccessful learners approach their studies. Nyikos (1987, in Oxford & Cohen, 1992: 2) observed that less successful language learners sometimes have no idea what strategies they use or rely on a few non-communicative techniques such as translation, rote memorisation and repetition. It was argued that, if application of strategies distinguished the successful learner, strategy instruction should become part of language learning programmes.

However, researchers have also pointed out the problems inherent in an approach which encourages learners to adopt the strategies of 'good language learners'. McDonough (2005) summarises the difficulties which many researchers have with the concept of teaching learning strategies in the first place and in evaluating the effectiveness of such teaching. For example, Rees-Miller (1993) expresses concern that this approach is far too simplistic, ignoring the influence on strategy use of cultural differences, age, educational background, beliefs about language learning and differing cognitive styles. Chamot (2001: 32) notes a recurrent finding in investigations of language learner strategies: that less successful learners often use strategies as frequently as successful learners but use them differently and do not appear to select appropriately. A study by Schrafnagl and Fage (1998) found widespread use of a very limited range of strategies among Open University students studying a level 1 French course, but this did not prevent those students from being successful. Therefore, it is argued, it is hard to define a set of strategies which characterise 'good language learners' in general, and strategy use *per se* doesn't necessarily lead to success.

Further doubts have been voiced by researchers with a socio-cultural perspective on learning. Gillette (1994) argues that the kinds of language learning strategy which people deploy reflect the significance which languages and language study have for their lives. She suggests that this explains why it may be difficult to teach positive learning strategies to ineffective language learners. Lantolf (2001: 148) expands this argument. Individual learners experience language tasks and activities in very different ways. They may be in the same group, apparently doing the same task, but cognitively they are not engaged in the same activity, because the activity and its significance to the individual are shaped by their motivations. Donato and McCormick (1994: 454) also argue that since learning strategies develop in the course of goal-directed, 'situated' activity, it makes no sense to expect to be able to teach them via separate, explicit instruction.

Nevertheless, language teachers and course writers have found the notions of 'good language learner' characteristics and learning strategies 'intuitively appealing' (Rees-Miller, 1993: 687). Kinoshita (2003: 3) drawing on O'Malley and Chamot (1995) distinguishes what she terms 'uninformed' and 'informed' instruction. In uninformed strategy instruction, learners work through materials and activities designed to elicit the use of specific strategies, but without being informed of the name, purpose or value of the strategy. Informed instruction ensures learners are aware of the value and purpose of learning strategies and helps them to use, identify and develop these strategies in a systematic way as they learn the target language. The first, and probably best-known, example of a course book for 'informed' instruction was Ellis and Sinclair's (1989) *Learning to Learn English: A Course in Learner Training*. A range of packs and study modules have followed, which generally have the same overall goals. Dörnyei (2005: 174) has summarised these as:

> to raise learners awareness about learning strategies and model strategies overtly [...]; to encourage strategy use and give a rationale for it; to offer a wide menu of relevant strategies for learners to choose from; to offer controlled practice in the use of some strategies; and to provide some sort of post task analysis which allows students to reflect on their strategy use.

McDonough (2005: 156) notes a basic instructional framework shared by many authors comprising four stages:

(1) preview (a) materials for useful strategies, (b) the students' own current repertoire;
(2) present a strategy by naming it and explaining why and when to use it;
(3) model the strategy and provide practice opportunities;
(4) develop students' ability to evaluate strategy use and develop skills to transfer strategy use to new tasks.

Despite apparently common frameworks and goals, the range of 'informed' teaching material can be sub-divided further according to whether the proposed intervention is:

- explicit, discrete strategy instruction within a separate study skills module or materials studied alongside the language;
- explicit strategy instruction within a framework of strategic awareness-raising to foster learner autonomy, integrated within a language learning programme.

As indicated in the introduction, the issue of which type of intervention, if any, is most effective is the subject of extensive debate.

The Effectiveness of Explicit Strategy Instruction

A series of surveys have examined the outcome of research studies to establish whether explicit strategy instruction can actually improve language proficiency. Oxford and Cohen (1992: 2) considered that the strategy training studies which they examined had been successful, but not consistently so. McDonough (1999) examined the outcomes from a larger number of studies and suggested evidence for the success of strategy instruction was increasing. He concluded that 'the relationship between strategy use and proficiency is very complicated: issues such as frequency and quality of strategy use do not bear a simple linear relationship to achievement in a second language'. He also noted that studies of successful learners such as Naiman *et al.* (1978) and Gillette (1987) did not advocate that others should be taught to use their strategies, rather that students should be encouraged to look more closely at their own behaviour. Hassan *et al.* (2005) in a systematic review of strategy instruction found sufficient evidence to support claims that it is effective, but could not say whether the effects would be long-lasting. They were unable to clarify whether the explicit training activity in relation to specific strategies was responsible for these effects or whether they were due to the increased awareness that would result from a training programme. The research studies explored in all these surveys are for the most part focused on a single skill and a specific, often experimental, short-term learning strategy intervention.

Dörnyei (2005: 177) suggests that ultimately, interpretation of these findings comes down to personal disposition: sceptics warn against investing too much effort in strategy training as it is unlikely to be cost-effective, whereas proponents point to increasing positive evidence to support their position.

Arguments in Favour of Integrated, Explicit Strategy Instruction

Nevertheless, Dörnyei (2005: 177) supports McDonough's view (1999: 13) that although explicit strategy training may not be universally successful, research shows that it can be so, particularly when incorporated as part of the normal teaching programme. Opportunities to put learning strategies into practice for authentic purposes are essential, as researchers have demonstrated that simply raising awareness of, or presenting strategies is not enough (Chamot, 1993; Cohen, 1998; Matsumoto, 1996; Ridley, 1997). Wood *et al.* (1998) found that learners typically use the least sophisticated strategy to achieve a goal, even when they have a variety available and no matter how advanced they are. Macaro (2001: 187) emphasises that learners need to be shown strategies explicitly and repeatedly through modelling within the language learning programme, which enables them to see how they might use a particular strategy in combination with others. They then need opportunities to try strategies out and become confident in using them in order to be able to make choices and apply strategies appropriately. Chamot's (2001) concerns about the strategy use of less successful learners led her to agree that learning about specific strategies and practising them may not develop learners' ability to select them appropriately and this skill is more likely to be developed if the strategy instruction is integrated within the language learning programme, providing natural opportunities for learners to make choices.

Holec (1996: 99) argues that integration reinforces the relevance of strategies and provides those regular opportunities for use that are necessary if they are to be proceduralised in a meaningful way. The issue of relevance is also important on a more pragmatic level. In a study of adult distance language learners at the Open University (UK), Murphy (2005: 36) found that learners are less likely to engage with materials or modules that are perceived to be an 'extra', rather than part of the language learning programme.

Arguments in Favour of Integrated Strategy Instruction within a Framework of Strategic Awareness-Raising

For some time, researchers in other areas of education have suggested that separate study skills packs or modules are not as effective as programmes or interventions which seek to raise learners' awareness of how they are approaching their study. Even before the main explosion of interest in language learning strategy instruction, Gibbs (1981) criticised the teaching of study strategies and techniques, advocating instead activities which enable students to reflect on the purpose and nature of their study and take a more active approach to their learning.

More recently, many language teaching researchers have advocated the encouragement of reflection and strategic metacognitive awareness-raising within the subject context, for example, Gremmo and Riley (1995), Little (1995, 1996), Holec (1996), Ridley (1997), Cohen (1998) and Benson (2001). This can also be seen as part of an increasing emphasis on self-regulation as outlined by Dörnyei (2005: 190). Macaro (2001: 264) illustrates this point: 'One thing seems to be increasingly clear and it is that, across learning contexts, those learners who are proactive in pursuit of their language learning appear to learn best'. Self-regulation in this context, or the capacity to choose and deploy strategies appropriately, is more likely to be achieved, it is argued, where strategic awareness-raising, and any explicit strategy instruction required, is integrated in language learning programmes. Little (1996) argues strongly for strategy instruction to be within a framework of communicative tasks which offer learners a chance to choose and deploy strategies appropriately and promote learner autonomy. His view is supported by Chamot *et al.* (1999: 99, cited in Harris, 2001: 71) who state that

> effective strategies instruction is not an add-on, but rather a way to support language learning in an existing curriculum. Students should

practise strategies while working on authentic, meaningful language tasks that are part of the language programme. (Chamot *et al.*, 1999: 99, cited in Harris, 2001: 71)

This integration provides a framework for practice, real reasons for selecting and using strategies and evaluating their effectiveness from an individual learner's perspective.

At the same time, Macaro (2001: 239) argues that because self-regulation implies choice of action, learners should be able to both accept or discard a strategy on the basis of having applied it in different combinations of strategies and in a variety of task types, although they may need coaching or a framework of guidance in order to articulate conscious choices.

The Challenges of Integration

Although there are many arguments in favour of integrating strategy instruction and strategic awareness-raising within learning programmes to enable learners to make informed choices about their strategy use, there are nevertheless a number of challenges which concern researchers and practitioners. They can be summarised as: the balance between strategy instruction and language instruction; the issue of progression or which strategies are appropriate at which levels; and the design of appropriate practice tasks which require the deployment of the strategies taught.

Balance

A number of researchers have raised questions about the balance between explicit strategy instruction and language learning. Holec (1996: 99) expresses concern that where strategy development is integrated within the subject, there is a danger that it will be sidelined. Alternatively, Sinclair (1996: 149) points out the difficulty in incorporating strategy instruction and encouraging learners to be aware of how they are learning, without swamping the language learning aims of a course or presenting the learners with too many hurdles. Macaro (2001: 266) states that 'too much strategy instruction will lead to a disconnection from the actual process of learning a language'.

Harris (2001: 122) points out that the reaction of learners to strategy instruction varies. She reports that both high and low attainers can be both responsive and unresponsive. High attainers may simply not feel they have any need for strategy instruction. Low attainers may be too preoccupied with language problems to see the benefits, although the attributional theory of achievement, motivation and emotion set out by Weiner (1985) suggests it could be helpful to them to realise that failures may be due to lack of strategies rather than lack of ability. This highlights the importance of arguments by Grenfell and Harris (1999: 140) for ensuring that strategy instruction focuses on raising awareness, enabling learners to expand their repertoire and make choices, capitalising on their preferred learning styles, rather than on trying to change learners' approach or behaviour. In other words, integrated strategy instruction within a framework of strategic awareness-raising appears the most effective way to maintain a language/strategy balance and respond to learner differences.

Learners at any level may feel they cannot 'waste time' that would otherwise be used for language learning. Little (1999) suggests that the strength of student expectation of learning time dedicated to language learning can mean teachers and course designers hesitate to risk devoting a lot of time and space to strategy instruction. But, as Harris (2001: 118) points out, strategy instruction should actually save time by enabling learners to apply their efforts more effectively. The prospect of 'smarter working' can be a selling point for sceptical, busy, adult learners reluctant to spend time thinking about the strategies they use (Murphy, 2005: 34).

Strategy instruction in the target language is often suggested as a way to avoid it being seen as a diversion from language study. Discussing and evaluating learning, sharing tips and talking about strategy use promotes genuine communication. For distance or other independent learners, online synchronous or asynchronous conferences or discussion forums offer opportunities to engage in such exchanges. Dörnyei (2005: 174) suggests that this kind of 'sharing' is often the most inspiring and instructive part of strategy instruction because students can gain fresh insights by listening to the experiences of their peers. However, there are also concerns about whether learners, particularly at lower levels, have the target language necessary to understand explanations about the nature and purpose of specific strategies or to discuss their experience. The apparent drawbacks of encouraging use of learners' first or preferred language for this purpose may be outweighed by the benefits of increasing understanding and motivation for strategy use.

A note of caution is sounded by Beaty *et al.* (1997) who point out that students study to maximise achievement, but within their own definition of what this means, which may not coincide with that of the teacher or course designer. McCune and Entwistle (2000) examined the perspectives of first-year undergraduate psychology students at a university in the UK via a longitudinal programme of in-depth interviews. The study explored reasons for the apparent ineffectiveness of attempts to raise awareness and provide study advice. The researchers conclude that this may be related to the persistence of existing attitudes and habits, the nature of the students' goals and the level of marks achieved. Students achieving what they perceive as reasonable grades may feel no need to examine their approach. This illustrates the concerns expressed by researchers such as Lantolf, noted earlier, suggesting that activity and its significance to the individual are shaped by personal motivations rather than programmes of strategy instruction or awareness-raising.

Progression

Researchers such as Grenfell and Harris (1999), Harris (2001) and Macaro (2001) have considered which strategies learners should be made aware of and at which point in the learning programme. Grenfell and Harris suggest that

> just as some parts of language are easier to learn than others, so some strategies are easier to use than others. [...] This point may also imply that easier strategies are acquired early by learners, the more difficult ones come later. (Grenfell & Harris, 1999: 46)

They point out that successful learners have been found to use a wide range of strategies appropriately and use them in combination rather than in isolation. Grenfell and Harris propose the continua in strategy use reproduced in Table 16.1, where the 'easy' column reflects the strategic behaviour that may be adopted by learners early on in their language studies and continue to be used by low attainers, whereas the 'hard' column reflects strategic behaviour developed later and deployed by high attainers. In reality, the picture is likely to be more complex as, for example, beginner learners may use top-down interpretation strategies in reading to compensate for a lack of vocabulary knowledge.

Grenfell and Harris anticipate that every learner, at every developmental stage of their learning, has a particular strategy profile. Strategies

Table 16.1 Continua in strategy use

Easy	Hard
Less frequent use	More frequent use
Narrow range	Wider range
Less helpful strategies	More helpful strategies
Bottom-up	Bottom-up and top-down
Word for word	Meaning
Translation	Inferencing
Repetition	Applying rules
Formulaic phrases	Monitoring phrases

Source: Grenfell and Harris (1999) *Modern Languages and Learning Strategies; In Theory and Practice.* London: Routledge. Reproduced here by kind permission of Taylor and Francis Books Ltd.

developed in the early stage of learning will be internalised through practice and use, then complemented by further strategies to facilitate a higher level of competence. Harris (2001) and Macaro (2001) have also proposed sequences for strategy instruction. Both subscribe to Macaro's (2001: 266) view that 'strategy training is a gradual, recursive and longitudinal process'. Nevertheless, the issue is still considered problematic because the sequences of language and strategy acquisition do not necessarily run in parallel, such instruction sequences do not appear to take account of the strategies which learners may have developed in their first language, and empirical research is needed to validate proposed strategy continua.

Grenfell and Harris (1999: 47–48) point out that rather than basing strategy intervention on language level, it may be better to consider learning style preferences. For example, inferencing strategies may be best employed by learners who prefer inductive methods and in contexts where there is high contact with other speakers of the target language, whereas those who prefer an analytical approach may favour more academic, deductive strategies. They conclude that cognitive style, cultural background and gender may affect the strategies used by an individual and how effectively they are deployed.

Consideration of learning style, cultural background and gender, alongside level of achievement adds weight to arguments in favour of strategy instruction within a framework of metacognitive awareness-raising, enabling learners to make their own choices and capitalise on their strengths, in other words to become self-regulated autonomous language learners.

Task design

Samuda (2005: 231) notes that findings from studies of task performance suggest the way a task is designed may have differential effects on the kinds of opportunities that are created for language use, supporting Hurd's (2000: 65) suggestion that the nature of the language learning activities and assessments can determine the nature and extent of learners' strategy use. Chamot *et al.* note that

> for a language task to be effective for learning a new strategy, it should be authentic and moderately challenging. If the task is too easy, students will not need strategies to succeed; they may therefore see the strategies as a waste of time. However, if the task is too difficult, students may not be able to succeed, even when using appropriate strategies. (Chamot *et al.*, 1999: 99, cited in Harris, 2001: 71)

Robinson (2001) considers the relationship between task complexity and task difficulty and their influence on fluency and accuracy in language production. He suggests that complex 'monologic' tasks lead to greater learner attention to accuracy than fluency, whereas complex 'interactive' tasks lead to more negotiation, although the language is not necessarily complex, and a focus on fluency. This highlights the way task type affects learner focus and activity and, as a result, strategy use. Therefore the design of learning activities has to balance the demands of both language and strategy practice, which adds a further layer of complexity to an already complex and relatively under-researched process (Samuda, 2005: 230).

Integration in Practice

The final part of this chapter presents examples of 'informed' strategy instruction (Kinoshita, 2003) designed for independent or distance learners. The first is an example of explicit, discrete strategy instruction. The second is an example of integrated strategy instruction within a framework of strategic awareness-raising. The examples are examined in relation to issues discussed in the previous sections, that is:

- instructional framework;
- relationship between strategy and language instruction;
- development of self-regulation;
- task design (natural opportunities for strategy use with reflection on outcomes).

(1) Explicit discrete strategy instruction within a separate study skills module or materials studied alongside the language: *DIY Techniques for Language Learners* (Fernández-Toro & Jones, 2001)

As its title suggests, this book aims to give practical support for self-instructed language learners and advice on how to learn effectively by selecting from recommended strategies or techniques to suit individual language learning needs and styles. It does not offer language instruction directly, but is to be used in conjunction with whatever language course or other materials the independent learner has available, whether text, audio or other speakers of the language. All the explanations and examples are in English.

Part 1 of the book supports learners in exploring their learning style, their strengths and 'challenges' depending on the type of learner they feel they are and how to get started. It includes a series of diagnostic questionnaires related to different language skill areas and depending on the outcomes, learners are referred to relevant sections in Part 2 of the book. These explain what each skill involves and offer a range of strategies and techniques to try out. Table 16.2 shows an example from the section on Reading.

This sample activity uses the instructional framework set out by McDonough (2005). The preview stage is not included in this activity, but the first part of the book could be said to constitute a general preview.

Integrating Strategy Instruction into Learning Materials

Table 16.2 Predicting questions in a text (Fernández-Toro & Jones, 2001: 80)

R10 Predicting questions in a text

What is it good for?

If you know what information to look for in a text, you are more likely to find it. This technique activates your existing knowledge to predict what questions are likely to be answered in a text. It also means that you no longer have to rely on a teacher setting reading comprehension questions for you.

How to proceed

(1) Look at the text that you want to read. Look at the title or use the skimming technique (→ **[R1]** *Basic reading techniques*) to figure out the topic.
(2) On the basis of this, make up five questions (in English or the target language) that a text of this type is most likely to address.

- *Example*: For a newspaper report about a football match: (1) What two teams were playing? (2) When? (3) Where? (4) Who won? (5) What are the implications of this result for each of the teams?

(3) Read the text and try to answer your questions. Tick off the ones for which the text provides an answer.
(4) If some of your questions are not answered in the text, cross them out.
(5) Write two more questions that are particular to this text.
(6) A few days later try to answer all your questions *before* reading the text, then check in the text.

How to assess progress

Give yourself 100% if you managed to answer all five questions. Take of 20% for every question that you had to cross out.
Try to arrive at a more or less 'universal' set of questions that would work for every text of this kind (e.g. the five questions on 'football matches' above) and try it out a few days later on a similar kind of text (e.g. another football match).

The strategy is presented and explained, then modelled through specific practice. Learners are given an explicit way to assess their progress in applying the strategy, and suggestions are made to help them transfer the strategy to other reading activities. The strategy can be applied in English or the target language. The focus is very much on the strategy but in the context of reading the target language material selected by the learner. Although this is an example of discrete, explicit strategy instruction, it is set within a clear context of awareness-raising for independent, self-directed learners, inviting them to evaluate their experience and strengths in order to choose which skill areas to work on through activities which provide clear explanations of the purpose and uses for the strategies and techniques concerned. On the other hand, the task design is determined by the strategy which is to be presented and practised. It therefore does not constitute a natural opportunity for the learner to choose and use strategies which they feel are most appropriate for the task in hand or to reflect on their choice. As noted earlier, it is this ability to choose and apply strategies appropriately which leads to effective strategy use.

(2) Strategy instruction within a framework of strategic awareness-raising to foster learner autonomy: *Rundblick* (The Open University, 2003)

Since the first French language course (*Ouverture*) was produced by The Open University in 1995, course writing teams have been looking at ways to integrate strategy instruction into a distance language learning programme. At first, courses simply offered learners tips for developing particular language skills or activities which prompted the use of specific strategies such as scanning for information or listening for gist, 'uninformed' strategy instruction (Kinoshita, 2003). More recently, course teams have worked to provide explicit strategy instruction within a framework of metacognitive awareness-raising where students are helped to examine their goals, their achievements and their approach to language skill development (Murphy, 2008).

Recent courses adopting this approach include the beginners' German course *Rundblick*. The course has explicit objectives 'to develop your ability to choose and use strategies which enhance your learning' and 'to develop your ability to monitor and evaluate your progress'. Before they begin studying, students are advised to spend some time on activities to find out what type of learner they are, which learning style suits them best and why this self-knowledge is important. They are also advised to work through specific activities to help them understand the importance of reflecting on their learning, how to do it and how to set and review their own learning goals.

The overview of each month's study includes learning strategies which are taught or practised alongside the topic, grammar, vocabulary, pronunciation or cultural content to be studied. The strategies are selected according to the needs of beginner language learners.

Table 16.3 shows an example from *Rundblick*, Unit 8, towards the end of Book 1. Students are taken through a series of activities focusing on listening and reading strategies which they have been encouraged to use already. Activities 8.1–8.3 guide them to extract information from authentic audio recordings by (1) using snippets of material that are understood, and (2) working out the context using background noises and key information from announcements. Activities 8.4–8.7 guide students to extract information from texts by identifying text types, scanning for key points, and examining texts in more detail. Table 16.3 shows the introduction and final activity in this *Lerneinheit* or Unit, where work on listening and reading strategies is drawn together.

Table 16.3 Strategies for listening and reading in another language

Lerneinheit 8
In this *Lerneinheit* you think about the strategies you need when listening to, or reading in, another language. You listen to authentic announcements and conversations and read some short documents.
Übung 8.8 (Activity 8.8)
The purpose of the final activity is to draw your attention to how you listen and read in a foreign language. You have read and listened to quite a lot of German during the course so far. In this *Lerneinheit* all materials were entirely authentic, that is to say not simplified or adapted in any way. How did you tackle them? Which of the following statements apply most to what you did when listening and reading?
Listening
I tried to understand:
by listening to the background noises ☐
by listening to the speakers' intonation ☐
by concentrating on the words I've learned in the course ☐
by concentrating on words that are similar to English ☐
by guessing ☐
by looking at the transcript ☐
Other:
Reading
I tried to understand
by looking at the format of the text ☐
by assuming that timetables, hotel brochures etc. contain the same kind of information as they would in English ☐
by looking at the headings first ☐
by picking out all the words I know ☐
by concentrating on words which are similar to English ☐
by guessing ☐
by looking up some words in the dictionary ☐
Other:
Lösung (Answer)
All the strategies listed are good ways of trying to start understanding a foreign language. If you hadn't thought of some of the ideas listed, you could try them next time.
(There is, of course, no transcript available in a 'real' situation – it may therefore be better to try listening without looking at the transcript first. Relying too much on a dictionary could also prevent you from trying to find out what you do understand first, but it's a useful tool for checking and looking up the occasional word which you think might be important.)

Source: Rundblick, Book 1: 38 and 43 © The Open University, 2003

In this example, the basic instructional framework is a little different from that outlined by McDonough (2005). The preview and presentation stages are delayed as students first tackle activities which demand the use of strategies such as skimming/scanning/listening for gist. These strategies are not presented beforehand, although the introduction alerts the student to the fact that strategies will be a focus in this *Lerneinheit*. Having worked through those activities where the focus is on understanding German in a variety of authentic contexts, and strategies are applied naturally, students are asked to reflect on the strategies they used. The tick list provides an opportunity to 'present' students with a range of strategies, some of which they might not have been familiar with. There are opportunities for transfer by applying these strategies later in the course, but students are expected to choose which to use and when, in the expectation that they will be able to manage their own learning. It can be argued, however, that students do not in fact get practice in applying unfamiliar or new listening or reading strategies at this point, and so may simply stick to what they used initially.

To some extent, this is addressed at the end of each *Thema* or Block of the course, when students are encouraged to think about their learning over the whole topic and develop their capacity for self-regulation. A regular feature – *Rückblick* (Review) – helps them to do this by suggesting techniques and strategies for organising and storing vocabulary, and invites students to try them out and decide which one to use:

> Here are suggestions to help you organise the language you have studied so far and to select what is particularly relevant to you. You don't have to do all the activities. Choose the ones which you find useful to reinforce and summarise your learning. At the end, you should have a summary of the most important things you have learned from this *Thema*. (*Rundblick*, Book 1: 54)

Suggested strategies and examples are then presented under four headings: *Nützliche Ausdrücke* (useful phrases); *Grammatik* (grammar); *Kulturelles* (cultural learning); *Lernstrategien* (learning strategies). In the early stages students concentrate on memorisation strategies.

For example, under *Grammatik* (see Figure 16.1):

> One way to learn verbs is to find ways of showing the pattern in a more creative way Here is a suggestion. Have you got any other ideas?' (*Rundblick*, Book 1: 54)

A further example presented under *Lernstrategien* for *Thema* 2 focuses on how to learn vocabulary:

> As the course progresses, you will soon build up a considerable store of vocabulary. In order not to forget the vocabulary from previous

Integrating Strategy Instruction into Learning Materials 317

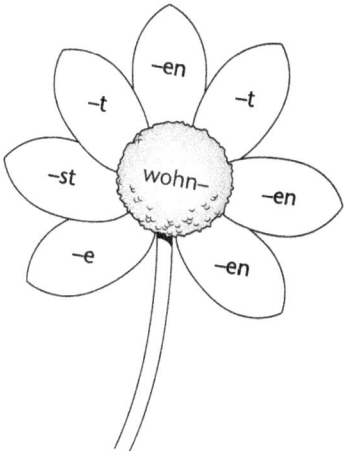

Figure 16.1 An activity for learning verbs (*Rundblick*, Book 1: 54) © The Open University, 2003

> *Themen*, you have to organise, practise and revise the words you need. [...] Here is a list of some of the things learners have found useful.
> - organise your vocabulary according to the topic area,
> - draw mind maps (write one word in the centre and write words or phrases you associate with this word all round it,
> - keep a spoken diary: say 10 words you want to learn and record them, then listen – add more words at regular intervals,
> - record your vocabulary on cards and go through them every week,
> - organise your cards according to how well you know the word.
>
> Choose one of the suggestions from the list and try it out.
> Are there any other strategies for learning, which you found useful while studying this course (or while studying other languages in the past)? (*Rundblick*, Book 1: 117).

The examples above illustrate a way of raising awareness, explaining and modelling strategies, while giving students opportunities to practice and evaluate these strategies and decide which to use. The activities combine language learning and strategy instruction and have been chosen for that purpose, but overall, the focus is firmly on language learning. At this language level, the course writers decided to use English for explanations, but learners put the strategies into practice in target language activities. Despite the warnings in relation to 'extras' and separate strategy instruction materials mentioned earlier, OU beginner students are referred to another publication, *Success with Languages* (Hurd & Murphy, 2005) for more detailed explanations, advice, additional strategies and practice activities. This is because there is a strict limit to the amount of material that can be included in a distance learning course. *Success with Languages* is a set book for the courses, but time for using the book is not explicitly built into the timetable after the initial stages. There is also no attempt to include strategy development in the course assessment schemes, an approach which can result in learners perceiving this aspect of their study as not actually valued after all, a lack of what Biggs (1999: 11) terms 'constructive alignment'. Reliance on the 'extra' material returns to the difficult issue of how much time to devote to strategy instruction within language materials and whether this can be handled by encouraging individuals to take control and concentrate on what they need in order to achieve their goals.

Conclusion

This chapter has set out arguments in favour of integrating strategy instruction, and provided some examples of how this may be achieved in learning materials for distance and other independent learners. However, it also highlights a need to explore the most appropriate sequences for strategy instruction at different levels and to resolve the difficulty of balancing language and strategy instruction through the design of tasks which naturally prompt strategy use. Another area for research is the ways in which deployment of language learning strategies might be assessed if they are to be perceived as a valued aspect of a programme, and the impact which assessment might have. However, if explicit strategy instruction is shown to be most effective within a framework of strategic awareness-raising to enable learners to take control and select strategies that work for them, then these issues may be less significant. As McDonough (2005: 163) concludes 'in such a complex area [...] there can never be a "one-size fits all" policy for language teaching'.

References

Beaty, L., Gibbs G. and Morgan, A. (1997) Learning orientations and study contracts. In F. Marton, D. Hounsell and N. Entwistle (eds) *The Experience of Learning* (2nd edn) (pp. 72–86). Edinburgh: Scottish Academic Press.

Benson, P. (2001) *Teaching and Researching Autonomy in Language Learning*. Harlow, Essex: Pearson Education.

Biggs, J. (1999) *Teaching for Quality Learning at University: What the Student Does*. Buckingham: Society for Research into Higher Education and Open University Press.

Chamot, A.U. (1993) Student responses to learning strategy instruction in the foreign language classroom. *Foreign Language Annals* 26 (3), 308–321.

Chamot, A.U. (2001) The role of learning strategies in second language acquisition. In M.P. Breen (ed.) *Learner Contributions to Language Learning* (pp. 25–43). Harlow, Essex: Pearson Education.

Cohen, A.D. (1998) *Strategies in Learning and Using a Second Language*. Harlow: Longman.

Donato, R. and McCormick, D. (1994) A sociocultural perspective on language learning strategies: The role of mediation. *The Modern Language Journal* 78 (4), 453–464.

Dörnyei, Z. (2005) *The Psychology of the Language Learner: Individual Differences in Second Language Acquisition*. Mahwah, NJ: Lawrence Erlbaum Associates Inc.

Ellis, G. and Sinclair B. (1989) *Learning to Learn English: A Course in Learner Training*. Cambridge: Cambridge University Press.

Fernández-Toro, M. and Jones, F. (2001) *DIY Techniques for Language Learners*. London: The National Centre for Languages (CiLT).

Gibbs, G. (1981) *Teaching Students to Learn: A Student-centred Approach*. Milton Keynes: Open University Press.

Gillette, B. (1987) Two successful language learners: An introspective approach. In C. Faerch and G. Kaspar (eds) *Introspection in Second Language Research* (pp. 268–279). Clevedon: Multilingual Matters.

Gillette, B. (1994) The role of learner goals in second language success. In J.P. Lantolf and G. Appel (eds) *Vygotskian Approaches to Second Language Learning* (pp. 195–213). New Jersey: Ablex Publishing Corporation.

Gremmo, M. and Riley, P. (1995) Autonomy, self-direction and self-access in language learning: The history of an idea. *System* 23 (2), 151–164.

Grenfell, M. and Harris, V. (1999) *Modern Languages and Learning Strategies: In Theory and Practice*. London: Routledge.

Harris, V. (2001) *Helping Learners Learn: Exploring Strategy Instruction in Language Classrooms Across Europe*. Strasbourg: Council of Europe Publishing.

Hassan, X., Macaro, E., Mason, D., Nye, G., Smith, P. and Vanderplank, R. (2005) Strategy training in language learning: A systematic review of available research. In *Research Evidence in Education Library*. London: EPPI-Centre, Social Science Research Institute, University of London.

Holec, H. (1996) Self-directed learning: An alternative form of training. In H. Holec, D. Little and R. Richterich (eds) *Strategies in Language Learning and Use (Modern Languages): Studies towards a Common European Framework of Reference for Language Learning and Teaching* (pp. 77–127). Strasbourg: Council of Europe.

Hurd, S. (2000) Distance language learners and learner support: Beliefs, difficulties and use of strategies. *Links and Letters* 7, 61–80.

Hurd, S. and Murphy, L. (2005) *Success with languages*. London: Routledge, in association with the Open University.

Kinoshita, C.Y. (2003) Integrating language learning strategy instruction into ESL/EFL lessons. *The Internet TESL Journal* 9 (4). On WWW at http://iteslj.org/Techniques/kinoshita-Strategy.html. Accessed 21.03.07.

Lantolf, J.P. (2001) (S)econd (L)anguage (A)ctivity theory: Understanding second language learners as people. In M.P. Breen (ed.) *Learner Contributions to Language Learning* (pp. 141–158). Harlow, Essex: Pearson Education Ltd.

Little, D. (1995) The dependence of learner autonomy on teacher autonomy. *System* 23 (2), 175–181.

Little, D. (1996) Strategic competence considered in relation to strategic control of the language learning process. In H. Holec, D. Little and R. Richterich (eds) *Strategies in Language Learning and Use (Modern Languages): Studies towards a Common European Framework of Reference for Language Learning and Teaching* (pp. 11–37). Strasbourg: Council of Europe.

Little, D. (1999) Learner Autonomy is more than a western cultural construct. In S. Cotterall and D. Crabbe (eds) *Learner Autonomy in Language Learning: Defining the Field and Effecting Change* (pp. 11–18). Frankfurt am Main: Lang.

Macaro, E. (2001) *Learner Strategies in Second and Foreign Language Classrooms*. London: Continuum.

Matsumoto, K. (1996) Helping L2 learners reflect on classroom learning. *ELT Journal* 50 (2), 143–149.

McCune, V. and Entwistle, N. (2000) *The Deep Approach to Learning: Analytic Abstraction and Idiosyncratic Development*. University of Edinburgh, paper presented at Innovations in HE Conference, Helsinki, Finland. On WWW at http://www.ed.ac.uk/etl. Accessed 10.01.02.

McDonough, S. (1995) *Strategy and Skill in Learning a Foreign Language*. London: Arnold.

McDonough, S. (1999) Learner strategies: State-of-the-art. *Language Teaching* 32, 1–18.

McDonough, S. (2005) Training language learning expertise. In K. Johnson (ed.) *Expertise in Second Language Learning and Teaching* (pp. 150–164). Basingstoke: Palgrave.

Murphy, L. (2005) Critical reflection and autonomy: A study of distance learners of French, German and Spanish. In B. Holmberg, M. Shelley and C. White (eds) *Distance Education and Languages: Evolution and Change* (pp. 20–39). Clevedon: Multilingual Matters.

Murphy, L. (2008) Supporting learner autonomy: Developing practice through the production of courses for distance learners of French, German and Spanish. *Language Teaching Research* 12 (1), 83–102.

Naiman, N., Froehlich, M., Stern, H.H. and Todesco, A. (1978/1996) *The Good Language Learner*. Clevedon: Multilingual Matters.

O'Malley, J.M. and Chamot, A.U. (1995) *Learning Strategies in Second Language Acquisition*. Cambridge: Cambridge University Press.

Oxford, R.L. and Cohen, A.D. (1992) Language learning strategies: Crucial issues of concept and classification. *Applied Language Learning* 3 (1), 1–35.

Rees-Miller, J. (1993) A critical appraisal of learner training: Theoretical bases and teaching implications. *TESOL Quarterly* 27 (4), 679–689.

Ridley, J. (1997) *Reflection and Strategies in Language Learning*. Frankfurt am Main: Peter Lang GmbH.

Robinson, P. (2001) Task complexity, task difficulty and task production: Exploring interactions in a componential framework. *Applied Linguistics* 22 (1), 27–57.

Rubin, J. (1975) What the "Good Language Learner" can teach us. *TESOL Quarterly* 9, 41–50.

Samuda, V. (2005) Expertise in pedagogic task design. In K. Johnson (ed.) *Expertise in Second Language Learning and Teaching* (pp. 150–164). Basingstoke, Palgrave.

Schrafnagl, J. and Fage, J. (1998) *The Good Distance Language Learner*. Unpublished study into the background, learning experience and strategies of students in the Open University London region studying L120.

Sinclair, B. (1996) Materials design for the promotion of learner autonomy: How explicit is "explicit"? In R. Pemberton, E.S.L. Li, W.W.F. Orr and H.D. Pierson (eds) *Autonomy in Language Learning* (pp. 149–165). Hong Kong: Hong Kong University Press.

Stern, H.H. (1975) What can we learn from the good language learner? *Canadian Modern Language Review* 31, 304–318.

The Open University (1995/2002) *L120 Ouverture*. Milton Keynes: The Open University.

The Open University (2003) *Rundblick*. Milton Keynes: The Open University.

Weiner, B. (1985) An attributional theory of achievement motivation and emotion. *Psychological Review* 92 (4), 548–573.

Wood, E., Motz, M. and Willoughby, T. (1998) Examining students' retrospective memories of strategy development. *Journal of Educational Psychology* 90 (4), 698–704.

Index

Page numbers in *italics* refer to tables and figures.

achievement strategies 52
active participation of learners 51-2
active and passive vocabulary 160, 161, 173
activity theory 31-2
ACTs *see* autonomous controlled tasks
affect
– and cognition 218-20
– management 223-5
affective strategies 14, 29, 35, 52, 53, 57, 58, 184, 218, 220-3, 224, 227, 232, 242, 286, *287*, 292
– computer-mediated communication (CMC) 224, 286-8, 291-6
– Tandem project 242, 247, *248*
– think-aloud protocols (TAPs) 225-32
agency 49
– experience and 34-6
   see also autonomy
Ahmad, I.S. and Asraf, R.M. 69, 73, 76
Ajideh, P. 70, 77
Aljaafreh, A. and Lantolf, J.P. 262, 266, 279
Álvarez, I. and Garrido, C. 179
Amer, A.A. 70, 74
analysis
– grammatical development 149-51, 154
– of word parts 91-2, 166-7
Angelo, T.A. and Cross, K.P. 104, 110, 116
anxiety 14, 35, 53, 54, 94, 151, 159, 170, 210, 218, 219, 220, 221, 222, 223, 224, 225, 227, 228, 231, 232, *248, 257, 260, 287,* 292, 293,
apologies 120-2, 127, 128, 129-30, 133, 137
Arabic language study 147-8
Argentina 34-5
Arnold, J. 219-20
– and Brown, H.D. 219, 220
Asian cultures 50
asynchronous computer-mediated communication 126, 213, 224, 247, 250, 284, *287*, 289, *291,* 293, 295, 309
Atkinson, D. 104-5
attention
– selective 147, 173, 201
– self-correction 265
attitudes
– intercultural competence 180, 181, 190
– self-correction 266-9, 274
audio journals 209-10, 214-15

audio texts 92
audiographic conferencing and blogging 290, *291*, 293-6, 300-2
aural/oral skills 96-7, 98, 213-15
Australia, Chinese students 35-6
authentic language texts 77-8, 93
autobiographical study 35-6
automaticity, think-aloud protocols (TAPs) 225-6
autonomous controlled tasks (ACTs) 11-12
autonomy
– decision-making 47-8, 57-8
– future research 58-9
– and independence 6
– individual vs social 48-51
– intercultural competence 190-1
– learner development for 54-5
– listening 90
– metaphors for 44-7
– and motivation 224
– multiple autonomies 44-7, 49
– and self-assessment 112-13
– and self-correction 273-4
– and strategies 51-5, 56-8, 68
– Tandem learning principle 239
– theories 42-51
   see also independent language learning

Bailey, K.M. 37, 263
balance, strategy instruction 308-10
Barnett, M. 69-70, 73, 104
Barnett, R. 202
Bartlett, F.C. 70
Bateman, B.E. 181-2, 184
Beaven, T.
   see Hurd *et al*.
Beliefs 7, 14, 17, 27, 31, 41, 50, 55, 181, 183, 187, 190, 192, 274, 293, 304
– motivation and strategy use 3, 26, 28, 29
– self-correction 266-9
Beliefs About Language Learning Inventory (BALLI) questionnaire 28
Bell, F. and LeBlanc, L. 68
Belz, J.A. 288, 289, 294
Benson, P. 4, 5, 50, 51, 55, 307
– and Lor, W. 7
– and Nunan, D. 34

321

– and Voller, P. 4, 49, 55
Bialystok, E. 149-50, 154
bilingual vs monolingual dictionary use 167-8
biological variables 27
– and interacting variables 29-30
Block, D. 285
Block, E. 73, 76, 231
blogging and audiographic conferencing 290, *291*, 291-6, 300-2
bottom-up approaches to reading 68-9, 71, 73, 76
Boud, D. 6
– *et al.* 200, 202
– and Walker, D. 202
Bown, J. 10, 14
Brammerts, H. 206, 238
Brantmeier, C. 68, 69-70, 71, 72-3, 81
Broady, E. and Kenning, M. 4
Buckwalter, P. 276-8
Byram, M. 179, 180-1, 184, 209

Canada 32
Carnegie Mellon University, US 288
Carson, J. and Longhini, A. 12-13, 34-5, 36, 37-8, 144-5
case studies 11, 34-6, 144
CEF *see* Council of Europe *Common European Framework of Reference*
Centre for Advanced Research on Language Acquisition (CARLA), University of Minnesota 126-7
Centre for Independent Language Learning (CILL), Hong Kong Polytechnic University (HKPU) 48
Centre for Language Education and Research (CLEAR), Michigan State University 126
Chamot, A.U. 159, 190, 192, 273-4, 283, 297, 304, 306-7
– *et al.* 55, 307-8, 311
– and O'Malley, J.M. 55
– O'Malley, J.M. and 8, 51, 84-90, 106-7, 108, 109, 110, 111, 143-4, 148-9, 182, 220, 221, 304-5
character maps 74-5, *76*
Chastain, K. 67, 68, 103, 115
Chinese students 32-3, 35-6, 203-4, 210-11
co-operative learning 264
cognition and affect 218-20
cognitive strategies 12, 29, 52, 53, 57, 72-3, 85, 87, 184, 303
– affect 223
– grammar 143, 148, 149
– listening 90
– and metacognitive strategies 90, 116, 221
– Tandem project 241, 242, 248, *249*
– vocabulary 169-70, 174
– writing 103, 104, 106, 107-15, 116

see also think-aloud protocols (TAPs)
Cohen, A.D. 8-9, 19, 51, 55, 122, 123, 126, 129, 183, 186-7, 189, 190, 212, 222, 297, 306, 307
– and Brooks-Carson, A. 108, 112
– *et al.* 123, 125, 179, 180, 182, 187, 191
– and Ishihara, N. 123, 125, 126-7
– and Olshtain, E. 120-1, 125
– Oxford, R.L. and 303, 304, 305-6
– and Sykes, J.M. 125, 126-7, 128, 135, 136
– Weaver, S. and 8
– and White, C. *15*, 19
collaborative learning 264
collaborative strategies 184, 185, 239, 242-3, 288-90
compensation strategies 8, 12, 28, 35, 186, 242, 247-8
comprehension monitoring 73
comprehension strategies 18, 73
computer technology 18, 54, 55, 56, 57-8
– affective strategies 224, 286-8, 291-6
– audiographic conferencing and blogging 290, *291*, 293-6, 300-2
– challenges 283-4, 296-8, 309
– e-journals 19, 210
– email exchange *see* Tandem
– grammar 150
– listening 92, 98
– reading 79-80, 81
– self-correction 271-2
– social strategies 242, 250-1, 252-3, 286-8, 291-6
– Spanish language study 128-36, 238
– speech and pragmatic ability 126-36
– telecollaboration, French language study 288-98
– theoretical background 285-6
– vocabulary 76-8
conscious and unconscious processes *see* implicit and explicit knowledge/learning
context
– awareness 228-9
– critical reflection 202
– independent language learning 4-5, 10-19
– individual variation 27-8, 30-3
– learner-context interface theory 7-8, 9, 17-18, 38
– vocabulary learning strategies 171-3
control
– of learning 6-7, 149-51
– locus of 49, 90, 232
– of emotions 14, 53, 321-3
Cotterall, S. 48, 50, 141, 142, 201
– and Crabbe, D. 42, 55
Council of Europe *Common European Framework of Reference* (CEF) 184-5
critical reflection 200-3
– self-correction 273, 274

Croquelandia (online virtual world) 131, *132*
cultural issues
– learner background 29, 30
– Western vs non-Western concept of autonomy 48-51
see also intercultural competence
Cumming, A. 107, 108, 111, 112
cumulative process of learning 36, 160-1

Dam, L. 273
'Dancing with Words', Spanish language study website 131, 133-6
Dantas-Whitney, M. 209, 210, 214
Davis, P. 205-6
de Charms, R. 49
Debski, R. 224, 283
decision-making 3, *45-6*, 47-8, 57-8, 279
deep
– processing 145, 164, 165
– strategies vs surface/shallow strategies 52, 164
DeKeyser, R. 153, 154, 155
determination strategies, vocabulary 166-8
development of language learning strategies 15-19
'dialogue journals' 214
diaries 11, 12, 13, 16, 34-5
– grammar 144-6
– listening 93, 94
see also learning logs and journals
Dickens, A. 205
Dickinson, L. 5, 6, 48, 90, 224, 263, 273
dictionary use 167-8
direct strategies 8, 72, 241
discovery-consolidation distinction, vocabulary 165
distance learners 9, 16-18, 38, 39
– affective aspects 53, 219, 223-4, 225
– development for autonomy 54-5, 125-6
– cognitive strategies 169
– grammar 142, 147
– think-aloud protocols (TAPs) study 225-32
– vs face-to-face learners' metacognitive strategies 13, 52, 125, 274
– writing 109, 203
Donato, R. and McCormick, D. 31-2, 304
Dörnyei, Z. 8, 25, 26-7, 29, 90, 221, 222, 223, 232, 305, 306, 307, 309

e-learning *see* computer technology; Tandem
Ehrman, M.E. 219, 220
– *et al.* 25, 218, 223
– and Oxford, R.L. 269
elaboration, pre-writing strategy 109-10
Ellis, G. and Sinclair, B. 8, 201, 305
Ellis, N.C. 142, 149, 153, 154
– and Beaton, A. 169

Ellis, R. 8, 25, 26, 27, 29, 141, 142, 146, 148, 149, 151, 162, 201, 220, 223, 264, 284, 286
– and Yuan, F. 108
emotions *see* affect; affective strategies
English language study
– Chinese students 32-3, 35-6, 203-4, 210-11
– Palestine 28-9
– self-correction 278-9
– Taiwan 28
– Tandem project 240-5, 246-54
– US 214
– websites 57-8
– word parts analysis 166-7
errors, self-correction 265-6, *267-8*
Europe
– Council of Europe *Common European Framework of Reference* (CEF) 184-5
– 'Open the Door to Language Learning' (OdLL Project Partners) 204-6
European Language Portfolio 200
evaluation
– listening *87*, 95-8
– planning, monitoring and 56, 85, 92, 143, 199, 203-10, 263, 272
– self-assessment 203-10
see also self-evaluation
experience and agency 34-6
explicit learning *see* implicit and explicit knowledge/learning
explicit strategy instruction 305-7, 312-14
external and internal influences on strategy use 25-30

face-to-face learners
– vs computer-mediated communication (CMC) learners 294, 297
– vs distance learners 13
feedback *15*, 16, 57, 79, 92, 134, 143, 148, 159, 209, 225, 232, 242, *245*, *251*, 261, 262, *267*, 269-72
Fernández-Toro, M. and Jones, F.R. 312
form
– focus on 264-5
– and meaning 144-8, 152-3
French language study
– self-correction 269
– telecollaboration 288-98
– think-aloud protocols (TAPs) 225-32

Galloway, V. 179, 182, 183, 184, 186, 187
Gao, X. 31, 32-3
Garrido, C.
– Alvarez, I. and 179
Gascoigne, C. 69, 70, 74, 76, 78
gender 28-9
genetic explanation 31
German language study 57, 151, 166, 237, *245*, 272, 314-17
– Tandem project 240-5, 246-54

Gillette, B. 31, 231, 304, 306
Goettsch, K. 214
Goh, C. 85, 90, 93, 97, 210-11
– and Taib, Y. 93
– Vandergrift, L. and 94
Goodman, K.S. 70
Graham, S. 84, 96, 230
grammatical development 141-3
– current theoretical frameworks 148-54
– future research 155
– hypotheses, generating and testing 143-4, 149, 151
– learner accounts: meaning and form 144-8
greetings 119-20
Grenfell, M. and Harris, V. 308-9, 310, 311
Grenfell, M. and Macaro, E. 8, 9
Griffiths, C. 223
Group Reading Diary 213
grouping, pre-writing strategy 109-110
Gu, P.Y. 31, 173, 174, 220, 222, 223
Gu, Y. and Johnson, K. 164, 165, 170
guided approach
– listening 97
– proofreading 114

Hampel
– et al. 224, 289, 290
– Lamy and 224, 283
Harmer, J. 50
Harris, C. 9, 14, 219, 222
Harris, V. 15, 17-18, 54-5, 187, 190, 191, 206, 218, 307-8, 309, 310, 311
– Grenfell. M. and 310, 311
Hauck, M. 284, 286, 295, 297
– and Hurd, S. 224, 284, 294, 297
He, A. 35-6
Holec, H. 4, 8, 42, 47-8, 263, 307, 308
Holec et al. 4
Holliday, A. 49, 50, 55
Holmes, J. 120
Holmes, V.L. and Moulton, M.R. 214
Hong Kong 16, 35-6, 56, 203-4, 211
– CILL 48
Horning, A. 80, 81
Horwitz, E.K. 28, 223, 293
Horwitz, E.K. et al. 219,223, 293
Hsiao, T. and Oxford, R. 182, 220, 222
Hulstijn, J.H. 91, 92, 162, 167, 169, 173
– Laufer B. and 173
Hurd, S. 4, 8, 13, 15, 116, 125, 218, 219, 222, 223, 224, 225, 232, 262, 263, 269, 274, 279, 284, 294, 311
– et al. 16-17, 112, 115, 125-6, 187
– Hauck, M. and 284, 297
– and Murphy, L. 20, 317-18
Hyland, F. 15, 16, 104, 105, 108
hypertext 79-80
hypotheses, generating and testing 143-4, 149, 151

Ikeda, M. and Takeuchi, O. 212
immersion context 12-13
implicit and explicit knowledge/learning
– grammar 141-2, 148-50, 151-2, 153-4
– intercultural competence 186-7, 189-90
– vocabulary 162-3
in-country strategies, intercultural competence 188-9
incompleteness, think-aloud protocols (TAPs) 226
independent language learning
– conceptualizing 7-8
– dimensions of 4-6
– emergence of 4-7
see also autonomy; strategies
indirect strategies 241
individual autonomy vs social autonomy 48-51
individual variation
– contexts and tasks 30-3
– experience and agency 34-6
– internal and external influences on strategy use 25-30
– quantitative vs qualitative research 26, 33, 36-8
'informed consumers' 19
'informed' strategy instruction 312-18
– vs 'uninformed' instruction 304-5
innate–acquired distinction 27
integrated strategy instruction see strategy instruction
interaction, teacher–learner 264
interactional and compensation strategies 186
interactive models for reading 71-2
intercultural competence 179-80
– autonomous 190-1
– culture and language learning 180-2, 192
– learning about other cultures 183-4
– learning to engage with people from other cultures 184-6
– strategy inventories 188-90
– strategy training 186-8, 192
– taxonomy of learning strategies 182-3
interdependence 6, 47, 239
– models: reader and text 68-72
interest and motivation, intercultural competence 190
internal and external influences on strategy use 25-30
Internet Internet 42, 80, 127, 211, 238, 284, 285, 288, 291
see also computer technology; Tandem
Ioup, G. et al. 147-8
Israel 30, 120-1

Japanese language study 123, 127-8, 129, 212-13
Jokikokko, J. 181
Jones, A. and Isaroff, E. 285

Jones, B. 188, 193
Jones, F. 10, 11, 12, 34, 144, 145, 146
– Fernandez-Toro and 312, *313*
journals
– audio 209-10, 214-15
– e- 19, 210
– listening 211
– online 214
– reflective 199, 202, 203, *204*
Juffer, K.A. 187, 191

K-W-L (know, want to know, learned) charts 109-10
keyword technique 168, 169
Kinoshita, C.Y. 304-5, 312, 314
knowledge
– intercultural competence 180, 181
– self-knowledge 16-17, 222, 224, 274, 314
– types and strategies 116
    see also implicit and explicit knowledge/learning; metacognitive knowledge
Knutson, E.M. 107, 108, 112, 183-4
Kolb, D.A. 200
Konishi, M. 68, 73, 76, 79-80, 81
Kramsch, C. 179, 181
– and Andersen, R.W. 26
Krashen, S.D. 67, 142, 148, 149, 151-2, 162, 163

L1
– use in writing strategy 107, 108, 111, 112
– use in monitoring L2 performance 143
– use in vocabulary development 162, 168
Lally, C. 67, 69, 76, 103, 107, 108, 112
Lamb, T. and Reinders, H. 6
Lantolf, J.P. 304, 309-10
– Aljaafreh, A. and 262, 266, 279
– and Pavlenko, A. 33, 34, 149
Larsen-Freeman, D. 25, 26, 28
learner–context interface theory 7-8, 9, 17-18, 38
learners
– attributes 4, 5-6, 7, 20, 26-7
– perspectives 7-8
– successful 9, 12, 14, 116, 143, 146-8, 151, 152-3, 163-4, 192, 201, 220, 253, 273, 283, 285, 303-4, 306, 310-11
– successful distance 224, 274
learning cycle/spiral 47, 95, *96*, 97,200, 201
learning logs
– critical reflection 200-3
– definition 199-200
– in development of metacognitive strategies 203-10
– in development of specific language skills 210-15
– learning theories and 200-1
    see also diaries

learning/learner support 5, *15*, 42, 205, 223, 231-232
learning environments 3,
– independent 16, 19, 52, 92, 98,
– virtual/online 20, 224, 293-4, 295, 297
– synchronous and asynchronous 289
Leow, R.P. 264
Leow, R.P. and Morgan-Short, K. 226
Leung, C.Y. 212-13
Levine, A. *et al.* 30
Lewis, T. and Walker, L. 4, 238
list learning 164, 169, 170
listening
– metacognitive knowledge 92-4
– metacognitive strategies 85-91
– strategies 84-5, 94-8
– word segmentation skills 91-2
'listening diary' 210-11
Little, D. 4, 6, 42, 47, 142, 190, 201, 239, 262, 263, 273, 274, 307, 309
– and Brammerts, H. 289
Littlewood, W. 6, 50, 59, 273
locus of control 49, 90, 232
Lyceum conferencing system 290, *291, 292-3, 293, 295-6, 300*

Macaro, E. 125, 221-2, 306, 307, 308, 310, 311
– Grenfell, M. and 8, 9
Macdonald, J. 224
McDonough, S. 8, 107, 142, 226, 231, 303, 304, 305, 306, 312, 316, 318
McEnery, A.M. *et al.* 150
Macianskiene, N. *et al.* 187, 190
MALQ *see* Metacognitive Awareness Listening Questionnaire
Mareschal, C. 97-8
Martinez-Lang, A. 69
meaning
– and form 144-8, 152-3
– negotiation of 186, 238
mediation/mediated 31-2, 33, 37, 44, 77, 262, 284
– socioculturally-mediated 31
– teacher-mediated 3, 9, 20
– technologically/computer-mediated 44, 79-80, 108, 126, 131, 150, 224, 271, 284, 285, 286
Melka Teichroew, F.J. 160
memory 219
– affect, learning and 219, 220
– short-term 225
– strategies 241, 242, 246, 247, 254, *255, 258,* 286
– vocabulary startegies 5, 168-9
Metacognitive Awareness Listening Questionnaire (MALQ) 93-4, 95, 97-8, 101-2
metacognitive knowledge 5, 8, 13, 18, 222, 274

– grammar 141-2, 147, 148
– listening 92-4, 98
– self-correction 274
metacognitive skills 275, 279
metacognitive strategies 8, 13, 35, 52-3, 56, 57, 58, 125, 143, 144, 201, 241, 284, 286
– and affect 220, 221-2
– and cognitive strategies 90, 116, 220, 221, 231, 276
– and critical reflection 201-3
– grammar 143-4, 150, 151, 154
– learning logs 203-10
– listening 84, 85-91, 98
– online 297-8
– reading 72, 73, 76, 80
– self-correction 274, 276, 279
– speaking 124
– Tandem project 242, 249-50
– vocabulary 170-1
– writing 106, 116
metapragmatic strategies 123, 124
Milton, J. 278-9
mistakes, self-correction 55, 114, 204, 210, 223, 242, 243, 244, 245, 263, 265-6, 267-8
Monitor Model 148, 151-2
monitoring see self-monitoring
motivation 8, 14, 17, 26, 27, 46, 52, 53, 55, 192, 205, 214, 218, 220, 224, 225, 238, 273, 303, 309-10
– and anxiety 219, 223, 231-2
– beliefs and strategy use 28, 29, 174, 183, 223, 309
– and interest 190
– listening 90, 93
– reading 167
see also affective strategies
multimedia courses 56-7
multimedia programmes 18, 92, 272
multiple autonomies 44-7, 49
Murphy, J.M. 90
Murphy, L. 4, 142, 147, 203, 213-14, 274, 307, 309, 314
– Hurd, S. and 20, 317-18

Naiman, N. et al. 143, 144, 154, 192, 303, 306
Nation, I.S.P. 160, 162, 164, 165, 166-7, 170, 173
– Hu, M. and 172
– and Meara, P. 166, 169
– and Wang, K. 172
negative emotions, control of 14, 52, 53, 232
negotiation of meaning 186, 238
Nicol, D.J. et al. 297
noticing 92, 142, 154, 212
– and attention 265. 267
– hypothesis 151-3
– strategies 162
Nunan, D. 4, 44-7
– Benson, P. and 34

– and Lamb 221
– et al. 203-4, 211

O'Dowd, R. and Ritter, M. 240, 288-9, 294
O'Malley, J.M.
– and Chamot, A.U. 8, 51, 84-90, 106-7, 108, 109, 110, 111, 143-4, 148-9, 182, 220, 221, 304-5
– Chamot, A.U. and 55
– et al. 85
online learning see computer technology; Tandem
Open University, UK 16, 57, 125-6, 214-15, 226, 240-1, 275-6, 288, 289, 304, 307, 314
oral/aural skills 96-7, 98, 213-15
Oxford, R.L. 25, 30, 49, 51, 55, 103, 108, 115, 165, 182, 187, 189, 190, 192, 219, 220-1, 222, 223, 241, 242, 246-7, 255, 264, 286, 291
– and Burry-Stock, J.A. 226, 232
– and Cohen, A.D. 304, 305-6
– Cohen, A.D. and 303, 304, 305-6
– and Crookall, D. 190
– Ehrman, M.E. and 269
– et al. 31
– Hsiao, T. and 182, 220, 222
– and Leaver, B.L. 55
– Scarcella, R. and 108
– and Shearin, J. 221

Palestine 28-9
Parks, S. 31
– and Raymond, P.M. 31, 32, 33
Paul, R. 5
peer assessment 206-9
philosophy of independent language learning 5-6
Phipps, A. and González, M. 192
Paige, R.M. et al. 15, 18-19, 188, 189
planning
– learning logs 203-10
– monitoring and evaluation 56, 85, 92, 143, 199, 203-10, 263, 272
see also entries beginning pre-
portfolios 199-201, 212
post-process approach to writing 104-5
post-study-abroad strategies 188-189
pre-departure strategies 188
pre-listening activities 94-5
pre-writing activities 104, 107, 108-11
predictions
– listening 93, 95, 97
– reading 70, 81
print-based materials 54-5
problem-solving
– listening 85, 93, 95, 96
– self-correction 264
– writing strategies 107, 111-12
– vocabulary 167

Index 327

process model 104-5, 222, 266-9
productive learning *see* receptive and productive learning
progression, strategy instruction 308, 310-11
proofreading 113-4
psychological types and interacting variables 29-30
Pujolà, J. *15*, 18, 272

quantitative research vs qualitative research 13, 19, 26, 33, 36-8, 58, 134, 151, 290
questionnaires 19, 26, 27, 28, 29, 30-1, 93-4, 97-8, 105, *105-6*105-6

Ramnani, N. 220
re-entry strategies, intercultural competence 189
reactivity, think-aloud protocols (TAPs) 225-6
reading 67-8
– global strategies 79-81
– interdependence models: reader and text 68-72
– interdependent strategies 72-3
– logs 74-5, *77*, 212-13
– technologically-mediated 74
– technologically-mediated environments 79-80, 81
– transferring tools and techniques to promote interactive 73-9
– vocabulary acquisition 171-3
receptive and productive learning
– cultural 184-5
– skills 127, 213
– vocabulary 160, 163
reciprocity, Tandem learning principle 239
recombining 166, *249*, *255*, *258*
– writing strategy 113, 115
reflection *see* critical reflection
rehearsal 159, 169, 170, 221, 276, 293
rereading
– reading strategy 72, 73,
– writing strategy 111, 113, 114
resource(s) 108-9, 111, 114-15, 191
– centres 56-7, 127
– online 56, 122
– resource-based learning 4
revising strategies
– reading 80
– writing 104, 107, 108, 111, 112-15
rhetorical organisation/structure 74, 78-9, 104
Richards, J. and Renandya, W. 14
Ridley, J. 212, 269, 306, 307
Riley, K. 199, 203, 204
Rivers, W. 144, 145
Robinson, M.A, 125
Robinson, P. 153, 231, 232, 311-12
role-model writing analysis 108-9

Rossiter, M.J. 219, 222
rote learning 169, 170
Rowsell, L. and Libben, G. *10*, 11-12, *15*, 146
Rubin, J. 4, 143, 144, 151, 154, 182, 220, 222, 274, 303
– Wenden, A. and 187, 220, 286
rules *see* grammatical development

Saricoban, A. 73, 76
Savignon, S.J. and Sysoyev, P.V. 186, 187-8
'scaffolding' 70, 128, 264, 269, 271
schema
– frameworks 52
– theory 70-1, 168
Schmeck, R. 52, 192
Schmidt, R. 151-2, 154, 162, 186, 265
– and Frota, S.N. 34, 144, 145, 151
Schmitt, N. 160-1, 164-5
– and Schmitt, D. 171
SCMC *see* synchronous computer-mediated communication
selective attention *86*, *88*, 93, *96*, 147, 162, 164, 173, 201, *267*, 275, 276, *277*, 279
self-access *see* resource(s)
self-assessment 16, 57, 112, 201, 203-10, 211, 263, 271
self-awareness 104, 181-2, 184, 210, 228-9, 230, 274, 286
self-concept 182, 190, 219
self-correction 16, 113, 115, 143, 262-3
– examples 275-9
– and learner autonomy 273-4
– pedagogical and research perspectives 264-72
self-direction 104, 201, 210
self-discovery 188
self-efficacy 49
self-encouragement 14, 221, 222, 223, 229-30, 231
self-evaluation 16, 113, 116, 127, 187, 191, 201, 203, 209-10, *249*, *257*, *260*, 266, 274, 276, *277*, 279
self-knowledge 16-17, 222, 224, 274, 314
self-management/regulation 11, 13, 14, 18, 44, 55, 90, 125, 159, 163, 165, 222, 239, 247, 263, 266, 271, 274, 276, 277, 283, 286, 279, 286, 297, 303, 307-8, 312, 316,
self-monitoring 73, 95, 148, 151-2, 165, 187, 201, 202, 203-9
see also planning, monitoring and evaluation
semantic associations 168-9
semantic maps 110, 112
shallow/surface strategies vs deep strategies 52, 164
Sheerin, S. 4, 5, 59
Shmais, W.A. 28-9
short-term memory 225
SIE *see* Synthetic Immersive Environment

SILL *see* Strategy Inventory for Language Learning
Sinclair, B. 308
– Ellis, G. and 8, 305
Singapore 93, 210-11
situational variables, and interacting variables/factors 26, 28, 29-30
skills 35, 44, 143
– auditory discrimination 98
– computer 240
– critical reflection 274
– decoding 92
– empathising 294
– intercultural competence 179-184
– interpersonal 150, 253
– language 4, 19, 67, 84, 144, 171, 187, 199, 209, 210
– learning 7, 8, 16, 20, 153, 168, 220, 239, 273
– listening 84, 90, 92, 97, 210-1
– metacognitive 275, 279
– pragmatic 119, 135
– presentation 209
– procedural 13
– processing 92
– reading 67, 68, 69, 72, 73, 74, 80, 81, 212-3, 238
– social 264, 284, *287*, 297
– self-correction 115
– speaking 119, 131, 136, 213-5, 271
– study 305
– thinking 44
– word building 166
– word perception 90, 92, 94, 96
– word recognition 92, 96, 97, 98
– word segmentation 91-2
– writing 12, 104, 105, 114-5, 213-5, 238
slips, self-correction *244*, 265-6, *267-8*
social autonomy vs individual autonomy 48-51
social constructivist theory
– critical reflection 201
– intercultural competence 183
– stages of development 44, 47
social relationships 221, 297
social strategies 33, 34, 221
– computer-mediated communication (CMC) 242, 250-1, 252-3, 286-8, 291-6
– Tandem project 242, 250-1, 252-3
social variables/factors 27, 28
– and interacting variables 29-30
social-interactive strategies 52, 53-4, 57, 58
socio-environmental strategies 284, 295-6
sociocultural perspective 31-3, 36-7, 51
Spanish language study 12
– computer-mediated 125, 127-36, 238
– diaries 34-5, 214-15
– self-correction 275-8
– Tandem 237-8

speaking
– independent language learning strategies 125-6
– pragmatic ability 119-22
– role of technology 126-36
– taxonomy of learning and performing strategies 123-5
see also skills
speech acts 50, 119, 120, 122, 123-9, 131, 133, 134, 136, 137
stage theories 44-7
Stevick, E.W. 141-2, 144, 220
story grammar 71, 74
story maps/frames 74, 75
strategic awareness-raising 307-8, 309, 312, 314-18
strategies
– and autonomy 51-5, 56-8, 68
– contribution of 8-10
– development of 15-19
– problem of definition 8-9
– use in independent learning 10-15
– value of 51-2
see also achievement, affective, cognitive, collaborative, compensation, comprehension, deep, determination, direct, global, in-country, indirect, , interactional, interdependent. listening, metacognitive, metapragmatic, post-study-abroad, pre-departure, reading, re-entry, revising, social, social-interactive, socio-environmental, speaking, study abroad, surface, vocabulary, writing
strategy instruction 303-5
– challenges 308-12
– explicit 305-7, 312-14
– strategic awareness-raising 307-8, 309, 312, 314-18
Strategy Inventory for Language Learning (SILL) 8, 25, 27, 28-9, 34, 220-1
strategy taxonomies 8, 52-4, 241, 165, 166, 182, *255-7*, *258-61*
– computer-mediated communication 286-8
– individual variation 27, 28-9
– intercultural competence 182-3
– speaking 123-5
– vocabulary 165
study abroad strategies 18-19
substitution, writing strategy 111-13
successful learners 9, 12, 14, 116, 143, 146-8, 151, 152-3, 163-4, 192, 201, 220, 253, 273, 283, 285, 303-4, 306, 310-11
successful distance learners 224, 274
surface/shallow strategies vs deep strategies 52, 164
Swaffar, J.K. *et al.* 67, 71-2, 73, 74, 75-6, 78-9

Index

synchronous computer-mediated communication (SCMC) 107, 126, 131, 206, 224, 284, *287*, 288-294, 295, *296*, 309
Synthetic Immersive Environment (SIE) 131, *132*, 133, 134

Taiwanese 28
Tandem
– German/English project 240-5, 246-54
– main features 238-9
– partnerships 206-9
– specific strategies *243-5*, 247-252
TAPs *see* think-aloud protocols
task design, strategy instruction 311-12
teacher–learner interaction 262, 264
teacher-led discussions 93
teachers/tutors
– mediation 17, 18, 20
– roles and interventions 16, 55, 73, 104, 154, 163, 187, 192, 201, 214, 219, 222, 224, 231, 225, 249, 264, 269-72, 289
– websites for 127
telecollaboration, French language study 126, 284, 288-98
text structure/organisation 71, 73, 74-5, 79
text–reader relationship 68-72
think-aloud protocols (TAPs) 225-32
top-down approaches to reading 69-71, 72, 73, 76, 310
Truman
– Ros-i-Solé and 266, 279

unconscious and conscious processes *see* implicit and explicit knowledge/learning
'uninformed' instruction vs 'informed' instruction 304-5
United States (US)
– Carnegie Mellon University 288
– Centre for Advanced Research on Language Acquisition (CARLA), University of Minnesota 126-7
– Centre for Language Education and Research (CLEAR), Michigan State University 126
– English language study 214
Ushioda, E. 14, 221, 224

Van Patten, B. 147, 152-3, 155
Vandergrift, L. 85-90, 92-3, *96*, 97, 187
– *et al.* 8, 93
– and Goh, C. 94
Vanijdee, A. 4, 68
Vann, R.J. and Abraham, R.G. 146-7
videotext 91-2
Virtual English Language Advisor (VELA) 56
visual aids 91-2
vocabulary 159-60
– explicit learning 166-71
– implicit and explicit learning 162-3
– implicit learning from context 171-3
– 'knowing' a word 160-1
– learning strategies 163-5
– recognition 76-9
– strategy taxonomies 165
Volkschochsule Ostkreis Hannover (HVS) 240-1
Vygotsky, L.S. 44, 47, 201, 262

Walker, L. 206, 207
– Lewis and 4, 203
Walz, J. 67, 80, 81, 114
Weinstein, C.E. and Mayer, D.K. 116
Wenden, A. 4, 7, 8, 27, 42, 68, 142, 143-4, 189, 190, 219, 220, 273, 274
– and Rubin 187, 220, 286
Western vs non-Western concept of autonomy 48-51
White, C. 4, 5, 7, 8, 10, 11, 13, 17, 38, 52-3, 68, 97, 125, 218, 219, 222, 224, 225, 232, 262, 266, 269, 274, 279
– Cohen, A.D. and *15*, 19
– *et al.* 10
Willems, G.M. 179
Williams, J. 264, 265
Williams, M. and Burden, R.L. 51-2
word cards 169-170
word segmentation/parts analysis 84, 91-2, 166-7
writing 103-4
– cognitive strategies 107-15, 116
– strategies 106-7, 111-12
– theoretical background 104-5

Yang, N-D. 7, 28, 29, 187, 190
Yen-Ren, T. 213

'zone of proximal development' (ZPD) 150, 201, 262, 263, 266, 269, 271

For Product Safety Concerns and Information please contact our EU Authorised Representative.

Easy Access System Europe

Mustamäe tee 50

10621 Tallinn

Estonia

gpsr.requests@easproject.com

www.ingramcontent.com/pod-product-compliance
Lightning Source LLC
Chambersburg PA
CBHW071152300426
44113CB00009B/1183